Also by Angela J. Davis

Arbitrary Justice: The Power of the American Prosecutor

Criminal Law
(author, with Katheryn Russell-Brown)

Trial Stories
(coeditor, with Michael E. Tigar)

Basic Criminal Procedure
(coauthor, with Stephen A. Saltzburg and Daniel J. Capra)

Policing the Black Man

Policing the Black Man

Arrest, Prosecution, and Imprisonment

**Edited and with an introduction by
Angela J. Davis**

Pantheon Books, New York

Library of Congress Cataloging-in-Publication Data
Names: Davis, Angela J., [date] editor.
Title: Policing the black man : arrest, prosecution, and imprisonment /
edited and with an introduction by Angela J. Davis.
Description: First edition. New York : Pantheon Books, a division of Penguin
Random House LLC [2017]. Includes bibliographical references and index.
Identifiers: LCCN 2016055965 (print). LCCN 2017006758 (ebook).
ISBN 9781101871270 (hardcover : alk. paper). ISBN 9781101871287 (e-book).
Subjects: LCSH: Discrimination in criminal justice administration—
United States. African American criminals.
Classification: LCC HV9950 P64 2017 (print). LCC HV9950 (ebook).
DDC 364.3/496073—dc23.
LC record available at lccn.loc.gov/2016055965

www.pantheonbooks.com

Jacket design by Oliver Munday
Book design by M. Kristen Bearse

Printed in the United States of America
First Edition
2 4 6 8 9 7 5 3 1

For the black men in my life, past and present—
my grandfather, Robert L. Harris; my father, Eddie Walter Jordan;
and my husband, Howard Neil Davis

Contents

Acknowledgments

This book would not have been possible without the hard work and dedication of so many people. I thank Erroll McDonald for his guidance, editorial assistance, and expert advice. I also thank Shawnta Albro, Gabrielle Best Husband, Sheryl Dublin, Layla Medina, Meaghan E. Mixon, and Summer Woods for their outstanding research assistance and Dean Camille A. Nelson and my colleagues at American University Washington College of Law for their support throughout the process. I owe a special debt of gratitude to Randall Kennedy, who generously suggested that I be offered the opportunity to edit this important anthology. Finally, I thank my dear husband, Howard Neil Davis, and all of my family and friends for their love, patience, and encouragement.

I am deeply grateful to Bryan Stevenson, Marc Mauer, Kristin Henning, Renée McDonald Hutchins, Katheryn Russell-Brown, Tracey Meares, Tom Tyler, Roger A. Fairfax, Jr., Ronald F. Wright, Sherrilyn A. Ifill, Jin Hee Lee, Jeremy Travis, and Bruce Western for their extraordinary contributions to this book and for all they do to ensure fairness for poor people and people of color in the criminal justice system. I thank them and the many lawyers, activists, scholars, teachers, and artists who are fighting every day to assure that Black Lives Matter.

Introduction

ANGELA J. DAVIS

Michael Brown, Eric Garner, Tamir Rice, Walter Scott, Freddie Gray, Sam DuBose, Alton Sterling, Philando Castile, and Terence Crutcher are just some of the names on a long list of unarmed black boys and men who were killed by police officers in recent years. Although black men have been the victims of violence at the hands of the state since the time of slavery, technology and social media now permit us to literally bear witness to many of these killings, repeatedly. Millions of people have watched the video of a police officer choking Eric Garner to death as he struggled for air. Similarly, millions have watched the video of a police officer shooting Walter Scott in the back as he ran for his life. Who can ever forget the grainy footage of Tamir Rice—the twelve-year-old boy who was shot by a police officer while he played alone with a toy gun in a park near his home? Two videos—one from a police helicopter and another from a police dashboard camera—show Terence Crutcher walking away from police officers with his hands raised high in the air just before he was shot and killed. These images have evoked feelings of fear, sadness, and outrage and serve as a reminder that the lives of black men and boys continue to be devalued and destroyed with impunity at the hands of the state. To date, not one of the police officers who killed these men and boys has been convicted of a single crime.

From the arrival of the first slaves in Jamestown in 1619 to the lynchings of the nineteenth and twentieth centuries to the present day—black boys and men have been unlawfully killed by those who were sworn to uphold the law and by vigilantes who took the law into their own hands. The National Museum of African American History and Culture, which opened its doors on September 24, 2016, includes exhibits that tell the story of many of these killings. Yet these killings are not just a part of African American history. They have continued well into the twenty-first century—almost four hundred years after the beginning of slavery—and persist with remarkable frequency and brutality during a time when America elected its first African American president.

Many of these race-based killings have inspired and reinvigorated movements for change. The brutal killing of fourteen-year-old Emmett Till in Mississippi in 1955, the murder of civil rights activist Medgar Evers in 1963, and the assassination of Martin Luther King in 1968 all serve as markers on the civil rights movement timeline, as did so many other killings of black men by white racists. Each tragic killing sparked nationwide protests and renewed activism in the struggle for civil rights and racial justice in the United States.

The killing of seventeen-year-old Trayvon Martin in 2012 was a pivotal marker of racial violence against black men in the twenty-first century. Martin was killed by George Zimmerman, a white man who called the police when he saw Martin walking in his neighborhood. Zimmerman, a member of a neighborhood crime watch group, reported to the police that Martin looked "suspicious" and that he looked like he was "up to no good or on drugs or something." Ignoring the dispatcher's warning that he should not follow Martin, Zimmerman ultimately shot and killed him. Martin was unarmed and was on his way back to his father's house after buying snacks at a local convenience store. Initially Zimmerman was not even charged with a crime, but after nationwide protests, he was charged with Martin's murder. A jury ultimately acquitted him.[1]

The killing of Trayvon Martin, the initial failure of the prosecutor to charge Zimmerman with a crime, and Zimmerman's ultimate acquittal captured the attention of the nation. President Obama even weighed in, stating, "Trayvon Martin could have been me 35 years ago."[2] Martin's killing also inspired the phrase "Black Lives Matter." The phrase trended on Twitter and all forms of social media and was displayed on posters carried in protests after Martin's killing and after every killing of a black man or woman by a police officer from that day forward. Black Lives Matter ultimately became a social justice movement with chapters throughout the United States and Canada.

Many unarmed black men and boys have been killed since Trayvon Martin's tragic death five years ago. Many of the killings occurred after police officers arguably engaged in racial profiling—stopping and harassing these men for no explainable reason other than the color of their skin. In all of the cases where black men were shot and killed, the officers claimed that they felt threatened, even though the men were unarmed and often running away or retreating. In almost all of the cases, the police officers were never arrested or charged with a crime.

The tragic killings of Trayvon Martin, Michael Brown, Eric Garner, Walter Scott, Tamir Rice, Freddie Gray, and others served as the catalyst for this anthology. But these killings also inspired the contributing authors to think about all of the ways that black men are "policed"—in the broad sense of the word— heavily and harshly at every step of the criminal process. In fact, black men are policed and treated worse than their similarly situated white counterparts at every step of the criminal justice system, from arrest through sentencing. These unwarranted disparities exist whether black men are charged with crimes or are victims of crimes. Police officers stop, search, and arrest black men far more frequently than white men engaged in the same behavior. Prosecutors charge black men more frequently and with more serious crimes than white men who engage in the same behavior. And there are disproportionate numbers of black men in the nation's prisons and jails. Criminal defendants, regardless of their race, are punished less harshly when their victims are black men. This anthology explores and explains the "policing" of black men—from slavery to the present day and at every stage of the criminal process and beyond.

Why Black Men?

Black men are not the only people of color to be treated worse than their similarly situated white counterparts at every step of the criminal process. Black women, Latino/a men and women, Native Americans, and other people of color also experience violence at the hands of the state and discriminatory treatment in the criminal justice system, as do people who are gay, lesbian, and/or transgender.[3] This book's focus on black men in no way trivializes the experiences of all people who face these harms.

While acknowledging that other groups have been and continue to be oppressed and discriminated against, this book focuses on black men. In many ways, the experience of black men in the criminal justice system is unique. The most noticeable difference is that they are impacted more adversely than any other demographic in the United States—at every stage of the process.

Black Boys Are Disproportionately Arrested and Detained

Black boys are more likely to be referred to the juvenile justice system than any other children. In 2011, black boys represented the greatest percentage of children placed in juvenile detention—903 black boys per 100,000 were sent to detention as compared to 125 black girls.[4] A Rhode Island study found that black boys were 9.3 times more likely to spend time in juvenile detention than white boys.[5]

Over half the students arrested at school in the United States and referred to the juvenile justice system are black or Hispanic.[6] While black students represent only 16 percent of student enrollment, they represent 27 percent of students referred to law enforcement and 31 percent of students subjected to in-school arrests.[7] Black male students alone make up 18 percent of all referrals and arrests.[8]

Black Men Are Disproportionately Arrested

African Americans are 2.5 times more likely to be arrested than whites[9] and 49 percent of black men can expect to be arrested at least once by age twenty-three compared to 44 percent of Hispanic men and 38 percent of white men.[10] Police officers are permitted to stop and frisk individuals if they have "reasonable suspicion" that crime is afoot and that the person is armed and dangerous.[11] However, numerous studies have shown that the practice of racial profiling has resulted in black men being targeted and disproportionately stopped, frisked, and arrested.

For example, the New York Civil Liberties Union analyzed the New York Police Department's 2011 stop-and-frisk database and found that 41.6 percent of all stops were of black and Latino men between the ages of fourteen and twenty-four, even though they make up only 4.7 percent of the population of New York.[12] The same study found that no crime had been committed in 90 percent of the stops.[13] Black men were disproportionately stopped. The number of stops of black men exceeded the city's entire population of black men by 9,720.[14]

Black Men Are More Likely to Be Killed or Injured During a Police Encounter

While more whites are killed by law enforcement than people of color, African Americans are killed at a disproportionate rate. In fact, black men are 21 times more likely to be killed by police than white men.[15] Between 2010 and 2012, black boys ages fifteen through nineteen were killed at a rate of 31.17 per million compared to 1.47 per million for white boys of the same age group.[16] In addition, a significant number of black men killed by police were unarmed. Data collected from January 1, 2015, to May 31, 2015, revealed that African Americans killed by the police were twice as likely to be unarmed as whites.[17] An overwhelming 95 percent of these victims were men.[18]

Not all violent encounters with the police result in death, but black men fare worse in nonfatal encounters as well. A study conducted by the Justice Department's Bureau of Justice Statistics (BJS) examined police use of nonfatal force between 2002 and 2011. The study found that African Americans were more likely to experience nonfatal force at the hands of police officers than either Hispanics or whites.[19]

Black Men Are Disproportionately Imprisoned and Receive Longer Sentences

African Americans make up approximately 35 percent of the prison population in the United States,[20] and by the end of 2015, black *men* constituted 34 percent of the American prison population.[21] In 2015, 5,165 in 100,000 black men ages twenty-five to twenty-nine were imprisoned compared to 2,165 Hispanic men and 921 white men of the same ages.[22] Remarkably, the number of black men in prison or jail, on probation, or on parole by the end of 2009 roughly equaled the number enslaved in 1850.[23] One in three black men born in 2001 can expect to be incarcerated in his lifetime.[24]

Black men serve more time for their crimes than others similarly situated. Data collected by the U.S. Sentencing Commission between December 2007 and 2011 revealed that black men in federal prisons received sentences 19.5 percent longer than white men sentenced for the same crime.[25] Blacks are also disproportionately sentenced to death. As of 2014, the national death row population is approximately 42 percent black, while the overall black population is only 13.6 percent.[26]

. . .

For all of these reasons, this anthology focuses on the plight of black men and boys. The extraordinarily disproportionate mistreatment of black boys and men at every step of the criminal process is explored in depth. As the essays make clear, the issues and problems are complex, as are the solutions. The authors are scholars, lawyers, and activists who have studied and, in some instances, personally experienced the phenomena about which they write. In these informative, well-researched, and sometimes poignant essays, the authors examine and explain the policing of the black man.

Policing the Black Man: The Essays

A Presumption of Guilt: The Legacy of America's History of Racial Injustice

In the book's deeply moving introductory essay, Bryan Stevenson traces the policing of black men from slavery to the present day. He explains how slavery firmly entrenched the regime of white supremacy in the United States. Stevenson makes it clear that the Black Codes passed after the Civil War and the shocking practice of convict leasing were the precursors of current discriminatory criminal laws and the modern-day policing of black men. His chilling examination of lynching and other forms of racialized terror present the sordid history of the criminal justice system's treatment of black men who were victims of the most violent crimes. Stevenson reveals the seamless link between lynching and capital punishment and discusses the continuing well-documented racial disparities in the implementation of the death penalty. He closes with a discussion of the importance of this country's confronting and acknowledging its history of racial violence. This essay lays a solid foundation for the remainder of the book and is essential to the reader's understanding of how and why the American criminal justice system continues to police black men.

The Endurance of Racial Disparity in the Criminal Justice System

In this essay, Marc Mauer provides an overview of most of the issues that are specifically addressed in the remaining chapters of the book. He describes the stark racial disparities that exist at every step of the criminal process, from arrest through sentencing. Mauer also explains the complex confluence of circumstances that resulted in these disparities—from harsh sentencing laws and policies to rising crime rates to discretionary decision-making by criminal justice officials. He discusses how race-neutral decisions result in unwarranted racial disparities. Mauer addresses all of these issues with a focus on black men, establishing that they have been more adversely affected than any other group. The essay ends with practical suggestions for reform and sets the stage for an exploration of the issues addressed in the remainder of the book.

Boys to Men: The Role of Policing in the Socialization of Black Boys

Kristin Henning's essay on the policing of black boys is fundamental to understanding the policing of black men. As she states early in the essay, "Black boys are policed like no one else, not even black men." Police officers persistently target, stop, and harass black boys wherever they are—on the street, in school, in stores—and no matter what they are doing. Henning explains how police officers see black boys not as children, but as dangerous criminals, even when they are not engaging in criminal or even suspicious behavior. She discusses a fascinating study that found that police officers tend to overestimate the age of black boys while underestimating the age of white boys. Henning explains the impact of this constant harassment on the psyche of black boys and the role that it plays in shaping their views of police officers. She then discusses how police officers respond when black boys react to the harassment, including the role of implicit bias. As a result of this treatment, black boys grow up with negative impressions of police officers and carry these impressions into adulthood. Henning's explanation of how these interactions impact interactions between black men and the police is illuminating. She concludes the essay with concrete proposals for reform.

Racial Profiling: The Law, the Policy, and the Practice

Racial profiling is at the very core of the policing of black men. Almost every stop, frisk, search, assault, or killing of black boys and men starts with racial profiling. Renée McDonald Hutchins defines and explains racial profiling and provides heart-wrenching examples that illustrate why this troubling phenomenon is so painful and damaging. She discusses the role of implicit bias and provides a comprehensive account of how the Supreme Court's rulings have permitted police officers to continue to engage in this practice that is illegal in name only. Hutchins explains why the Court's jurisprudence has made it so difficult to challenge racial profiling in the lower courts and concludes the essay with a discussion of recent efforts to end the practice.

Black Men and the Police: Making Implicit Bias Explicit

Many of the essays in this anthology refer to the phenomenon of implicit bias—the unconscious bias that results from exposure to negative stereotypes and attitudes. In this essay, Katheryn Russell-Brown explains implicit bias and its role in police officers' interactions with black men. She discusses the so-called "shooter studies" that indicate that police officers perceive black men as more threatening and dangerous than white men and are therefore more inclined to shoot unarmed black men than similarly situated white men. Russell-Brown examines recommendations for reform within police departments and the need to address implicit bias at its core through a revamping of the K–12 curriculum in public schools.

Policing: A Model for the Twenty-first Century

In this essay, Tracey Meares and Tom Tyler explore the relationship between the police and communities of color. They discuss why communities of color tend to trust police officers less than white communities and propose a model of procedural justice to improve the level of trust. Meares and Tyler examine the obvious and not-so-obvious reasons why it is important to close this deficit of trust—for the benefit of both the communities and the police officers. Drawing on Meares's service on President Obama's Task Force on 21st Century Policing, they present ideas for a new model that will improve the relationship between police and communities of color while addressing the legitimate concerns of both.

The Prosecution of Black Men

In this essay, I explain how and why prosecutors are the most powerful officials in the criminal justice system. I discuss their discretion and power in the charging and plea-bargaining process before setting forth the ways in which these decisions impact the lives of black men—as criminal defendants and as victims of crimes. I use hypothetical and real examples to illustrate how prosecutorial decisions result in black men being treated worse than their similarly situated white counterparts. I also explore the dearth of African American prosecutors and discuss whether the race of the prosecutor has an impact on the treatment of black men. I conclude with a discussion of the Vera Institute of Justice's Prosecution and Racial Justice Program, a project that sought to address the role of prosecutors in the unwarranted racial disparities in the criminal justice system.

The Grand Jury and Police Violence Against Black Men

Grand juries decide whether an individual should face criminal charges. The vast majority of grand juries almost always bring charges against defendants, primarily because the standard for charging is so low ("probable cause") and because grand juries are entirely controlled by the prosecutor. Yet in cases involving police officers who kill black men, grand juries rarely return an indictment. In this essay, Roger A. Fairfax Jr. explains the history and purpose of the grand jury before exploring the grand jury's problematic role in the investigation of police officers involved in the killings of black men. Fairfax discusses the grand jury investigations of the killings of Freddie Gray, Michael Brown, Eric Garner, Walter Scott, Tamir Rice, and Laquan McDonald. He explains why most of the police officers were not indicted and concludes with suggestions for reform of the grand jury in cases involving police shootings.

Elected Prosecutors and Police Accountability

The prosecutors who were criticized for their failure to criminally charge police officers who killed unarmed black men and boys were all elected officials. In this essay, Ronald F. Wright examines the complex relationship between elected prosecutors and police officers and the problems associated with holding prosecutors accountable through the electoral process, especially the difficulty of challenging incumbents. He discusses and compares the elections of prosecutors in jurisdictions where police officers were involved in the deaths of unarmed black men. Wright explores the challenges African American voters face in prosecutorial elections and suggests reforms to make prosecutors more responsive to minority voters.

Do Black Lives Matter to the Courts?

African Americans have always looked to the Supreme Court for protection from discrimination and all forms of injustice. In this essay, Sherrilyn A. Ifill and Jin Hee Lee demonstrate how the Court has often failed to safeguard the rights of African Americans. They outline the Court's "sordid history dealing with race in this country," beginning with the infamous *Dred Scott* decision. Ifill and Lee discuss how Justice John Marshall Harlan's declaration that "our Constitution is color-blind" in his dissent in *Plessy v. Ferguson* was turned on its head in the modern-day reverse discrimination cases that ignore the specific history of racism against black individuals. They persuasively argue that, by requiring discriminatory intent by a specific actor, the Court fails to acknowledge structural racism and fails to provide viable legal remedies to black men who are the victims of police violence.

Poverty, Violence, and Black Incarceration

The last essay provides important insight into the relationship between poverty, violence, and the incarceration of black men. Jeremy Travis and Bruce Western discuss the research that shows how the overincarceration of black men grew out of poverty and violence. They argue that the overuse of incarceration has created a social inequality that has prevented African Americans from fully participating in American life. Travis and Western maintain that mass incarceration has not had an appreciable impact on public safety and has resulted in devastating consequences for the African American community that have the potential to last for generations. They call for a criminal justice reform agenda that advances peace and justice in African American communities.

NOTES

1. Lizette Alvarez and Cara Buckley, "Zimmerman Is Acquitted in Trayvon Martin Killing," *New York Times*, July 13, 2013, http://www.nytimes.com/2013/07/14/us/george-zimmerman-verdict-trayvon-martin.html?_r=0.

2. James S. Brady, "Remarks by the President on Trayvon Martin," news release, July 19, 2013, https://www.whitehouse.gov/the-press-office/2013/07/19/remarks-president-trayvon-martin.

3. Terrence Rogers, "Using International Human Rights Law to Combat Racial Discrimination in the U.S. Criminal Justice System," *Scholar: St. Mary's Law Review on Minority Issues* 14 (Winter 2011): 389–405; Sally Kohn, "Greasing the Wheel: How the Criminal Justice System Hurts Gay, Lesbian, Bisexual, and Transgendered People and Why Hate Crime Laws Won't Save Them," *New York University Review of Law and Social Change* 27 (2001–2002): 260–64; Kimberlé Williams Crenshaw and Andrea J. Ritchie, *Say Her Name: Resisting Police Brutality Against Black Women* (New York: African American Policy Forum, 2015); Teri A. McMurtry-Chubb, "#SayHerName #BlackWomensLivesMatter: State Violence in Policing the Black Female Body," *Mercer Law Review* 67 (2016): 651; Mike Males, "Who Are Police Killing?" Center on Juvenile and Criminal Justice website (Aug. 26, 2014), http://www.cjcj.org/news/8113.

4. "Juvenile Detention," *Child Trends*, accessed August 20, 2015, http://www.childtrends.org/?indicators=juvenile-detention.

5. *The School-to-Prison Pipeline in Black and White* (American Civil Liberties Union of Rhode Island, 2015), 6.

6. Catherine E. Lhamon and Jocelyn Samuels, *Dear Colleague Letter: Nondiscriminatory Administration of School Discipline* (U.S. Department of Justice and U.S. Department of Education, 2014), 3–4, http://www.justice.gov/sites/default/files/crt/legacy/2014/01/08/dcl.pdf.

7. *Civil Rights Data Collection: Data Snapshot: School Discipline* (U.S. Department of Education Office for Civil Rights, 2014), 6, http://ocrdata.ed.gov/Downloads/CRDC-School-Discipline-Snapshot.pdf.

8. "2011–12 Discipline Estimations by Discipline Type," U.S. Department of Education, Office for Civil Rights, Civil Rights Data Collection, accessed August 20, 2015, http://ocrdata.ed.gov/StateNationalEstimations/Estimations_2011_12.

9. Jamal Hagler, "8 Facts You Should Know About the Criminal Justice System and People of Color," *Center for American Progress*, May 28, 2015, https://www.americanprogress.org/issues/race/news/2015/05/28/113436/8-facts-you-should-know-about-the-criminal-justice-system-and-people-of-color/.

10. Robert Brame, et al., "Demographic Patterns of Cumulative Arrest Prevalence by Ages 18 and 23," *Crime & Delinquency* (January 2014): 474–76.

11. *Terry v. Ohio*, 392 U.S. 1 (1968).

12. "New NYCLU Report Finds NYPD Stop-and-Frisk Practices Ineffective, Reveals Depth of Racial Disparities," *New York Civil Liberties Union*, May 9, 2012, http://www.nyclu.org/news/new-nyclu-report-finds-nypd-stop-and-frisk-practices-ineffective-reveals-depth-of-racial-dispar.

13. Ibid.

14. Ibid.

15. Ryan Gabrielson, Ryann Grochowski Jones, and Eric Sagara, "Deadly Force, in Black and White," *ProPublica*, October 10, 2014, http://www.propublica.org/article/deadly-force-in-black-and-white.

16. Ibid.

17. Jon Swaine, Oliver Laughland, and Jamiles Lartey, "Black Americans Killed by Police Twice as Likely to Be Unarmed as White People," *The Guardian*, June

1, 2015, http://www.theguardian.com/us-news/2015/jun/01/black-americans-killed -by-police-analysis.

18. Ibid.

19. U.S. Department of Justice, Bureau of Justice Statistics, *Police Use of Nonfatal Force, 2002–11*, by Shelley Hyland, Ph.D, Lynn Langton, Ph.D., and Elizabeth Davis. NCJ 249216 (Washington, DC: U.S. Government Printing Office, 2015), 1, http://www.bjs.gov/content/pub/pdf/punf0211.pdf.

20. U.S. Department of Justice, Bureau of Justice Statistics, *Prisoners in 2015*, by E. Ann Carson and Elizabeth Anderson. NCJ 250229 (Washington, DC: U.S. Government Printing Office, 2016), 1, http://www.bjs.gov/content/pub/pdf/p13.pdf.

21. Ibid., 13 (citing 501,300 as the total number of black male sentenced prisoners).

22. Ibid.

23. Michelle Alexander, *The New Jim Crow: Mass Incarceration in the Age of Colorblindness* (2010), 180.

24. U.S. Department of Justice, Bureau of Justice Statistics. *Prevalence of Imprisonment in the U.S. Population, 1974-2001*, by Thomas Bonczar. NCJ 197976 (Washington, DC: U.S. Government Printing Office, 2003), 1, https:www.bjs.gov/content/pub/pdf/piusp01.pdf.

25. Joe Palazzolo, "Racial Gap in Men's Sentencing," *Wall Street Journal*, Feb. 14, 2013, http://www.wsj.com/articles/SB1000142412788732443200457830446378 9858002.

26. Deborah Fins, *Death Row U.S.A.* (Criminal Justice Project of the NAACP Legal Defense and Education Fund, 2016), 1, http://www.naacpldf.org/files/publica tions/DRUSA_Summer_2016.pdf; Matt Ford, "Racism and the Execution Chamber," *The Atlantic*, June 23, 2014, http://www.theatlantic.com/politics/archive/2014/06/ race-and-the-death-penalty/373081/.

Policing the Black Man

A Presumption of Guilt

The Legacy of America's History of Racial Injustice

BRYAN STEVENSON

LATE ONE NIGHT several years ago, I got out of my car on a dark midtown Atlanta street when a man standing fifteen feet away pointed a gun at me and threatened to "blow my head off." I'd been parked outside my new apartment in a racially mixed but mostly white neighborhood which I didn't consider a high-crime area. As the man repeated the threat, I suppressed my first instinct to run and fearfully raised my hands in helpless, terrifying submission to the barrel of a handgun. I tried to stay calm, begged the man not to shoot me, repeating over and over again, "It's all right, it's okay."

As a young criminal defense attorney, I knew that my survival required careful, strategic thinking, I had to stay calm. I'd just returned home from my law office in a car filled with legal papers, but I knew the man holding the gun wasn't targeting me because he thought I was a young professional. Since I was a young, bearded black man dressed casually in jeans, most people would not assume I was a lawyer with a Harvard Law School degree; I looked like most young black men in America. I had filled my head as a college philosophy major with the nonviolent teachings of King and Gandhi; I even thought of myself as "peace-loving." But to the Atlanta police officer threatening to shoot me I looked like a criminal, someone dangerous and guilty.

There was no legitimate reason for a police officer to point a gun at my head and threaten to shoot me in front of my apartment. I had been sitting in my beat-up Honda Civic for over fifteen minutes listening to music which could not be heard outside the vehicle. There was a delicious Sly and the Family Stone retrospective playing on a local radio station that had so engaged me I couldn't turn the radio off. It had been a long day at work. A neighbor must have been alarmed by the sight of a black man sitting in his car and called the police. My getting out of my car to explain to the police officer that this was my home and nothing criminal was taking place is what prompted the officer to pull his weapon and start making threats. Having drawn his weapon, the officer and his partner justified their threat of lethal force by dramatizing their fears and suspicions about me. They threw me on the back of the vehicle, they searched my car illegally, and they kept me on the street for fifteen humiliating minutes while neighbors gathered to view the dangerous criminal in their midst. When no crime was discovered and nothing incriminating turned up after a computerized background check on me, I was told by the police officers to consider myself lucky. While this was said as a taunt and threat, they were right: I was lucky.

People of color in the United States, particularly young black men, are burdened with a presumption of guilt and dangerousness. Some version of what happened to me has been experienced by millions of black people because of this racially biased presumption. In too many situations, black people are presumed to be offenders incapable of being victims themselves. As a consequence of this country's historic failure to address effectively its legacy of racial inequality, this presumption of guilt and the racial narrative that created it have significantly shaped every institution in American society, especially our criminal justice system.

The issue of racially motivated police violence or racial disparities in sentencing can't be viewed simply as a consequence of bad police officers or racially biased judges. There are deep historical forces that have created the problems so clearly seen in America's criminal justice system.

There is a narrative of racial difference that contaminates the thinking of most Americans. We are burdened by our history of racial injustice in ways that shape the way we think, act, and enforce the law. Without understanding this narrative, confronting it truthfully and repairing the damage created by our history, we will never truly experience the equality and fairness we value so highly in our legal system. As in South Africa, Rwanda, and Germany, America desperately needs to commit itself to a process of truth and reparation. We need to own up to the way racial bias and legalized racial subordination have compromised our ability to implement criminal justice. In the wake of decades of our avoiding or minimizing our history of racial injustice, communities from Ferguson to Charleston to Baltimore now bear witness to what we have wrought.

Birth of a Nation: Roots of the Presumption of Guilt

From the moment white settlers reached this continent, color emerged as the defining feature that would shape the cultural, social, political, and economic development of the United States. The indigenous people that Europeans encountered in America were not white. White settlers viewed native people as inferior and unworthy of the wealth, resources, and opportunity this land possessed. The differences between white Europeans and Native Americans weren't just geographic; they quickly became racial, resulting in decades of exploitation and violence. Over the course of two centuries, the native population of America was decimated by Europeans. This genocide reduced the population of more than ten million indigenous tribal people in America to less than 500,000.[1] While disease spread by Europeans accounts for most of the deaths suffered by Native people, war, violence, and forced migration also played a part. The birth of the United States was defiled by the willingness to exploit people of color despite vaunted norms, values, and principles of equality.

Slavery created an even deeper injury to America. Beginning in the seventeenth century, millions of African people were kidnapped, enslaved, and shipped across the Atlantic under horrific conditions: starvation and death were the rule. For the next two centuries the enslavement of black people created wealth, prosperity, and growth for free people of European descent while an elaborate and enduring mythology about the racial inferiority of black people took hold to legitimate, perpetuate, and defend slavery. The ideology of white supremacy survived the Civil War and endures in ways that are evident even today.

Slavery in America and the Ideology of White Supremacy

The racialized caste system of American slavery that originated in the British colonies was unique in many respects vis-à-vis forms of slavery that existed in other parts of the world.[2] In the Spanish and Portuguese colonies, for example, slavery was a class category or form of indentured servitude—an "accident" of individual status that could befall anyone and could be overcome after a completed term of labor or assimilation into the dominant culture.[3]

American slavery began as such a system. When the first Africans were brought to the British colonies in 1619 on a ship that docked in Jamestown, Virginia, they held the legal status of "servant."[4] But as the region's economic system became increasingly dependent on forced labor, and as racial prejudice became more ingrained in the social culture, the institution of American slavery developed as a permanent, hereditary status tied to race.[5]

Over the next two centuries, American slavery grew from and reinforced racial prejudice.[6] Advocates of slavery argued that science and religion supported the fact of whites' racial superiority: white people were smart, hardworking, and more intellectually and morally evolved, while black people were dumb, lazy, childlike, and in need of guidance and supervision. In 1857, for example, Mississippi governor William McWillie denounced anti-slavery critics and insisted:

"[T]he institution of slavery, *per se*, is as justifiable as the relation of husband and wife, parent and child, or any other civil institution of the State, and is most necessary to the well-being of the negro, being the only form of government or pupilage which can raise him from barbarism, or make him useful to himself or others; and I have no doubt but that the institution, thus far in our country, has resulted in the happiness and elevation of both races; that is, the negro and the white man. In no period of the world's history have three millions of the negro race been so elevated in the scale of being, or so much civilized or Christianized, as those in the United States, as slaves. They are better clothed, better fed, better housed, and more cared for in sickness and in health, than has ever fallen to the lot of any similar number of the negro race in any age or nation; and as a Christian people, I feel that it is the duty of the South to *keep them in their present position*, at any cost and at every peril, even independently of the questions of interest and security."[7]

Under this worldview, black people's lifelong and nearly inescapable enslavement in the United States was defended not only as a justifiable necessity but also as a *kindness* through which whites exposed their less-evolved human chattel to discipline, hard work, and morality. Though American slavery was often brutal and barbaric, the myth of black people's racial inferiority developed and persisted as the system's very reason for being. This was so through the Civil War, the 1863 Emancipation Proclamation, and the adoption in 1865 of the Thirteenth Amendment.

The ending of slavery hardly did away with the racist ideology created to defend it.[8] "Freeing" the nation's masses of enslaved black people without undertaking the hard work of deconstruct-ing the narrative of their inferiority doomed those freedmen and -women and their descendants to a fate of subordination and second-class citizenship. In place of slavery, belief in a racial hierarchy took virulent expression in newly defined social norms, including lynching and other forms of racial terrorism; segrega-tion and Jim Crow; and unprecedented mass incarceration.

Denying and Perpetuating the Racial Construct

When eleven southern states seceded from the Union to form the Confederate States of America, sparking the Civil War in 1861, they made no secret of their ultimate aim to preserve the institution of slavery. As Confederate vice president Alexander H. Stephens explained, the ideological "cornerstone" of the new nation they sought to form was "that the negro is not equal to the white man," and that "slavery—subordination to the supe-rior race—is his natural and normal condition."[9]

Slavery had been an increasingly divisive political issue for generations, and though United States president Abraham Lin-coln personally opposed slavery, he had rejected abolitionists' calls for immediate emancipation. Instead, Lincoln favored a gradual process of compensated emancipation and voluntary colonization that would encourage freed black people to immi-grate to Africa.[10] Once the nation was in the throes of civil war, Lincoln feared that any federal move toward emancipa-tion would alienate border states that permitted slavery but had not seceded. Lincoln's cabinet and other federal officials largely agreed, and shortly after the war's start, the House of Represen-tatives passed a resolution emphasizing that the purpose of the war was to preserve the Union, not to eliminate slavery.[11]

As the Civil War dragged on, however, increasing numbers of enslaved African Americans fled and relocated behind Union lines; the cause of emancipation now became more militarily and politically expedient. On January 1, 1863, President Lincoln issued the Emancipation Proclamation,[12] which declared enslaved people residing in the rebelling Confederate states to be "then, thenceforward, and forever free."[13] The proclamation did not apply to the roughly 425,000 enslaved people living in Tennessee, Delaware, Kentucky, Missouri, and Maryland—states that had not seceded or were occupied by Union forces.

In most Confederate states where the proclamation *did* apply, resistance to emancipation was inevitable, and there was almost no federal effort to enforce the grant of freedom.[14] Southern planters attempted to hide news about Lincoln's proclamation from their slaves, and in many areas where federal troops were not present, slavery remained the status quo well after 1863.[15] Even as the Confederacy faced increasingly certain defeat in the war, southern whites insisted that Lincoln's wartime executive order was illegal and that slavery could only be formally banned by a legislature or a court. Many used deception and violence to keep slaves from leaving the plantation.[16]

Formal nationwide codification of emancipation came in December 1865 with ratification of the Thirteenth Amendment, which prohibited slavery throughout the United States "except as punishment for crime." Several states continued symbolically to resist into the twentieth century: Delaware did not ratify the Thirteenth Amendment until 1901; Kentucky until 1976; and Mississippi until 1995.[17]

The legal instruments that led to the formal end of racialized chattel slavery in America did nothing to address the racial hierarchy that sustained slavery, nor did they establish a national commitment to the alternative ideology of racial equality. Black people might be free from involuntary labor, under the law, but that did not mean white people across the nation recognized them as fully human. In many parts of this country, white identity was grounded in a belief that whites were inherently superior to African Americans; following the war, whites in the South reacted violently to the notion that they would now have to treat their erstwhile property as equals and pay for their labor. In numerous recorded incidents, plantation owners attacked black people simply for claiming their freedom.[18] This contempt for black people was not confined to the South. New York governor Horatio Seymour openly campaigned for president of the United States as the "white man's candidate." At the New York Democratic Convention, Seymour argued that black people "are in form, color, and character unlike the whites . . . an ignorant and degraded race." Frontier western states like Idaho passed racial integrity laws making it illegal for a white person to marry or have sex with a black person even though the state was 99.8 percent white.

At the Civil War's end, black autonomy expanded but white supremacy remained deeply rooted. The failure to unearth those roots would leave black Americans exposed to terrorism and racial subordination for more than a century. Two incidents in 1866 foretold terrifying days to come for African Americans. On May 1, 1866, in Memphis, Tennessee, white police officers began firing into a crowd of African American men, women, and children that had gathered on South Street, and afterward white mobs rampaged through black neighborhoods with the intent to "kill every Negro and drive the last one from the city." Over three days of violence, forty-six African Americans were killed (two whites were killed by friendly fire); ninety-one houses, four churches, and twelve schools were burned to the ground; at least five women were raped; and many black people fled the city permanently.[19]

Less than three months later, in New Orleans, a group of African Americans—many of whom had been free before the Civil War—attempted to convene a state constitutional convention to extend voting rights to black men and repeal the racially discriminatory laws known as the Black Codes. When the delegates convened at the Mechanics' Institute on July 30, 1866, groups of black supporters and white opponents clashed in the streets.

The white mob began firing on black marchers, indiscriminately killing convention supporters and unaffiliated black bystanders. Instead of maintaining order, white police officers attacked black residents with guns, axes, and clubs, arresting many and killing several. By the time federal troops arrived to suppress the white insurgency, as many as forty-eight black people were dead and two hundred had been wounded.[20]

The Black Codes: Using the Criminal Justice System to Maintain Racial Hierarchy

Before the end of the nineteenth century, states looked to the criminal justice system to construct policies and strategies to maintain white supremacy and racial subordination. Law enforcement officers were tasked with menacing and controlling black people in ways that would shape policing and the criminal justice system in America for the next century.

Convict leasing, the practice of "selling" the labor of state and local prisoners to private interests for state profit, utilized the criminal justice system for the economic exploitation and political disempowerment of black people. State legislatures passed discriminatory criminal laws, or "Black Codes," which created new criminal offenses such as "vagrancy" and "loitering." This led to the mass arrest and incarceration of black people. Then, relying on language in the Thirteenth Amendment that prohibits slavery and involuntary servitude "except as punishment for crime," lawmakers empowered white-controlled governments to extract black labor in private lease contracts or on state-owned farms.[21] "While a Black prisoner was a rarity during the slavery era (when slave masters were individually empowered to administer 'discipline' to their human property) the solution to the free black population had become criminalization. In turn, the most common fate facing black convicts was to be sold into forced labor for the profit of the state."[22]

Beginning as early as 1866 in states like Texas, Mississippi, and Georgia, convict leasing spread throughout the southern states and continued throughout the late nineteenth and early twentieth centuries.[23] In contrast to white prisoners, who were routinely sentenced to the penitentiary, leased black convicts faced deplorable, unsafe working conditions and brutal violence when they attempted to resist or escape bondage.[24]

An 1887 report by the Hinds County, Mississippi, grand jury recorded that, six months after 204 convicts were leased to a man named McDonald, twenty were dead, nineteen had escaped, and twenty-three had been returned to the penitentiary disabled, ill, and near death.[25] The penitentiary hospital was filled with sick and dying black men whose bodies bore "marks of the most inhuman and brutal treatment . . . so poor and emaciated that their bones almost come through the skin."[26] Under this grotesquely cruel system that lasted decades, countless black men, women, and children lost their freedom—and often their lives. "Before convict leasing officially ended," writes historian David Oshinsky, "a generation of black prisoners would suffer and die under conditions far worse than anything they had ever experienced as slaves."[27]

More enduring was the mythology of black criminality and the way America's criminal justice system adopted a racialized lens which menaced and victimized people of color, especially black men. The presumptive identity of black men as "slaves" evolved into the presumptive identity of "criminal," and we have yet to fully recover from this historical frame.

The explicit use of race to codify different kinds of offenses and punishments was challenged as unconstitutional, and criminal statutes were modified with language that contained no explicit racial references, but the enforcement of the law didn't change. Black people were targeted for a wide range of "offenses," some of which were never used to charge whites. African Americans endured these challenges and humiliations and continued to rise up from slavery by seeking education and working hard under difficult conditions. But the more black people no longer acted as slaves, the more most white people were provoked and agitated. This tension created an era of racial terror, lynching, and violence that traumatized black people for decades.

Nowhere was the animus toward black people more evident than in the criminal justice system. The deep racial hostility that permeated America from the 1860s through the 1940s often served to focus suspicion on black communities after a serious violent crime was discovered, whether evidence supported that suspicion or not. Whites' accusations of rape or murder were rarely subject to serious scrutiny when they were lodged against black people. In a strictly maintained racial caste system, just the suggestion of black-on-white violence was often enough to spark outrage, mob violence, and murder before even a biased judicial system could act. After all, in this society, white lives held heightened value, while the lives of black people held little or none.

Lynching in America: The Legacy of Racial Terror

Between the Civil War and World War II, thousands of African Americans were lynched in the United States. Lynchings were violent, public acts of torture that traumatized black people throughout the country and were largely tolerated by state and federal officials. These lynchings were terrorism. "Terror lynchings" were at their peak between 1880 and 1945 and claimed the lives of African American men, women, and children who were forced to endure the fear, humiliation, and barbarity of this widespread practice.

Lynching had a profound impact on race relations in the United States and shaped the geographic, political, social, and economic conditions of African Americans in ways that are still evident today. Terror lynchings sparked the mass migration of millions of black people from the South into urban ghettos in the North and West throughout the first half of the twentieth century. Lynching created an environment where racial subordination and segregation could be maintained for decades with limited resistance. Most critically, lynching reinforced a legacy of racial inequality that has never been adequately addressed in America. In particular, the administration of criminal justice is tangled with the history of lynching in profound and important ways that continue to compromise the integrity and fairness of the justice system.

Of the hundreds of black people lynched under accusations of rape and murder, very few were legally convicted of an offense, and many were demonstrably innocent. In 1918, for example, after a white woman was raped in Lewiston, North Carolina, a black man named Peter Bazemore was accused of the crime and lynched by a mob before an investigation revealed that the real perpetrator had been a white man wearing black face makeup.[28]

Hundreds more black people were lynched based on accusations of far less serious crimes, like arson, robbery, nonsexual assault, and vagrancy,[29] many of which would not have been punishable by death even if the defendants had been convicted in a court of law. In addition, African Americans were frequently lynched for noncriminal violations of social customs or racial expectations, such as speaking to white people with less respect or formality than observers believed due.[30]

Many African Americans were lynched, not because they committed a crime or social infraction, and not even because they were accused of doing so, but simply because they were black and present when the preferred party could not be located. In 1901, Ballie Crutchfield's brother allegedly found a lost wallet containing $120 and kept the money. He was arrested and about to be lynched by a mob in Smith County, Tennessee, when, at the last moment, he was able to break free and escape. Thwarted in their attempt to kill the suspect, the mob turned their attention to his sister and lynched Ms. Crutchfield in her brother's stead though she was not even alleged to have been involved in the theft.[31]

The Equal Justice Initiative (EJI) in Montgomery, Alabama—of which I am founder and executive director—spent five years and hundreds of hours documenting and researching terror lynchings in the twelve most active lynching states in America: Alabama, Arkansas, Florida, Georgia, Kentucky, Louisiana, Mississippi, North Carolina, South Carolina, Tennessee, Texas, and Virginia. We distinguished "racial terror lynchings" from hangings or mob violence that followed some sort of criminal trial process or were committed against non-minorities without the threat of terror. Those lynchings were a crude form of punishment that didn't have the features of "terror lynchings" directed at racial minorities who were being threatened and menaced in multiple ways.

We also distinguished "terror lynchings" from other racial violence and hate crimes that were prosecuted as criminal acts. Although criminal prosecution for hate crimes committed against black people was rare before World War II, such prosecutions ameliorated those acts of violence and racial animus. The lynchings we documented were acts of terrorism because these were murders carried out with impunity, sometimes in broad daylight. These terror lynchings were horrific acts of violence, often as Sherrilyn Ifill explains "on the courthouse lawn,"[32] whose perpetrators were never held accountable. They were not "frontier justice," because they generally took place in communities where there was a functioning criminal justice system that was deemed too good for African Americans. Some "public spectacle lynchings" were even attended by the entire white community and conducted as celebratory acts of racial control and domination.

EJI's research generated several findings which are relevant to criminal justice policy today. First, racial terror lynching was much more prevalent and common than has been previously reported. EJI documented several hundred more lynchings than had been identified in the most comprehensive work done on lynching to date. Sociologists Stewart Tolnay and E. M. Beck did extraordinary work on lynching and provided an invaluable resource for our work, as did the collected research at Tuskegee University in Tuskegee, Alabama, assembled by Professor Monroe Nathan Work. These two sources are widely viewed as the most comprehensive collections of research data on the subject of lynching in America. EJI did extensive analysis of these data and then did supplemental research and investigation of lynchings in each of the states covered by this report. We reviewed local newspapers, historical archives, and court records, and we conducted interviews and exhaustively examined reports in African American newspapers published during the era. EJI has documented more than four thousand racial terror lynchings between the end of Reconstruction in 1877 and 1950 in just twelve southern states. This represents at least eight hundred more than had been previously reported.[33]

There were six kinds of terror lynchings most common from Reconstruction until World War II: (1) lynchings that resulted from a wildly distorted fear of interracial sex; (2) lynchings based on casual social transgressions; (3) lynchings based on allegations of serious violent crime; (4) public spectacle lynchings, which could involve any of the allegations named above; (5) lynchings that escalated into terroristic violence that targeted the African American community as a whole; and (6) lynchings of sharecroppers, ministers, and other community leaders who resisted mistreatment, which were most common between 1915 and 1945.

Our research confirmed that many victims of terror lynchings were murdered without being accused of committing a crime; they were killed for minor social transgressions or for asserting basic rights. Racial terror lynching was a tool used to enforce Jim Crow laws and racial segregation. These lynchings were a tactic for maintaining racial control more than a way of punishing particular crimes; their purpose was to victimize the entire African American community, not just the alleged perpetrator of a crime.

Our conversations with the survivors of lynchings led us to recognize that the phenomenon of lynching and racial terror played a key role in the forced migration of millions of black Americans out of the South. Thousands of people fled north for fear that some minor social transgression might provoke a mob to show up and take their lives. Parents and spouses sent their loved ones away in frantic, desperate acts of survival and suffered what they characterized as "near-lynchings."

The decline of lynching in America relied heavily on the increased use of capital punishment following court trials and accelerated, unreliable legal process in state courts. The death penalty's roots are clearly linked to the legacy of lynching.

Death and the Racially Motivated License to Kill

As early as the 1920s, lynchings were falling out of favor for the "bad press" they attracted. Southern legislatures looked to shift to capital punishment as a means of using ostensibly legal and unbiased court proceedings to reach the same goal as vigilante violence: satisfying the lust for revenge.[34]

In what is likely the most famous attempted "legal lynching," the "Scottsboro Boys" were nine young African Americans charged with raping two white women in Alabama in 1931. During the trial, white mobs outside the courtroom demanded the boys' executions. Represented by incompetent lawyers, the nine were convicted by all-white, all-male juries within two days, and all but the youngest were sentenced to death. When the NAACP and others launched a national movement to challenge the cursory proceedings, "the white people of Scottsboro did not understand the reaction. After all, they did not lynch the accused; they gave them a trial."[35] In reality, many defendants of the era learned that the prospect of being executed rather than lynched did little to increase the fairness of trial, reliability of conviction, or justness of sentence.

Though northern states had abolished public executions by 1850, some in the South authorized the practice until 1938.[36] The hangings were often racialized displays intended more to deter mob lynchings than to deter individual crimes.[37] Following Will Mack's execution by public hanging in Brandon, Mississippi, in 1909, the *Brandon News* reasoned: "[P]ublic hangings are wrong, but under the circumstances, the quiet acquiescence of the people to submit to a legal trial, and their good behavior throughout, left no alternative to the board of supervisors but to grant the almost universal demand for a public execution."[38] Even in southern states that had outlawed public hangings much earlier, mobs often successfully demanded them.

In Sumterville, Florida, in 1902, a black man named Henry Wilson was convicted of murder in a trial that lasted just two hours and forty minutes. To mollify the mob of armed whites that filled the courtroom, the judge promised a death sentence would be carried out in a public hanging—despite state law prohibiting public executions. Even so, when the execution was set for a later date, the enraged mob threatened, "We'll hang him before sundown, governor or no governor."[39] In response, Florida officials moved up the date, authorized Mr. Wilson to be hanged before a jeering mob, and congratulated themselves on having "avoided" lynching.

By the end of the 1930s, court-ordered executions outpaced lynchings in the former slave states for the first time ever.[40] Two-thirds of those executed that decade were black,[41] and the trend continued: as African Americans fell to just 22 percent of the southern population between 1910 and 1950, they constituted 75 percent of those executed in the South in those years.[42]

In the 1940s and 1950s, the NAACP's Legal Defense Fund (LDF) began what would become a multi-decade litigation strategy to challenge the American death penalty—which was most active in the South—as racially biased and unconstitutional.[43] They won in *Furman v. Georgia* in 1972, when the United States Supreme Court struck down Georgia's death penalty statute, holding that capital punishment still too closely resembled "self-help, vigilante justice, and lynch law" and "if any basis can be discerned for the selection of these few to be sentenced to die, it is the constitutionally impermissible basis of race."[44]

Southern opponents immediately decried the decision and set to writing new death penalty statutes.[45] In 1976, in *Gregg v. Georgia*, the Supreme Court upheld the demand for Georgia's new death penalty statute and reinstated the American death penalty, capitulating to the claim that legal executions were needed to prevent vigilante mob violence.[46]

The new death penalty statutes continued to result in racial imbalance, and constitutional challenges persisted. In the 1987 case of *McCleskey v. Kemp*, the United States Supreme Court considered statistical evidence demonstrating that Georgia decision-makers were more than four times as likely to impose death for the killing of a white person than a black person. Accepting the data as accurate, the Court accepted racial bias in sentencing as "an inevitable part of our criminal justice system,"[47] and upheld Warren McCleskey's death sentence because he had failed to identify a "constitutionally significant risk of racial bias"[48] in his particular case.

Today, race remains a salient factor in capital sentencing. African Americans make up less than 13 percent of the national population, but nearly 42 percent of those currently on death row in America are black,[49] and 34 percent of those executed since 1976 have been black.[50] In 96 percent of states where researchers have completed studies examining the relationship between race and the death penalty, results reveal a pattern of discrimination based on the race of the victim, the race of the defendant, or both.[51] Meanwhile, capital trials remain proceedings with little racial diversity, where the accused is often the only person of color in the courtroom and illegal racial discrimination in jury selection also remains widespread. This is especially true in the South and in capital cases; in Houston County, Alabama, prosecutors have excluded 80 percent of qualified African Americans from serving as jurors in death penalty cases.[52]

More than eight in ten American lynchings between 1889 and 1918 occurred in the South, and more than eight in ten of the more than 1,400 legal executions carried out in this country since 1976 have been in the South.[53] Modern death sentences are disproportionately meted out to African Americans accused of crimes against white victims; efforts to combat racial bias and create federal protection against racial bias in the administration of the death penalty remain thwarted by familiar appeals to the rhetoric of states' rights; and regional data demonstrates that the modern American death penalty mirrors racial violence of the past.[54] As contemporary proponents of the American death penalty focus on form rather than substance, tinkering with the aesthetics of lethal punishment to improve process and methods, capital punishment remains rooted in racial terror and is "a direct descendant of lynching."[55]

America's comfort with lethal violence in response to suspected black criminality cannot be disconnected from police violence today and a range of contemporary racial justice issues in law enforcement policy. This nation's racial history has nurtured an impulse to shoot or kill black men in ways that can't be justified or defended. Our history has created a resistance to acknowledging the victimization of black people, and the explicit and implicit bias in this history can be seen in law enforcement and criminal justice policy throughout this nation.

In the face of this national ignominy, there is still an astonishing absence of any effort to acknowledge, discuss, or address lynching. Many of the communities where several lynchings took place have gone to great lengths to erect markers and memorials to the Civil War, to the Confederacy, and to events and moments when local power was violently reclaimed by white southerners. These communities celebrate and honor the architects of racial subordination and political leaders known for their beliefs in white supremacy. There are very few, if any, significant monuments or memorials that address the history and legacy of lynching in particular or the struggle for racial equality in general. Most communities have no active or visible awareness of the way in which race relations in their communities were formed and shaped by terror and lynching. As Sherrilyn Ifill has brilliantly argued in her seminal book on the topic, *On the Courthouse Lawn*, the absence of memorials to lynching has deepened the injury to African Americans and left the rest of the nation indifferent to black victimization.

The Legacy of Lynching

When the era of racial terror and widespread lynching ended in the mid-twentieth century, it left behind a nation and an American South fundamentally altered by the preceding decades of systematic community-based violence against black Americans. The effects of the lynching era echoed throughout the latter half of the twentieth century. African Americans continued to face violent intimidation when they transgressed social boundaries or asserted their civil rights, and the criminal justice system continued to devalue black life and operate as a tool to subordinate African Americans. These legacies have yet to be confronted.

After the number of lynchings abated, the central feature of the era of racial terror—violence against black Americans—found expression in new ways. The social forces and racial animus that made lynching a frequent occurrence and constant threat in the late nineteenth and early twentieth centuries remained deeply rooted in American culture, and violent intimidation continued to be used as a means of preserving social control and white supremacy. Unable to rely on the justice system for protection, African Americans faced violence, threats, and intimidation in myriad areas of daily life.

Black southerners who had survived the lynching era still lived under the established legal system of racial apartheid known as Jim Crow. African Americans in other parts of the country generally lived in the margins of newly organized political structures. As organized resistance to this racial caste system began to swell in the early 1950s, black demonstrators' efforts were met with violent opposition from white police officers and community members. Black activists protesting racial segregation and disenfranchisement through boycotts, sit-ins, voter registration drives, and mass marches consistently faced physical attacks, riots, and bombings from whites.

As a leader of the nonviolent protest movement, the Reverend Dr. Martin Luther King Jr. faced white law enforcement officials and private citizens who issued death threats, physically assaulted him at public lectures, and even bombed his Montgomery, Alabama, home while his wife and infant daughter were inside. Police also attacked demonstrators in highly publicized events like Bloody Sunday in Selma, Alabama, in 1965. Even black children were at great risk of harm and death: in 1963, four young girls were killed when the Sixteenth Street Baptist Church in Birmingham, Alabama, was bombed, and that same year, more than seven hundred black children protesting racial segregation in the city were arrested, blasted with fire hoses, clubbed by police, and attacked by police dogs.

Police in Mississippi facilitated the extrajudicial murders of civil rights workers Andrew Goodman, James Chaney, and Michael Schwerner in 1964 by delivering the men to waiting white mobs after detaining them for an alleged traffic violation. A mob of Ku Klux Klansmen who had gathered during the several hours the three young men were held in jail were ready and waiting to pursue, seize, and murder them upon release.[56] Just as lynchings had been justified in the preceding decades, these violent incidents were defended as necessary to maintain "law and order."

Transitional Justice and the Way Forward

America has never systematically and publicly addressed the effects of racial violence, the criminalization of African Americans, and the critical role these phenomena have played in shaping the American criminal justice system. The Civil Rights Act of 1964, arguably the signal legal achievement of the civil rights movement, contains provisions designed to eliminate discrimination in voting, education, and employment, but does not address discrimination in criminal justice. Though the most insidious engine of racial subordination throughout the era of racial terror and its aftermath, the criminal justice system remains the institution in American life least affected by the civil rights movement. Similarly, the system's links to and existence as a legacy of racist myths of black criminality have never been meaningfully acknowledged or confronted. The unprecedented levels of mass incarceration in America today stand as a continuation of these past distortions and abuses, still limiting opportunities in our nation's most vulnerable communities.

The civil rights movement should have been followed by a process of truth and reparation that focused on recovery. We needed diagnosis and treatment for what decades of racial subordination and segregation—which followed decades of racial terror and violence, which followed two hundred years of brutal, racialized slavery—had done to us. The trauma, the bigotry, the miseducation and distortions required therapy and management so we could move forward and reconcile ourselves to a better future informed by the mistakes and human rights abuses of the past. Instead, a toxic era shaped by the politics of fear and anger followed the civil rights movement and sustained racial inequality. We retreated from racial and economic justice and opted for mass incarceration and a misguided "war on drugs" that has left many poor and minority people marginalized, incarcerated, and condemned.

We can't change our history, but we can acknowledge it and better shape our future. The United States is not the only country with a violent history of human rights atrocities and oppression. Many nations have been burdened by legacies of racial domination or tribal conflict resulting in massive human rights abuses or genocide. Apartheid in South Africa shaped that nation in ways that are profound. The horrific genocide in Rwanda created wounds that will last for generations. The Holocaust in Germany was a twentieth-century nightmare with unprecedented features. What distinguishes the United States from these other nations is our unwillingness to confront our history in a public and meaningful way.

Th commitment to truth and reconciliation in South Africa was critical to that nation's recovery. In Rwanda, there is an understanding that there must be transitional justice for the nation to heal. Today in Berlin, Germany, visitors encounter markers and stones at the homes of Jewish families who were abducted and taken to the concentration camps. The Germans want everyone to go to the camps and reflect soberly on the history of the Holocaust; they have created legal structures to eliminate and repel the return of Nazism.

In America, we do the opposite. We don't acknowledge the history and legacy of slavery; instead we have littered the landscape with misguided markers, memorials, and pride in the Confederacy. We have done nothing to recognize the era of lynching. We have done very little to atone for decades of legally sanctioned racial subordination.

We are long overdue for a commitment to transitional justice in this country. We need to engage in truth-telling about our history with the hope that the truth might inspire us to address a range of contemporary issues in a different way. In *Between Vengeance and Forgiveness*, Martha Minow outlines the complex demands of truth and justice when societies seek to recover from massive human rights abuses and atrocities. What emerges from Minow's work and others in the transitional justice community is that silence and inaction in the aftermath of horrific abuse yield continuing frustration and distrust. As the International Center for Transitional Justice has noted:

> A history of unaddressed massive abuses is likely to be socially divisive, to generate mistrust between groups and in the institutions of the State, and to hamper or slow down the achievement of security and development goals. It raises questions about the commitment to the rule of law and, ultimately, can lead to cyclical recurrence of violence in various forms.[57]

Lynching scholars like Sherrilyn Ifill have recognized that this process is vital for recovery. The Equal Justice Initiative has begun a project to erect markers across the nation that recognize the history of slavery. No one should be able to travel to Memphis, New Orleans, Montgomery, Natchez, Charleston, Richmond, Savannah, or Washington, D.C., without being forced to confront the history of slavery in America. To confront our violent past and resolve to never repeat it, EJI wants to mark every lynching site in America. At the dedication of each of these markers, law enforcement leaders ought to be present to apologize to communities of color because public safety officials throughout our history failed to protect black people from racially motivated violence and persecution.

We are building a national memorial to the victims of lynching where the names of victims and the communities that allowed this terror will be recorded for our nation to see and reflect upon. We want to create a space where we can soberly acknowledge the terror that fed racial hierarchy and violence so we can better understand the challenges we face. We are opening a museum named From Enslavement to Mass Incarceration so visitors can understand the connections between our past and the issues we face today.

We could make different policy decisions about a host of contemporary issues. The threshold question concerning capital punishment is not whether people deserve to die for the crimes they commit but rather do we deserve to kill. Given the racial disparities that still define the death penalty in this country, we should eliminate capital punishment and expressly identify our history of racially biased lethal violence as a basis for its abolition. Confronting implicit bias within police departments should be seen as essential in twenty-first-century policing. If we don't proactively confront the challenges our history of racial injustice has created, we will be doomed to another century of inequality and abuse.

What threatened to kill me on the streets of Atlanta when I was a young attorney wasn't just a misguided police officer with a gun, it was the force of America's history of racial injustice and the presumption of guilt it created. In America, no child should be born with a presumption of guilt, burdened with expectations of failure and dangerousness because of the color of her or his skin or a parent's poverty. Black people in this nation should be afforded the same protection, safety, and opportunity to thrive as anyone else. But, alas, that won't happen until we confront our history and commit to engaging the past that continues to haunt us.

NOTES

1. See Tanya H. Lee, "The Native American Genocide and the Teaching of U.S. History," Truthout, April 1, 2015. Available at http://www.truth-out.org/news/item/29954-the-native-american-genocide-and-the-teaching-of-us-history.

2. For example, in the Spanish and Portuguese colonies of South America, freed

black people did not retain a stigma of inferiority after slavery ended there, the way they did in the United States. Frank Tannenbaum, *Slave and Citizen: The Negro in the Americas* (New York: Alfred A. Knopf, 1947), 65.

3. Roman law, which remained influential in countries like Spain and Portugal in the seventeenth and eighteenth centuries, viewed slavery as a mere accident, of which anyone could be the victim. As such, it tended to forestall the identification of the black man with slavery, "thus permitting the Negro to escape from the stigma of his degraded status once he ceased to be a slave." Carl Degler, "Slavery and the Genesis of American Race Prejudice," *Comparative Studies in Society and History* 2, no. 1 (Oct. 1959): 50. "Yet, of course, ancient [Roman] slavery was fundamentally different from modern [American] slavery in being an equal opportunity condition—all ethnicities could be slaves—and in seeing slaves as primarily a social, not an economic, category." Philip D. Morgan, "Origins of American Slavery," *OAH Magazine of History* 19, no. 4 (July 2005): 51.

4. "The status of the Negroes was that of servants, and so they were identified and treated down to the 1660s." Oscar and Mary Handlin, "The Origins of the Southern Labor System," *William & Mary Quarterly* 2, no. 3 (April 1950): 203.

5. "Slavery was not an isolated economic or institutional phenomenon; it was the practical facet of a general debasement, without which slavery could have no rationality. (Prejudice, too, was a form of debasement, a kind of slavery in the mind.) Certainly the urgent need for labor in a virgin country guided the direction which debasement took, molded it, in fact, into an institutional framework. That economic practicalities shaped the external form of debasement should not tempt one to forget, however, that slavery was at bottom a social arrangement, a way of society's ordering its members in its own mind." Winthrop D. Jordan, "Modern Tensions and the Origins of American Slavery," *Journal of Southern History* 28, no. 1 (Feb. 1962): 30. "[S]lavery became indelibly linked with people of African descent in the Western hemisphere. The dishonor, humiliation, and bestialization that were universally associated with chattel slavery merged with blackness in the New World. The racial factor became one of the most distinctive features of slavery in the New World." Morgan, "Origins of American Slavery," 53.

6. "[A]s slavery evolved as a legal status [in America], it reflected and included as a part of its essence, this same discrimination which white men had practiced against the Negro all along and before any statutes decreed it . . . As a result, slavery, when it developed in the English colonies, could not help but be infused with the social attitude which had prevailed from the beginning, namely, that Negroes were inferior." Degler, "Slavery and the Genesis of American Race Prejudice," 52.

7. "Extracts from the Message of Gov. McWillie, of Mississippi, to the Legislature of the State," *The Liberator* (Dec. 11, 1857).

8. French researcher Alexis de Toqueville observed that slavery was on the decline in some regions of the United States, but "the prejudice to which it has given birth is immovable."Alexis de Tocqueville, *Democracy in America*, trans. Henry Reeve (1840), 460. Writing more than a century later, American historian Carl Degler noted, "[I]t is patent to anyone conversant with the nature of American slavery, particularly as it functioned in the nineteenth century, that the impress of bondage upon the character

and future of the Negro in the United States has been both deep and enduring." Degler, "Slavery and the Genesis of American Race Prejudice," 49.

9. Alexander H. Stephens, Cornerstone Address (March 21, 1861), available at http://teachingamericanhistory.org/library/document/cornerstone-speech/.

10. Doris Kearns Goodwin, *Team of Rivals: The Political Genius of Abraham Lincoln* (New York: Simon & Schuster, 2005), 91, 369.

11. Ibid., 369–70.

12. See ibid., 462–72.

13. Abraham Lincoln, Emancipation Proclamation (Jan. 1, 1863), available at http://www.loc.gov/resource/lprbscsm.scsm1016/#seq-1.

14. Goodwin, *Team of Rivals*, 464; , *infra*. 4.

15. Leon F. Litwack, *Been in the Storm So Long: The Aftermath of Slavery* (New York: Alfred A. Knopf, 1979), 172–74.

16. Ibid., 182–83.

17. John W. Blassingame, *The Slave Community: Plantation Life in the Ante-bellum South*, rev. ed. (New York: Oxford University Press, 1979), 261; Equal Justice Initiative, *Slavery in America: The Montgomery Slave Trade* (2013), 27 & n108 (noting that despite the Mississippi legislature's voting finally to ratify the Thirteenth Amendment in 1995, the necessary paperwork was not submitted to federal authorities for nearly eighteen years, so the state's official ratification was not recorded until 2013).

18. Litwack, *Been in the Storm So Long*, 182, 194–96.

19. T. W. Gilbreth, "The Freedmen's Bureau Report on the Memphis Race Riots of 1866" (May 22, 1866), available at http://teachingamericanhistory.org/library/document/the-freedmens-bureau-report-on-the-memphis-race-riots-of-1866/; U.S. Congress, House Select Committee on the Memphis Riots (July 25, 1866), available at https://babel.hathitrust.org/cgi/pt?id=ucl.c054751926;view=1up;seq=13; Herbert Shapiro, *White Violence and Black Response: From Reconstruction to Montgomery* (Amherst: University of Massachusetts Press, 1988), 6–7.

20. James G. Hollandsworth Jr., *An Absolute Massacre: The New Orleans Race Riot of July 30, 1866* (Baton Rouge: Louisiana State University Press, 2001), 3, 104–5, 126; Donald E. Reynolds, "The New Orleans Riot of 1866, Reconsidered," *Louisiana History* 5 (Winter 1964): 5–27.

21. "The Mississippi Black Codes were copied, sometimes word for word, by legislators in South Carolina, Georgia, Florida, Alabama, Louisiana and Texas." David M. Oshinsky, *Worse Than Slavery: Parchman Farm and the Ordeal of Jim Crow Justice* (New York: Simon & Schuster, 1996), 21.

22. Jennifer Rae Taylor, "Constitutionally Unprotected: Prison Slavery, Felon Disenfranchisement, and the Criminal Exception to Citizenship Rights," *Gonzaga Law Review* 47, no. 2 (2011): 365, 374.

23. Douglas A. Blackmon, *Slavery by Another Name: The Re-enslavement of Black Americans from the Civil War to World War II* (New York: Anchor Books, 2008), 54–55.

24. Oshinsky, *Worse than Slavery*, 35–36.

25. "Prison Abuses in Mississippi: Under the Lease System Convicts Are Treated with Brutal Cruelty," *Chicago Daily Tribune*, July 11, 1887, 26.

26. Ibid.

27. Oshinsky, *Worse than Slavery*, 35.

28. "Southern Farmers Lynch Peter Bazemore," *Chicago Defender*, March 30, 1918; "Short Shrift for Negro," *Cincinnati Enquirer*, March 26, 1918.

29. Stewart E. Tolnay and E. M. Beck, *A Festival of Violence: An Analysis of Southern Lynchings, 1882–1930* (Urbana: University of Illinois Press, 1995), 47.

30. Ibid., 31.

31. Crystal N. Feimster, *Southern Horrors: Women and the Politics of Rape and Lynching* (Cambridge, MA: Harvard University Press, 2009), 165; Ralph Ginzburg, *100 Years of Lynchings* (Baltimore: Black Classic Press, 1962), 38–39.

32. Sherrilyn Ifill, *On the Courthouse Lawn: Confronting the Legacy of Lynching in the Twenty-First Century* (Boston: Beacon Press, 2007).

33. Equal Justice Initiative, "Lynching in America: Confronting the Legacy of Racial Terror in America" (2015).

34. Stephen B. Bright, "Discrimination, Death and Denial: The Tolerance of Racial Discrimination in Infliction of the Death Penalty," *Santa Clara Law Review* 35 (1995): 440; see also Charles David Phillips, "Exploring Relations Among Forms of Social Control: The Lynching and Execution of Blacks in North Carolina, 1889–1918," *Law and Society Review* 21 (1987): 372 (finding evidence for the conclusion that, prior to disenfranchisement, lynchings and executions were used in concert to suppress the black population, but once blacks were politically neutralized, lynching became a "costly and unnecessary form of repression" and legal executions then became sufficient to punish deviance within the black population).

35. Bright, "Discrimination, Death and Denial," 440–41.

36. Stuart Banner, "Traces of Slavery: Race and the Death Penalty in Historical Perspective," in *From Lynch Mobs to the Killing State: Race and the Death Penalty in America*, ed. Charles J. Ogletree Jr. and Austin Sarat (New York: New York University Press, 2006), 106.

37. Amy Louise Wood, *Lynching and Spectacle: Witnessing Racial Violence in America*, 1890, https://www.pinterest.com/1940 (2009), 38.

38. Ibid., 47.

39. Margaret Vandiver, *Lethal Punishment: Lynchings and Legal Executions in the South* (2006), 101.

40. James W. Clarke, "Without Fear or Shame: Lynching, Capital Punishment and the Subculture of Violence in the American South," 28 *British J. of Pol. Sci.* 269 (April 1998), 284.

41. Bright, "Discrimination, Death and Denial," 440.

42. Clarke, 287.

43. David Garland, *Peculiar Institution: America's Death Penalty in an Age of Abolition* (Cambridge, MA: Belknap Press of Harvard University Press, 2010), 218–19.

44. *Furman v. Georgia*, 408 U.S. 238, 310 (1972) (Stewart, J., concurring).

45. Following *Furman*, Mississippi senator James O. Eastland accused the Court of "legislating" and "destroying our system of government," while Georgia's white supremacist lieutenant governor, Lester Maddox, called the decision "a license for anarchy, rape, and murder." In December 1972, Florida became the first state after *Furman* to enact a new death penalty statute, and within two years, thirty-five states

had followed suit. Proponents of Georgia's new death penalty bill unapologetically borrowed the rhetoric of lynching, insisting: "There should be more hangings. Put more nooses on the gallows. We've got to make it safe on the street again . . . It wouldn't be too bad to hang some on the court house square, and let those who would plunder and destroy see." State representative Guy Hill of Atlanta proposed a bill that would require death by hanging, to take place "at or near the courthouse in the county in which the crime was committed." Georgia state representative James H. "Sloppy" Floyd remarked, "If people commit these crimes, they ought to burn." Garland, *Peculiar Institution*, 232, 247–48.

46. *Gregg v. Georgia*, 428 U.S. 153, 184 (1976).

47. *McCleskey v. Kemp*, 481 U.S. 279, 313 (1987).

48. Ibid.

49. Current Death Row Populations by Race, Death Penalty Information Center, http://www.deathpenaltyinfo.org/race-death-row-inmates-executed-1976#deathrow pop (accessed June 22, 2014).

50. Annual Estimates of the Resident Population by Sex, Race, and Hispanic Origin for the United States, States, and Counties: April 1, 2010 to July 1, 2012, U.S. Census Bureau, https://factfinder.census.gov/faces/tableservices/jsf/pages/productview .xhtml?pid=PEP_2012_PEPSR6H&prodType=table (accessed June 23, 2014).

51. Facts About the Death Penalty, Death Penalty Information Center, http://www.deathpenaltyinfo.org/documents/FactSheet.pdf (accessed June 19, 2014).

52. Equal Justice Initiative, *Illegal Racial Discrimination in Jury Selection: A Continuing Legacy* (2010), 5.

53. Number of Executions by State and Region Since 1976, Death Penalty Information Center, http://www.deathpenaltyinfo.org/number-executions-state-and-region -1976 (accessed June 21, 2014).

54. Bright, "Discrimination, Death and Denial," 439.

55. Ibid.

56. James P. Marshall, *Student Activism and Civil Rights in Mississippi: Protest Politics and the Struggle for Racial Justice, 1960–1965* (Baton Rouge: Louisiana State University Press, 2013), 101–103.

57. International Center for Transitional Justice, "What Is Transitional Justice?" https://www.ictj.org/about/transitional-justice.

The Endurance of Racial Disparity in the Criminal Justice System

MARC MAUER

Introduction

Clarence Aaron was a twenty-three-year-old college student from Mobile, Alabama, with no criminal record. In 1992 he introduced a classmate whose brother was a drug dealer to a cocaine seller he knew from high school. He was subsequently present for the sale of nine kilograms of cocaine and was paid $1,500 by the dealer. After police arrested the drug group, the others testified against Aaron, describing him as a major dealer, which led to his being sentenced to three terms of life imprisonment in federal prison.

In the era of mass incarceration and the harsh mandatory sentencing laws imposed disproportionately on black men, stories such as Aaron's are unfortunately all too familiar. Aaron was fortunate, though, in having his injustice recognized; after twenty years in prison, he became one of a modest number of individuals to receive a sentence commutation from President Obama.

While the complicated relationship between black men and the criminal justice system has endured throughout American history, the experience of the past half century marks a shift of historic proportions. In 1954, the year the historic *Brown v. Board of Education* decision marked the symbolic launching of the modern-day civil rights movement, there were fewer than 100,000 black men incarcerated in the nation's prisons and jails. Since that time there has been a substantial opening of social and economic opportunity for many people of color who had previously been denied access to full participation in American society. This progress is reflected even within the criminal justice system, where there is a much greater diversity of leadership in many areas. It is now not unusual to see a black man or woman heading a police force or a state corrections system.

Yet despite these societal gains, if we examine other developments in the criminal justice system since the day of the *Brown* decision, the situation is profoundly troubling. The number of black males behind bars is now more than 600,000,[1] a proportionally far greater increase than that of the overall black male population since 1954. As a result, the life prospects of a substantial number of black men have been profoundly affected, severely limiting their opportunities for future employment, education, and overall participation in society. And as a result of the compounding effect of mass incarceration on African American communities these developments hold substantial potential to become part of the life experiences of the generation of black boys growing up today as well.

On the surface, these trends are confounding. Why is it that overlapping with a period of substantial progress toward civil rights and economic progress we see such an unprecedented expansion of the role of the criminal justice system in the lives of black men? To understand these shifts we need to examine both the racial dynamics of the criminal justice system as well as the profound political and economic shifts of the past several decades that created the environment in which the mass incarceration of black men became possible.

In exploring the disproportionate incarceration rates of black men the proximate cause is seemingly a higher rate of involvement in certain crimes. As we shall see, while available data support this correlation to some extent, the data are more complex than they appear at first and also tell us little about how these factors were shaped by the political environment.

Beyond these factors the effect of practitioner decision-making within the justice system continues to shape differential outcomes, whether as a result of overtly racist behavior or the implicit bias which affects all of us. These decisions are compounded as well by a set of "race-neutral" policies which inevitably produce distorted outcomes in justice as a result of the failure to project the ways in which such initiatives will not in fact be race-neutral when implemented.

In telling this story I hope it will become clear that while socioeconomic changes created the *possibility* of a mass incarceration response, it was only due to American society's racial assumptions about crime that made this the outcome of choice. Whether these perceptions were conscious or not, they resulted in policymakers and the public creating a systemic approach that not only reinforced distorted assumptions of criminal behavior, but solidified the second-class status of so many black men in disadvantaged communities. And in large part due to the persistence of racial segregation in housing and other areas of social life, the broad-ranging effects of the mass incarceration of African American males now contributes to declining life opportunities for the next generation of children.

Setting the Stage for the Mass Incarceration of Black Men

While the prison population, and black male incarceration, began its historic rise in 1973, clearly the antecedents of that moment were long in the making. A centuries-long history of brutal racism beginning with slavery and progressing through Jim Crow in all its permutations throughout the nation set the stage for a modern-day version of oppression in response to developing social and economic conditions in American society.

Those shifts in part took the form of rising rates of crime beginning in the mid-1960s. To what extent crime rates rose is not entirely clear, since data collection on crime at the time was much less comprehensive than it is today. But at the very least we can note that murder rates—historically the most well-reported crime—nearly doubled, from 5.0 per 100,000 population in 1960 to 9.8 per 100,000 by 1974.[2]

Various factors explain this rise in violent crime, as well as crime in general. First is the impact of the coming of age of the "baby boom" generation in the 1960s. Since young males in the 15–24 age group commit crimes at higher rates, it should not have been surprising that a bulge in this part of the population would affect crime rates. Second, urbanization, another factor that is generally correlated with higher crime rates, increased at a rapid rate in this period. And third, despite the general decline in unemployment during these years, the disproportionate effect of rising unemployment on nonwhite youth was "sufficient to explain increasing crime rates for youths" in the 1960s, according to economists Llad Phillips and Harold Votey.[3]

Coincident with these trends was the emergence of crime as a national issue. While it now seems rather commonplace, prior to the 1960s crime was largely perceived as a local issue. By and large crime took place in local communities and was responded to by local police agencies. Sensational events, such as the exploits of gangsters like Al Capone, attracted national attention, but these were hardly run-of-the-mill crimes.

Seeking to gain political advantage by focusing on rising crime, Republican presidential candidate Barry Goldwater in 1964 articulated the need to deal with "law and order," followed by more vigorous rhetoric four years later in the themes of Richard Nixon's presidential campaign. As framed by Nixon, this was a sweeping call to action, responding to street crime, but also to the perceived threats to public order posed by the burgeoning civil rights and antiwar movements. Not coincidentally, this campaign theme was marked by not very subtle racial overtones, from the candidate promising to save (white) America from (black male) "criminals" and civil rights disrupters. Thus, while the image of black male criminality had long been a feature of American racism, the emerging political initiatives now refashioned these perceptions for what would become an unprecedented, and unforeseen, explosion in the U.S. prison population.

This shifting political environment would become more significant with the broad economic transitions in the United States that began in the 1970s. The rapid postwar recovery beginning in the late 1940s, made possible in large part by the relatively limited war damage in the United States, paved the way for a dramatic leap in American manufacturing. Largely provided by the auto and steel industries, union wage jobs in the Upper Midwest and elsewhere attracted large numbers of African American and white working-class men, often migrating from Appalachia or the South in search of economic opportunity. These jobs laid the foundation for workers to buy a house, gain access to employer-sponsored health care, and enable their children to have an entryway into middle-class America.

This was not accomplished without conflict, of course. Spurred on by the civil rights movement and growing labor militancy, black workers in particular organized to demand both better working conditions and racial justice in the workplace. Movements such as the Detroit-based DRUM (Dodge Revolutionary Union Movement) drew the connection between the rights of workers and the still-unmet economic needs of many communities of color.

But the hard-fought gains of union workers in these and other manufacturing industries were about to suffer from an economic disruption that would remain a defining feature of American society to this day and further set the stage for the development of mass incarceration. Beginning in the early 1970s the three-decade expansion of the economy fueled by war production needs in the 1940s and by the leading position of the United States in the world economy began a sharp decline. American manufacturers initially faced competition from Japanese auto and steel companies, and subsequently adopted a globalization strategy of seeking lower-wage markets for their production. With an initial shift to Latin American workforces and later a move to Asian nations, the once-robust high-wage production jobs in the United States began a precipitous decline that contributed in large part to the expansion of a lower-wage service economy and growing inequality.

Hardest hit in these transitions were the working-class communities of the Upper Midwest. Detroit, for example, lost 90,000 blue-collar jobs in the 1970s, and Chicago 120,000. The sons and daughters of auto and steel workers were now more likely to be employed at a fast-food chain than at the local auto plant, with a consequent sharp decline in earnings potential. These effects were felt disproportionately in African American communities, where the millions who had traveled north through the Great Migration experienced a sharp setback in their newfound economic opportunity. African American high school graduates in metropolitan areas suffered a 20 percent decline in employment and those who were high school dropouts experienced a 30 percent decline.[4]

So, by the early 1970s we saw the confluence of rising rates of crime, the growing influence of the conservative political movement and its challenge to social welfare policies, and the increasing identification of black males as "the crime problem" in the minds of many Americans. With crime and violence rising, it was not inappropriate to develop strategies to address the problem. The means chosen to do so, though, reflected the racial identification of crime in ways that prioritized punishment over prevention, and individual responsibility over collective action. None of this was inevitable, and the consequences of this profound shift in ideology and practice remain with us today in the era of mass incarceration.

Crime Rates and the Imprisonment Rate of Black Men

One might assume that examining the scale of incarceration, or the degree to which different demographic groups experience imprisonment, would be a function of the degree of involvement in criminal activity for those populations. All things being equal, a greater likelihood of committing crime should lead to an increased likelihood of arrest and conviction, and subsequent incarceration. But as we have seen over a period of several decades, this seemingly commonsense observation actually tells us little about the mass incarceration of black men, or incarceration overall.

How a society chooses to advance public safety is very much a function of how it conceptualizes the problem and the means of producing the outcomes it desires. Prison is but one aspect of the broader criminal justice system, which in turn is only one element of any comprehensive crime strategy. Overall, public safety is a product of family and community environments, access to opportunity, educational and health care services, and many other interventions, including criminal justice initiatives.

As I will describe later, the fundamental shift leading to mass incarceration—and the dramatic incarceration of black men— beginning in the 1970s was a function of the set of decisions made to treat the crime problem in disadvantaged communities primarily as a criminal justice problem. One can argue about the degree to which racism may have motivated this shift, but at the very least we can conclude that this was a form of benign neglect. That is, as outsourcing and the search for low-wage labor markets abroad brought about a substantial decline in the manufacturing sector, this was almost inevitably going to impact urban communities of color very directly. This in turn contributed to the development of illicit drug distribution economies in subsequent years. And while these developments should have been entirely predictable, one would be hard-pressed to find any indication that policymakers or corporate leaders considered these impacts in advance or proposed any policy initiatives to ameliorate the community disruption that would ensue.

Given that mass incarceration—whether articulated or not—became the method of choice for addressing the disadvantaged life circumstances of black men in low-income communities, some would argue that this might be unfortunate but merely reflected a greater degree of criminal behavior. Several layers of analysis are necessary to understand these dynamics.

In analyzing degrees of involvement in crime there is less precision than one might imagine. Since most crimes go undetected and there are few self-report surveys of crime involvement (with the exception of some surveys of juveniles), arrest data become the best proxy for measuring criminal behavior. With the significant exception of drug crimes, which will be addressed later, arrest reports have generally been found to offer a reasonable reflection of crime involvement. One limitation, though, is that while the Uniform Crime Reports (UCR) publications of the FBI contain information on race and gender, these are reported separately, and so we cannot routinely examine data for black men in particular. (In addition, Latinos are characterized as an ethnic group, and so are largely included within the white and black racial categories for these purposes.)

UCR data for 2015 show that African Americans constituted 28 percent of persons arrested for property crimes and 36 percent of those arrested for violent crimes, clearly disproportionate to their 13 percent share of the total U.S. population.[5] But what might appear at first glance to be a race effect on crime in fact is essentially a socioeconomic measure, an outgrowth of the disadvantages brought about by the concentrated poverty that afflicts many African American communities. The problem in trying to break out the degree to which crime involvement (or other outcomes) is a function of race and/or class is that disadvantaged whites are far less likely to reside in situations of concentrated poverty that are so prevalent for African Americans.

A study by Lauren Krivo and Ruth Peterson looking at "extremely disadvantaged" neighborhoods concluded that rates of violence were considerably higher in these areas regardless of race. The authors concluded that "it is these differences in disadvantage that explain the overwhelming portion of the difference in crime, especially criminal violence, between White and African American communities."[6]

Looking at racial disparities in incarceration, a series of studies over time have explored the question of the degree to which disparities in imprisonment reflect involvement in crime. As pioneered by criminologist Alfred Blumstein, a study of the 1979 prison population concluded that 80 percent of the prison disparities could be explained by arrest patterns, while a follow-up study of the 1991 population concluded that the figure had declined to 76 percent. Blumstein found that the incarceration of drug offenders in particular was far less correlated with crime involvement (at least to the extent that one can measure by estimates of drug use and drug selling).[7]

Of the findings of 20 percent and 24 percent disparities, respectively, that could not be explained by arrest proportions, Blumstein stated that these could reflect relevant criminal justice variables such as prior criminal record or they could be a function of racially disparate processing decisions within the justice system. Research over time suggests that disparate outcomes in decision-making are more likely to be present in less serious cases. This is because decision-makers—prosecutors, judges, parole officials—generally have more discretion in such cases, which can manifest in differences in charging, plea negotiations, and sentencing practices in particular.

While these findings would be interpreted by some to suggest that most of the disparity in imprisonment rates is in fact due to greater involvement in crime among black men, two factors strongly mitigate against this. First, as we shall see, the racially skewed impact of drug law enforcement and sentencing has substantially affected these outcomes. And second, the racially influenced nature of punishment for all offenses exacerbates these impacts as well.

The racial disparities we observe in the prison system are also mirrored in the juvenile justice system. While there has been a substantial decline in the number of juveniles held in residential placement over the past decade, racial disparities persist at a disturbing level. A study examining processing in the system concluded that "disparity is most pronounced at the beginning stages of involvement with the juvenile justice system. When racial/ethnic differences are found, they tend to accumulate as youth are processed through the system."[8] Given that juvenile justice involvement is so highly correlated with future imprisonment, these disparities are of particular relevance to the mass incarceration of black men.

Practitioner Decision-Making and Racial Disparities

The criminal justice system has changed substantially in recent decades. Not least among these shifts has been the evolution toward diversity in leadership and staffing in criminal justice agencies. While these advances still fall short of representing the population as a whole, they nonetheless mean that it is now not unusual for people of color and women to be heading major agencies in law enforcement and corrections, and to be substantially represented in the ranks of many of these institutions.

Despite these developments there has perhaps been no moment in recent decades when there has been less trust and confidence in the criminal justice system among African American communities than there is now. In recent years this has clearly been a function in large part of the tragic circumstances surrounding the high-profile killings of so many black men by police—Eric Garner, Freddie Gray, Walter Scott, and others.

The outrage at these tragedies begins with the fact that these events have largely received national attention because of cell phone technology and the dramatic videos that have quickly gone viral through social media. And while many people, and certainly African Americans, believe that the only aspect of these killings that is new is that they have been captured on camera, shockingly we have no way of knowing whether this is in fact the case. No governmental institution tracks killings of civilians by police, and it was not until 2015 that two leading newspapers— the *Washington Post* and the *Guardian*—undertook their own surveys of the frequency of such episodes.

The anger that has surfaced in cities across the country calls into question the experience of the community policing movement of recent decades. Since the 1980s, pioneered by scholars such as Herman Goldstein and others, the law enforcement community has largely embraced the concept of problem-oriented policing. While this has taken a variety of forms in different jurisdictions, typically it is described as an approach that does not measure success based on the number of arrests, but rather on solving problems through community engagement. At the national level, support for this approach was enhanced by the establishment of the COPS (Community Oriented Policing Services) office through the 1994 federal crime bill, along with President Clinton's pledge to fund 100,000 new community policing officers.

The extent to which problem-oriented policing has taken hold is far from clear. A 2003 study examining these developments concluded that "[t]he police still cling to an institutional definition that stresses crime control and not prevention," and that "police organizations . . . have not been radically or even significantly altered in the era of community policing and problem-oriented policing."[9] While there are no doubt cities in which this approach has produced constructive relationships, the eruption in so many African American communities across the nation suggests that success has been much more modest than claimed by many.

Also, as articulated by so many of the protesters and civil

rights leaders, the tension between law enforcement and African American communities is but the flashpoint for a broad critique of the apparatus of mass incarceration and its profound impact on black men in particular. As spending time in prison has become almost an inevitable part of the life cycle for black boys growing up in disadvantaged communities, the criminal justice system broadly has come to be viewed by many not as an institution designed to advance public safety but as an oppressive bureaucracy implementing a twenty-first-century version of racial hierarchy.

While the racial disparities produced by the system have complex origins and are far less likely to appear as outwardly racist as in the days of Jim Crow, they nonetheless are pervasive at each stage of the system. And despite the noted increased diversity in the justice system leadership, centuries of racism in American society continue to affect criminal justice practitioners, as it does all Americans, in decision-making, allocation of resources, and adoption of "race-neutral" policies with unambiguously racially disparate outcomes.

We can see this at each level of the criminal justice system. In law enforcement, it was not until extensive data became available in the 1990s that the racial profiling so prevalent in traffic stops by law enforcement officers came to broad public attention, though black motorists had been keenly aware of these practices since the invention of the automobile. Litigation brought about through extensive data collection in states such as New Jersey, Maryland, and Florida confirmed that the degree to which black drivers were stopped on highways far exceeded their share of motorists who were driving above the speed limit or had other violations related to their vehicles. Further, the "hit rates" resulting from searches during these stops failed to show that black drivers were any more likely to be carrying drugs or illegal weapons in their cars. More recent data from the Department of Justice show that white, black, and Hispanic drivers are now stopped at comparable rates, but that black and Hispanic drivers are more than three times as likely as whites to be searched by police following a stop.[10]

Some law enforcement officials have argued that racially disparate traffic stops have been the result of "a few bad apples" within police agencies—officers who account for a disproportionate amount of stops of black drivers. Whether or not that is a plausible explanation in a given jurisdiction, the widespread practice of "stop and frisk" in many large cities is clearly a conscious strategy of police departments, growing out of the "broken windows" theory of crime control, which produces broad disparities as a direct consequence of policy decisions.

New York has been the city with the greatest attention focused on its "stop and frisk" policy, largely as a result of the litigation that ultimately led to the policy being found unconstitutional in 2013. From a figure of about 97,000 pedestrian stops in 2002, the police department ratcheted up the practice in subsequent years, reaching a level of 685,000 stops annually by 2011. Of the total, 87 percent of those stopped were African American or Latino, a rate that resulted in many teenage boys being able to recount multiple experiences with these practices.[11] The effect of the policy on public safety appears to have been quite minimal at best. Of the 191,000 stops in 2013, 92 percent did not result in an arrest and guns were found in less than 1 percent of all cases.[12] Black and Latino New Yorkers were more likely than whites to be frisked following a stop, yet were only about half as likely to be found in possession of an illegal weapon.[13] Following the decision by federal judge Shira Scheindlin to reduce the number of stops dramatically, no significant increase in crime resulted in the following year.

Such practices came to be seen as even more calculating in some jurisdictions through the revelations that surfaced in Ferguson, Missouri, in the wake of the Michael Brown killing. Not only were police stops and ticketing skewed against black residents, but they actually served as a primary revenue strategy of local government through the fines and fees imposed for traffic and other infractions. Similar allegations about debtors' prisons have since surfaced in Alabama, Louisiana, and elsewhere.

Troubling racial outcomes have also been well documented in prosecutorial charging and plea negotiating practices. With the expansion of determinate and mandatory sentencing, which has restricted the discretion afforded to judges at sentencing, prosecutors have become particularly influential in determining the consequences of criminal activity. This can perhaps be seen most directly in studies of the impact of mandatory sentencing for drug offenses in the federal justice system.

Promoted by lawmakers in the 1980s as a "tough on crime" measure that would "send a message" to potential drug sellers that they would face stiff mandatory penalties, the reality is that such penalties are not in fact inevitable and are also racially skewed in their application. Research by the U.S. Sentencing Commission has documented that in cases where the facts of the case suggested that a mandatory minimum could apply, 63.7 percent of white defendants were able to plead to a charge that didn't carry a mandatory minimum, compared to just 39.4 percent of black defendants.[14]

Several factors help to explain these outcomes. One is the way in which the federal sentencing "safety valve" functions. Adopted by Congress as part of the 1994 crime bill, the safety valve permits judges to sentence certain individuals below the applicable mandatory minimum. The criteria for doing so include being charged with drug crimes that do not involve any violence or possession of a weapon, limited criminal history, and cooperation with the prosecution. Because in certain locales African Americans are more likely to have a greater criminal history than whites, they qualify for the safety valve exception less often.

A further analysis by Sonja B. Starr and M. Marit Rehavi illustrates the role of practitioner decision-making in these outcomes as well. Their analysis finds that controlling for relevant factors, black males received federal prison terms 10 percent longer than white males. Further, in examining the imposition of mandatory minimums, they found that prosecutors charged black men with offenses carrying mandatory penalties twice as often as they did comparable white men.[15]

We can see sentencing decision-making broadly following these patterns. These are most pronounced at the deep end of the system, the application of the death penalty. Dating back to the 1980s, a series of studies originally pioneered by David Baldus[16] have demonstrated the key role of race in the determination of which capital defendants receive the death penalty, as opposed to life imprisonment or a lesser penalty. Consistently the research has shown that when the victim of the killing is white it is far more likely that the perpetrator will be sentenced to death than when the victim is black. No one in the courtroom necessarily articulates such a biased perspective, and it is likely that in most cases both judges and jurors would deny any intentional bias, yet an unchecked and unexplored unconscious bias is broadly at work.

An enlightening example of how this plays out can be seen in the findings of a study of decision-making by probation officers in the juvenile justice system in a northwest state.[17] Examining the narrative section of pre-sentence reports prepared by the officers, researchers assessed the ways in which black and white juveniles were described in this subjective assessment. White youth tended to be described as having "environmental" problems—not getting along with their family, acting out at school, peer pressure, etc. But black youth were more likely to be assessed as having an "antisocial" personality. The consequences of these distinctions are critical. For teenagers having adjustment problems the court can engage counselors and therapists to help them work through these challenges. But for those defined as having an antisocial personality, there is no obvious intervention, and so the goal of public safety will be more likely to suggest incapacitating the youth in some type of residential placement.

Research in a variety of jurisdictions documents similar biased impacts among a range of criminal justice practitioners as well. Defense attorneys, for example, may exhibit racial bias in how they triage their substantial caseloads; judges are more likely to impose longer prison terms on people of color than on whites; and all-white juries deliberate for shorter periods of time than racially diverse juries. None of these outcomes necessarily suggest that these dynamics result from conscious racist motives among practitioners. Rather, as is true of all persons raised in a society with a centuries-long history of racism, the often unconscious biases and attitudes that we all carry within us influence our thinking and behavior in complex ways.

The Impact of "Race-Neutral" Policies

Just as criminal justice practitioners make decisions that, consciously or not, disadvantage black men in the system, so too do public policy decisions have racially biased outcomes even if apparently "race-neutral" on the surface. These decisions have come about in large part due to the failure of policymakers to analyze the unintended impacts of policies developed in the name of public safety. In so doing they have frequently exacerbated the effect of practitioner decision-making on African American men.

Many of these effects can be seen in policies adopted through the war on drugs in recent decades. At the level of policing, a wealth of evidence, generally acknowledged by law enforcement leadership, has documented that drug law enforcement has disproportionately focused on communities of color. Police leaders will frequently justify this by stating that while they are aware that there are substance abuse violations in communities of all socioeconomic levels, in disadvantaged neighborhoods drug use and selling are more likely to take place at street-corner drug markets. Thus, compared to more well-off communities where drug transactions largely take place behind closed doors, the outdoor markets are more disruptive to the community.

While there is some validity to this argument, it presupposes that a heavy-handed law enforcement approach is the only, or most effective, means of responding to this concern. In so doing, it implicitly rejects policy responses that might prioritize creating economic opportunity, improving educational outcomes, expanding substance abuse treatment centers, or other measures. And while some might argue that such approaches seem reasonable in the abstract but are not politically viable, consider the response to the rise in heroin overdoses of recent years. Increasingly, the focus has been on prevention and treatment, rather than punishment, and one cannot help but observe that "the problem" is overwhelmingly seen as one affecting white Americans.

The purportedly race-neutral effects of drug policy extend into the sentencing area as well. The most well-known instance relates to the mandatory penalties for crack cocaine offenses enacted by Congress in 1986. Coming as the crack cocaine "epidemic" was developing, the legislation was adopted in record time, with virtually no discussion about approaches to the problem other than harsh penalties. Here, too, the racial imagery was inescapable. As portrayed on the cover of news magazines and other media, "the problem" was identified as one of black men using and selling crack. As a consequence, the penalties adopted for crack cocaine offenses—80 percent of which were applied to African Americans—were far more punitive than those for powder cocaine, a drug more widely used by whites and Latinos.

Other seemingly rational policies implicitly incorporate racially disparate effects as well. Consider the increased penalties for repeat offenders present in every state through some mix of habitual offender laws, "three strikes and you're out" policies, and other measures. While judges have long taken into account a defendant's prior record in imposing sentence, the effect of this consideration in the new generation of such policies can result in dramatically different outcomes. Under the original version of California's three strikes law, for example, a third felony conviction for stealing golf clubs from a sporting goods store resulted in a prison term of twenty-five years to life, far in excess of what would have been imposed in the absence of the three strikes law.

The racial impact of such laws results from the fact that African American men in general are more likely to have prior convictions than other racial groups. While in various situations this may be a function of racist policing, greater involvement in certain crimes, or other factors, it means that black men will be more likely to be subject to these enhanced penalties upon conviction.

A 1998 case in federal court in Boston illustrates these dynamics. Alexander Leviner, an African American man, was found guilty of being a felon in possession of a weapon. At sentencing, Judge Nancy Gertner examined Leviner's prior convictions and found that several of them had resulted from traffic stops by Boston police. Knowing of the history of disparate policing in the city, Judge Gertner concluded that as a black man Leviner was more likely than white drivers to be stopped by police and thereby acquire a more substantial criminal record. So while she did not dispute the validity of the prior convictions, she essentially discounted part of this criminal record and sentenced Leviner to 2.5 years in prison rather than the four to six years called for in the sentencing guidelines.[18]

Extreme racial disparities can also be seen in the implementation of drug-free school zone laws that exist in every state. These policies, adopted under the goal of deterring drug selling on school grounds, generally call for stiffer penalties for drug offenses committed within a designated school zone. The school zones, defined by a radius from a school property, typically extend at least one thousand feet from a school, but can be as much as three miles, as in Alabama. One of the many problems with such policies is that individuals can be subjected to these penalties even if they had no knowledge that they were within the school zone district.

The racial impact of these policies grows out of housing patterns. In densely populated urban neighborhoods a much higher proportion of the city area lies within a school zone than in more spread out suburban or rural neighborhoods. Thus, drug crimes in cities, where African Americans are frequently clustered, are more likely to result in enhanced school zone penalties. In New Jersey, an analysis of persons sentenced under this policy in 2005 found that 96 percent of all drug crimes charged with school zone enhancements involved either African American or Latino defendants.[19] As a result, the state legislature subsequently restored discretion to judges in sentencing for these offenses.

Race and the Severity of Punishment

As the preceding discussion has made clear, what might appear to be a relationship between race and higher levels of engagement in violent and property crime is in large part a function of socioeconomic disadvantage, and the unique ways in which African Americans are subject to concentrated poverty. Nevertheless, some would argue that while this supports efforts to address these issues in the long term, it doesn't negate the need to punish offenders today in the interest of public safety. But even to the extent that punishment responds to levels of involvement in crime, the relative severity of punishment is intimately related to racial perceptions of crime.

We have seen how this has played out during the drug war, but similar dynamics accompany the development of punishment policies broadly. Key research by Ted Chiricos and colleagues has identified how racial perceptions of crime influence the degree of public support for harsh penalties. Analyzing responses to a 2002 survey ascertaining support for policies such as "making sentences more severe for all crimes" and "locking up more juvenile offenders," they found that whites—but not African Americans or Latinos—who attributed higher proportions of violent crime, burglary, or robbery to blacks were significantly more likely to support punitive policies.[20] Other research has found similar patterns among whites who agree that "African Americans pose a greater threat to public order and safety than other groups,"[21] as well as support for harsher juvenile sanctions.

These findings are troubling in their suggestion that support for punishment among white Americans (and presumably white policymakers as well) increases to the extent that respondents perceive crime as a "black problem." But this is further compounded by broad misperceptions of actual levels of racial involvement in crime. Although African Americans are disproportionately engaged in crime (as measured by arrest rates, the closest proxy), whites in particular believe that these rates are even higher than is the case. A 2010 survey, for example, asked white respondents to estimate the proportion of burglaries, drug sales, and juvenile crime committed by African Americans, and found that they overestimated these rates by 20 percent to 30 percent.[22] These inaccurate perceptions of crime derive from various sources, which include media imagery and political demagoguery, and contribute not only to distorted political debate but also to harsher punishment not only for black men, but for others as well.

Impact of Mass Incarceration on Black Men

The stated rationale for the development of mass incarceration is that it has been necessary to subject millions of Americans to lengthy periods of imprisonment to promote public safety.

Whether through incapacitation, deterrence, or some other means, prison walls separate dangerous people from society and are meant to deter potential lawbreakers. And in the minds of many, it may be unfortunate if black men are overly represented within this population but this is just the result of a "do the crime, do the time" ethos. In this scenario, if we want to see fewer black men in prison then black men should stop committing so much crime.

There are certainly many people behind bars—one can think of Charles Manson, among others—who would likely be a threat to the community if they were not imprisoned. But if we examine the overall effect of mass incarceration, it is clearly lacking as a successful strategy for addressing crime.

The complexity of examining the relationship between crime rates and policy initiatives is challenging overall. But perhaps the most succinct assessment of this effect comes from the comprehensive analysis of the growth of incarceration in the United States produced by the National Research Council in 2014. The well-regarded body of experts assembled for that review concluded that "panel data studies support the conclusion that the growth in incarceration rates reduced crime, but the magnitude of the crime reduction remains highly uncertain and the evidence suggests that it was unlikely to have been large."[23]

This conclusion may seem puzzling at first since one could easily assume that incarcerating a world-record number of people would surely have a major effect on crime. But there are in fact a number of factors that help us to understand why this is not the case. First, as the pool of offenders sentenced to prison expands, there is a tendency to incarcerate an increasing number of less serious offenders, thereby diminishing the "cost-effectiveness" of any given prison term. Second, the broad use of life imprisonment—which now accounts for one of every nine people in prison today—means that there are many individuals in prison who are well past the point at which people "age out" of crime, and therefore it produces diminishing returns as well. Third, mass incarceration has a destabilizing effect in disadvantaged communities of color; the endless cycle of young black men heading off to prison and returning home years later tears at the fabric of community relationships, economic security, and the informal social controls that are critical to public safety.

While it is not unreasonable to ask whether incarceration has a significant effect on crime, in many respects that is not a very useful line of inquiry. A more fruitful undertaking would be to ask what mix of social interventions, including but not limited to incarceration, are effective in reducing crime. That is, imagine that we have a choice of spending a million dollars on public safety. How much crime reduction would be produced by building prisons and how much by expanding preschool education? Or substance abuse treatment, or affordable housing, or Medicaid expansion? This is an intellectual exercise, but also a guide for what policymakers should be engaged in on a routine basis, as opposed to competing for sound bites on tough crime policies.

A second frame of analysis should be to examine incarceration not only for any crime-reducing benefits, but for its unintended consequences and harm to individuals and communities. As a consequence of both the societal stigma for those with a criminal record and political initiatives of recent decades that have erected further barricades for citizens returning home from prison, the impact of a criminal record for black men and others is now a lifelong stain. So, for the black men who have been to prison—who overwhelmingly suffered from poor educational attainment, high rates of substance abuse, and mental health issues—the prospects for obtaining gainful employment, decent housing, and a legitimate opportunity in society have become increasingly more difficult.

These barriers extend to the communities around them as well. With so many black men "missing" from the community and/or with limited economic prospects, family formation suffers as well. Record rates of incarceration mean that black boys in many communities are growing up with the recognition that going off to prison is a far more likely part of their life course than the prospect of entering college. These are certainly not healthy developments for any community.

Reframing Public Policy

Mass incarceration is increasingly being framed as a chief civil rights issue of the twenty-first century. As American society evolves toward a more fair and just community in many respects, the growing inequality and related phenomenon of mass imprisonment stand out as striking reminders that racism has not gone away, but merely takes new forms in new generations.

As challenging as the current moment is, there is nonetheless some reason for hope. In recent years the political environment has undergone a significant shift in regard to criminal justice policy. As a result of lowered crime rates since the 1990s, along with a growing critique of the excesses of the war on drugs, leaders across the political spectrum are now calling for an end to mass incarceration and a scaling back of some of the excessive sentencing policies that have been a major factor in producing the current situation.

While the shift in the public discussion is most welcome, results to date are more modest. As measured by the number of people behind bars, the best one can say is that since 2009 the incarcerated population has declined modestly. This development is certainly a stark contrast to the 1980s and 1990s, when prison populations experienced as much as double-digit growth in some years. But stabilizing at a world-record level of incarceration clearly does not represent anything close to the scale of what is necessary to reverse these trends.

Within these developments, though, there are broad variations in incarceration trends. Since 2000 a handful of states have achieved substantial reductions in their prison populations, reaching 25 percent or more in New Jersey, New York, Rhode Island, and California. Given that much of the change has come about through reduced incarceration of drug offenders, these declines have disproportionately benefited black men because of their overrepresentation among these offenders. These shifts have come about through a mix of policy change and practitioner decision-making, and have emerged through a growing recognition that no single initiative in itself can substantially reduce prison populations in itself.

Much more needs to be done to challenge racism and mass incarceration. Practitioners at each level of the system have the ability to assess and respond to unwarranted racial disparities as they perform their job functions. This includes making decisions regarding the location of drug arrests, disparate charging and plea-negotiation practices by prosecutors, support for indigent defense programs, sentencing policy disparities, and parole decision-making.

Policy change needs to take place in all states and at the federal level. Most significantly, we need to engage in a reassessment of the scale and wisdom of extreme punishment that has been the hallmark of mass incarceration for decades. The United States incarcerates a greater proportion of its population for a variety of reasons, but among them the severity of punishment is a key factor. Such a reevaluation needs to begin at the top of the scale. The United States is one of the only industrialized nations that still maintains the death penalty; this both casts a stain on our moral standing and exerts an upward pressure on the severity of punishment across the board. Thus, not only are serious offenses punished more harshly than in comparable nations, but so too are persons convicted of crimes such as burglary and car theft. There is no criminological justification for such policies, and the human costs are overwhelming.

This scope of policy change will not be easy to achieve, of course. But in some respects the opportunity to make such a shift has never been more timely. As the tragic, and highly visible, killings of black men by police has made clear, the racial tensions within the criminal justice system are quite high, and they are not sustainable. So there is at least an opportunity for dialogue, and a chance for all of America to consider what we mean by "Black Lives Matter."

And as we have that national conversation, we should do it in the context of the historical underpinnings of mass incarceration and its racial dynamics, whether developed consciously or not. So yes, this is a problem of the criminal justice system, but more so it is a societal problem that challenges us to consider how we should address the twin goals of pursuing public safety and challenging inequality. The extent to which we can do that successfully will tell us how much in fact black lives *do* matter.

NOTES

1. All corrections population figures taken from various data reports of the Bureau of Justice Statistics unless otherwise noted.

2. Marc Mauer, *Race to Incarcerate* (New York: The New Press, 2006), 29.

3. Elliot Currie, *Confronting Crime: An American Challenge* (New York: Pantheon, 1985), 111.

4. Howard L. Rosenthal and David J. Rothman, *What Do We Owe Each Other?* (Piscataway, NJ: Transaction Publishers, 2008), 103.

5. Federal Bureau of Investigation, Uniform Crime Reports: Arrest Tables, https://ucr.fbi.gov/crime-in-the-u.s/2015/crime-in-the-u.s.-2015/tables/table-43.

6. Lauren J. Krivo and Ruth D. Peterson, "Extremely Disadvantaged Neighborhoods and Urban Crime," *Social Forces* 75 (1996): 642.

7. Alfred Blumstein, "On the Racial Disproportionality of the United States' Prison Populations," *Journal of Criminal Law and Criminology* 73 (1982): 1259–81; Alfred Blumstein, "Racial Disproportionality of U.S. Prison Populations Revisited," *University of Colorado Law Review* 64 (1993): 743–60.

8. Eileen Poe-Yamagata and Michael A. Jones, "And Justice for Some: Differential Treatment of Minority Youth in the Justice System," 1, http://files.eric.ed.gov/fulltext/ED442882.pdf.

9. Jack R. Greene, "Community Policing and Organizational Change," in *Community Policing: Can It Work?*, ed. Wesley G. Skogan (Belmont, CA: Wadsworth, 2003), 49, quoted in John L. Worrall and *Tomislav v. Kovandzic*, "COPs Grants and Crime Revisited," *Criminology* 45, no. 1 (2007): 163.

10. Lynn Langton and Matthew Durose, "Police Behavior During Traffic and Street Stops, 2011," Bureau of Justice Statistics, http://www.bjs.gov/content/

pub/pdf/pbtss11.pdf (2013): 3; Christine Eith and Matthew R. Durose, "Contacts Between Police and the Public, 2008," Bureau of Justice Statistics, http://www.bjs .gov/content/pub/pdf/cpp08.pdf (2011): 7.

11. New York Civil Liberties Union, Stop-and-Frisk Data, http://www.nyclu.org/ content/stop-and-frisk-data.

12. New York Civil Liberties Union, Stop and Frisk 2013, http://www.nyclu.org/ files/publications/8.26.14_Stop-and-Frisk_2013_final.pdf.

13. Ibid.

14. U.S. Sentencing Commission, *Report to the Congress: Mandatory Minimum Penalties in the Federal Criminal Justice System* (Washington, DC: GPO 2011), 133.

15. S. B. Starr and M. M. Rehavi, "Mandatory Sentencing and Racial Disparity: Assessing the Role of Prosecutors and the Effects of Booker," *Yale Law Journal* 123, no. 2 (2013): 2–80.

16. David C. Baldus, Charles Pulaski, and George Woodworth, "Comparative Review of Death Sentences: An Empirical Study of the Georgia Experience," *Journal of Criminal Law and Criminology* 74, no. 3 (1983).

17. G. Bridges and S. Steen, "Racial Disparities in Official Assessments of Juvenile Offenders: Attributional Stereotypes as Mediating Mechanisms of Juvenile Offenders," *American Sociological Review* 63 (1998): 554–71.

18. Marc Mauer, "Addressing Racial Disparities in Incarceration," *The Prison Journal* 91, no. 3 (2011): 95S.

19. Ibid.

20. T. Chiricos, K. Welch, and M. Gertz, "Racial Typification of Crime and Support for Punitive Measures," *Criminology* 42, no. 2 (2004): 369.

21. R. D. King and D. Wheelock, "Group Threat and Social Control: Race, Perceptions of Minorities and the Desire to Punish," *Social Forces* 85, no. 3 (2007): 1255–80.

22. J. T. Pickett, T. Chiricos, K. M. Golden, and M. Gertz, "Reconsidering the Relationship Between Perceived Neighborhood Racial Composition and Whites' Perceptions of Victimization Risk: Do Racial Stereotypes Matter?" *Criminology* 50, no. 1 (2012): 145–86.

23. National Research Council of the National Academies, *The Growth of Incarceration in the United States* (Washington, DC: National Academies Press, 2014), 155.

Boys to Men

The Role of Policing in the Socialization of Black Boys

KRISTIN HENNING[1]

On September 15, 2015, sixteen-year-old black male Emilio Mayfield was on his way to school when an officer stopped him for jaywalking in a bus lane in Stockton, California.[2] An officer told Emilio to sit down, but he refused and continued walking toward the bus he was trying to catch. The officer eventually grabbed Emilio's arm and Emilio pulled away. After forcing Emilio to sit on the sidewalk, the officer grabbed Emilio's ankles and pushed him backward onto the ground by pinning his ankles against his upper body and hitting him with a baton. The encounter escalated as nine officers became involved, at least four of whom piled on top of Emilio after slamming him to the ground. The irony—jaywalking isn't an arrestable offense in Stockton. Emilio was later cited for trespassing and resisting arrest.

On Memorial Day, in May 2013, fourteen-year-old black male Tremaine McMillian was at the beach with his family, friends, and puppy when an officer forced him to the ground and held him in a choke hold so tight that he wet his pants.[3] His transgression? Clenched fists and dehumanizing stares. The backstory—Tremaine had been roughhousing with a friend on the beach when a Miami-Dade police officer told him to stop. Tremaine asked "Why?" and the officer ordered him to point out his mother. As Tremaine walked toward his mother with his puppy in his arms, the officer followed him in an ATV, jumped out, and

put him in the choke hold. Tremaine was charged with a felony count of
resisting arrest with violence and disorderly conduct.

THESE ARE JUST two stories that made the news. Consider the
many abuses, transgressions, and unnecessary intrusions that
young black males experience in the United States that are never
reported to the media. Consider the many reports of injustice
that are passed by word of mouth in black families, schools,
churches, and communities.

These narratives have a profound impact on the way black
boys learn to think about and interact with the police. Because
adolescence is a time when initial impressions of the justice system become fixed in a child's mind, early encounters with the
police—both personal and vicarious—have an enduring impact
on the way young black males respond to the law and law enforcement as they transition into adulthood. Perceived injustices like
those shared by Emilio and Tremaine undermine police legitimacy and erode the child's willingness to obey the law, report
criminal activity, assist the police in investigations, and cooperate with the police during future face-to-face encounters. Over
time, negative police interactions with black boys have cascading
consequences for public safety, officer safety, and ultimately the
mortality of black boys and men.

The Black Juvenile Super-predator, Implicit Racial Bias, and Perceptions of Innocence

Black boys are policed like no one else, not even black men.
Youth in general are more likely than adults to have contact with
the police as they play in the streets, congregate in public spaces,
hang out past curfew, drink alcohol, ride around in cars, and talk
loudly.[4] Because youth may be arrested for minor crimes, such as
curfew violations and being incorrigible with authorities, their
contacts are also more likely to be police-initiated and adversar-

ial.[5] Young black males who move in crowds, "jone," and play-fight, like Tremaine McMillian and his friend, are even more likely than young white men, young minority women, and older minority men to attract attention from the police and experience verbal abuse, excessive force, unwarranted street stops, and other negative interactions with police.[6] Further, although black girls are far from immune to the harmful effects of negative police contact—especially those involving sexual mistreatment—black girls and women are socialized to play differently, tend to have less contact with the police, and are more likely than black boys to benefit from discretionary, lenient behavior by the police.[7]

The reality is that we live in a society that is uniquely afraid of black boys. Consider the 1990s rhetoric surrounding the black juvenile super-predator. In numerous articles and television interviews, Princeton professor John Dilulio Jr. predicted that "a new generation of street criminals is upon us—the youngest, biggest and baddest generation any society has ever known."[8] "America is now home to thickening ranks of juvenile 'super-predators'—radically impulsive, brutally remorseless young-sters, including ever more preteen boys who murder, assault, rape, rob, burglarize, deal deadly drugs, join gun-toting gangs and create serious communal disorders."[9] Dilulio was not alone in promoting this demographic theory, which gained extraordi-nary traction in the media and among politicians seeking to earn a reputation as being tough on crime.

Notwithstanding his own acknowledgment that demography is not fate and criminology is not pure science,[10] Dilulio man-aged to sensationalize his theory with such reckless abandon that even his academic peers worried that he had become a patsy for conservative politicians.[11] Even worse, the super-predator myth was racialized in explicit and unapologetic ways as evident from Dilulio's now infamous 1996 *City Journal* headline that boldly proclaimed "My Black Crime Problem, and Ours."[12] Dilulio predicted that "not only is the number of young black criminals likely to surge, but . . . as many as half of these juvenile super-predators could be young black males." Describing the black children who inspire fear among white Americans as not "merely unrecognizable, but alien," Dilulio appeared to sympathize with them when he said:

> Not that we can't understand where they come from . . . [T]hink about how many inner-city black children are without parents, relatives, neighbors, teachers, coaches, or clergymen to teach them right from wrong, give them loving and consistent discipline, show them the moral and material value of hard work and study, and bring them to cherish the self-respect that comes only from respect for the life, liberty and property of others. Think how many black children grow up where parents neglect and abuse them, where other adults and teenagers harass and harm them, where drug dealers exploit them. Not surprisingly, in return for the favor, some of these children kill, rape, maim, and steal without remorse.[13]

Dilulio dubbed his argument "the theory of moral poverty"—the poverty of being without loving, capable, responsible adults who teach you right from wrong; the poverty of growing up in the absence of people who teach morality through their own example and insist that you follow suit.[14] In an effort to jus-tify white fears and denounce claims of racism in the criminal and juvenile justice systems as unreasonable paranoia by blacks, Dilulio argued, "If blacks are overrepresented in the ranks of the imprisoned, it is because they are overrepresented in the criminal ranks—and the violent criminal ranks, at that."[15] "Espe-cially in urban America, white fears of black crime—like black fears of black crime—are rational far more than reactionary or racist."[16]

It took a religious conversion on Palm Sunday in 1996 for

Dilulio to abandon his theory.[17] By then it was too late. As even Dilulio himself admits, "once [the myth] was out there, there was no reeling it in."[18] The damage has been unyielding. Notwithstanding statistical evidence that by 2001 had firmly disproven the predictions of an imminent juvenile super-predator, children as young as thirteen and fourteen are still being tried as adults, and hundreds of juveniles have been sent to prison for life without the possibility of parole in the wake of horrific legislation designed to stave off the impending black threat.

More troubling is the lingering and pervasive influence of the super-predator myth on the psyche of the police and the public. Although it is impossible to trace any one event to the image police have of black youth, it is hard to believe that Dilulio's rhetoric did not emblazon the image of violent black boys running amok on the minds of those who police our streets. Think about Tamir Rice, the twelve-year-old Cleveland boy who was killed by police on November 22, 2014. Why do police keep talking about Tamir's size? The shooting unfolded shortly after a witness from a nearby recreation center called 911, reporting "a guy with a pistol" that was "probably fake."[19] Since the shooting, police have been emphatic that Tamir looked much older than twelve, weighing 170 pounds, standing five feet seven inches tall, and wearing size 36 pants and a man's extra-large jacket.[20] Apparently, the baby face we see in photos after Tamir's death did little to alert officers to Tamir's true age.

We should not allow Tamir's physical features to obscure the role of implicit bias in the officers' perceptions. In a study on police perceptions of childhood innocence, researchers showed police officers a series of photographs of young white, black, and Latino males, advised them that the children in the photographs were accused of either a misdemeanor or a felony, and asked them to estimate the age of each child.[21] While the officers overestimated the age of adolescent black felony suspects by five years, they underestimated the age of adolescent white felony suspects by one year. Moreover, the older an officer thought a child was, the more culpable the officer perceived the child to be in his suspected crime. Further nuancing their study, researchers asked officers to take a "dehumanizing" implicit association test to determine the extent to which the officers associated black people with apes. This study found that the more readily participants implicitly associated blacks with apes, the higher their culpability ratings were for both black misdemeanor and black felony suspects. In a related experiment with university students, the same researchers found that study subjects perceived youth aged 0–9 as equally innocent regardless of race, but began to think of black children as significantly less innocent than other children at every age group thereafter.[22] The perceived innocence of black children aged 10–13 was equivalent to that of nonblack children aged 14–17, and the perceived innocence of black children aged 14–17 was equivalent to that of nonblack adults aged 18–21.

So what do these distorted perceptions mean for young black males? They mean that black boys are more likely to be treated as adults much earlier than other youth and less likely than white boys to receive the benefits and special considerations of youth.[23] In the context of policing, these perceptions mean that black boys are more likely to be stopped and arrested for normal adolescent behavior, more likely to be harassed and assaulted for typical adolescent transgressions, and more likely to be perceived as culpable and deserving of punishment.[24]

Even if politicians no longer bandy about the term "superpredator," the recent shootings of black males provide substantial evidence that the fear of black boys has not subsided since 1996. The number of black *boys* who have been shot by the police is staggering: Tamir Rice, twelve; Stephon Watts, fifteen; Cedrick LaMont Chatman, seventeen; Laquan McDonald, seventeen. Add to that the number of eighteen- and nineteen-year-olds who have been shot and the count is unconscionable.

Conditioning a Generation of Black Men

Legal Socialization and Procedural Justice

Tamir's story is significant not only for the tragic devaluing of life it conveys, but also for the message it sends to black boys. Adolescence is a critical time during which norms and values, including beliefs about law and legal institutions, are formed.[25] It is a time when young people's initial impressions of the justice system are translated into conscious and subconscious expectations about how police will treat them and how they should respond. Negative attitudes about the police acquired during childhood and adolescence have a "lasting" effect on adults' opinions about police.[26] Thus, youths' experiences and perceptions of fairness and justice during adolescence may have a substantial impact on their risk of offending and of having dangerous and hostile encounters with police as they transition to adulthood.

Legal socialization is the process by which individuals come to understand and appreciate the law, the institutions that create those laws, and the people who enforce those laws.[27] Effective legal socialization occurs when youth develop a healthy respect for legal authority and internalize the social norms that prohibit illegal behavior. Positive legal socialization is achieved over time by fair and "procedurally just" social interactions with legal authorities."[28] When authorities enforce rules and make decisions in a way that is fair, people are more likely to support and cooperate with those authorities and ultimately to obey their rules.[29]

Individuals evaluate procedural justice based on four primary variables: voice and participation, which refers to the degree to which people feel they are given the opportunity to express their opinions and concerns during a decision-making process; impartiality, which refers to the perceived neutrality and consistency of a decision-making process; respect and dignity, which relates to the way people perceive they are being treated; and trust-worthiness and perceived benevolence of the officers' motives.[30] Procedural justice has a significant impact on the perceived legitimacy of the police and, ultimately, on an individual's willingness to obey the law. When people believe an institution or legal authority such as the police is proper, they are willing to accept the power of authority and feel it is their duty to obey authority's rule.[31]

These principles apply to youth and adults. Studies involving youth have found a strong correlation between youths' perceptions of legitimacy and self-reported compliance with the law.[32] The more youth perceive police to behave fairly, the more likely they are to view the police as legitimate, the less cynical they are likely to be about the laws, and the more likely they are to comply with the rules.[33]

The Black Family: What Black Parents Teach Their Black Boys

Legal socialization starts early for black boys. Young people's attitudes about the police develop from the personal interactions they have with the police as well as the direct and indirect lessons they internalize from the social environments in which they live.[34] School and home are likely two of the most important environments that contribute to the legal socialization of young black males. Because African Americans are more likely to have family members who have been verbally or physically abused by the police,[35] it is no surprise that black families have been proactive in transmitting norms on dealing with law enforcement. Black parents tell their children to "always keep your hands where they can see them," "avoid sudden movements," and "behave in a courteous and respectful manner toward officers."[36] "Don't do nothing, don't say nothing smart. Don't play with BB guns."[37] In an interview with *Democracy Now*, Roots member Ahmir "Questlove" Thompson recalls his father telling him, "If you're ever in this position, you're to slowly keep your hands up," and notes that his father "did it in sort of a humorous way that Richard Pryor did."[38]

But these lessons are not all conveyed through humor. For many black boys, these lessons mean the difference between life and death. Journalist Ta-Nehisi Coates's warning to his son was much more bleak: "And you know now, if you did not before, that the police departments of your country have been endowed with the authority to destroy your body. It does not matter if the destruction is the result of an unfortunate overreaction. It does not matter if it originates in a misunderstanding. It does not matter if the destruction springs from a foolish policy."[39]

Just as these lessons may keep some children safe, they also transfer negative attitudes and resentments created by the police from one generation to the next.[40] In his 2015 TED talk, poet and educator Clint Smith highlights the blatantly racist nature of police interactions when he tells his son, "Son, I'm sorry you can't act the same as your white friends. You can't pretend to shoot guns. You can't run around in the dark."[41] These narratives are not new. Blacks have had a long and tortured relationship with the police, arising from the enforcement of the Fugitive Slave Act, the Black Codes, and unjust Jim Crow laws as well as the excessive force and brutality used to curtail the social and racial protests of the 1960s civil rights movement. Blacks have long spoken out against police brutality and racism, and black children have long internalized family stories about negative experiences with the police, often reliving them vicariously.

COPS in Schools: Race and School Discipline

Legal socialization is intensified for black boys who attend schools with a significant police presence. Police surveillance strategies, such as metal detectors, security cameras, and school resource officers, surged considerably after several high-profile school shootings in the 1990s. School resource officers (SROs), typically defined as certified, sworn police officers employed by a local police agency but permanently assigned to work in local schools, are now pervasive in cities with more than 100,000 residents.[42] This growth is attributable in no small measure to federal funding. In 1999, the Office of Community Oriented Policing Services (COPS) initiated the COPS in Schools grant program to facilitate the hiring of SROs in primary and secondary schools.[43] Federal support was renewed by the Obama administration in response to yet another school shooting in Connecticut in 2012.[44] Ironically, SROs are especially common in urban public schools in impoverished communities, notwithstanding evidence that most recent mass shootings have occurred in schools and other venues dominated by middle-class whites.[45]

Many policymakers advocate for the presence of SROs in schools as a strategy for deterring violence and delinquency. Others have loftier goals. They hope that SROs will improve the image of police generally and increase the level of respect that young people have for the law and the role of law enforcement.[46] Notwithstanding these worthy objectives, evidence suggests that the current proliferation of police in schools has done little to improve police-community relations as SROs remain deeply entrenched in their traditional law enforcement and crime control roles.[47] For those students who are first exposed to police through school resource officers, overly aggressive officers who treat students "like criminals" have a negative effect on the students' respect for law enforcement and willingness to follow the rules.[48] Students perceive their oppressive interactions with SROs as representative of how all officers will treat them. For students who have already been exposed to police outside of school, SROs have been unable to dislodge the youths' already negative opinions and attitudes about law enforcement.[49]

The problem is that police are always police. Those who take the oath are police officers 24 hours a day, 7 days a week, 365 days a year.[50] In schools, community policing goals are outweighed by traditional law enforcement objectives such as increasing the flow of information between schools and police; gathering and exchanging information about gangs, drug dealers, and other allegedly "problematic" students; referring youth to juvenile courts; investigating suspected criminal activity; making arrests; and reporting misconduct to probation officers.[51]

The visual presence of the police—many of whom patrol schools in uniforms with guns, pepper spray, and batons at their waist[52]—merely reinforces students' image of the police in their traditional roles. In the extreme, schools like those in California's Compton Unified School District recently authorized its police officers to carry military-grade assault rifles, converting schools into correctional facilities or military zones.[53] These images confirm for students that police are there to criminalize their behavior and may alienate students instead of fostering cooperation. At its worst, hostility toward SROs may lead some students to act out further.

Historically, most crime committed at school was not reported to police. More recently, the presence of SROs has increased arrests for low-level offenses, including non-serious assaults typical of an adolescent school fight or disorderly conduct.[54] Whereas teachers, parents, and principals once had primary responsibility for the socialization of youth, many school administrators now eagerly relinquish their disciplinary and rule enforcement responsibilities to police. As expected, school-based arrests disproportionately affect black boys and contribute significantly to the "school-to-prison pipeline." Studies show that schools with higher percentages of black and Hispanic students are more likely to employ school resource officers or other security personnel.[55]

Racial disparities in school-based arrests likely communicate to black students that society does not value them.[56] Perceived bias and discrimination undermine police legitimacy and weaken officers' moral authority among black youth.[57] Consider a study of school-based arrests in McKinney, Texas, which found that disorderly conduct and disruption of class were the most common offenses charged by SROs from 2012 to 2015.[58] Even more troubling, the study found that while African American students made up only 13 percent of the total school population in McKinney, they accounted for 53 percent of the disorderly conduct arrests and 43 percent of the disruption of class offenses charged. In this way, SROs significantly increased the racial disparity that already existed in McKinney's student arrests. Similar stories can be told all over the country. In Delaware, black students accounted for 67 percent of all students arrested although they made up only 32 percent of the student body.[59] As in Texas, black students in Delaware were disproportionately arrested for disorderly conduct and fighting.

On-the-Street Encounters: Personal and Vicarious Trauma

Beyond family and school, youth come to understand the law and the role of law enforcement through their own personal and vicarious experiences with the police. Because black boys may hear about more instances of police violence than they actually see or experience, their perceptions of law enforcement are also shaped by the collective group experiences of African Americans.[60] National and international media attention to racial profiling and racially discriminatory policing in the United States has increased considerably since the deaths of unarmed black men like Michael Brown and Eric Garner. With the increase of camera phones and personal videos, the dissemination of these stories is pervasive and the vicarious trauma experienced from videotaped beatings and killings is extensive. These indirect and vicarious contacts with the police play a significant role in shaping black boys' long-term attitudes and future behaviors toward the police.

Given the myriad of negative direct and indirect contacts young black males have with the police, it is no surprise that black boys have an especially low opinion of the police, particularly in socioeconomically disadvantaged communities where friction between the police and citizens is common. Research shows that while youth in general have less favorable attitudes toward the police than adults, black youth have even less favorable attitudes toward the police than white youth.[61] Frequent contact between police and teenagers increases the risk of conflict and contributes to the negative attitudes that many young people have.[62] However, unlike white youth, who tend to see police misconduct as an aberration, black male youth experience that misconduct as ubiquitous.[63]

Black boys are angered not only by the sheer number of police officers patrolling their neighborhoods, but also by the frequency with which they are stopped and the treatment they experience or observe during these stops.[64] In a recent qualitative study involving young black males in St. Louis, boys complained of persistent pedestrian stops, vehicle stops, and the assignment of specialized units and detectives to patrol their neighborhoods, making their friends and relatives reluctant to visit.[65] Children grow up watching their friends and family members accosted for minor infractions like not wearing a seat belt, having the windows too tinted, and playing the radio too loud.[66] Black boys describe their neighborhoods as besieged by police who stop them "like five, six times a day. Just to pat [them] down and ask questions."[67] The experiences in St. Louis mirror those of youth in Washington, D.C., where youth who have been arrested once are often harassed repeatedly thereafter by the same officers. In one case, twin brothers were arrested four times by the same officers in a few short weeks for the most petty of offenses.[68] At some point, even the prosecutors stopped charging the youths because it was clear the officers had a grudge against the boys, who were never engaged in any serious criminal behavior.

Under the guise of "reasonable articulable suspicion," police stop black boys on the vaguest of descriptions. Black boys running. Two black males in jeans, one in a gray hoodie. Black male in athletic gear. Black male with a bicycle. Young black males are treated as if they are "out of place" not only when they are in white, middle-class neighborhoods, but also when they are hanging out in public spaces or sitting on their own front porches.[69] Black boys who congregate on the "corner" attract the attention of the police at all times of the day or night. Young black males cannot escape police surveillance even when they dress nicely or drive nice cars since such signs of wealth among black youth are presumed to be associated with drug dealing.[70]

When black boys are stopped, police pepper them with questions like "Where are you coming from?," "Where are you going?," and "Where is your mother?" Consider Tremaine McMillian's encounter with the Miami-Dade officer who demanded that Tremaine point out his mother, suggesting that he did not believe the fourteen-year-old was legitimately visiting the beach with his family. The pervasiveness of these intrusions is debilitating for black boys.

The boys in St. Louis maintain that officers treat them as if they are always "criminal." Black boys and girls complain that police are mean and disrespectful and do not know how to talk to people—especially black people.[71] Just pull up any one of the recent police shootings or assaults captured on video and you will see officers who are visibly hostile, speaking rudely and creating such a negative tone that virtually any child would respond with resistance and disrespect. Black boys describe police as belligerent and antagonistic and are especially outraged by the officers' use of inflammatory language, including racial slurs, profanity, and demeaning terms like "punk" and "sissy."[72] Racial slurs and profanity have been particularly damaging to youths' perceptions of police legitimacy and moral authority.[73]

Black boys also take particular exception to being told to "assume the position," "put [their] hands on the hood/wall/car," or "sit or lie on the sidewalk."[74] They resent strip searches and cavity probes and being told to pull down their pants or take off their clothes, especially when there is no obvious rationale for such an order. Black boys are almost never allowed to question the officers' conduct and are rarely allowed to explain why they are present and engaged in a particular activity.[75] When they are allowed to explain, the police do not believe them. Moreover, despite their admitted involvement in minor and sometimes serious delinquent behavior, the black boys in St. Louis reported that the "vast majority of their involuntary police contacts—and harassment from the police—occurred when they weren't doing anything wrong."[76] With frustration at the "officers' apparent inability to distinguish law-abiding residents from those engaged in crime,"[77] the boys resented stops that seemed arbitrary and baseless and quickly learned that obeying the law does little to insulate them from police interference and even physical violence. In fact, as the researchers in St. Louis concluded, being innocent could actually increase a young man's chance of being assaulted, as he is more likely to challenge the inappropriateness of the officers' actions.[78]

Police stops involving black boys are routinely initiated by some physical contact such as grabbing, pushing, shoving, pulling, or tackling the youth to the ground. Once on the ground, black boys like Emilio Mayfield are often held down by multiple officers who sit or lie on them while other officers kick, punch, or mace them. Even more violent encounters include billy clubs, like the one that was pressed against Emilio's neck as he was jaywalking on his way to school, or choke holds like the one that killed Eric Garner in New York or the one that caused Tremaine McMillian to wet his pants on the beach in Miami. Other aggressive policing strategies include teams of plainclothes officers called "jump outs" who drive up fast to street corners, jump out to grab and search youth on the streets, and shove their hands in the youths' mouths in search of drugs.[79] Fear of violence by police is now the norm for black boys. Instead of looking to police for protection, young black males see police as a primary source of potential danger and are conditioned to expect mistreatment.

Even when black boys know police are justified in stopping them, they are often angered by the way police treat them during the encounters. They complain of harassment, physical violence, and other forms of police misconduct as extreme as taking money from suspects, driving suspects around the city instead of taking them to the police station, and dropping suspects off in unfamiliar or rival neighborhoods.[80] Sadly, these rides sound eerily similar to the "rough ride" that Freddie Gray experienced in Baltimore leading up to his tragic death from injuries.[81] From the observers' perspective, rarely do the offenders' illegal activities justify the police violence and killings that have become so pervasive today.[82]

In interview after interview, young black males speak of policing in black neighborhoods as repressive, obtrusive, and insidious. They describe the exercise of police discretion as arbitrary and racially biased. Not only are they frustrated by what they perceive to be countless unjustified and unwarranted encounters with the police, but they are also bothered by what they see as slow response times and an outright failure of police to respond to and investigate crimes reported by victims in black communities.[83] The cumulative impact of these experiences erodes police legitimacy at an early age among black boys and weakens the value of law and order. The net result is that black youth come to *expect* unfair treatment and carry these feelings and expectations into adulthood.[84] As young black males internalize the lessons they acquire about police from their families, schools, and communities, they bring strong psychological and emotional reactions into their future encounters with the police. Over time, their views and reactions to the police become unconscious and automatic.[85]

How Black Boys Respond

Adolescent Anger and Resistance

Current affairs have created a crisis in police legitimacy. The consequences of aggressive policing and police bias—perceived or real—with young black males are significant. Collectively, the heightened media attention to police-on-black violence and the pervasive impact of personal and vicarious discriminatory experiences with the police produce unfavorable preconceived opinions about law enforcement and cause young black males to be hostile—if not outright confrontational—with police in each subsequent encounter. When police legitimacy is compromised, black youth have little reason to respect or engage with the police.

The long history of negative interactions with the police has socialized a generation of black boys to avoid contact with the police whenever possible. Young black males now routinely run from police to avoid face-to-face contact, decline to seek police assistance when they have been injured, and refuse to assist police during criminal investigations. Many black boys would rather settle disputes on their own than initiate contact with the police, and norms against snitching are so strong in some black communities that black boys often refuse to report crimes—even when they are the victim or the victim's friend or neighbor.[86] The ripple effects may be felt throughout the justice system when blacks refuse to testify as witnesses in criminal proceedings, reject jury service, or decline to convict black defendants who are clearly guilty.[87] Street violence may also increase as black boys resort to self-defense or preemptive attacks to ward off actual or anticipated threats to their safety. When the state's law enforcement authority loses legitimacy, private violence becomes an "acceptable or even necessary alternative" to the police.[88] Eventually, an illegitimate police force may become as useless as no police force at all.

Of course, black boys cannot entirely avoid the police. Those who cannot avoid them may resist.[89] Resistance can be subtle or violent, verbal or nonverbal, extemporaneous or planned. Boys may resist with their voices by speaking out against seemingly arbitrary intrusions, unfair treatment, and other perceived injustices. In their verbal resistance, boys may curse, disparage the officers, or simply question an officer's decision to stop and detain them. Boys may challenge officers' orders to turn down "loud" music that is not that loud, to pull over for no reason at all, or to move on from a particular location when there is no criminal activity occurring.[90]

Black boys who believe they will be discredited both because they are young and because they are black have little, if any, faith in more formal grievance procedures.[91] Reporting police misconduct to internal affairs is of little use to black boys who recognize that police are rarely, if ever, held accountable by their peers for the mistreatment of blacks. The boys' reluctance to seek reform within the justice system is likely even greater today given the recent failures of grand juries to indict police in high-profile shootings of black males. Society's presumptive association of black boys and crime appears to lend credence to the officers' purported justifications for violence against black boys and insulates police against complaints of bias. Over time, the lack of accountability for aggressive police conduct allows officers to internalize those behaviors as appropriate and ultimately gives them a monopoly on state-sanctioned violence against black boys.

Unfortunately, parents' efforts to keep children safe by teaching them to stay clear of the police has had only minimal success, as is evident from news accounts of Tamir Rice's toy gun, Emilio Mayfield's refusal to sit when the officer ordered him to do so, and Tremaine McMillian's clenched fist as he walked away from the officer on the beach. Kids will be kids—impetuous, emotional, and reactive. This is what any parent knows, and this is what the neurological and developmental research confirms. Neurological studies show that the section of the brain responsible for logical reasoning, planning, self-regulation, and impulse control are the last to mature and develop.[92] Similarly, developmental studies assessing youths' capacity for self-regulation indicate that adolescents have a more difficult time than adults tempering their emotions, controlling their impulses, and suppressing their aggression.[93] Children are also particularly sensitive to issues of fairness and respect and are more susceptible to peer influence than adults.[94] Thus, even when children remember their parents' advice and know it is dangerous to talk back to the police, they often cannot help it, especially in fast-paced, emotionally charged situations like those involving the police.[95] In the heat of the moment, adolescents have a hard time focusing on the likely consequences of their actions and making rational decisions.

Reckless behavior is so common among adolescents that it has been described as "virtually a normative characteristic of adolescent development."[96] Like any other group of adolescents, black boys will be reckless. They will curse, talk back, become hostile, and sometimes even fight those who mistreat them.

Police Perception of Disrespect

To resist is proactive, maybe even revolutionary, for a child. Resistance seeks to change police behavior. Unfortunately, neither resistance nor avoidance has been particularly effective in preventing abuses and rectifying injustices against black youth. In fact, resistance may contribute to violent—and sometimes deadly—confrontations with the police. Resistance in the form of flight, for example, has been particularly problematic for black boys, not only because it leads the police to retaliate, but also because it adds a layer of suspicion to the officers' assessment of reasonable articulable suspicion and probable cause under the Fourth Amendment.[97] Flight from the police allows the officers, and later the courts, to make peremptory assumptions about the guilt of the one who runs. At its worst, flight may convert a routine encounter into a deadly pursuit.

Like youth, police officers bring their own social and psychological assumptions into each encounter they have with young people. Those assumptions dictate what officers will expect and often cause them to develop conscious or subconscious schema for handling juveniles.[98] Police expect youth to be anti-authoritarian.[99] They expect black boys to be dangerous.[100] Unfortunately, black boys' hostility toward police affirms what police expect.

A child's demeanor contributes significantly to how police will respond to him or her.[101] Police perceive disrespect in simple questions like "What did I do?" and "Why are you stopping me?" Videotaping, cursing, "ill-chosen" words, ignoring an officer's orders, and flight are all seen as forms of disrespect.[102] Even innocuous behavior by black boys is perceived as threatening. Several studies on implicit bias have found that individuals are more likely to interpret ambiguous behavior by blacks as more aggressive and consistent with violent intentions while the same behavior by whites is seen as harmless.[103] In one study, researchers asked participants to view a brief movie clip in which a target's facial expression morphed from unambiguous hostility to unambiguous happiness and a second clip where the target's expression did the reverse.[104] Participants with higher levels of implicit bias took longer to perceive the change of black faces from hostile to friendly, but not that of white faces. In the second clip, those same participants perceived the onset of hostility much earlier for black faces than for white faces. In another study, researchers asked participants to view a series of black or white faces and then determine whether some object was crime-related or neutral.[105] Study participants were more likely to see crime-related objects when associating the object with a black face than with a white face.

Perceived resistance during face-to-face encounters only provokes greater hostility, disrespect, and ultimately physical force from the police.[106] As to be expected, black youth are more likely to experience a use of force than white youth. For example, according to Bureau of Justice Statistics, one in ten black youth surveyed between 1996 and 2005 had contact with the police, and one in four of those contacts involved police force.[107] Young black males do not have the luxury of "talking back" or voicing displeasure. Black boys who talk back and ask questions are told to shut up and sit down. Anger and criticism of the police are privileges reserved for whites. Consider Stockton police officer Joe Silva's response to the aggressive arrest of sixteen-year-old Emilio Mayfield: "If everyone would just learn to comply with the lawful orders from police officers and not try to hold or grab any of our weapons force would never have to be used."[108] To be clear, videos posted on the internet show that Emilio held on to the officer's baton only when the officer forced it up against his body and hit him with it. When the officer pulled the baton away, Emilio never again tried to reach for it.

Perceived and overt resistance also causes police to arrest youth for offenses with overly broad statutory definitions, such as resisting arrest, assaulting a police officer, disturbing the peace, and disorderly conduct. Youth in St. Louis and the District of Columbia routinely complain of being charged with resisting arrest in situations where the officer was not justified in making the stop or using force in the first place.[109] A child in the District of Columbia may be arrested for assault on a police officer for little more than refusing to put his arms out for handcuffing or lying on the ground with his arms underneath him so the officers cannot reach them. Recall that Emilio Mayfield was charged in Stockton with trespassing and resisting arrest. Tremaine McMillian was charged with a felony count of resisting arrest with violence and disorderly conduct.

Ultimately, the way youth perceive police and the way police perceive youth will determine the type and outcome of their interactions.[110] Police expect trouble from black boys, and black boys expect to be disrespected and harmed by the police. Suspicion and distrust are mutual.[111] Is there any way forward? The seminal question is whether we can ever alter the preconceived negative opinions and attitudes that black boys and police have about each other. Whatever strategies we employ must start early in a child's life, before the negative views are entrenched and intractable.

Reforms: Finding a Way Forward

Mistrust and alienation between young black males and the police are so deeply entrenched that we need radical, sweeping change. Our quest for reform will require us to rethink the presence of police in schools and envision a new space for genuine and meaningful positive interactions between black youth and the police. Reform must also include officer training on adolescent development, procedural justice, and implicit bias and require deep shifts in police policy, procedure, and infrastructure. Reform should also require us to rethink how courts interpret race and adolescent behavior under the Fourth Amendment.

Rethinking COPS in Schools

Any effort to improve relations between black boys and the police must attend to the role of schools in socializing children's views of law enforcement. Given the failure of SROs to prevent mass shootings and the relatively low success SROs have had in altering the views of police among youth, schools should rethink their recent hyper-dependence on police in schools. Recommendations for reform range from entirely removing officers from schools to keeping officers in schools, but refocusing their objectives.

Some schools have increased training for SROs while simultaneously decreasing the scope of disciplinary issues SROs can address—specifically limiting them to drug and weapons possession in schools. The Denver Public Schools, for example, entered into an agreement with the Denver Police Department to prevent officers from writing tickets for minor misbehavior such as bad language and to require officers to participate in training on topics such as teenage psychology and cultural competence.[112] In Philadelphia, in 2014, the police chief instructed his officers to stop arresting youth for minor infractions such as school yard fights and possession of small amounts of marijuana, which together accounted for about 60 percent of all school-based arrests.[113] While these are important and necessary reforms, they probably do not go far enough to permanently alter the perception of police among young black males.

On the other end of the spectrum, youth advocates have called for the removal of all SROs from schools, leaving discipline up to administrators and involving police only when absolutely necessary.[114] Alternative school safety strategies include hiring school administrators, counselors, social workers, and mental health professionals who are particularly trained to identify and assist troubled youth.[115]

Cities committed to improving the attitudes and behaviors of police and young black males might consider programs that truly take police out of their traditional disciplinary and law enforcement roles and encourage them to engage positively with children at very young ages. Policymakers might consider Connecticut's success in funding Police and Youth Interaction Programs in seven communities during the 2011–2012 school year.[116] Each program allowed youth to participate in fun extracurricular activities and community service with police officers in a non–law enforcement and non-teaching environment. Results from surveys administered before and after the program revealed that youths' attitudes and opinions of the police improved during the program. Although the surveys did not reveal any significant change in the officers' attitudes about youth after the program, all of the officers rated the program as "excellent" or "good," and evidence suggests that officers who participated in the program already had positive views of youth before the program started. Cities might also consider youth-police sports leagues, team-building or leadership-development courses, and other opportunities for informal engagement in a local recreation facility.

Police Training: Procedural Justice, Adolescent Development, and Implicit Bias

Broad-based reform must start with police training. Young black males are a unique demographic and police must account for all three critical aspects of their makeup: their youth, their race, and their basic human dignity. Positive interactions with black boys require police not only to engage them with the same dignity and respect they show other civilians, but also to understand the role of implicit bias in decision-making and develop special skills in working with adolescents.

As discussed above, procedural justice and police legitimacy have a significant impact on a youth's sense of obligation to obey the law and respect legal authority. Thus, it is critical that police enhance their legitimacy by providing fair and procedurally just treatment to everyone with whom they interact. Simple changes like explaining the reasons for a stop and allowing boys to ask questions and respond may help increase a youth's sense of participation and procedural justice.[117]

Notwithstanding outrage over the recent police shooting of Laquan McDonald in Chicago, the Chicago Police Department has had some success in developing a training curriculum to improve police-citizen contacts through procedural justice.[118] The training seeks to enhance public trust and confidence in the police by teaching officers to treat people with dignity and respect, make decisions that are based on facts instead of inappropriate factors such as race, give people a voice by allowing them to tell their side of the story, and act in a way that encourages the community to believe they will be treated fairly and with goodwill in the future. Police departments that employ these principles ideally experience higher levels of cooperation in resolving crime, greater compliance with the law, more public support for the police, and greater deference to police in face-to-face interactions with civilians.

The Chicago curriculum has been adapted and implemented in three California cities. Police departments there and in Chicago have enhanced the original curriculum to include scenarios and role plays, input from community leaders, real-life examples of how procedural justice has been effective in practice, and videos illustrating the value of procedural justice. In Oakland, California, community leaders joined the team of trainers to share their own firsthand experiences and unique perspectives on race and policing.[119] In Salinas, California, one officer described an experience he had when he was called to the scene with a teenager who had a gun in his waistband.[120] As the officer responded to the scene, he yelled aggressively to two onlookers to get them to back away. As he was leaving the scene, the officer was motivated by his procedural justice training to go back and explain his behavior to the two onlookers. One of the onlookers thanked him for coming back and asked him for help dealing with alcoholism. That same onlooker later came forward as an essential witness in an officer-involved shooting.

Police departments have also begun to think about new procedurally just "scripts" or protocols to guide officers in their routine activities.[121] New protocols might govern the execution of search warrants, stop-and-frisk encounters, and traffic stops. Protocols would require officers to show greater respect for civilians, listen, make fair decisions, build trust, and demonstrate goodwill toward civilians. In the world's first randomized field test of applied procedural justice, researchers "operationalized" and tested the four key components of procedural justice: citizen participation, dignity and respect, neutrality, and trustworthy motives.[122] Using a random allocation of participating officers at sixty planned roadblocks, between three hundred and four hundred drivers were engaged in either a standard traffic stop with a breath test or an experimental traffic stop that employed principles of procedural justice before and after the breath test. Officers in the experimental traffic stop used scripts to enhance civilians' sense of having been treated with dignity and respect.[123] To demonstrate their trustworthy motives, police in the experimental traffic stops explained why they were doing the roadblock testing and informed drivers about the number of deaths from road accidents. To convey neutrality, the officers in the experimental stops told drivers they had been stopped randomly. Although all drivers were mandated by law to take the breath tests, the officers attempted to provide drivers with an opportunity for "citizen participation" by engaging them in a short conversation that elicited their ideas and advice about problems facing the police in their community. After each traffic stop, police provided drivers with a sealed envelope and asked them to complete a survey regarding their experience. Study results revealed that drivers who were engaged in the experimental traffic stop were significantly more likely to report that their views on drinking and driving had changed and to indicate a greater willingness to comply with the law. The study also suggested that even short, procedurally just encounters like these have indirect effects on people's general perceptions of police legitimacy, satisfaction, and willingness to cooperate with law enforcement.

To address the unique interplay between police and young black males, the procedural justice training should be paired with trainings on adolescent development. Recent studies have found that police who participate in training to enhance their knowledge of normal adolescent development hold more favorable attitudes toward youth after the training.[124] A few innovative programs have been launched across the country.[125] In Philadelphia, new and experienced law enforcement officers participated in a training to help them understand the key features of normal adolescent development, youth culture, and youth coping skills and to distinguish between normal adolescent behavior and criminal conduct.[126] In separate sessions, youth learn how respect impacts their interactions with police and discuss strategies for creating positive and safe encounters with law enforcement. The training also engages minority youth and experienced officers in facilitated discussions about policing and mutual mistrust and allows participants to suggest recommendations for improving youth-police relations. Finally, youth and police engage in role playing, allowing officers to practice what they have learned.

To facilitate more nationwide reforms, Lisa Thurau founded Strategies for Youth (SFY) to develop a national curriculum for training police on how to work effectively with youth.[127] SFY recognizes that youth respond differently to social cues and interpersonal interactions and that a child's developmental stage affects how he or she will perceive, process, and respond to the police. SFY trainings teach officers to draw upon their knowledge of adolescent development and respond with empathy, patience, and techniques designed to de-escalate youth outbursts. SFY offers courses such as Policing the Teen Brain, Policing the Teen Brain in School, Policing Youth on Public Transit, and Policing Youth Chronically Exposed to Trauma and Violence. To reduce the officers' reliance on force and arrest, SFY has also developed "how-to" cards to guide officers during arrests and prepare them for effective conversations with youth. The trainers rely on community-based youth-serving organizations to assist with role plays during trainings.

While training in procedural justice and adolescent development will likely begin to ameliorate the disproportionate rates of arrest for young black males, police should also participate in trainings about implicit racial bias. Studies suggest that well-intentioned actors can overcome automatic or implicit biases, at least to some extent, when they are made aware of the stereotypes and biases they hold, have the cognitive capacity to self-correct, and are motivated to do so.[128] Other research suggests that implicit bias can be diminished when actors are repeatedly exposed to positive images of and develop relationships with people in a previously stereotyped or devalued group.[129] One longitudinal study on strategies to reduce implicit racial bias found success in the simultaneous implementation of five corrective strategies: stereotype replacement, counter-stereotypic imaging, individuation, perspective-taking, and increased opportunities for contact.[130] Stereotype replacement would require officers to replace stereotypical responses to black boys with non-stereotypical responses. Thus, instead of responding in anger to a child's hostility and questions about why he is being stopped, the officer would explain the reason for the stop and patiently answer the youth's questions. Counter-stereotypic imaging would require officers to imagine black boys in counter-stereotypic ways. Police departments might periodically identify and share success stories about young black males from the local community, including stories about youth who have enrolled in college, secured employment, or excelled in academics or sports. Individuation would require officers to obtain more specific information about a young black male before making any inferences about him or his behavior. In practice, officers would need to observe, inquire, and investigate more before making a stop or an arrest. Perspective-taking would require officers to assume the first-person perspective of a young black male during a stop. Officers participating in the adolescent development training should have an opportunity to engage in role-playing that helps them to understand the attitudes and feelings of young black males who are frequently stopped. Finally, officers seeking increased opportunities for positive contact with black boys may engage in the community service and extracurricular activities like those organized in Connecticut.

Ultimately, each form of training requires buy-in from the top down, with chiefs and sergeants actively participating and advocating for reform. To ensure long-term organizational change, law enforcement leaders should translate training and the principles they teach into meaningful and lasting reforms of policy, general orders, infrastructure, periodic performance reviews, and mandatory requirements for promotion.

Race and Age in the Assessment of Fourth Amendment Reasonable Articulable Suspicion

Reform must be grassroots, legislative, and systemic. It must also be judicial. When the courts are not rigorous in reviewing police stops, arrests, and other physically aggressive encounters with civilians, they become complicit in affirming the aggressive behavior of police.

Much of the aggressive policing we see today is made possible by the permissive nature of the U.S. Supreme Court's 1968 ruling in *Terry v. Ohio*. Although the Fourth Amendment was originally interpreted to prohibit state intrusions absent probable cause to believe a person was committing or had recently committed a crime, *Terry* permits officers to engage civilians in an "investigatory stop" based on a much lower and arguably even more ambiguous standard of "reasonable articulable suspicion." In determining whether there is reasonable suspicion for a stop, the police may consider the time and location of the purported offense as well as information about the suspect's behavior, including flight, which may convey a consciousness of guilt, or furtive gestures, which may suggest the suspect has something to hide.[131] Although courts have long given lip service to the notion that civilians have a right to avoid police and go about their business,[132] that notion has been undermined by less than rigorous determinations that a suspect is engaged in some "headlong flight" that manifests a real consciousness of guilt.

Judicial reform should require courts to consider the race and age of a suspect in interpreting the suspect's behavior in the context of reasonable articulable suspicion. A child's flight from the police is a clear example of how race and age might negate the inference of guilt that might otherwise follow. As the Supreme Court has recognized, "the determination of reasonable suspicion must be based on commonsense judgments and inferences about human behavior."[133] Flight may be imminently reasonable for an adolescent who is impulsive and often does not engage in the same commonsense judgments and behaviors as adults. A child's age, as is evident to anyone who has ever been a child, including police officers and judges, "generates commonsense conclusions about behavior and perception."[134] A child's flight can be impulsive, emotional, and rebellious, particularly in the face of perceived unfairness.

When we add race to adolescent indiscretions, the link between flight and consciousness of guilt becomes even more tenuous. A black boy's flight from the police is just as likely to be a protective measure to avoid police violence as it is to result from consciousness of guilt. That flight is also just as likely to reflect a personal desire to avoid contact with a corrupt system as it is to be a sign of criminal activity. Black boys who live in a society where police-on-black shootings are commonplace have every reason to run from the police. Taking race and youth into account in the assessment of flight and reasonable articulable suspicion should significantly mitigate any inference that a black boy's flight manifests a consciousness of guilt.

Conclusion

There is now a wealth of empirical and qualitative evidence demonstrating that the cumulative impact of racial discrimination affects how young black males evaluate the law and law enforcement officials. The negative personal and vicarious experiences black boys have with the police not only undermine their perceptions of the police, but also decrease their willingness to cooperate with the law and increase the likelihood of their own arrest and abuse at the hands of police. The aggressive and abusive policing of young black males sends a message that black boys are to be feared and are unworthy of police protection. The collateral outcomes are troubling for everyone. Society suffers when black youth refuse to obey the law and turn to violence to protect themselves. Police suffer when black boys refuse to help them investigate crimes, testify in court, or cooperate in face-to-face encounters. Youth suffer emotionally from the persistent and debilitating indignities and injustices they experience and observe with police, and they suffer physically when they retaliate against officers whom they perceive as a threat to their safety.

Given this reality, we must all be attentive to the enduring impact of police-youth relations as black boys transition into adulthood. School officials and legislators need to rethink their current reliance on police in schools and create other opportunities for young black males to engage in positive and meaningful encounters with the police. Law enforcement leaders should train their officers in adolescent development, implicit racial bias, and procedural justice and modify policies, procedures, and infrastructure to ensure that all youth are treated with dignity and respect. Finally, courts should rigorously protect the Fourth Amendment rights of black youth by accounting for a suspect's race and age in their evaluation of the officer's reasonable articulable suspicion for a stop. While none of these strategies alone will prevent the unnecessary killing of young black males, collectively they should make significant improvements in the state of youth-police relations and begin to dismantle the mutual and long-standing mistrust and suspicion that exists between them.

NOTES

1. Professor of Law and Director, Juvenile Justice Clinic, Georgetown University Law School. I would like to thank Brittany Harwell and Jenadee Nanini for their invaluable research.

2. "Teen Who Was Brutally Beaten and Arrested by 9 Cops for Jaywalking Speaks Out," *Counter Current News*, Sept. 21, 2015.

3. "Tremaine McMillian, 14-Year-Old with Puppy, Choked by Miami-Dade Police Officer over 'Dehumanizing Stares,'" *Huffington Post Miami*, May 31, 2013.

4. Terrance J. Taylor, K. B. Turner, Finn-Aage Esbensen, and L. Thomas Winfree Jr., "Coppin' an Attitude: Attitudinal Difference Among Juveniles Toward Police," *Journal of Criminal Justice* 29 (2001): 296; Yolander Hurst, James Frank, and Sandra Browning, "The Attitudes of Juveniles Toward the Police," *Policing* 23 (2000): 40.

5. Hurst, Frank, and Browning, "Attitudes of Juveniles," 40.

6. Ronald Weitzer and Rod K. Brunson, "Strategic Responses to the Police Among Inner-City Youth," *Sociological Quarterly* 50 (2009): 235; Taylor, Turner, Esbensen, and Winfree, "Coppin' an Attitude," 302.

7. Taylor, Turner, Esbensen, and Winfree, "Coppin' an Attitude," 297–98; Lyn Hinds, "Building Police-Youth Relationships: The Importance of Procedural Justice," *Youth Justice* 7 (2007): 197.

8. Elizabeth Becker, "An Ex-Theorist on Young 'Super-predators,' Bush Aide Has Regrets," *New York Times*, Feb. 9, 2001.

9. Ibid.

10. John J. Dilulio Jr., "The Coming of the Super-predators," *Weekly Standard*, Nov. 27, 1995.

11. Becker, "Ex-Theorist on Young 'Super-predators.'"

12. John J. Dilulio Jr., "My Black Crime Problem, and Ours," *City Journal*, Spring 1996, http://www.city-journal.org/html/6_2_my_black.html.

13. Ibid., 5.

14. Dilulio, "The Coming of the Super-predators."

15. Dilulio, "My Black Crime Problem, and Ours," 5.

16. Ibid., 12.

17. Becker, "Ex-Theorist on Young 'Super-predators.'"

18. Clyde Haberman, "When Youth Violence Spurred 'Super-predator' Fear," *New York Times*, April 6, 2014.

19. Ashley Fantz, Steve Almasy, and Catherine E. Shoichet, "Tamir Rice Shooting: No Charges for Officers," CNN.com, Dec. 28, 2015.

20. Christopher Ingraham, "Why White People See Black Boys Like Tamir Rice as Older, Bigger, and Guiltier Than They Really Are," *Washington Post*, Dec. 28, 2015.

21. Phillip A. Goff, Matthew C. Jackson, Brooke Allison, L. Di Leone, Carmen M. Culotta, and Natalie A. DiTomasso, "The Essence of Innocence: Consequences of Dehumanizing Black Children," *Journal of Personality and Social Psychology* 106 (February 2014): 526–45.

22. Ibid., 529.

23. Ibid., 527.

24. See, e.g., Sandra Graham and Brian S. Lowery, "Priming Unconscious Racial Stereotypes About Adolescent Offenders," *Law & Human Behav*ior 28 (October 2004): 483–504 (finding that police officers primed with words related to black ethnicity were more likely to perceive a suspect as culpable and deserving of punishment in a low-level property offense or assault crime and less likely to judge the offender as immature); Birt L. Duncan, "Differential Social Perception and Attribution of Intergroup Violence: Testing the Lower Limits of Stereotyping of Blacks," *Journal of Personality and Social Psychology* 34 (1976): 590, 591 (finding that when there is more than

one appropriate response, implicit bias can cause subjects to react more forcefully in interacting with blacks than whites); Joshua Correll, Bernadette Park, and Charles M. Judd, "The Police Officer's Dilemma: Using Ethnicity to Disambiguate Potentially Threatening Individuals," *Journal of Personality and Social Psychology* 83 (2002): 1314, 1315–17 (finding that participants in a shooter-paradigm video game with photographs of individuals holding an object were quicker to shoot when the target was black as compared to white and made more mistakes and shot more unarmed black targets than unarmed white targets).

25. Jeffrey Fagan and Tom R. Tyler, "Legal Socialization of Children and Adolescents," *Social Justice Research* 18, no. 3 (September 2005): 217–41.

26. Hinds, "Building Police-Youth Relationships," 196; Fagan and Tyler, "Legal Socialization of Children," 218–19.

27. Rick Trinkner and Ellen S. Cohn, "Putting the 'Social' Back in Legal Socialization: Procedural Justice, Legitimacy, and Cynicism in Legal and Nonlegal Authorities," *Law & Human Behavior* 38 (2014): 602.

28. Ibid., 602; Fagan and Tyler, "Legal Socialization of Children," 222.

29. Trinkner and Cohn, "Putting the 'Social' Back in Legal Socialization," 603.

30. Fagan and Tyler, "Legal Socialization of Children," 222.

31. Trinkner and Cohn, "Putting the 'Social' Back in Legal Socialization," 604; Fagan and Tyler, "Legal Socialization of Children," 221.

32. Trinkner and Cohn, "Putting the 'Social' Back in Legal Socialization," 606–608; Erika K. Penner, Jodi L. Viljoen, Kevin S. Douglas, and Ronald Roesch, "Procedural Justice Versus Risk Factors for Offending: Predicting Recidivism in Youth," *Law and Human Behavior* 38 (2014): 225–34.

33. Trinkner and Cohn, "Putting the 'Social' Back in Legal Socialization," 608; Penner, Viljoen, Douglas, and Roesch, "Procedural Justice Versus Risk Factors," 234.

34. Hinds, "Building Police-Youth Relationships," 198.

35. Ronald Weitzer and Steven Tuch, "Perceptions of Racial Profiling: Race, Class, and Personal Experience," *Criminology* 40, no. 2 (2002).

36. Ulysses Burley III, "A Letter to My Unborn [Black] Son," *The Salt Collective*, http://thesaltcollective.org/letter-unbornblack-son/; Celia K. Dale, "A Letter to My Black Son," *Atlanta Black Star*, Nov. 25, 2014, http://atlantablackstar.com/2014/11/26/letter-son/; Geeta Gandbhir and Blair Foster, "A Conversation with My Black Son," *New York Times*, Op Doc, March 17, 2015, http://www.nytimes.com/2015/03/17/opinion/a-conversation-with-my-black-son.html?_r=0; Ronald Weitzer, "Citizens' Perceptions of Police Misconduct: Race and Neighborhood Context," *Justice Quarterly* 16 (1999): 833.

37. Weitzer and Brunson, "Strategic Responses," 250.

38. "Questlove on Police Racial Profiling, Stop & Frisk, the Message He Took from Trayvon Martin Verdict," *Democracy Now*, Aug. 14, 2013.

39. Ta-Nehisi Coates, "Letter to My Son: Excerpts from *Between the World and Me*," *The Atlantic*, July 4, 2015.

40. Weitzer and Brunson, "Strategic Responses," 250.

41. Clint Smith, "How to Raise a Black Son in America," TED Talk, March 2015, https://www.ted.com/talks/clint_smith_how_to_raise_a_black_son_in_america.

42. Brad A. Myrstol, "Public Perceptions of School Resource Officer (SRO)

Programs," *Western Criminology Review* 12, no. 3 (2011): 21; Matthew T. Theriot, "School Resource Officers and the Criminalization of Student Behavior," *Journal of Criminal Justice* 37 (2009): 281.

43. Myrstol, "Public Perceptions of School Resource Officer Programs," 21.

44. "Police in Schools: Arresting Developments," *The Economist*, Jan. 9, 2016; Nathan James and Gail McCallion, "School Resource Officers: Law Enforcement Offices in Schools," *Congressional Research Service*, June 26, 2013, 1.

45. "Police in Schools," *The Economist*.

46. Arrick Jackson, "Police-School Resource Officers' and Students' Perception of the Police and Offending," *Policing* 25, no. 3 (2002): 633.

47. Myrstol, "Public Perceptions of School Resource Officer Programs," 35.

48. Ibid., 21. Nicole L. Bracy, "Student Perceptions of High-Security School Environments," *Youth & Society* 43 (2011): 365–95; Lawrence F. Travis III and Julie K. Coon, "The Role of Law Enforcement in Public School Safety: A National Survey" (Washington, DC: National Institute of Justice, 2005), https://www.ncjrs.gov/pdffiles1/nij/grants/211676.pdf.

49. Jackson, "Police-School Resource Officers' and Students' Perceptions," 637, 645–46. See also Myrstol, "Public Perceptions of School Resource Officer Programs," 35.

50. Myrstol, "Public Perceptions of School Resource Officer Programs," 36.

51. Jackson, "Police-School Resource Officers' and Students' Perceptions," 631–50.

52. "Police in Schools," *The Economist*.

53. Bethany J. Peake, "Militarization of School Police: One Route on the School-to-Prison Pipeline," *Arkansas Law Review* 68 (2015): 196.

54. Theriot, "School Resource Officers," 286–87 (finding increase in disorderly arrests, but a decrease in assaults and weapons); Chongmin Na and Denise C. Gottfredson, "Police Officers in Schools: Effects on School Crime and the Processing of Offender Behaviors," *Justice Quarterly*, (2011), 24, http://www.tandfonline.com/doi/abs/10.1080/07418825.2011.615754 (percentage of non-serious violent crimes reported to law enforcement increased).

55. Simone Robers, Anlan Zhang, Rachel E. Morgan, and Lauren Musu-Gillette, *Indicators of School Crime and Safety: 2014* (Washington, DC: U.S. Department of Education and Office of Justice Programs, U.S. Department of Justice, 2015): 162 (Table 20.3).

56. See Jacinta M. Gau and Rod K. Brunson, "Procedural Injustice, Lost Legitimacy, and Self-Help: Young Males' Adaptions to Perceived Unfairness in Urban Police Tactics," *Journal of Contemporary Criminal Justice* 31, no. 2 (2015): 136.

57. Rod K. Brunson, " 'Police Don't Like Black People': African-American Young Men's Accumulated Police Experiences," *Criminology & Public Policy* 6, no. 1 (2007): 85.

58. "Data Analysis: Most Commonly Charged Offenses by McKinney Police Department's School Resource Officers, Disaggregated by Student Race: January 2012–June 2015" (Texas Appleseed, 2015), https://www.texasappleseed.org/sites/default/files/McKinneyPDFact%20Sheet_2012-2015.pdf.

59. Kerrin C. Wolf, "Booking Students: An Analysis of School Arrests and Court Outcomes," *Northwestern Journal of Law and Social Policy* 9 (Summer 2013): 77–78.

60. Hurst, Frank, and Browning, "Attitudes of Juveniles," 49; Weitzer and Tuch, "Perceptions of Racial Profiling," 435–36.

61. Taylor, Turner, Esbensen, and Winfree, "Coppin' an Attitude," 298, 300, 302; Brunson, " 'Police Don't Like Black People,' " 74; Hurst, Frank, and Browning, "Attitudes of Juveniles," 44–46.

62. Hurst, Frank, and Browning, "Attitudes of Juveniles," 41.

63. See, e.g., Weitzer and Brunson, "Strategic Responses," 252.

64. Ibid., 241.

65. Ibid., 241.

66. Rod K. Brunson and Jody Miller, "Gender, Race and Urban Policing: The Experience of African American Youths," *Gender and Society* 20, no. 4 (2006), 543.

67. Brunson, " 'Police Don't Like Black People,' " 84.

68. The author is a juvenile defense attorney in Washington, D.C. These are examples from the author's practice.

69. Hurst, Frank, and Browning, "Attitudes of Juveniles," 40–41; Brunson and Miller, "Gender, Race and Urban Policing," 540, 549.

70. Brunson, " 'Police Don't Like Black People,' " 84.

71. Brunson and Miller, "Gender, Race and Urban Policing," 539.

72. Weitzer and Brunson, "Strategic Responses," 240; Brunson and Miller, "Gender, Race and Urban Policing," 539.

73. Weitzer and Brunson, "Strategic Responses," 244.

74. Brunson, " 'Police Don't Like Black People,' " 81, 85; Brunson and Miller, "Gender, Race and Urban Policing," 540 (consistent with this author's experience with clients in D.C.).

75. Brunson, " 'Police Don't Like Black People,' " 85, 86.

76. See e.g., Gau and Brunson, "Procedural Injustice," 141.

77. Ibid., 142.

78. Brunson, " 'Police Don't Like Black People,' " 96.

79. Ibid., 88.

80. Ibid., 83, 86–87.

81. Justin Fenton and Kevin Rector, "Officer Goodson, Driver of Freddie Gray, Faces the Most Serious Charges," *Baltimore Sun*, Jan. 9, 2016.

82. Brunson, " 'Police Don't Like Black People,' " 90.

83. Ibid., 81; Brunson and Miller, "Gender, Race and Urban Policing," 534.

84. Hurst, Frank, and Browning, "Attitudes of Juveniles," 41.

85. Samantha A. Goodrich and Stephen A. Anderson. "Evaluation of a Program Designed to Promote Positive Police and Youth Interactions," *OJJDP Journal of Juvenile Justice* (January 2014): 87.

86. Weitzer and Brunson, "Strategic Responses," 241–43.

87. See Paul Butler, "Racially Biased Jury Nullification: Black Power in the Criminal Justice System," *Yale Law Journal* 105 (1995) 677–725.

88. Gau and Brunson, "Procedural Injustice," 136.

89. Weitzer and Brunson, "Strategic Responses," 237.

90. Ibid., 244, 247.

91. Ibid., 246, 248.

92. See *Brief for the American Medical Association and the American Academy of Child and Adolescent Psychiatry as Amici Curiae Supporting Neither Party* at 14–36, *Miller v. Alabama*, 132 S. Ct. 2455 (2012) (Nos. 10-9646, 10-9647) (collecting and summarizing studies); Elizabeth S. Scott and Thomas Grisso, "Developmental Incompetence, Due Process, and Juvenile Justice Policy," *North Carolina Law Review* 83 (2005): 793, 812.

93. Elizabeth Cauffman and Laurence Steinberg, "(Im)maturity of Judgment in Adolescence: Why Adolescents May Be Less Culpable than Adults," *Behavioral Science & Law* 18 (2000): 741, 748–49, 754 (table 4); Laurence Steinberg et al., "Age Differences in Sensation Seeking and Impulsivity as Indexed by Behavior and Self-Report: Evidence for a Dual Systems Model," *Developmental Psychology* 44 (2008): 1764, 1774–76.

94. Jennifer L. Woolard, Samantha A. Harvell, and Sandra Graham, "Anticipatory Injustice Among Adolescents: Age and Racial/Ethnic Differences in Perceived Unfairness of the Justice System," *Behavioral Sciences & the Law* 26 (2008): 207–26; Elizabeth S. Scott and Laurence Steinberg, *Rethinking Juvenile Justice* (Cambridge, MA: Harvard University Press, 2008), 38.

95. Dustin Albert and Laurence Steinberg, "Judgment and Decision Making in Adolescence," *Journal of Research on Adolescence* 21 (2011): 216–20; Laurence Steinberg, Elizabeth Cauffman, Jennifer Woolard, Sandra Graham, and Marie Banich, "Are Adolescents Less Mature than Adults? Minors' Access to Abortion, the Juvenile Death Penalty, and the Alleged APA 'Flip-Flop,'" *American Psychologist* 64 (2009): 586.

96. Jeffrey Arnett, "Reckless Behavior in Adolescence: A Developmental Perspective," *Developmental Review* 12 (1992): 350–51.

97. *Illinois v. Wardlow*, 528 U.S. 119 (2000).

98. Jackson, "Police-School Resource Officers' and Students' Perceptions," 638.

99. Goodrich and Anderson, "Evaluation of a Program," 87.

100. Brunson and Miller, "Gender, Race and Urban Policing," 532, 534.

101. Goodrich and Anderson, "Evaluation of a Program," 87; John Liederbach, "Controlling Suburban and Small-Town Hoods: An Examination of Police Encounters with Juveniles," *Youth Violence and Juvenile Justice* (2007): 111.

102. Deborah Sontag and Dan Barry, "Challenge to Authority: A Special Report; Disrespect as a Catalyst for Brutality," *New York Times*, Nov. 19, 1997.

103. Song Richardson, "Arrest Efficiency and the Fourth Amendment," *Minnesota Law Review* 95 (2011): 2046–48; Justin D. Levinson and Danielle Young, "Different Shades of Bias: Skin Tone, Implicit Racial Bias, and Judgments of Ambiguous Evidence," *West Virginia Law Review* 112 (2010): 310 (when mock jurors were primed with a black perpetrator, they were significantly more likely to find ambiguous evidence to be more indicative of guilt than with a white perpetrator).

104. Kurt Hugenberg and Galen V. Bodenhausen, "Facing Prejudice: Implicit Prejudice and the Perception of Facial Threat," *Psychological Science* 14, no. 6 (2003): 640.

105. Jennifer L. Eberhardt et al., "Seeing Black: Race, Crime, and Visual Processing," *Journal of Personality and Social Psychology* 87 (2004): 886.

106. Robin Engel, "Explaining Suspects' Resistance and Disrespect Toward Police," *Journal of Criminal Justice* 31 (2003): 475–92; Michael Reisig, John McCluskey, Stephen Mastrofski, and William Terrill, "Suspect Disrespect Toward the Police," *Justice Quarterly* 17 (2004): 607–29.

107. Lisa H. Thurau, "Rethinking How We Police Youth: Incorporating Knowledge of Adolescence into Policing Teens," *Children's Legal Rights Journal* 29 no. 3 (2009): 32.

108. Andrew Blankstein, Becky Bratu, and Alastair Jamieson, "Stockton, Calif. Cops Under Fire over Teen's Jaywalking Arrest," nbcnews.com, Sept. 18, 2015.

109. Brunson, "'Police Don't Like Black People,'" 89.

110. Jackson, "Police-School Resource Officers' and Students' Perceptions," 638–39.

111. Gau and Brunson, "Procedural Injustice," 144.

112. Sadie Gurman, "Agreement Keeps Denver Police Out of Most School Discipline Problems," *Denver Post*, Feb. 19, 2013.

113. "Police in Schools," *The Economist*.

114. Amanda Petteruti, *Executive Summary Education Under Arrest: The Case Against Police in Schools* (Washington, DC: Justice Policy Institute, 2011).

115. Jackson, "Police-School Resource Officers' and Students' Perceptions," 631.

116. Goodrich and Anderson, "Evaluation of a Program."

117. Lorraine Mazerolle, Emma Antrobus, Sarah Bennett, and Tom R. Tyler, "Shaping Citizen Perceptions of Police Legitimacy: A Randomized Field Trial of Procedural Justice," *Criminology* 51, no. 1 (2013): 33–63; Penner, Viljoen, Douglas, and Roesch, "Procedural Justice Versus Risk Factors," 234.

118. Mazerolle, Antrobus, Bennett, and Tyler, "Shaping Citizen Perceptions of Police Legitimacy," 33–63; Daniela Gilbert, Stewart Wakeling, and Vaughn Crandall, "Procedural Justice and Police Legitimacy: Using Training as a Foundation for Strengthening Community-Police Relationships," https://www.bja.gov/bwc/pdfs/Procedural-Justice-and-Police-Legitimacy-Paper-CPSC-Feb-2015.pdf; Bruce Lipman and Mark Sedevic, "Procedural Justice and Police Legitimacy: Participant Guide," Chicago Police Department: Education and Training Division, February 2013.

119. Gilbert, Wakeling, and Crandall, "Procedural Justice and Police Legitimacy," 9.

120. Ibid.

121. Ibid., 12.

122. Mazerolle, Antrobus, Bennett, and Tyler, "Shaping Citizen Perceptions of Police Legitimacy," 33–63.

123. Ibid., 40–41.

124. Valerie LaMotte, Kelly Oullette, Jessica Sanderson, Stephen A. Anderson, Iva Kosutic, Julie Griggs, and Marison Garcia, "Effective Police Interactions with Youth: A Program Evaluation," *Police Quarterly*, 13, no. 2 (2010).

125. *Law Enforcement's Leadership Role in Juvenile Justice Reform: Actionable Recom-*

mendations for Practice and Policy, MacArthur Foundation and International Association of Chiefs of Police, July 2014.

126. Ibid.

127. See the Strategies for Youth website: http://strategiesforyouth.org.

128. John F. Irwin and Daniel L. Real, "Unconscious Influences on Judicial Decision-Making: The Illusion of Objectivity," *McGeorge Law Review* 42 (2010): 8–9 (summarizing research on strategies to reduce implicit judicial bias); Jerry Kang, "Trojan Horses of Race," *Harvard Law Review* 118 (2005): 1529–30 and n. 207; Jeffrey J. Rachlinski et al., "Does Unconscious Racial Bias Affect Trial Judges?," *Notre Dame Law Review* 84 (2009): 1195, 1196–97, 1221 (indicating that judges are able to control implicit biases when they are aware of them and motivated to do so).

129. Nilanjana Dasgupta and Anthony G. Greenwald, "On the Malleability of Automatic Attitudes: Combating Automatic Prejudice with Images of Admired and Disliked Individuals," *Journal of Personality and Social Psychology* 81 (2001): 800, 802, 806–807; Anthony G. Greenwald and Linda Hamilton Krieger, "Implicit Bias: Scientific Foundations," *California Law Review* 94 (2006): 945, 964.

130. Patricia G. Devine, Patrick S. Forscher, Anthony J. Austin, William T. L. Cox, "Long-Term Reduction in Implicit Race Bias: A Prejudice Habit-Breaking Intervention," *Journal of Experimental Psychology* 48, no. 6 (2012): 1267.

131. *Illinois v. Wardlow*, 528 U.S. 119.

132. See *Florida v. Royer*, 460 U.S. 491, 497–98 (1983); *Smith v. United States*, 558 A.2d 312, 316 (D.C. 1989).

133. *Illinois v. Wardlow*, 528 U.S. 125.

134. *J.D.B. v. N. Carolina*, 131 S. Ct. 2394, 2403 (2011). See also *Yarborough v. Alvarado*, 541 U.S. 652, 674 (2004) (Breyer, J., dissenting).

Racial Profiling: The Law, the Policy, and the Practice

RENÉE MCDONALD HUTCHINS[1]

Introduction

In 2004, Jay-Z released the hit single "Ninety-Nine Problems," in which he complained of being targeted by police because he was "young," and "black," and his hat was "real low."[2] Jay-Z's artistic expression of frustration over the influence of race on policing was not new. In the modern era, not a decade has passed without a lyrical critique of race-based policing. In the early 1960s, James Baldwin wrote, "I might have pitied [the police] if I had not found myself in their hands so often and discovered, through ugly experience, what they were like when they held power and what they were like when you held the power."[3] In the 1970s, Gil Scott-Heron wrote in his classic anthem "The Revolution Will Not Be Televised," "There will be no pictures of pigs shooting down brothers in the instant replay."[4] In the 1980s, the rap group N.W.A. caused controversy with its rap song "F**k the Police." The song boasted lyrics that lamented the fate of young black men in the hands of police officers who "think they have the authority to kill a minority."[5] In the 1990s, hip-hop artist KRS-One connected the racial violence of slavery with modern-day policing when he compared the power once wielded by overseers to a police officer's "right to arrest, and if you fight back they put a hole in your chest."[6] These artists, and many others, gave voice to the lived reality of many black men (and women) in America—a reality in which skin color is too often a factor in police decision-making.[7]

Race-based decision-making has been a part of American policing at least since the Fugitive Slave Acts of the pre–Civil War period. This pair of acts (one in 1793 and the other in 1850) authorized the capture and re-enslavement of runaways on little more than a slaveholder's word.[8] Following the Fugitive Slave Acts, the "Black Codes" of the late nineteenth century were used to force many blacks back into slavery-like conditions after Emancipation.[9] More recently, the "war on drugs" has resulted in shockingly disparate rates of imprisonment for racial minorities.[10] A recent report by the NAACP found that as a result of the war on drugs, "in counties with the worst disparities, African Americans were up to 30 times more likely than their white counterparts to be arrested for marijuana offenses."[11]

While wealth and education certainly insulate some racial minorities from the harshest impacts of racialized policing, it would be naïve to suggest that prosperity provides immunity. The arrests of Harvard professor Henry Louis "Skip" Gates Jr. on the front porch of his Cambridge, Massachusetts, home, and of television personality Bryant Gumbel's son on the Upper East Side of Manhattan are recent evidence that affluence is an ineffectual antidote. In the last few years, well-publicized, in-custody deaths of unarmed black men, women, and children have reignited a national conversation about issues that for many years received little attention outside of the affected communities. One of the questions raised by the national debate is: how did we get here? How can America embrace a societal ideal of equal justice under law at the same time that there is widespread acknowledgment that race matters when it comes to policing?

One answer is that the U.S. Supreme Court has accepted the use of race in police decision-making. Two constitutional limits on police authority are the Fourth Amendment and the Fourteenth Amendment's Equal Protection Clause. However, the Court has not interpreted either of these amendments to prohibit racialized policing. As to the Fourth Amendment, the Court has found that (outside of border checkpoints) police officers cannot be motivated *exclusively* by race when targeting suspects. There is no Fourth Amendment problem, though, with police officers using race as one of many motivations for everyday police actions. Similarly, while discriminatory policing can be attacked as violating the Equal Protection Clause, the Court has made it nearly impossible to bring a successful claim on these grounds.

The alarming reality is that (as currently interpreted) few, if any, constitutional sanctions prevent the practice of singling out young black men for suspicion and investigation. In joining the long-running scholarly conversation around this issue, this chapter makes no pretense to neutrality. Racial profiling creates more societal harm than benefit. The practice is detrimental even when it is not motivated by racial hatred.

This chapter does four things. First, it defines racial profiling in all its forms. Second, it analyzes the Supreme Court's treatment of the practice. Third, it explores some proposals for reform. And fourth, it suggests additional interventions that may move us closer to eradicating racial profiling.

In the Streets: A Look at Racial Profiling in Practice

A single definition of racial profiling is hard to come by despite substantial evidence that the practice exists. Definitions are important. Clearly identifying the boundaries of a problem allows for the crafting of effective remedies. And there is no doubt effective remedies are needed. The harm caused by racial profiling is documented in the stories of those victimized by the practice and the empirical studies of their suffering. Studying the problem makes it clear that it is not just transparent racial hatred we must be concerned about. Certainly, some racial profiling can be explained as a direct result of explicit racial animus. But it would be inaccurate to suggest that such hatred motivates all (or even most) race-based policing.[12] Implicit bias plays, perhaps, an even more central role in racialized policing.

Defining Racial Profiling

The term "racial profiling" was first used in a February 19, 1990, *New York Times* article to describe the New Jersey state police practice of stopping black men on the New Jersey Turnpike in a poorly conceived law enforcement effort to combat drug trafficking.[13] Since then, the term has become widely accepted. A majority of white Americans (56 percent) and an overwhelming majority of black Americans (77 percent) believe that racial profiling exists.[14] However, since September 11, 2001, a single, universally accepted definition of racial profiling has been more difficult to agree upon. There are at least three ways racial profiling has been popularly defined.

On the narrowest end of the spectrum, racial profiling is understood to include only the conduct of police officers who consciously view black men as suspicious for no reason other than race. Indeed, some state legislatures have written their racial profiling laws to prohibit the use of race to target suspects only when race is the *sole* justification for police action.[15] Some law enforcement agencies have urged a similarly restricted view of the term, arguing that absent racial animus the use of race to target suspects is simply an efficient use of limited resources.[16]

This narrow "race-only" understanding of what constitutes racial profiling is consistent with Supreme Court precedent. However, defining racial profiling to include such a limited swath of police conduct limits reform efforts. It is a rare instance where a police officer will concede that he or she stopped a person based on nothing more than the suspect's race.

The 1991 stop of four young black men just outside of Philadelphia illustrates how easy it is for police to come up with alternate justifications for even transparently race-based stops. The four young men were stopped by police on I-95, near the Philadelphia airport. For nearly an hour, the officers detained the men. Despite thorough searches of the car and the men, the police found no drugs or other contraband. After being released, one of the men asked why they had been stopped. An officer answered: "[B]ecause you are young, black and in a high drug-trafficking area, driving a nice car."[17] Not surprisingly, the officer's candid admission didn't make it into the official record—the stop was instead justified by a written traffic warning. The basis for the warning? That the car's windshield was "obstructed" by a piece of string hanging from the rearview mirror. If racial profiling is limited to the narrow definition described above, the stop of the men escapes scrutiny because the "obstruction" of the windshield provides a lawful (albeit laughable) justification for police action.

Moving past the narrowest understanding of the term, racial profiling can next be defined to include police conduct that is driven only in part by race. For example, a police officer might become suspicious of a person because of the neighborhood where the person is walking, because the person is looking into parked cars, and because the officer has a generalized belief that most car thieves are young black men. This "race-plus" definition of racial profiling is found (among other places) in the *Oxford English Dictionary*, which defines racial profiling broadly to include "the use of race or ethnicity as grounds for suspecting someone of having committed an offense." The "race-plus" definition is also deployed by some law enforcement agencies and intermediate appellate courts. For example, the Arizona Attorney General's Office has determined that "any reliance on race and/or ethnicity in articulating reasonable suspicion is prohibited, except in investigations in which race or ethnicity is part of an identifying description of a specific suspect."[18]

The Maryland attorney general issued similar direction to law enforcement officers in August 2015.[19] The Arizona and Maryland rules echo guidance originally issued by then–United States attorney general Eric Holder to federal law enforcement officers in December 2014.[20]

An example of the "race-plus" form of racial profiling is also found in the facts of a 1992 Kansas City case.[21] In *United States v. Weaver*, police officers in Kansas City were at the airport looking for drug traffickers who were primarily members of L.A.-based street gangs. Weaver became a target of suspicion "because he was a 'roughly dressed' young black male who was carrying two bags and walking rapidly, almost running, down the concourse toward a door leading to a taxi stand."[22] An arresting officer testified that Weaver's appearance and behavior were consistent with what the officer knew of the street gang members who imported drugs into the city. After the officers approached Weaver, they determined that he had two carry-on bags but no checked luggage, that he appeared extremely nervous, and that he carried no identification.[23] Weaver later challenged his stop and search as violations of the Fourth Amendment. There is no question race was part of the officers' justification for stopping Weaver. Thus, if a "race-plus" definition of racial profiling had been applied in that case, the police treatment of Weaver would have been prohibited. Instead, the *Weaver* court applied the narrow "race-only" definition. This definition, which is the dominant understanding of racial profiling in our nation's courts, led the *Weaver* court to find the police conduct unobjectionable. The court wrote that "had [the officer] relied solely upon the fact of Weaver's race as a basis for his suspicions, we would have a different case before us."[24] But where race was just one of many reasons for Weaver's detention, the court found the stop was reasonable.[25]

A third and final definition of racial profiling is even broader than the "race-plus" definition described above. Advocates of "race-plus" prohibitions on racial profiling often carve out an exception for the use of race if the police are investigating a specific crime and are relying on credible information that makes race relevant to the investigation (for example, an eyewitness's description of his attacker). Under the third and final definition of racial profiling, even an eyewitness-generated reliance on race would be objectionable if the ensuing police suspicion sweeps large numbers of innocent people into the investigatory net for no reason other than the shared characteristic of race. For example, imagine for a moment that the victim of a carjacking tells police that her assailant was an elderly white woman with short blond hair. The police set out to investigate based on this description. Under this final definition, racial profiling will be found if the investigation is conducted in a manner that sweeps large numbers of innocent white women into the investigatory net simply because they are white.

This final definition of racial profiling is subject to vigorous debate. Scholars, law enforcement agencies, and courts have each declined to prohibit police conduct that is based on a credible description of the suspect.[26] For example, as noted, the Arizona Attorney General's Office specifically exempts from its definition any racially targeted investigations that are based on a witness description. Groups like the American Civil Liberties Union have adopted a similar approach.[27] Likewise, when asked to evaluate the constitutionality of a police sweep that ensnared virtually all of the young black men in one upstate New York town, a federal appellate court found it determinative that the police were acting on a description provided by the victim. The case was *Brown v. City of Oneonta*.[28]

In *Brown*, an elderly woman was attacked in the home where she was staying. The woman described her attacker as black, male, and young. She also indicated that she fought with her attacker over his knife. Blood evidence found at the scene led the police to believe the attacker had cut himself during the struggle.[29] In the days after the attack, the police rounded up more than two hundred young black men (and one young black woman) for questioning. The police interrogated each detained person and asked to inspect his (or her) hands and arms. Those targeted by the police sweep sued, alleging violations of their equal protection rights.[30] The Second Circuit rejected the claim because the sweep was based on an eyewitness description: "Here, the police were not routinely patrolling [for possible criminal activity]. Instead, it is alleged that they were searching for a particular perpetrator of a violent assault, relying in their search on the victim's description of the perpetrator as a young black man with a cut on his hand."[31]

For purposes of this chapter, the term "racial profiling" is meant to encompass all of the above. The "race-only" definition is insufficient because the harm of racial profiling is not restricted to the harm caused by officers acting in individual spasms of racial hatred.[32] As scholars have noted, "The core of the problem is not individual racism among a few officers. It is not simply officers' isolated discretionary choices to stop black people and, increasingly, Latinos and other minorities."[33] The second "race-plus" definition is similarly insufficient where many who use it exclude from its reach *any* police action that is based on a victim's description. Such blanket exclusion ignores two realities. First, even where a victim has provided a description, that description may be so devoid of detail that it fails to narrow the targeted population in any meaningful way. For example, a witness might describe his assailant simply as "a white man." While such a description certainly includes race and one other identifier—gender—it defines a group of potential matches that is so large as to be essentially meaningless. A second and related problem with exempting *any* search based on a victim's description is that the police investigation based on the description (particularly where the description is not detailed) may be executed in a manner that causes a large number of people to be swept into police surveillance for little reason other than their race. Finally, the third definition standing alone is inadequate where it only reaches particular applications of racialized police surveillance based on a victim's account. Each of the above definitions describes conduct that raises cause for concern. Accepting all of the definitions and thereby defining racial profiling to include any policing that subjects individuals to greater scrutiny based in whole or in part on race helps better expose the true scope of damage caused by the practice.[34]

Examples of Racial Profiling and the Harm It Causes

Though repeated studies suggest that widespread, racially targeted investigatory stops do little to reduce crime,[35] there is evidence that police departments across the country engage in extensive race-based policing and have been doing so for some time. For example, on the New Jersey Turnpike—where the term "racial profiling" was first applied—studies in the late 1990s revealed that black drivers constituted 42 percent of the stops and 73.2 percent of the arrests, even though they constituted only 15 percent of all turnpike drivers. These statistics persisted despite the fact that black and white drivers violated traffic laws at almost identical rates.[36] The statistics were supported by subsequent studies and a report issued by the state attorney general.[37]

Similar targeting of racial minorities during traffic stops has been documented in other states, including Florida, Illinois, Ohio, and Pennsylvania.[38] Systemic racial bias in the execution of traffic stops has been documented in Massachusetts and Maryland as well.[39] And the phenomenon is not a historic relic of an unfortunate but bygone era. A study published in 2014 confirmed that black drivers continue to be more likely to be stopped and more likely to be stopped multiple times in any given year.[40] Furthermore, after an investigatory stop happens, the police are five times more likely to search the vehicle if the driver is black than if the driver is white, even though the so-called "hit rate"—the rate at which contraband is found—for blacks is less than half of what it is for whites.[41]

Racial profiling is not limited to traffic stops. Pedestrians are also affected by the practice. For example, in 2012, the New York City Police Department stopped more than 700,000 New Yorkers.[42] Nearly 85 percent of these stops were of young black or Latino men.[43] In a class-action lawsuit, victims of the stops challenged the racially disproportionate impact of the police action. The trial court found the racial makeup of the stops could not be attributed to differential crime statistics.[44] In other words, the racial imbalance of the stops could not be justified by the notion that young black men simply commit more crimes.[45] Indeed, of the 4.4 million people stopped in New York over the eight-year stretch between 2004 and 2012, almost 90 percent of the stops resulted in the targeted individual being released at the scene after no evidence of wrongdoing was found.[46]

Moving past the numbers, narratives provide additional insight into the lived experience of racial profiling. For example, a black man named Kenneth described an encounter he had with the police. His account is unfortunately representative of stories told by so many other young black men:

> I was riding down the street and I saw the police going in the other direction. And I pulled over. I stopped to talk to some friends. He [the officer] was going the opposite direction, like, in another street . . . and he came back around a block. He stopped and sat down the street for a few minutes and then he came down the street. And then he was, "Everybody hands up. Give me your ID"—that kind of thing, you know? Now you know, obviously there was no reason for him to stop because the tags and the registration, it was good on the car, you know.
>
> He asked what was I doing down there with these guys.

I mean, these guys are guys I grew up with. You know what I mean? It wasn't a drug area, nothing like that. It was just six black guys standing, you know, in front of a house.[47]

Darrell, another black man, described his experience with police officers when he was just a teen. According to Darrell, he was pulled over by the police as he was driving through a pre-dominantly white neighborhood with friends. The police officer told Darrell and his friends they matched the description of a suspect who had recently burglarized a home in the neighbor-hood:

Yeah, he asked us for [our] driver's license and all that stuff. Then he asked if we lived around here because, I guess, my driver's license address wasn't from around where we was. Then he asked us where we lived and why we were over here. And he made us get out of the car and stuff. I mean I just kept cool about it, I guess. I kept my composure. Because I didn't want to make something out of nothing. I mean it was something, now that I look at it. But I didn't wanna, you know, give him a reason to do anything else. So I just play along with it. But after all, I felt really bad. We just had to sit outside on the curb for like an hour. . . . Yeah, they put us in handcuffs. And we sat outside for about an hour, and then they just let us go.[48]

Echoing Darrell's sense of frustration, another target of racial profiling succinctly explained, "When you're young and you're black, no matter how you look, you fit the description."[49]

Targeting citizens on the basis of race is something that stands at odds with American notions of equal justice. Nonetheless, it can be easy for many to ignore a call for reform where the direct harm of such stops is perceived as localized, and broader damage is seen as primarily philosophical. Such a framing is a mistake.

Racial profiling has social costs that reach well beyond individual stories or abstract notions of equality. Even scholars who favor aggressive police tactics have conceded that "the long term social costs of proactive police stops and arrests may overwhelm their short term crime fighting benefits."[50]

The societal harms caused by racial profiling were recently cataloged in a study of the practice that focused on traffic stops. Among other conclusions, the study confirmed that fear and distrust of the police increase among black Americans as a result of racial profiling. Importantly, individual experience with the practice is not necessary for a person to develop negative feelings about the police. Instead, the sense of fear and distrust spreads through the targeted group's collective awareness. This fear and distrust, in turn, can reduce willingness to cooperate with law enforcement—a phenomenon that tends to destabilize communities if it is sufficiently widespread. As decades of research have found, "crime is controlled primarily by communities working with the police, not by police working on their own."[51]

Another harm of racial profiling is that it contributes negatively to notions of racial identity and racial hierarchy by more deeply entrenching destructive notions of race. Racialized policing has been credited with marking those targeted as less than full citizens—blacks who were the subject of such policing were reminded of their subordinate social status and felt "more black," while whites who had been targeted were temporarily stripped of privilege and reported feeling "less white."[52] As a general rule, "[p]olice stops confirm whites' common assumption that they are full citizens deserving respect and leniency; they teach African Americans that they are targets of suspicion."[53]

Professor Sherry Colb described it as "targeting harm." This harm is the result of being the focus of repetitive and inescapable suspicion.[54] Such targeting, Professor Bernard Harcourt has explained, exacts substantial societal costs "by turning increasing numbers of the targeted groups into convicted criminals or innocent but distrustful subjects of surveillance who feel treated like criminals—and by giving others the comparative freedom from such control."[55]

The targeting of racial minorities for enhanced surveillance is also corrosive of democratic fundamentals. "[W]hen people's experience in government is limited to programs with arcane rules and arbitrary decision-making, they come to believe that government in general is arbitrary and unfair and that they have little efficacy in shaping their own fate in its hands."[56] In fact, some scholars have gone so far as to suggest that voting may be suppressed by the negative experience of racial profiling in police stops. Still others have compared the corrosive societal effects of race-based investigatory stops to the pass laws in South Africa during apartheid.[57]

Finally, the above harms are exacerbated by the fact that racial profiling depends upon large numbers of police-citizen contacts if even limited success is to be achieved. One law enforcement authority noted in the context of investigatory vehicle stops, "criminal patrol in large part is a numbers game; you have to stop a lot of vehicles to get the law of averages working in your favor."[58] Another harm of the practice is therefore that a large number of innocent people are swept into an investigatory net.[59] As history demonstrates, most racially targeted stops produce no evidence of any crime. In New York, years of rampant stop-and-frisk practices resulted in millions of blacks and Latinos being investigated by the New York City Police Department though there was no evidence to suggest they were engaged in any criminal wrongdoing.[60]

Professor Randall Kennedy has deftly summarized the harms of racial profiling, writing that the hostility and estrangement caused by racial profiling "gives rise to witnesses who fail to cooperate with the police, citizens who view prosecutors as 'the enemy,' lawyers who disdain the rules they have sworn to uphold, and jurors who yearn to 'get even' with a system that has, in their eyes, consistently mistreated them."[61]

The Role of Implicit Bias

Explicit racial animus is certainly responsible for some racial disparity in policing. But in modern America it is only the most politically tone-deaf police officer who would admit to targeting black men simply because they are black. Far more than overt racial animus, implicit bias better explains a greater percentage of the racial differences in policing outcomes.

The presence of implicit bias means that "an officer might evaluate behaviors engaged in by individuals who appear black as suspicious even as identical behavior by those who appear white would go unnoticed."[62] Indeed, a study conducted for the National Institute of Justice confirms the conclusion that implicit bias and not overt racism drives many racially disparate policing outcomes. In the study, researchers accompanied officers on 132 tours. The researchers documented 174 instances where these officers became suspicious of an individual during their tours. Black men accounted for 71 percent of the instances in which police officers identified an individual as worthy of suspicion. But in each instance individual officers maintained that race was not the basis for suspicion. Instead, officers reported targeting individuals for greater scrutiny because of the person's behavior or appearance.[63]

Implicit biases against black Americans are confirmed by decades of scientific research.[64] For example, studies demonstrate that observers perceive chaos and turmoil in black neighborhoods more readily than they do in comparable white ones.[65] Black men are routinely perceived as more aggressive, violent, and dangerous than other people. And the more stereotypically black one's phenotype, the more likely one is to be labeled a criminal. Studies have found that even children are impacted—ambiguous conduct is perceived as more threatening when performed by black boys.[66]

Unfortunately, it is difficult for anyone to escape the pervasive stereotypes of black aggression and criminality in our society. Once primed, implicit negative stereotypes inform decision-making regardless of race or political leanings.[67] The broad cultural saturation of these stereotypes then results in implicit biases that inform behavior.[68]

When these implicit biases are imposed on top of the training of police officers to be hypersuspicious, differential policing outcomes are a natural result. Police officers must necessarily be more suspicious than anyone else.[69] "Policemen are indeed specifically trained to be suspicious, to perceive events or changes in the physical surroundings that indicate the occurrence or probability of disorder."[70] Police officers are also on the alert for disrespect. Studies and anecdotal evidence confirm that a police officer's decision to detain a person is guided by how disrespected the officer feels by the subject.[71] These tendencies toward suspicion and high attention to disrespect operate simultaneously within a cultural atmosphere where stereotypes of young black men as dangerous, violent, aggressive, and criminal are prevalent.[72]

In the Court: The Role of the Law

Racial discrimination in policing decisions can be challenged under two constitutional provisions: the Fourth Amendment and the Equal Protection Clause. However, both such challenges have been largely foreclosed by limitations imposed by the U.S. Supreme Court.

In the context of ordinary street policing and the Fourth Amendment, the Court has instructed that an officer's racial motivation will not render subsequent police action unconstitutional so long as the officer also has individualized suspicion unrelated to race.[73] Consequently officers have a great deal of leeway when making decisions about who to target. For equal protection claims, the Court has imposed almost insurmountable burdens of proof before defendants may even secure a right to discovery in such cases. The combination of these two analytical lines has meant that only the most blatant racial misconduct in policing is challenged in courts. However, before turning to consider what the Court has said more recently in the context of the Fourth Amendment and equal protection, it is important to remember just how long the Court has been willing to tolerate racial profiling. One of the Court's earliest treatments of racial profiling arose during the Second World War.

Korematsu

In *Korematsu v. United States*,[74] the Supreme Court was asked to consider a clear example of law enforcement activity motivated purely by the race of the targets. However, rather than condemning the practice, the *Korematsu* Court expressed a tolerance for the impact of race on criminal procedure that has carried forward into the modern era. In *Korematsu*, the Court upheld the criminal conviction of Toyosaburo Korematsu after he failed to vacate his home in violation of an exclusion order that applied only to Japanese Americans. The *Korematsu* Court wrote, "[A]ll legal restrictions which curtail the civil rights of a single racial group are immediately suspect. That is not to say that all such restrictions are unconstitutional. . . . Pressing public necessity may sometimes justify the existence of such restrictions; racial antagonism never can."[75] Applying this logic to the facts before it, the Court found that Congress could lawfully require Korematsu (and all other Japanese Americans on the West Coast) to leave home and report to so-called "relocation centers" for internment. Recognizing that the law impacted only those Americans of Japanese ancestry, the Court nonetheless concluded the hardship was justified by "circumstances of direst emergency and peril"—namely the war.[76]

Three dissenting justices separately denounced the majority's logic as an unmitigated endorsement of racism.[77] And Justice Frankfurter sought to blunt the impact of the case, writing in a separate opinion that the majority's tolerance of racialized policing should not be understood as anything more than a function of the wartime in which the decision was written.[78] However, Justice Jackson powerfully foreshadowed that the Court's explicit endorsement of race as a factor in criminal justice decision-making would not remain confined to times of war.

> [O]nce a judicial opinion rationalizes such an order to show that it conforms to the Constitution, or rather rationalizes the Constitution to show that the Constitution sanctions such an order, the Court for all time has validated the principle of racial discrimination in criminal procedure . . . The principle then lies about like a loaded weapon ready for the hand of any authority that can bring forward a plausible claim of an urgent need.[79]

Justice Jackson's caution rang true as future Courts repeatedly permitted a role for race in policing decisions even in peacetime. In each case, the Court's approval of the challenged practice was (as Justice Jackson predicted) grounded in the government's claim of direst law enforcement necessity.

The Fourth Amendment and Race

Following *Korematsu*, one of the first broad expansions of police power following a claim of dire law enforcement need was *Terry v. Ohio*.[80] Notwithstanding language condemning overbearing police conduct,[81] the Court's 1968 decision in *Terry v. Ohio* is plausibly seen as one of the cases most responsible for current instances of racial discrimination in street-level policing. At the time of the *Terry* decision, the country was in a period of social upheaval. The civil rights movement was transitioning from the courts into the streets,[82] and a younger generation of civil rights leaders was advocating increasingly combative methods to ensure racial equality.[83] At the same time, popular support for the movement among nonblacks was eroded by conservative politicians who characterized civil rights protesters as lawless and the source of the nation's criminal unrest.[84] Race riots that broke out in response to charges of actual and rumored police brutality created even greater tension with white Americans, as images of armed black activists and cities in flames played into a perception that the nation was becoming dangerous and in need of more policing.[85] In the same month as a gun battle between black activists and police officers in Oakland, California, civil rights leader Martin Luther King Jr. was shot and killed as he stood on the balcony of a motel in Memphis, Tennessee.[86] Following King's assassination, the nation exploded in a spasm of racial violence that erupted from Washington to Watts. In the end, more than 120 American cities were jolted by the rioting.[87]

It was in this frenzied climate that the *Terry* Court approved temporary stops and frisks of civilians even if the police did not have probable cause to believe criminal activity was afoot.[88] Prior to the Supreme Court's decision in *Terry v. Ohio*,[89] probable cause was understood to be the minimum level of suspicion police officers would need before a warrantless stop was appropriate. In *Terry*, the Court upended this time-honored reasoning and awarded the police more "flexibility" in on-the-street encounters by allowing reasonable suspicion (a lower level of suspicion) to justify a limited police encounter.[90] Moreover, though the *Terry* decision made almost no mention of race, that aspect of the case was well understood to be at the center of the underlying facts.

Since *Terry*, the Court has become more explicit in its acceptance of the influence of race on some police work. In *United States v. Brignoni-Ponce*, a case that commentators have called "the Supreme Court's most significant immigration stop decision in the last fifty years,"[91] the Court considered the Border Patrol's authority to stop cars at or near the U.S.-Mexico border using so-called "roving patrols." Much like the frenzied national environment that gave birth to *Terry*, America was in an analogous spasm of national anxiety over immigration at the time of *Brignoni-Ponce*. The country was facing deep recession, and there was a sense that we were being "overrun" by undocumented immigrants.[92] As one commentator has noted, "[R]eports in the press expressed deep concern with 'the flood of illegal aliens' and 'almost uncontrollable' immigration from Mexico."[93] In this environment, the *Brignoni-Ponce* Court found the governmental interests at stake were substantial.

Estimating that "there may be as many as 10 or 12 million aliens illegally in the country," the Court wrote, "these aliens create significant economic and social problems, competing with citizens and legal resident aliens for jobs, and generating extra demand for social services."[94] Balancing the "valid public interest" in deterring illegal immigration against the "modest" intrusion entailed by a limited detention, the Court concluded that "when an officer's observations lead him reasonably to suspect that a particular vehicle may contain aliens who are illegally in the country, he may stop the car briefly and investigate the circumstances that provoke suspicion."[95]

In describing facts that might generate the reasonable suspicion necessary to justify such a stop, the *Brignoni-Ponce* Court found that race was a perfectly permissible factor. The Court wrote, "The likelihood that any given person of Mexican ancestry is an alien is high enough to make Mexican appearance a relevant factor, but standing alone it does not justify stopping all Mexican-Americans to ask if they are aliens."[96] Because suspected nationality was the only thing the Border Patrol agents knew about Brignoni-Ponce and his passengers before pulling them over, the Court found that the stop violated the Constitution.[97]

But, the next year, the Court went a step further and approved brief detentions at fixed checkpoints "even if it be assumed that such referrals are made largely on the basis of apparent Mexican ancestry."[98] In *United States v. Martinez-Fuerte*,[99] the Court considered the constitutionality of vehicle stops at two permanent checkpoints north of the U.S.-Mexico border. At one of the checkpoints, the narrowing of the traffic lanes brought cars to a virtual halt. A "point agent" standing between the lanes visually inspected each passing car. While most traffic was allowed to drive past without further inquiry, the point agent directed a handful of cars to a "secondary inspection area." At this secondary inspection area, another Border Patrol agent questioned the driver and any passengers about citizenship and immigration status.

Before assessing the constitutionality of the challenged checkpoint procedures, the Court commented on the "formidable law enforcement problems" created by illegal immigration. Reciting many statistics first presented in *Brignoni-Ponce*, the Court again reminded readers that "large numbers of aliens seek illegally to enter or to remain in the United States."[100] Against this "great" governmental interest, the Court balanced the "limited" intrusion being imposed on motorists—"a response to a brief question or two and possibly the production of a document evidencing a right to be in the United States."[101] Even in the absence of any individual suspicion of the motorists stopped, the Court found in favor of the detentions.[102] The Court's decision was similarly broad with regard to endorsing the use of race.

The *Martinez-Fuerte* Court was untroubled by the fact that race or ethnic appearance may have been the only basis for the selection of motorists diverted to the secondary inspection area. "As the intrusion here is sufficiently minimal that no particularized reason need exist to justify it, we think it follows that the Border Patrol officers must have wide discretion in selecting the motorists to be diverted for the brief questioning involved."[103] In other words, if the border agents needed no reason to act in the first instance, the fact that they may have acted chiefly for racial reasons was irrelevant according to the *Martinez-Fuerte* Court.

As the *Martinez-Fuerte* dissenters recognized, the majority's willingness to ignore the prominent role of race in the agents' referral of cars to the secondary inspection point eviscerated the Court's pronouncement in *Brignoni-Ponce* that "standing alone [racial appearance] does not justify stopping all Mexican-Americans to ask if they are aliens."[104] In one year, the Court thus went from disavowing the use of race as a stand-alone justification for law enforcement action to ignoring the substantial likelihood that race was being used in precisely that manner during fixed-checkpoint stops.[105]

Twenty years after *Martinez-Fuerte*, the Court considered race again in a street-level drug case that had nothing to do with immigration or the nation's borders. The case was *Whren v. United States*. The *Whren* defendants alleged that the officers' behavior toward them was racially motivated. But the Court found that the Fourth Amendment "allows certain actions to be taken in certain circumstances, *whatever* the subjective intent [of the officers]." This result perhaps should not have been unexpected in light of *Martinez-Fuerte*. "Once government embraces the use of race-based statistical probabilities as a law enforcement tool, the argument logically follows that the probabilities justify similar law enforcement techniques across the board."[106]

In *Whren*, plainclothes police officers were patrolling an area known for drug activity. The officers saw Michael Whren and James Brown sitting at a stop sign for what the officers thought was an unreasonably prolonged period. Brown, the driver, was looking down into Whren's lap. Both Whren and Brown were young black men. The officers made a U-turn to investigate. After Brown pulled off quickly and made a right turn without signaling, the officers caught up with the SUV and ordered Brown to put the car in park. As one of the officers approached, he saw

Whren holding two large plastic baggies of what appeared to be crack cocaine. Whren and Brown challenged the stop of their car as an unreasonable seizure under the Fourth Amendment.[107] In a terse eleven-page opinion, the Supreme Court found that it was not.

The *Whren* Court confirmed that automobile stops are governed by the Fourth Amendment and thus are required to conform to the "constitutional imperative" of reasonableness.[108] However, a unanimous Court found that "the decision to stop an automobile is reasonable where the police have probable cause to believe that a traffic violation has occurred."[109] Having found no violation of the Fourth Amendment, the Court suggested that Whren and Brown perhaps might look to the Equal Protection Clause to press their complaints: "We of course agree with petitioners that the Constitution prohibits selective enforcement of the law based on considerations such as race. But the constitutional basis for objection to intentionally discriminatory application of laws is the Equal Protection Clause, not the Fourth Amendment."[110]

What then of the Equal Protection Clause? The *Whren* Court directed litigants to the Equal Protection Clause as a possible source of relief. However, to the extent *Whren* did not completely dismantle every opportunity to challenge racialized policing under the Constitution, it was something of a Pyrrhic victory. This is because the Court, prior to *Whren*, had already erected near-insurmountable barriers to successful discrimination claims under the Equal Protection Clause.

Racialized Policing and Equal Protection

Equal protection of the laws is guaranteed by the Fourteenth Amendment. The amendment guarantees in part that the government will not treat people differently on the basis of race without a compelling reason for doing so.[111] It is not sufficient, though, to show that government action affects people of different races differently.[112] Known as "disparate impact," this showing is just one-half of the equation. In addition, "[p]roof of racially discriminatory *intent* or *purpose* is required to show a violation of the Equal Protection Clause."[113]

A selective enforcement claim is the way a person would raise an equal protection challenge to racial profiling (or other forms of racialized decision-making by the police and prosecutors). A selective enforcement claim challenges the process that draws the defendant into the criminal justice system.[114] Unfortunately for individual litigants such claims are exceedingly hard to bring. The month before *Whren* was decided, the Court issued a decision in *United States v. Armstrong*.[115] The *Armstrong* decision provides a good example of how difficult it is to successfully challenge government action on equal protection grounds in the criminal justice context.

Christopher Armstrong, who was black, was charged in federal court with conspiring to sell crack cocaine. He complained that because of his race he had been singled out for prosecution in the federal system, which carried harsher penalties than the state system.[116] Armstrong moved to dismiss his indictment and sought information from the government about the number of drug and firearm cases it had brought in federal court, the race of the defendants in those cases, and other information related to the investigation of the offenses. In support of his motion, Armstrong submitted an affidavit from an employee in the Office of the Federal Public Defender. The author of the affidavit maintained that the defendants in every one of the crack conspiracy cases the office had handled the preceding year were black.[117] After the trial court ordered the prosecution to produce documents and other evidence relevant to Armstrong's claims, the Supreme Court accepted the case for review.

The Court found that Armstrong was not entitled to discovery (the legal term for the information Armstrong sought). Before the government would be forced to disclose a single document, the Court insisted Armstrong needed evidence that whites in situations similar to his had not been prosecuted in federal court. It mattered not that this very information was located only in the government files nor that this was the same showing needed to triumph at the end of the case.

The *Armstrong* Court was quite candid that the burden it imposed was an intentional obstacle to litigation. As the Court announced, "[T]he showing necessary to obtain discovery should itself be a significant barrier to litigation of insubstantial claims."[118] At the same time, the Court insisted that the "similarly situated requirement does not make a selective prosecution claim impossible to prove."[119] In the Court's view, if Armstrong's claim was well founded, he should have been able to obtain evidence that whites had committed similar crimes but were not being prosecuted. It is difficult to imagine how Armstrong might have obtained this evidence absent discovery from the government. Nonetheless, the Court pointed to its then-110-year-old decision in *Yick Wo* as proof that success was not impossible.[120] It is telling that the only example of success the *Armstrong* Court could find was more than a century old and involved exceedingly particular facts . . . and a concession by the government.[121]

The *Armstrong* Court's declared purpose in imposing the high burden was not animosity toward litigants of racial discrimination. Rather, the Court said it was constrained by the broad discretion prosecutors are entitled to when enforcing the law.[122] In language that would be echoed a month later in *Whren*, the Court wrote, "[S]o long as the prosecutor has probable cause to believe that the accused committed an offense defined by statute, the decision whether or not to prosecute, and what charge to file or bring before a grand jury, generally rests entirely in his discretion."[123] It is presumed that a prosecutor's discretionary decisions are lawful, and that presumption, the Court found, should not be disturbed in the absence of clear evidence to the contrary.[124]

Beyond the serious uphill climb in terms of proof, it is

also true that an equal protection claim provides an ill-suited remedy for litigants embroiled in the criminal justice system. This is because even if a target of a racially motivated stop can overcome the substantial evidentiary burden imposed in *Armstrong*, the remedy for the equal protection violation would presumably not affect the progress of the criminal case. When the government violates the Fourth Amendment, as a general rule any evidence that was secured as a result of the constitutional abuse will be excluded from the criminal case. Put simply, if the police violate your Fourth Amendment rights and discover drugs and a gun, the government is prohibited from introducing the drugs and gun as direct evidence against you, which frequently compels the prosecutor to dismiss the criminal case. However, an equal protection violation would not afford similar relief. If the police violate your equal protection rights and discover drugs and a gun, you may ask for monetary damages or a declaration that the government was wrong, but you cannot ask for those drugs and gun to be kept out of a future prosecution.[125]

Over the years many justices have warned of the racially discriminatory impacts that might accompany expanded police authority. For example, in *Terry v. Ohio*, at the same time that it was broadening police powers, the Court acknowledged that expansive police authority might be used to disadvantage racial minorities.[126] Similar concerns about the racial impact of expanded grants of authority to the police were expressed years later in *Atwater v. City of Lago Vista*, where the Court authorized warrantless arrests for trivial criminal offenses punishable only by fines.[127] Justices O'Connor, Stevens, Ginsburg, and Breyer expressed profound concern over the future racial impacts the decision might have. In particular, the dissenting justices cautioned that the broad discretion granted the police might be used to harass racial minorities.[128] Notwithstanding these cautions, as the above discussion reflects, a majority of the

Court has repeatedly refused to step in and prohibit racialized policing.

Curbing the Role of Race in Street-Level Detentions

In the absence of intervention by the high court, the question then becomes what else can be done to curb the practice of racial profiling. There have been a number of proposals to end racial profiling in everyday policing. Some of these proposals have been advanced by scholars. Others have been put into action by elected officials. Still, others have been proposed by law enforcement or the courts.

On the political side of the ledger, state legislatures, in an effort to combat racial profiling, have "require[d] the collection of demographic and other data for drivers stopped by police, with the hope of compiling statistical evidence of impermissible profiling."[129] From New York to Oregon, police departments have begun amassing data to document the racial breakdown of police stops. One theory behind the data-collection-as-remedy approach is that officers who know they are being monitored will be more evenhanded in the execution of their duties. Indeed, even in the absence of legislation, many police departments are voluntarily collecting data related to race.[130]

Beyond data collection, there have also been numerous legislative proposals to prohibit any use of race in crime patrol activities. At the federal level, Representative John Conyers has, since 2001, repeatedly introduced the End Racial Profiling Act. The bill was recently reintroduced by the congressman in 2013, when he was joined by Senator Ben Cardin, who introduced the bill in the Senate chamber. Despite its repeated introduction, the act has never passed. Nonetheless, at the state level, legislative bans on racial profiling have become law in a majority of jurisdictions. Indeed, racial profiling has been explicitly prohibited in all but twenty states.[131] Unfortunately, as a report completed by the NAACP in 2014 found, these state laws are not adequate to eliminate the practice:

> Most state laws do not include a definition of profiling that is inclusive of all significantly impacted groups. They also tend to lack a ban of pretextual stops of pedestrians and motorists. . . . In addition, most state laws do not include a provision allowing individuals to seek court orders to stop police departments from engaging in racial profiling or obtain remedies for violations.[132]

In addition to legislation, several law enforcement agencies have issued guidelines to provide direction to officers. For example, the U.S. Justice Department in December 2014 issued guidance for federal law enforcement agents.[133] The Maryland attorney general issued similar direction to law enforcement officers in that state in August 2015.[134] And, the Arizona attorney general issued guidelines banning the use of racial profiling in law enforcement investigations based on Ninth Circuit case law.[135] One drawback to such guidelines is they are not independently enforceable, and thus what they provide is more in the way of suggestion than command.

Other law enforcement agencies have, building on notions of procedural justice, suggested politeness as a cure.[136] The suggestion here is not that a showing of civility will end racial profiling. Rather, the suggestion is that what is most offensive about race-based stops is the disrespect or discourtesy shown by the police officer to those stopped.[137] However, as others have noted, a fastidiously well-mannered officer will "not convert an otherwise offensive police stop into a fair and legitimate one. . . . Pervasive, ongoing suspicious inquiry sends the unmistakable message that the targets of this inquiry look like criminals: they are second-class citizens."[138]

On the scholarly side of the ledger, experts have advanced a range of approaches to the problem. To name just a few: Professor Randall Kennedy has proposed abandoning entirely racial profiling as a tool of law enforcement and permitting the consideration of race only when the police can demonstrate a compelling reason for doing so.[139] Alternatively, Professor Frank Cooper has suggested that a modified version of vulnerability theory[140] be applied. In short, Professor Cooper's suggestion is that our shared human condition of vulnerability imposes on the government "an affirmative duty to protect substantive equality of opportunity not only by preventing vulnerability to natural disasters but also by correcting for social hurdles rooted in cultural stereotypes."[141] And, policing expert Professor Kami Simmons has recommended a host of practical reforms ranging from legislation to investigation of local police departments by the federal government under the Department of Justice's pattern and practice authority.[142]

Finally, while the Supreme Court has done little to discourage the practice of racial profiling, some lower courts have been less restrained. For example, in New York, Judge Shira Scheindlin, who presided over repeated class-action challenges to the NYPD's stop-and-frisk practices, oversaw a settlement agreement that required a number of remedial efforts. These included data collection by the department and the adoption of an anti-racial-profiling policy, among other things. When these initial remedial efforts failed to produce results, Judge Scheindlin ordered the appointment of an independent monitor to manage reforms, and recommended the use of body cameras on a trial basis.

Many of the above proposals bear promise for eradicating the scourge of racial profiling. However, until we rethink the Court's current treatment of police authority in cases like *Terry* and *Whren*, efforts to do away with racial profiling will likely fall short. Consequently, I propose two additional changes to modify current law in an effort to provide additional relief.

First, the Supreme Court should reexamine its willingness to ignore race-plus thinking in forced police contacts that are justified by less than probable cause. As discussed above, in *Whren* the Court said that subjective motivations are irrelevant if a police officer has probable cause to believe a crime has been committed. In other words, in light of *Whren*, a police officer's "race-plus" thinking cannot be challenged under the Fourth Amendment so long as the "plus" amounts to probable cause. In *Ashcroft v. al-Kidd*,[143] however, the Court expanded the *Whren* rationale to include forced interactions where a police officer acts on a lesser showing of suspicion. Thus, since *al-Kidd*, "race-plus" thinking cannot be challenged even if the "plus" amounts only to reasonable suspicion. *Al-Kidd*'s extension of *Whren* should be revisited because it is inconsistent with the Court's earlier explanations of reasonable suspicion in *Terry* (and its progeny).

Prior to *Terry*, a police officer's authority under the Fourth Amendment was dependent upon the existence of probable cause and/or a warrant based on probable cause. In the pre-*Terry* era, the Court often repeated the caution that "reasonableness" under the Fourth Amendment should be equated with a warrant or probable cause. In that era, no balancing of "individual rights" against "law enforcement needs" was done if a warrant was present or probable cause existed. But in *Terry*, the Court deliberately introduced reasonableness balancing. In this balancing, the lawfulness of government action is determined by weighing the degree of infringement on a person's rights against the seriousness of the problem law enforcement seeks to address. Where the law enforcement needs are substantial and the infringement minimal, the government wins. When the converse is true, the citizen wins. Consequently, reasonable suspicion (the intermediate scrutiny created in *Terry*) must be understood to invite a more fact-sensitive inquiry than probable cause. Along the individual rights–versus–law enforcement needs continuum, the balance is quite different when a police officer seeks to stop and frisk a suspect because he is black and running in a high-crime area than when that same police officer seeks to stop and frisk a suspect who is suspected of criminal activity for objective reasons unrelated to race. This is particularly true where, on the needs side of the balance, racial profiling has proven to be less efficient and less successful than more traditional forms of policing. It is time to recognize that race-plus-probable-cause policing requires a different analysis than race-plus-reasonable-suspicion policing. It is time for the Court to find that the subjective racial motivations of a police officer are relevant to the reasonableness balancing required by *Terry*.

Second, it is time to consider a ban on so-called *Terry* stops, both pedestrian and vehicular,[144] for all drug and weapons possession offenses. Studies have found that racial imbalances in policing are most pronounced with police crime patrols that roam the streets looking for individuals in possession of contraband even though there have been no specific reports of criminal wrongdoing. The expanded authority granted by *Terry* vastly enhanced police officers' ability to engage in such proactive policing. Indeed, as programs like the NYPD's stop-and-frisk initiative in New York City demonstrate, millions of citizens can be swept into an investigatory net when *Terry*'s authority is interpreted broadly.

Part of the justification for expanding police power in *Terry* was the perceived urgency of preventing an imminent armed robbery. However, no similar justification for expanded police authority exists in run-of-the-mill possession cases. For such cases, the traditional limitations of the Fourth Amendment—including the warrant requirement and its well-defined exceptions—are sufficient. To reduce the numerous harmful effects of racial profiling, we must limit opportunities for the practice to take hold. One way of doing this is by narrowing the ability of police to forcibly stop suspects. In cases where an officer reasonably believes the suspect is engaged in nothing more than a possession offense, we should eliminate the expanded police authority defined in *Terry* and further expanded in later cases. This proposed narrowing of *Terry's* application will allow police to operate under the more lenient reasonable suspicion standard only in cases of the greatest need from a public safety perspective.

Conclusion

Professor Randall Kennedy wrote in a compelling deconstruction of racial profiling:

> The point here is that racial equality, like all good things in life, costs something; it does not come for free. Politicians often speak as if all that Americans need to do in order to attain racial justice is forswear bigotry. They must do that. But they must do more as well. They must be willing to demand equal treatment before the law even under circumstances in which unequal treatment is plausibly defensible in the name of nonracist goals. They must even be willing to do so when their efforts will be costly.[145]

Racial profiling causes "a collective erosion of civil rights, but only some groups feel the immediate impact."[146] In the immigration context, it is Mexicans and other Latin American natives who feel the brunt of removal decisions.[147] In the criminal justice context, it is black men (and to a somewhat lesser extent black women) who are disproportionately targeted. The consequence has been that "Blacks and Latina/os today are disproportionately represented among prison populations across the country—one of the few institutions in modern America in which these groups are over-represented as compared to their percentage of the general U.S. population."[148] Yet, despite this harm, the legal apparatus governing racial profiling has rendered successful challenges to the practice nearly impossible. It is time to rethink those rules.

NOTES

1. Jacob A. France Professor of Public Interest Law and Co-Director of the Clinical Law Program, University of Maryland Francis King Carey School of Law. I would like to thank Abigail Metzger, whose phenomenal research assistance made this work possible.

2. Jay-Z, "Ninety-Nine Problems," *The Black Album* (2004).

3. James Baldwin, *The Fire Next Time* (New York: Dial, 1963), 48.

4. Gil Scott-Heron, "The Revolution Will Not Be Televised," *Small Talk at 125th and Lenox* (Flying Dutchman Productions, 1970).

5. N.W.A., "F*** The Police," *Straight Outta Compton* (1988).

6. KRS-One, Sound of Da Police, *Return of the Boom Bap* (1993).

7. Many of the observations about the policing of black men in this essay apply with equal force to black women and Latinos.

8. Act of Feb. 12, 1793, 1 Stat. 302 (1793); Act of Sept. 18, 1850, 9 Stat. 462 (1850).

9. Randall Kennedy, *Race, Crime, and the Law* (New York: Pantheon, 1997), 151.

10. See generally *United States v. Shull*, 793 F. Supp. 2d 1048, 1052–57 (S.D. Ohio 2011).

11. NAACP, *Born Suspect: Stop-and-Frisk Abuses and the Continued Fight to End Racial Profiling in America*, September 2014, 7. Available at http://action.naacp.org/page/-/Criminal%20Justice/Born_Suspect_Report_final_web.pdf.

12. See generally Randall Kennedy, "Suspect Policy," *New Republic*, Sept. 13, 1999, 2–3 (pointing out that "[e]ven Jesse Jackson once revealed himself to be an amateur racial profiler. 'There is nothing more painful to me at this stage in my life,' he said in 1993, 'than to walk down the street and hear footsteps and start to think about robbery and then look around and see somebody white and feel relieved.' The reason Jackson felt relief was not that he dislikes black people. He felt relief because he estimated, probably correctly, that he stood a somewhat greater risk of being robbed by a black person than by a white person").

13. Samuel Gross and Deborah Livingston, "Racial Profiling Under Attack," *Columbia Law Review* 102 (2002): 1413, 1426; see also Joseph F. Sullivan, "New Jersey Police Are Accused of Minority Arrest Campaign," *New York Times*, Feb. 19, 1990; available online at http://www.nytimes.com/1990/02/19/nyregion/new-jersey-police-are-accused-of-minority-arrest-campaigns.html.

14. Will Lester, "Americans Think Racial Stops Are Widespread," *Philadelphia Inquirer*, Dec. 11, 1999, A14.

15. See, e.g., Md. Code Ann., Transp. § 25-113(g)(2) (banning the use of race in traffic stops only when race is the only justification for the stop).

16. Mia Nodeen Moody, *Black and Mainstream Press' Framing of Racial Profiling: A Historical Perspective at 2* (University Press of America 2008).

17. *Wilson v. Tinicum Township*, No. Civ. A. 92-6617, 1993 WL 280205 at *2 (E.D. Pa. July 20, 1993).

18. See Arizona Office of the Attorney General, "Racial Profiling Policy Guidance," available online at https://www.azag.gov/document/racial-profiling-policy-guidance (citing *United States v. Montero-Camargo*, 208 F.3d 1122 [9th Cir. 2000]).

19. In 2015, the Maryland attorney general issued a "guidance memorandum" prohibiting *any* use of race in "routine police activity unconnected to an investigation of a specific crime, organization or scheme." Where an officer was investigating a particular crime, the memorandum authorized the use of race only to the extent that the police are in "possession of credible information that makes the defining personal characteristic directly relevant to the investigation of a specific offense, organization, or scheme." Maryland Office of the Attorney General, "Guidance Memorandum: Ending Discriminatory Profiling in Maryland," August 2015, 4, 6.

20. See U.S. Department of Justice, "Guidance for Federal Law Enforcement Agencies Regarding the Use of Race, Ethnicity, Gender, National Origin, Religion, Sexual Orientation, or Gender Identity" (December 2014).

21. *United States v. Weaver*, 966 F.2d 391 (8th Cir. 1992).

22. *Weaver*, 966 F.2d at 392.

23. *Weaver*, 966 F.2d at 395.

24. *Weaver*, 966 F.2d at 394 n.2.

25. *Weaver*, 966 F.2d at 396.

26. See, e.g., Gross and Livingston, "Racial Profiling Under Attack," 1416.

27. On its website the American Civil Liberties Union (ACLU) defines racial profiling as "the discriminatory practice by law enforcement officials of targeting individuals for suspicion of crime based on the individual's race, ethnicity, religion or national origin." Unlike many, the ACLU also includes within its definition of the term the discriminatory failure to enforce the law against certain perpetrators because of their race.

28. *Brown v. City of Oneonta*, 221 F.3d 329 (2nd Cir. 1999).

29. *Brown v. State*, 45 A.D.3d 15 (N.Y. App. Div., 3rd Dept. 2007).

30. In addition to the equal protection claims, several of the plaintiffs also presented 42 U.S.C. § 1983 claims alleging a violation of their Fourth Amendment rights. These plaintiffs did not maintain that the use of race violated the Fourth Amendment directly. Rather, they maintained that their seizure by police officers was not based on either reasonable suspicion or probable cause where the police were simply looking for a young black man somewhere in the vicinity of the city of Oneonta. *Brown v. City of Oneonta*, 221 F.3d 329, 340 (1999).

31. *Brown*, 221 F.3d at 338; see also *Brown v. State*, 45 A.D.3d 15 (N.Y. App. Div. 3rd Dept. 2007) (dismissing parallel state claims on similar grounds).

32. Cf. David Rudovsky, "Law Enforcement by Stereotypes and Serendipity: Racial Profiling and Stops and Searches Without Cause," *University of Pennsylvania Journal of Constitutional Law* 3 (2001): 296, 307 (defending some racialized policing as justified by the "facts" "(1) that minorities commit more crime than whites . . . (2) that enforcement of criminal laws that are violated by whites and minorities in roughly proportionate numbers is disproportionate as to minorities because the location and social impact of the same types of crimes justifies a more aggressive response in minority communities; and (3) that current practices work").

33. Charles Epp, Steven Maynard-Moody, and Donald Haider-Markel, *Pulled Over: How Police Stops Define Race and Citizenship* (Chicago: University of Chicago Press, 2014), 159.

34. See generally Kennedy, "Suspect Policy," *7 (recommending that a "better

definition of racial profiling embraces a much more widespread police practice: using race as a factor in deciding whom to place under suspicion and/or surveillance").

35. Epp et al., *Pulled Over*, 154.

36. One group that studied traffic stops found a distinction between so-called "traffic-safety stops" and "investigatory stops." Traffic-safety stops are those that the police undertake when they are enforcing traffic-safety laws. In contrast, investigatory stops are driven by a more generalized focus on crime control and prevention. "In speeding stops, the most important influence on who is stopped is how fast you drive. In investigatory stops, the most important influence on who is stopped is not what you do but who you are: young black men are by far the most likely to be stopped." Epp et al., *Pulled Over*, 13–14.

37. *State v. Soto*, 734 A.2d 350, 360 (N.J. Super. Ct. Law Div. 1996); Peter Veniero and Paul H. Zoubek, "Interim Report of the State Police Review Team Regarding Allegations of Racial Profiling," April 20, 1999, 26–28, available at http://www.state.nj.us/lps/intm_419.pdf.

38. David Rudovsky, "Law Enforcement by Stereotypes·and Serendipity: Racial Profiling and Stops and Searches Without Cause," *University of Pennsylvania Journal of Constitutional Law* 3 (2001): 296, 299–302.

39. ACLU, "Black, Brown and Targeted: A Report on Boston Police Department Street Encounters from 2007–2010" (ACLU Foundation of Massachusetts, 2014); "ACLU Takes Battle to End Racial Profiling to the Turnpike," October 4, 2001, press release, available at https://www.aclu.org/racial-justice/aclu-takes-battle-end-racial-profiling-turnpike; David Harris, "The Stories, the Statistics, and the Law: Why 'Driving While Black' Matters," *Minnesota Law Review* 84 (1999): 277.

40. Epp et al., *Pulled Over*, 67.

41. Ibid., 105, 156.

42. Center for Constitutional Rights, "Stop and Frisk: The Human Impact" (2012), 3, available at http://ccrjustice.org/sites/default/files/attach/2015/08/the-human-impact-report.pdf.

43. Ibid.

44. *Floyd*, 959 F. Supp. 2d. at 585–86, 663.

45. For a defense of aggressively targeted policing policies, see generally Lawrence Rosenthal, "The Crime Drop and the Fourth Amendment: Toward an Empirical Jurisprudence of Search and Seizure," *NYU Review of Law & Social Change* 29 (2005): 641.

46. *Floyd v. City of New York*, 959 F. Supp. 2d. 540, 553 (S.D.N.Y. 2013).

47. Epp et al., *Pulled Over*, 63.

48. Ibid., 75.

49. Ross Tuttle and Erin Schneider, "Stopped and Frisked for Being a F**king Mutt," *The Nation*, Oct. 8, 2012, available at http://www.thenation.com/article/170413/stopped-and-friskedbeing-fking-mutt-video.

50. See Epp et al., *Pulled Over*, 33 (citing Lawrence W. Sherman et al., *Preventing Crime: What Works, What Doesn't, What's Promising: Report to the U.S. Congress* [National Institute of Justice, 1997]), and 153–54 (noting that "the benefits of investigatory stops are modest and greatly exaggerated, yet their costs are substantial and

largely unrecognized"); see also National Advisory Commission on Civil Disorders ("Kerner Commission"), *Report of the National Advisory Commission on Civil Disorders* (Washington, DC: Government Printing Office, 1968) (noting that urban riots were triggered in part by the racially disparate stop-and-frisk practices of the era).

51. Epp et al., *Pulled Over*, 156.

52. Ibid., 149–50.

53. Ibid., 157.

54. Sherry F. Colb, "Innocence, Privacy, and Targeting in Fourth Amendment Jurisprudence," *Columbia Law Review* 96 (1996): 1486.

55. Bernard Harcourt, *Against Prediction: Profiling, Policing and Punishing in an Actuarial Age* (Chicago: University of Chicago Press, 2006). See also Bernard Harcourt, *Illusion of Order: The False Promise of Broken Windows Policing* (Cambridge, MA: Harvard University Press, 2001).

56. Epp et al., *Pulled Over*, 15, 156. See also Joe Soss, "Lessons of Welfare: Police Design, Political Learning, and Political Action," *American Political Science Review* 93 (1999): 363–80.

57. Epp et al., *Pulled Over*, 16.

58. Charles Remsberg, *Tactics for Criminal Patrol: Vehicle Stops, Drug Discovery and Officer Survival* (Glen Ellyn, IL: Calibre Press, 1995), 27.

59. As discussed in greater detail in "Curbing the Role of Race in Street Level Detentions," below, the degree of impact a police tactic has on innocent citizens is relevant to the constitutionality of the tactic under the Fourth Amendment. For example, in *Delaware v. Prouse*, the Supreme Court rejected the government's request to conduct suspicion-less stops of cars to identify unlicensed drivers. In the Court's view, the discretionary spot checks were not a "sufficiently productive mechanism to justify the intrusion upon Fourth Amendment interests which such stops entail." *Delaware v. Prouse*, 440 U.S. 648, 659 (1979). The Court used this "sufficiently productive" line of reasoning in a somewhat perverse manner several years later in a racial profiling case. In approving the use of race to target only some cars for secondary inspection at a border checkpoint, the Supreme Court concluded in *Martinez-Fuerte* that selective referral tended "to advance some Fourth Amendment interests by minimizing the intrusion on the general motoring public." 428 U.S. 543, 560 (1976).

60. *Floyd*, 959 F.Supp. 2d at 553.

61. Kennedy, "Suspect Policy," *4.

62. Song Richardson, "Arrest Efficiency and the Fourth Amendment," *Minnesota Law Review* 95 (2011): 2035, 2039. See also Andrew Taslitz, "Police Are People Too: Cognitive Obstacles to, and Opportunities for, Police Getting the Individualized Suspicion Judgment Right," *Ohio State Journal of Criminal Law* 8 (2007): 9, 48.

63. Geoffrey P. Alpert, Roger G. Dunham, Meghan Stroshine, Katherine Bennett, and John MacDonald, *Police Officer Decision Making and Discretion: Forming Suspicion and Making a Stop: A Report to the National Institute of Justice* (October 2004), available online at https://www.ncjrs.gov/pdffiles1/nij/grants/213004.pdf.

64. Sophie Trawalter, "Attending to Threat: Race-Based Patterns of Selective Attention," *Journal of Experimental Social Psychology* 44 (2008): 1322.

65. Robert Sampson and Stephen Raudenbush, "Seeing Disorder: Neighborhood

Stigma and the Social Construction of 'Broken Windows,'" *Social Psychology Quarterly* 67 (2004): 319, 336; see also Song Richardson, "Cognitive Bias, Police Character, and the Fourth Amendment," *Arizona State Law Journal* 44 (2012): 267, 268.

66. See generally Epp et al., *Pulled Over*, 41–48 (reviewing implicit bias studies).

67. Ibid.

68. Mahzarin Banaji and Anthony Greenwald, *Blind Spot: Hidden Biases of Good People* (New York: Delacorte Press, 2013).

69. Jerome H. Skolnick, *Justice Without Trial: Law Enforcement in Democratic Society*, 3rd ed. (New York: Macmillan College Publishing, 1994), 46–47.

70. Ibid., 48.

71. Donald Black, "The Social Organization of Arrest," *Stanford Law Review* 23 (1971): 1087, 1097–101 (1971); William Westley, "Violence and the Police," *American Journal of Sociology* 59 (1953): 34, 38, table 1. The historical studies are consistent with modern narratives describing the experience of police force being "often used . . . in response to being asked the reason for a stop or an arrest." Center for Constitutional Rights, "Stop and Frisk," 5.

72. See, e.g., Jennifer L. Eberhardt, "Seeing Black: Race, Crime, and Visual Processing," *Journal of Personality and Social Psychology* 87 (2004): 876 ("The stereotype of Black Americans as violent and criminal has been documented by social psychologists for almost 60 years"); Victor M. Rios, *Punished: Policing the Lives of Black and Latino Boys* (New York: New York University Press, 2011).

73. *Ashcroft v. al-Kidd*, 563 U.S. 731 (2011); *Whren v. United States*, 517 U.S. 806 (1996).

74. *Korematsu v. United States*, 323 U.S. 214 (1944).

75. Ibid.

76. *Korematsu*, 323 U.S. at 220; see also 223 ("To cast this case into outlines of racial prejudice, without reference to the real military dangers which were presented, merely confuses the issue").

77. *Korematsu*, 323 U.S. at 226 (Roberts, J., dissenting) ("[This] is a case of convicting a citizen as a punishment for not submitting to imprisonment in a concentration camp, based on his ancestry, and solely because of his ancestry"); *Korematsu* at 233 (Murphy, J., dissenting) ("Such exclusion goes over 'the very brink of constitutional power' and falls into the ugly abyss of racism"); *Korematsu* at 243 (Jackson, J., dissenting) (noting that restrictions were imposed only on Japanese Americans, but not other potential national enemies—German Americans, Italian Americans, or those guilty of treason—and commenting that "[the] difference between their innocence and his crime would result, not from anything he did, said, or thought, different than they, but only in that he was born of different racial stock").

78. See, e.g., *Korematsu*, 323 U.S. at 224 (Frankfurter, J., concurring) (observing that "the validity of action under the war power must be judged wholly in the context of war. That action is not to be stigmatized as lawless because like action in times of peace would be lawless").

79. *Korematsu*, 323 U.S. at 247.

80. *Terry v. Ohio*, 392 U.S. 1 (1968).

81. See, e.g., *Terry*, 392 U.S. at 15.

82. The NAACP initially attacked Jim Crow in the courts using a coordinated

series of legal challenges to restraints on segregated education and voting rights. See, e.g., *Smith v. Allwright*, 321 U.S. 649 (1944), and *Brown v. Board of Education of Topeka*, 347 U.S. 483 (1954). By the 1960s, this strategy was being replaced with more public demonstrations like sit-ins, Freedom Rides, the Birmingham confrontation, and the March on Washington. For a brief description of the Freedom Riders, the confrontations in Birmingham, and the March on Washington, see generally Juan Williams, *Eyes on the Prize: America's Civil Rights Years, 1954–1965* (New York: Penguin, 1987), 144–61, 179–95, 197–205.

83. Ben W. Gilbert and the staff of the *Washington Post*, *Ten Blocks from the White House: Anatomy of the Washington Riots of 1968* (New York: Frederick A. Praeger, 1968), 5.

84. See Michelle Alexander, *The New Jim Crow* (New York: The New Press, 2010), 41; see also John Edgar Hoover, Federal Bureau of Investigation, *Crime in the United States: Uniform Crime Report—1964* (Washington, DC: Government Printing Office, 1965), 3–5 (documenting overall crime rate increase in the early 1960s), available at https://archive.org/stream/uniformcrimerepo1965unit/uniformcrime repo1965unit_djvu.txt.

85. See Stanley Lieberson and Arnold R. Silverman, "The Precipitants and Underlying Conditions of Race Riots," *American Sociological Review* 30 (1965): 887, 889; Walter C. Rucker and James N. Upton, eds., *Encyclopedia of American Race Riots*, vol. 2 (Westport, CT: Greenwood, 2006), 566–67; Robert M. Fogelson, "Violence as Protest," *Proceedings of the Academy of Political Science* 29 (1968) 25, 38–41; Robyn Meredith, "5 Days in 1967 Still Shake Detroit," *New York Times*, July 23, 1997, http://www.nytimes.com/1997/07/23/us/5-days-in-1967-still-shake-detroit.html (discussing the 43 people killed during the 1967 Detroit riots); "40 Years On, Newark Re-Examines Painful Riot Past," available online at http://www.npr.org/templates/story/story.php?storyId=11966375 (discussing the 26 fatalities of the 1967 Newark riot); Taylor Branch, *At Canaan's Edge: America in the King Years, 1965–1968* (New York: Simon & Schuster, 2006), 293–99 (discussing the triggering events and aftermath of the 1965 Watts riots); "The Raging Silence," *Philadelphia* (Sept. 20, 2006), http://www.phillymag.com/articles/philadelphia-magazine-the-raging-silence/ (describing the rumor of police abuse of a pregnant woman that precipitated the 1964 Philadelphia riot).

86. Earl Caldwell, "Martin Luther King Is Slain in Memphis," *New York Times*, April 5, 1968, A1.

87. Gilbert et al., *Ten Blocks from the White House*, 15–16.

88. Though the *Terry* Court provided official sanction of stop-and-frisk practices, they were not a new phenomenon. Scholar John Barrett suggests that stops and frisks may have been used by law enforcement in the early 1900s in an attempt to "control" Italian American immigrants in New York City. See John Q. Barrett, "*Terry v. Ohio*: The Fourth Amendment Reasonableness of Police Stops and Frisks Based on Less Than Probable Cause," in *Criminal Procedure Stories: An In-Depth Look at Leading Criminal Procedure Cases*, ed. Carol Steiker (New York: Foundation Press, 2006), 295, 299–300; see also generally Jennifer Guglielmo and Salvatore Salerno, eds., *Are Italians White? How Race Is Made in America* (New York: Routledge, 2003).

89. *Terry v. Ohio*, 392 U.S. 1 (1968).

90. *Sokolow*, 490 U.S. at 7.

91. Kevin R. Johnson, "How Racial Profiling in America Became the Law of the Land: *United States v. Brignoni-Ponce* and *Whren v. United States* and the Need for Truly Rebellious Lawyering," *Georgetown Law Journal* 98 (2010): 1005, 1009.

92. Immigration Reform and Control Act of 1983: Hearings on H.R. 1510 Before the Subcomm. on Immigration, Refugees, and International Law of the H. Comm. on the Judiciary, 98th Cong. 1 (1983).

93. Johnson, "How Racial Profiling," 1010.

94. *United States v. Brignoni-Ponce*, 422 U.S. 873 (1975).

95. *Brignoni-Ponce*, 422 U.S. at 881. But see *Almeida-Sanchez v. United States*, 413 U.S. 266 (1973) and *United States v. Ortiz*, 422 U.S. 891 (1975) (finding that roving patrols and permanent checkpoints around or at the border need probable cause to justify the search—as opposed to the brief detention—of suspect vehicles).

96. *Brignoni-Ponce*, 422 U.S. at 886–87.

97. Interestingly, what the Border Patrol agent suspected about Brignoni-Ponce's nationality was in fact wrong. Brignoni-Ponce was not of Mexican descent, but was instead Puerto Rican.

98. *United States v. Martinez-Fuerte*, 428 U.S. 543, 563 (1976).

99. Ibid., 428 U.S. 543 (1976).

100. Ibid., 428 U.S. at 551.

101. Ibid., 428 U.S. at 557–58 ("Neither the vehicle nor its occupants are searched, and visual inspection of the vehicle is limited to what can be seen without a search").

102. Ibid., 428 U.S. at 562.

103. Ibid., 428 U.S. at 563–64.

104. *Brignoni-Ponce*, 422 U.S. at 886–87.

105. *Martinez-Fuerte*, 428 U.S. at 572 (Brennan, J., dissenting) (finding that "checkpoint officials, uninhibited by any objective standards and therefore free to stop any or all motorists without explanation or excuse, wholly on whim, will perforce target motorists of Mexican appearance. The process will then inescapably discriminate against citizens of Mexican ancestry and Mexican aliens lawfully in this country for no other reason than that they unavoidably possess the same 'suspicious' physical and grooming characteristics of illegal Mexican aliens").

106. Johnson, "How Racial Profiling," 1072.

107. At the suppression hearing one of the officers was asked whether the fact that Whren and Brown were black was what actually motivated the stop. The officer answered that it was not. However, the suppression court noted that the officer "hesitated a long time" before answering the question. See Brief of Petitioners at 10 n. 11, *Whren v. United States*, 517 U.S. 806 (1996).

108. *Whren*, 517 U.S. at 810.

109. Ibid., 517 U.S. at 810.

110. Ibid., 517 U.S. at 813. In *Ashcroft v. al-Kidd*, 563 U.S. 731 (2011), the Court confirmed that *Whren* foreclosed Fourth Amendment challenges to all forms of racially motivated policing including *Terry* stops and other police stops justified by less than probable cause.

111. *Yick Wo v. Hopkins*, 118 U.S. 356 (1886).

112. *Washington v. Davis*, 426 U.S. 229, 235–36 (1976).

113. *Village of Arlington Heights v. Metropolitan Housing*, 429 U.S. 252 265 (1977).

114. *United States v. Armstrong*, 517 U.S. 456, 463 (1996).

115. *Armstrong* addressed a claim of selective prosecution, not selective enforcement. However, where the Court had drawn equivalence between the evidentiary hurdles required for both claims, the decision there is relevant.

116. *United States v. Armstrong*, 517 U.S. 456 (1996).

117. Ibid., 517 U.S. at 459.

118. Ibid., 517 U.S. at 464.

119. Ibid., 517 U.S. at 466.

120. Ibid., 517 U.S. at 466.

121. *Yick Wo* challenged an ordinance that banned laundries in wooden buildings. At the time of *Yick Wo*'s challenge there were approximately 320 laundries in the San Francisco area and most (310) were made of wood. Of the laundries 240 were owned by people of Chinese ancestry; the remainder were owned by others. In the year leading up to *Yick Wo*'s challenge, more than 150 laundry owners of Chinese ancestry were arrested for operating laundries in wooden dwellings. The approximately 80 laundry owners not of Chinese descent, however, were "left unmolested, and free to enjoy the enhanced trade and profits arising from this hurtful and unfair discrimination." *Yick Wo v. Hopkins*, 118 U.S. 356 (1886). After the city conceded *Yick Wo*'s claims, the Court had little trouble concluding that an equal protection violation had occurred. Thus, the *Armstrong* Court's suggestion that *Yick Wo* is proof that *Armstrong* doesn't create an insurmountable hurdle is belied by the unusual facts of the earlier case.

122. *Armstrong*, 517 U.S. at 464–65.

123. Ibid., 517 U.S. at 464 (citing *Bordenkircher v. Hayes*, 434 U.S. 357 [1978]).

124. Ibid., 517 U.S. at 465.

125. See Johnson, "How Racial Profiling," 1064.

126. *Terry*, 392 U.S. 1, 14–15 (1968) ("The wholesale harassment by certain elements of the police community, of which minority groups, particularly Negroes, frequently complain, will not be stopped by the exclusion of any evidence from any criminal trial").

127. *Atwater v. City of Lago Vista*, 532 U.S. 318, 354–55 (2001).

128. Ibid., 532 U.S. at 372 ("[A]s the recent debate over racial profiling demonstrates all too clearly, a relatively minor traffic infraction may often serve as an excuse for stopping and harassing an individual").

129. Johnson, "How Racial Profiling," 1071 (citing Matthew Hickman, U.S. Dept. of Justice, Traffic Stop Data Collection Policies for State Police 2004 [2005], 1–2).

130. See, e.g., Greg Stewart and Emily Covelli, "Stops Data Collection: The Portland Police Bureau's Response to the Criminal Justice Police and Research Institute's Recommendations" (2014), available at http://www.portlandoregon.gov/police/article/481668; Kami Simmons, "The Legacy of Stop and Frisk: Addressing the Vestiges of a Violent Police Culture," *Wake Forest Law Review* (2014): 849, 855 (discussing the collection of data by the NYPD).

131. German Lopez, "20 States Still Haven't Outlawed Racial Profiling. Has Yours?" (Sept. 26, 2014), available online at http://www.vox.com/xpress/2014/9/26/6844837/20-states-dont-prohibit-racial-profiling.

132. NAACP, *Born Suspect*.

133. See U.S. Department of Justice, Guidance for Federal Law Enforcement Agencies Regarding the Use of Race, Ethnicity, Gender, National Origin, Religion, Sexual Orientation, or Gender Identity (December 2014), available at https://www .justice.gov/sites/default/files/ag/pages/attachments/2014/12/08/use-of-race-policy. pdf.

134. See above, note 19 ["In 2015"].

135. See above, note 18 ["Arizona Office"].

136. See, e.g., William J. Stuntz, "Local Policing After the Terror," *Yale Law Journal* 111 (2002): 2174.

137. Epp, Maynard-Moody, and Haider-Markel, *Pulled Over*, 4 (citing Tom R. Tyler, *Why People Obey the Law* [New Haven, CT: Yale University Press, 1990]; Tom R. Tyler and Yuen J. Huo, *Trust in the Law: Encouraging Public Cooperation with the Police and the Courts* [New York: Russell Sage Foundation, 2002]; and E. Allen Lind and Tom R. Tyler, *The Social Psychology of Procedural Justice* [New York: Plenum Press, 1988]).

138. Epp, Maynard-Moody, and Haider-Markel, *Pulled Over*, 5. See also p. 6: "What makes inquisitive police stops so offensive to so many African Americans and Latinos is not that the officers carrying them out are impolite or even frankly bigoted, but that these stops are common, repeated, routine, and even scripted. This scripted practice treats its targets not as individuals worthy of dignity but as numbers to be processed in search of the small percentage who are carrying contraband or have an outstanding warrant."

139. Kennedy, "Suspect Policy," *6.

140. See generally Martha Fineman, "Beyond Identities: The Limits of an Antidiscrimination Approach to Equality," *Boston University Law Review* 92 (2012): 1713.

141. Frank Rudy Cooper, "Always Already Suspect: Revising Vulnerability Theory," *North Carolina Law Review* 93 (2015): 1339, 1344.

142. See Simmons, "Legacy of Stop and Frisk," 849, 855.

143. *Ashcroft v. al-Kidd*, 563 U.S. 731 (2011).

144. In *Pulled Over*, the study's authors found that investigatory traffic stops are far more racially biased than more traditional traffic safety stops. Epp et al., *Pulled Over*, 59–60, 160.

145. Kennedy, "Suspect Policy," *6.

146. Rudovsky, "Law Enforcement by Stereotypes," 335.

147. See U.S. Department of Homeland Security, Annual Report: Immigration Enforcement Actions: 2013 at 1, 6 and table 8 (2014), available at http://www.dhs .gov/sites/default/files/publications/ois_enforcement_ar_2013.pdf. See also Johnson, "How Racial Profiling," 1026 (citing U.S. Department of Homeland Security, Annual Report: Immigration Enforcement Actions: 2007, 4, table 2 [2008], available at http:// www.dhs.gov/xlibrary/assets/statistics/publications/enforcement_ar_07.pdf).

148. Johnson, "How Racial Profiling," 1047.

Making Implicit Bias Explicit

Black Men and the Police

KATHERYN RUSSELL-BROWN

Introduction

The 2014 case of Michael Brown represents the high-water mark of contemporary cases involving police violence against black men. Modern-day police killings and assaults have struck an uneasy chord across the country. The prominence of these incidents has created a kind of public death watch. Thanks to cell phone videos, online petitions, and Twitter postings, these cases take up ever larger spaces in the public consciousness. These technological tools allow us all to bear witness, putting us all on homicide watch. This new collective sight has created seismic rumblings about policing, race, and justice. It has become harder to dismiss police violence as random, unfortunate, "post-racial" aberrations. Adding to the weighty pall of these cases is their frequency. With each passing fortnight, another police-officer-kills-black-man case makes its way into the national headlines. The chorus of concern has become increasingly louder—expressions of dismay at the body count, concerns as to why it continues to happen, and pleas to make it stop.

The disproportionately high rate at which black men are killed by the police is a major social problem in the United States.

Confounding this problem is the fact that until recently, there was no effort to keep official statistics about these incidents.[1] In 2017, in response to criticism, the Department of Justice introduced a pilot program designed to gather national data on use of force by police. This data gap has been problematic for two reasons. One, the FBI gathers annual statistics on the number of law enforcement officers killed in the line of duty.[2] The failure to gather data on fatal police-citizen encounters sends the message that these deaths are not important, relatively speaking. Two, it left the work of collecting these statistics to agencies, organizations, and individuals whose findings are not official. Notably, two prominent news organizations have developed websites that track these data. *The Guardian* (U.S.) and the *Washington Post* have websites that count the number of people killed by law enforcement officers. Both sites provide data about each victim, including race, gender, age, region, and whether the victim was carrying a weapon.[3] In 2016, the *Washington Post* reported that 963 people were killed by police in the United States.[4] Of this number, 222 (23 percent) were black men. Based on these numbers, each month approximately eighteen black men are killed by law enforcement officers. Black men make up approximately 6 percent of the U.S. population.

While the mounting toll of cases is hard to ignore, blacks and whites continue to view these killings through different interpretive lenses. A 2015 survey by the Associated Press–National Opinion Research Council found that the overwhelming majority of blacks believe the police are too quick to use deadly force, particularly against someone black. In contrast, most whites believe that the police only use deadly force when necessary.[5]

Policy experts, scholars, and public officials have argued that an examination of implicit bias will help us understand and reduce police violence against black men. Implicit racial bias studies examine the workings of unconscious mental processes to uncover which traits and characteristics individuals associate with various racial groups. Psychologists have developed tests to measure hidden bias. The best known of these is the Implicit Association Test (IAT).[6]

The growing focus on implicit bias is driven partly by the popularity of the IAT, which has been taken by over 1.5 million people.[7] This online test allows people to test themselves to determine whether and to what degree they hold implicit racial biases. Participants are shown photographs of people from different racial groups and asked to quickly perform a series of tasks, since the responses are supposed to capture the participants' unconscious rather than conscious choices. One task requires participants to select the words they associate with various faces. The results range from findings that indicate that the test taker demonstrates a slight, moderate, or strong preference for a particular racial group.

This chapter is written with three goals in mind. The first goal is to highlight the fact that implicit racial bias is real and that it has real-world and sometimes deadly consequences. The second is to identify the strengths and weaknesses of the implicit bias analysis and to determine what it tells us and what else we need to know. The third is to establish that implicit bias analyses offer a critical area of inquiry and should be included as part of the racial checks and balances of the criminal justice system.

Why Implicit Bias Matters

Calls to determine how implicit bias influences individual actors within the justice system have been met with great interest and enthusiasm. Implicit bias has emerged as the go-to explanation for racial discrimination and racial bias within the justice system. Accounting for it, some argue, will help eliminate the racial ills of the criminal justice system. Further, it has been identified as an inroad to understanding racial disparity that persists across the justice system continuum, including arrest, bail decisions, prosecutorial charging decisions, jury selection, sentencing, and parole.

Before discussing what an analysis of implicit bias adds to our understanding of police shootings of black men, let us consider why this approach has become popular. In particular, what are the concerns and social costs associated with moving from an explicit to implicit bias approach? By definition, "implicit bias" refers to attitudes and beliefs that individuals do not consciously control. From one perspective, an implicit bias approach minimizes individual responsibility, establishing what Eduardo Bonilla-Silva refers to as "racism without racists."[8] An emphasis on hidden biases may promote a "racial innocence" that lets decision-makers within the justice system—police, prosecutors, judges, and jurors—off the hook.

Another issue is whether an implicit bias analysis has been promoted because it offers a nonthreatening explanation of racial bias. It may be that implicit bias has been embraced because of its universal applicability. In other words, implicit bias does not allow for racial finger-pointing and blame. It does not label whites as racists. Implicit bias is something that anyone, regardless of race, can have. Thus, part of the appeal of implicit bias is that everyone becomes part of "we"—as in "We are all (implicit) racists." In this way, implicit bias infuses race-neutrality into the study of racial bias.

While there are legitimate questions about the resonance of an implicit bias analysis, these concerns do not undercut its potential value. Implicit bias is a real psychosocial phenomenon and offers another way of examining how racial bias manifests itself within the legal system. Analyses of implicit bias complement and coexist with studies of explicit bias. The social costs are minimal given that attention to implicit bias has not diminished long-standing efforts to highlight and tackle explicit racial bias within the justice system. Studies of explicit racial bias continue to be the main focus of empirical research and policy prescriptions. Further, considerations of how implicit bias works may deepen our understanding of how racial bias works and help identify needed policy reforms. As well, the heightened interest in implicit bias has helped to keep the discussion of racial bias at the forefront of national discussions of the criminal justice system.

The History of Policing and African Americans

The tensions between African Americans and the police have deep historical roots. Slave patrols, which formally began during the 1700s, were the precursors of today's men and women in blue. Slave patrols began in South Carolina and spread across the slave states and colonies. The patrols emerged during slavery as the enforcement arm of the slave codes. Slave codes were the laws that regulated slave life, including where and when they could gather, what activities they were prohibited from engaging in, and the types of punishment they would receive for violating the codes. Patrollers, who were usually white slaveholders, observed and regulated all aspects of black life. When desired, slave owners were permitted to "hire out" their patrol duty. Laws typically allowed any white person between the ages sixteen and sixty to serve as a slave patroller. Some patrollers received pay while others volunteered.

The slave patrols were used to search slave cabins, keep slaves off the roadway, and ensure there were no gatherings of slaves. At their core, slave patrols were devised to thwart any activity that might upend the institution of slavery, especially escapes or uprisings. According to an early slave patrol act, militia captains were to locate men who would "ride from plantation to plantation . . . and take up all slaves, which they shall meet without their masters' plantation which have not a permit or ticket from their masters, and the same punish."[9] Under another act from the early eighteenth century, patrols were to "prevent all caballings amongst negroes, by dispersing of them when drumming or playing, and search all negro houses for arms or other offensive weapons."[10] Patrollers could also exact punishment. Here is an excerpt from a Tarborough, North Carolina, law:

> If any slave shall violate the . . . rules, the Patrol shall have power and it shall be their duty . . . to whip the . . . slave, either at the time of the offence . . . or at any time within three months thereafter.[11]

In effect, slave patrollers were roving slave masters.

Following the Civil War, slave patrols remained in force, only in a different form. At the beginning of Reconstruction, various groups joined what had been the slave patrols and were now the patrols designed to police the movements of newly freed slaves. The state militia, the federal military, and the Ku Klux Klan became the new, more violent slave patrols.[12]

The slave patrols were the first uniquely American form of policing and the first publicly funded police agencies.[13] This means that at its inception, American policing was designed to police black bodies, particularly black male bodies. Twenty-first-century cases involving police assaults and killings of black men are connected to this early history of U.S. policing. Contemporary cases can be added to the long list of cases that have coursed through the centuries—ones that highlight the too-often-fatal relationship between black men and the police.

Proof of Implicit Bias

Social psychologists have explored hidden bias for decades.[14] Early work by Else Frenkel-Brunswik examined how the mind creates and maintains categories.[15] Frenkel-Brunswik found that once these categories are set and the brain has established a framework, it is difficult to change perceptions. Patricia Devine's pioneering research set the stage for today's research on implicit bias.[16] In a 1989 article, she argued that social scientists should expand their study of racial bias to include implicit or subconscious bias. She observed distinctions between stereotypes and personal beliefs about race. Devine found that white subjects perceived blacks as hostile and aggressive. She also found that even undetected exposure to race-related material could trigger racial stereotypes in whites, including whites who had low levels of overt prejudice. Devine's early findings opened the door for contemporary research on implicit racial bias. An example is how the brain links attributes to a racial group, such as an association between "black" and "bad" or "white" and "good."

Over the years, researchers have broadened their interest in implicit bias beyond how it works as a psychological process, to examine how it impacts institutional structures. The criminal justice system is one of the institutional structures that has been of interest to researchers. A robust body of work has emerged that explores the impact of internalized racial stereotypes on people who work in the justice system, including police officers, judges, and jurors.[17] What follows is a look at the subset of this research that examines how a police officer's decision to shoot may be influenced by hidden racial bias.

Several empirical studies have analyzed how implicit bias impacts law enforcement encounters with the public. What do we know about the levels of implicit racial bias held by law enforcement officers compared with civilians? What information do we have about "shooter bias" and whether implicit bias operates to make police officers perceive black men as more threatening than other men? These studies reach strong and clear conclusions.

In a classic and memorable *Saturday Night Live* television sketch, comedians Richard Pryor and Chevy Chase engage in a word association game during a job interview. The game begins when Chase's character says "dog" and Pryor's character responds "tree." However, before long, the word game becomes heated as Chase's character uses an escalating variety of racial slurs and looks to Pryor's character to respond. The slurs include "tar baby" and "jungle bunny." The skit ends when Chase's character says "nigger" and Pryor's character responds "dead honky." The skit offers an example of how priming works.[18] Priming invites broad-stroke categorizations. Psychologists use priming to gauge responses to certain visual and verbal stimuli.

In a 2004 article, Jennifer Eberhardt and her colleagues discuss a series of studies they conducted on racial stereotypes. The research was designed to test how race-based stereotypes affected the perceptions of police officers and college students in their assessments of the association between race and criminality. One of the studies examined the reactions of sixty-one police officers. One-half of the officers were "primed" with words associated with crime (for example, "violent," "crime," "arrest," "shoot," "capture," and "chase").[19] The other half, who were not primed, were shown photos of black and white men. Later all the officers were asked to recall the faces. The findings indicated that priming did impact officers' perceptions of race and criminality. The officers who were primed with crime-related words were more likely to falsely identify faces considered more stereotypically black. The researchers conclude: "[P]riming police officers with crime caused them to remember Black faces in a manner that more strongly supports the association between Blacks and criminality."[20]

The article includes another study that examines police officers and implicit bias. One-half of the officers were shown forty photographs of black men. The other half were shown forty photographs of white men. The researchers tracked the responses of the 182 police officers involved in the study. The officers were told to categorize some photos. Their responses were then reviewed to determine how the officers rated "stereotypicality" and "criminality." The researchers found that race played a "significant role" in how the officers made judgments of criminality. The police officers linked blacks with the concept of crime. Of particular note, the researchers found that "Black faces looked more criminal to police officers; the more Black, the more criminal."[21]

Eberhardt and her colleagues found that the link between perceptions of criminality and blackness are bi-directional. "Black faces and Black bodies can trigger thoughts of crime [and] thinking of crime can trigger thoughts of Black people."[22] They concluded by noting that while visual processes may underscore stereotypical associations (for instance, linking "black" with "crime"), these processes are based on cultural understandings. As understandings change, new associations may develop and the world may change. In future centuries, perhaps blackness and criminality will no longer be linked.

In a 2005 study of fifty police officers, researchers used a computer simulation to test their decision to shoot.[23] The officers viewed a simulation that showed photographs of black or white men with either a gun or a neutral object (cell phone or wallet). The officers participating in the study were told that they would be viewing photos of criminals. They were told to select the button for "shoot" if the photo showed a person and a gun. They were told to push the button for "do not shoot" if the photo showed a person with a neutral object. The researchers E. Ashby Plant and B. Michelle Peruche discovered that officers were more likely to shoot if the unarmed suspect in the photo was black. However, they also found that repeated viewings of the simulation led to an elimination of racial bias. Multiple exposures to the computer simulation shifted the officers' decision criteria for black suspects. More practice led to fewer overall mistakes. More practice also made it less likely that officers would shoot an unarmed white suspect. The setup of the simulation included a kind of racial priming. Here the participants were told that they were going to be shown photos of criminal suspects. This overt linking of "criminal" and "black" may have worked to prime officers on racial perceptions. As well, in light of the findings of Eberhardt and her colleagues on bi-directionality, the reference to "criminal" may have triggered thoughts about black people for some participants.

In a follow-up article, the researchers continued their examination of how and when police officers decide to shoot a suspect.[24] The 2006 study examines implicit and explicit racial bias. Using a computer simulation, fifty officers were observed to see how they responded to pictures of black and white men holding an object (either a gun or a neutral item). Officers were instructed to hit the "shoot" key if a gun was present and to hit the "don't shoot" key if a neutral object was present. The officers also completed surveys that asked questions about their perceptions of blacks, their job-related experiences (which included questions about race and criminal suspects), and their contact with blacks in their professional and personal lives. Officers were initially more likely to shoot unarmed black suspects than unarmed white suspects. In a promising development, the researchers found that after extensive exposure to the simulation, racial bias by police officers faded away and they had similar shooting responses to white and black suspects. They also found that officers who had greater positive contact with blacks were able to eliminate racial bias in the shooting simulations.

In another important study of implicit bias, Joshua Correll and his colleagues explored the responses of police officers and civilians. A video game simulation was used to test how police and civilians would respond in shooter simulations involving criminals and noncriminals of different races.[25] The simulation included images of white and black men, some armed and some unarmed. Participants were told to "shoot" armed targets and "not to shoot" unarmed targets by pressing a button to indicate their selection. The findings were based on the responses of more than 250 police officers and more than 150 civilians.

The researchers observed stark differences between the responses of police officers and civilians. Officers were better at deciding to shoot an armed target (rather than an unarmed target) and did so at a faster speed than community members. The community members were more likely than the officers to shoot unarmed black targets. The researchers also found that community members were overall more likely to shoot black targets than white targets. They also found that officers and community members took longer to decide whether to shoot when there was a "stereotype-incongruent" target, such as an unarmed black man or an armed white man. However, while officers took longer to decide, they were not more likely to shoot black targets (contrary to the findings for community members). Correll and his colleagues suggest that the training police officers receive may explain the difference in findings between the two groups.

In a 2012 study involving video game simulations, Melody Sadler and her colleagues evaluated the role of implicit racial bias in police officers' decisions to shoot.[26] This study is notable because more than two hundred police officers participated, and the simulation included photos of Latino and Asian men.[27] The researchers drew several conclusions. One, police officers showed racial bias in their reaction times toward Latino targets (compared with Asian and white targets). Officers also showed racial bias in their reaction times toward white targets (compared with Asian targets). Two, police officers were better able to tell if a black or Latino target was holding a weapon or nonthreatening object (compared with Asian or white targets). Three, the degree of racial bias in officers' reaction times was related to their personal beliefs (for instance, cultural stereotypes). The researchers found that officers who overestimated the amount of crime in a community showed more bias toward Latinos (compared with whites). Officers who held stereotypical views of blacks and Latinos, and officers who had more contact with them, shot more quickly at blacks and Latinos during the simulation. The latter finding is problematic insofar as one would assume that increased contact would reduce implicit bias.

Several themes emerge from the research on implicit bias and police decision-making. First, police respond in a racially biased way toward black targets, when compared with targets from other racial backgrounds. Second, the decision to shoot is made more quickly when there is a black armed target rather than a white armed target. Third, police officers are more likely to "see" a black armed target when none exists. They are less likely to "see" a white armed target when one does exist. Fourth, when targets do not match stereotypes (they are "stereotype-incongruent"), police officers take longer to decide whether to shoot. For instance, officers take longer to decide not to shoot an unarmed black man than they take to decide not to shoot an unarmed white man. As Eberhardt and colleagues note, this has implications for police safety given the racial time "bonus" white targets receive. Fifth, when compared with members of the public, police demonstrate a more accurate ability to identify whether black and white targets are armed or unarmed. Sixth, studies that considered factors beyond the decision to shoot, such as officers' contact with members of racial minority groups and officers' personal beliefs, found that these factors affected the overall levels of implicit bias.

These studies raise additional questions for future research on how race impacts the decision to shoot. One issue is whether these findings are generalizable to police as a group. Further research will determine, for instance, whether the structure of police departments (racial diversity, number of officers, and location) impacts the existence of implicit bias. It would also be valuable to know whether a police officer's race is related to the existence and degree of implicit bias. This would address the conventional wisdom that police are neither black nor white, but "blue." Other officer-level characteristics should be examined, such as their number of years on the force and level of education.

As well, implicit racial bias research should expand to include police responses to Latinos, Asian Americans, and Middle Easterners.[28]

Future research should also examine whether implicit racial bias impacts other facets of police work. For instance, the work of undercover officers raises two particular concerns. First, based on the research, black undercover officers have a greater chance of being shot by officers who are more likely to mistake them for criminals. Second, an innocent black person may misperceive an approaching undercover officer as a potential attacker. A notable example involves the 1999 police shooting of Amadou Diallo, a twenty-three-year-old immigrant from Guinea. Diallo was shot and killed by undercover officers who mistook his wallet for a gun. It was widely speculated that Diallo may have believed the men were going to rob him and held out his wallet for that reason.

Training and Education

Training and education have been the popular responses to the problem of implicit racial bias. Interventions for police officers focus on how to eliminate implicit bias at a personal or structural level. At the individual level, studies show that officers are less likely to register implicit bias when they have greater contact with people outside of their racial group and when they have contact with people in other racial groups who do not fit racial stereotypes.[29] Correctives for implicit racial bias, however, have largely focused on training. In 2016, the Department of Justice announced that it will require implicit bias training for more than 28,000 federal law enforcement agents and prosecutors. This includes agents working for the FBI, the Bureau of Alcohol, Tobacco, Firearms, and Explosives, U.S. marshals, and the Drug Enforcement Administration. The training will help officers recognize and counter their own racial biases. Numerous police departments across the country have added training programs to address implicit bias.

One program, Fair and Impartial Policing, teaches officers about implicit bias, how it works, and how it may impact their decision-making skills regarding use of force.[30] Trainers work with officers through a series of role-playing exercises to uncover and mitigate hidden biases. The program has been used in over 250 police agencies and precincts.

In 2015, California's attorney general Kamala Harris established the first certified training program on implicit bias and procedural justice in the United States.[31] The program was developed for law enforcement leaders. In addition to implicit bias training, the plan calls for the development and implementation of a Department of Justice policy on implicit bias and requires all command-level staff and special agents to complete the Fair and Impartial Policing training program.

While there is some support for training programs as a way to moderate implicit bias,[32] some researchers are less optimistic. Robert Smith concludes that implicit bias training "may not be the best solution to prevent the death of the next Eric Garner or Michael Brown."[33] Smith points to research that shows that the police demonstrate lower levels of hidden racial bias than civilians.

Some reforms focus on changing police responses in particular situations. UCLA's Center for Police Equity (CPE) works with police departments to identify the causes of racially biased police practices. For instance, CPE worked with a police department seeking to reduce the amount of times force was used against minorities. They discovered that many of the incidents involving force occurred after an officer chased a suspect on foot. In response, CPE helped the department develop a protocol for officers to follow when chasing a suspect. CPE determined that it would be easier to change the protocol than an officer's reactions. CPE's approach is that unconscious bias exists and changes can be made to mitigate its impact. Rather than attempting to eliminate implicit bias, this approach works as a kind of intervention between implicit bias and police actions.

Another strategy for addressing implicit bias is increasing awareness about how unconscious bias works. U.S. District Judge Mark Bennett takes a novel approach to solving the problem of implicit bias.[34] He argues that anyone with decision-making power in the criminal justice system should be required to take the Implicit Association Test. The PowerPoint presentation he shows to lawyers before jury selection includes a slide on implicit bias. Judge Bennett also talks with jurors about implicit bias. Prior to opening arguments in all of the trials in his courtroom, Judge Bennett reads this jury instruction:

As we discussed in jury selection, growing scientific research indicates each one of us has "implicit biases," or hidden feelings, perceptions, fears and stereotypes in our subconscious. These hidden thoughts often impact how we remember what we see and hear and how we make important decisions. While it is difficult to control one's subconscious thoughts, being aware of these hidden biases can help counteract them. As a result, I ask you to recognize that all of us may be affected by implicit biases in the decisions that we make. Because you are making very important decisions in this case, I strongly encourage you to critically evaluate the evidence and resist any urge to reach a verdict influenced by stereotypes, generalizations, or implicit biases.[35]

Acknowledging the findings of "shooter bias" studies, Judge Bennett convincingly argues that interventions are required to mitigate the effects of implicit racial bias. His novel efforts underscore the need to address implicit bias across the justice system continuum, from police officers to correctional officers.[36]

Skin Tone, White Favoritism, and Educating
Children About Race

Skin Tone and Implicit Bias

There is an old expression in the black community: "If you're white you're all right; if you're brown, stick around; but if you're black, get back." The expression pointedly highlights the relationship between racial bias and skin color. Black skin evokes a different unconscious response than white skin. Given the unconscious association of blackness with deviance, how is bias connected to skin tone? Are people with physical traits most closely associated with being black—dark brown skin, a wide nose, and full lips—more likely to be perceived as dangerous? Research on skin tone explores whether a person's skin tone results in differential treatment (also known as colorism).[37] A determination of how skin tone impacts criminal justice system decision-making is important. For instance, anyone visiting a prison (or viewing a prison documentary) will likely be struck not just by the prevalence of African Americans, but by the salience of dark brown skin. Whether this reflects an unconscious bias against darker skin is a relevant research issue.[38]

A few studies have addressed the nexus between skin tone and criminal punishment. In a 2010 publication, Justin Levinson and Danielle Young examined whether potential jurors would perceive a criminal suspect with a darker skin tone as more likely to be guilty than a criminal suspect with a lighter skin tone.[39] This study tested their "Biased Evidence Hypothesis," which predicts that when racial stereotypes are triggered, jurors will "automatically and unintentionally evaluate ambiguous trial evidence in racially biased ways."[40] Researchers showed participants a series of crime-related slides. In one set of slides, the suspect, who is seen committing a store robbery, has a dark brown hand. The second set used the exact same photo, except the suspect's hand was a lighter color. Participants were randomly assigned to a group. Levinson and Young found that showing photos of dark-skinned perpetrators triggered racial bias and influenced the potential juror's evaluation of the evidence and ultimately whether they voted him guilty or not guilty. The racial cues were implicit and participants were unaware that negative stereotypes had been triggered by these cues.[41] The research supported their Biased Evidence Hypothesis.

Other studies have reached similar conclusions. In another 2010 article, Kimberly Barsamian Kahn and Paul Davies looked at whether participants were more likely to shoot at darker-skinned targets than lighter-skinned targets.[42] The researchers used a video game simulation to test whether the perceived race and features of the target would impact the decision to shoot.[43] Specifically, Kahn and Davies wanted to see whether participants were more likely to shoot at a black target with stereotypically black features, compared with a target that was either white or had less pronounced black features. They found that both whites and blacks were more likely to mistakenly shoot a black target who had pronounced black physical features than a white target or one with less pronounced black features.

A 2006 article examined whether darker-skinned inmates were more likely to have received longer prison sentences than black inmates with lighter skin tone.[44] Kwabena Gyimah-Brempong and Gregory Price used data from the Mississippi Department of Corrections. Their study was based on an evaluation of 403 cases. They used six skin shades—dark, dark brown, medium brown, light brown, light, and fair—to compare and measure the impact of skin tone on sentencing. Dark skin, they found, had a "large and significant effect" on prison sentences. A subsequent study supports these findings.

In a 2015 article, Traci Burch reviewed sentencing outcomes for first-time felony offenders in over 67,000 cases.[45] A comparison of white and black inmates revealed a racial disparity in prison sentences. The average sentence received by a white inmate was 270 days shorter than the average sentence received by a black inmate. However, this racial disparity increased when Burch took account of skin tone differences in black prisoners. The findings showed that darker-skinned blacks received sentences that were 400 days longer than sentences received by whites.[46]

The findings from these four studies are striking. Overall, they demonstrate that the sledgehammer of racial bias will have a disproportionate impact on those deemed "most" black.[47] While black men as a group face a particular threat of criminalization and disparate levels of lethal force when compared with white men, darker-skinned men are disproportionately targeted by the police. The majority of the high-profile cases involving police killings of black men bear out these findings. Case examples include Michael Brown (Missouri), Freddie Gray (Maryland), Walter Scott (South Carolina), Alton Sterling (Louisiana), Sam DuBose (Ohio), Philando Castile (Minnesota), and Corey Jones (Florida). Researchers should continue to examine the impact of skin tone on perceptions of criminal threat to determine whether darker-skinned blacks are more likely to be singled out for racial profiling, more likely to be perceived as dangerous, and more likely to be shot by police officers.

Implicit White Favoritism
Implicit favoritism refers to the process by which someone unconsciously links positive attributes with members of a particular group, leading to preferential treatment for members of the favored group. With regard to the criminal justice system, whites are the most favored racial group. This is another way of saying that within the justice system, implicit favoritism is white favoritism. Robert Smith and his colleagues have thoughtfully critiqued the concept of implicit white favoritism.[48] They contend that addressing this problem is critical to reducing implicit racial bias within the justice system.

Smith's argument is that implicit bias works in two directions. First, implicit racial bias may be expressed as a negative sentiment toward members of a particular racial group (for instance, blacks). Another way of describing this is *anti*-black implicit bias. The studies discussed in the previous section on skin tone fall into this category. Second, implicit racial bias may also be expressed as a *positive* sentiment toward members of a particular racial group (for instance, whites). Another way of describing this is *pro*-white implicit bias—or implicit white favoritism as it is labeled by Smith and colleagues. The impact of implicit white favoritism on the justice system has not been subject to rigorous testing or included in the discussion and calculation of how implicit racial bias works overall. The researchers make their case:

> Even if we could eliminate the bias that scholars have illuminated, racial disparities would persist because removing derogation is not the same as being race-neutral. If legislators, police officers, jurors and legal professionals implicitly favor White Americans then we still possess a racialized justice system. To gain a fuller understanding of what drives unjustified disparities, then, we must rotate the flashlight ever so slightly to reveal a rich and diverse form of implicit racial bias that has been overlooked in criminal law and procedure research.[49]

The researchers underscore that it is necessary to determine whether police are more likely to use lethal force (and more quickly) against black suspects (and other suspects of color) *and* whether and the degree to which police are less likely to use lethal force against white suspects.

Educating Children About Race

A promising long-term approach to addressing implicit bias is to restructure the way race and racial issues are addressed within the K–12 curriculum, particularly in the elementary grades. In the United States, more than fifty million children attend public schools. If the development of implicit racial biases can be interrupted or tempered in some way during a child's early years, negative racial biases will be less likely to take shape and fester.

There are numerous steps that might be taken to address race and racial issues more holistically in public education. The core suggestion made here is to enhance the primary curriculum to include a broader, more critical history of race and race relations in the United States. There is widespread ignorance of U.S. racial history.[50] In over twenty states, there are state codes that mandate that some aspect of race be addressed within the K–12 curriculum. Most state codes identify the need to include African American or Native American history. For instance, Florida's education code includes explicit language regarding the need to address race and bias within the curriculum. It states that education shall teach:

> The history of African Americans, including the history of African peoples before the political conflicts that led to the development of slavery, the passage to America, the enslavement experience, abolition, and the contributions of African Americans to society. Instructional materials shall include the contributions of African Americans to American society.[51]

After noting the importance of teaching Holocaust history, the Florida code states that this history should be taught "in a manner that leads to an understanding of the ramifications of prejudice, racism, and stereotyping."[52] In addition to state codes, some state constitutions mandate a race-based curriculum.[53] More can be done to expand the race-related curriculum in our public schools. Across the states, there are codes and constitutional language that support and encourage race studies in K–12 education. Enhancing the knowledge of young people about race and race relations is an important, long-term step in reducing racial bias. In turn, it may result in large-scale reductions in the levels of implicit bias by the public at large, including criminal justice officials.

Understanding implicit bias is essential to identifying and eliminating racial bias in policing. The existing studies confirm the existence of implicit bias and the role that it plays in police shootings of black men, but more research is needed. Additional research is also needed to explore the role of skin color in decision-making by criminal justice officials, including police officers, and the effectiveness of current police training and education programs. Because of the deep-seated nature of racial bias, especially implicit bias, meaningful education about race and racial bias should begin in elementary school and should be infused throughout the K–12 curriculum in public schools. Providing early education on race could go a long way toward tempering implicit racial bias for young people, including those who go on to become police officers.

RESOURCES

Banks, R. R., J. L. Eberhardt, and L. Ross. "Discrimination and Implicit Bias in a Racially Unequal Society." *California Law Review* 94 (2006): 1169.

Bennett, M. W. "Unraveling the Gordian Knot of Implicit Bias in Jury Selection: The Problems of Judge-Dominated Voir Dire, the Failed Promise of *Batson* and Proposed Solutions." *Harvard Law and Policy Review* 4 (2010): 149.

Correll, J., B. Park, C. M. Judd, B. Wittenbrink, M. S. Sadler, and T. Keesee. "Across the Thin Blue Line: Police Officers and Racial Bias in the Decision to Shoot." *Journal of Personality and Social Psychology* 92 (2007):1006.

"The Counted: People Killed by Police in the U.S., 2015," *The Guardian*. http://www.theguardian.com/us-news/ng-interactive/2015/jun/01/the-counted-police-killings-us-database#. Ongoing tabulation of people killed by police in the U.S., by race, gender, and state.

Devine, P. "Stereotypes and Prejudice: Their Automatic and Controlled Components." *Journal of Personality and Social Psychology* 56 (1989): 5.

Eberhardt, J., A. Goff, V. Purdie, and P. Davies. "Seeing Black: Race, Crime and Visual Processing." *Journal of Personality and Social Psychology* 87 (2004): 876–93.

Feingold, J., and K. Lorang. "Defusing Implicit Bias." *UCLA Law Review* 59 (2012): 210.

Fridell, L. "Racially Biased Policing: The Law Enforcement Response to the Implicit Black-Crime Association." In *Racial Divide: Racial and Ethnic Bias in the Criminal Justice System*, eds. M. Lynch, E. Patterson, and K. Childs, 39–59. Monsey, NY: Criminal Justice Press, 2008.

Gyimah-Brempong, K., and G. N. Price. "Crime and Punishment: And Skin Hue Too?" *American Economic Review* 96 (2005): 246.

Hadden, S. *Slave Patrols: Law and Violence in Virginia and the Carolinas.* Cambridge, MA: Harvard University Press, 2001.

Kahn, K. B., and P. G. Davies. "Differentially Dangerous? Phenotypic Racial Stereotypicality Increases Implicit Bias Among Ingroup and Outgroup Members." *Group Processes & Intergroup Relations* 14 (2010): 1–12.

Kirwan Institute for the Study of Race and Ethnicity. "State of the Science: Implicit Bias Review 2014." http://kirwaninstitute.osu.edu/wp-content/uploads/2014/03/2014-implicit-bias.pdf (last accessed Nov. 1, 2015).

Levinson, J. D., and D. Young. "Different Shades of Bias: Skin Tone, Implicit Racial Bias, and Judgments of Ambiguous Evidence." *West Virginia Law Review* 112 (2010): 307.

Mooney, C. "The Science of Why Cops Shoot Young Black Men." *Mother Jones*, Dec. 1, 2014.

Peruche, B. M., and E. A. Plant. "The Correlates of Law Enforcement Officers' Automatic and Controlled Race-Based Responses to Criminal Suspects." *Basic and Applied Social Psychology* 28, no. 2 (2006): 193–99.

Plant, E. A., and B. M. Peruche. "The Consequences of Race for Police Officers' Responses to Criminal Suspects," *Psychological Science* 16, no. 3 (2005).

Reichel, P. L. "Southern Slave Patrols as a Transitional Police Type." *American Journal of Police* 7 (1988): 51.

Richardson, L. S. "Police Racial Violence: Lessons from Social Psychology." *Fordham Law Review* 83 (2015): 2961.

Russell-Brown, K. *Underground Codes.* New York: New York University Press, 2004.

———. *The Color of Crime.* New York: New York University Press, 2009.

Sim, J., J. Correll, and M. Sadler. "Understanding Police and Expert Performance: When Training Attenuates (vs. Exacerbates) Stereotypic Bias in the Decision to Shoot." *Personality and Social Psychology Bulletin* 39, no. 3 (2013): 291–304.

Smith, R. J. "Reducing Racially Disparate Policing Outcomes: Is Implicit Bias Training the Answer?" *University of Hawai'i Law Review* 37 (2015): 295.

Smith, R. J., J. D. Levinson, and Z. Robinson. "Implicit White Favoritism in the Criminal Justice System." *Alabama Law Review* 66 (2015): 871.

Sommers, S., and S. Marotta. "Racial Disparities in Legal Outcomes: On Policing, Charging Decisions, and Criminal Trial Proceedings." *Policy Insights from the Behavioral and Brain Sciences* 1, no. 1 (2014): 103–11. Available at http://www

.thejuryexpert.com/2015/02/racial-disparities-in-legal-outcomes-on-policing
-charging-decisions-and-criminal-trial-proceedings/.

Spencer, K., A. Charbonneau, and J. Glaser. "Implicit Bias and Policing." *Social and Personality Psychology Compass* 10, no. 1 (2016): 50–63.

U.S. Department of Justice. "Department of Justice Announces New Department-wide Implicit Bias Training for Personnel." June 27, 2016. https://www.justice
.gov/opa/pr/department-justice-announces-new-department-wide-implicit-bias
-training-personnel.

Van Ausdale, D., and J. Feagin. *The First R: How Children Learn Race and Racism.* Lanham, MD: Rowman and Littlefield, 2001.

Washington Post. "991 People Shot Dead by Police in 2015." https://www.washington
post.com/graphics/national/police-shootings/ (last accessed March 8, 2017).

NOTES

1. Scholars have called for a national database of police uses of deadly force. See, e.g., D. Klinger, R. Rosenfield, D. Isom, and M. Deckard, "Race, Crime and the Microecology of Deadly Force," *Criminology & Public Policy* 15, no. 1 (2016): 193–222.

2. See, e.g., Uniform Crime Report (2014), "Law Enforcement Officers Killed & Assaulted, 2013," https://www.fbi.gov/about-us/cjis/ucr/leoka/2013/officers
-feloniously-killed/felonious_topic_page_2013.pdf. According to this report, in 2013 twenty-seven law enforcement officers were killed in the line of duty (this number includes sworn officers in city, county, state, tribal, federal, and college positions).

3. *Washington Post*: http://www.washingtonpost.com/graphics/national/police
-shootings/; *The Guardian*: http://www.theguardian.com/us-news/ng-interactive/
2015/jun/01/the-counted-police-killings-us-database#.

4. https://www.washingtonpost.com/graphics/national/police-shootings-2016/.

5. The Associated Press–NORC Center for Public Affairs Research (2015), "New Survey on Americans' Views on Law Enforcement, Violence and Race," http://www
.apnorc.org/PDFs/Police%20Violence/Race%20and%20Policing%20Press%20
Release.pdf.

6. The website for Project Implicit: https://implicit.harvard.edu/implicit/takeatest
.html.

7. Chris Mooney, "Across America, Whites Are Biased and They Don't Even Know It," *Washington Post* Wonkblog, Dec. 8, 2014, https://www.washingtonpost
.com/news/wonk/wp/2014/12/08/across-america-whites-are-biased-and-they-dont
-even-know-it/ (last accessed, Nov. 11, 2015).

8. See Eduardo Bonilla-Silva, *Racism without Racists* (Lanham, MD: Rowman and Littlefield, 2003). Bonilla-Silva begins his book by discussing this duality: "Nowadays, except for members of white supremacist organizations, few whites in the United States claim to be 'racist.' Most whites assert they 'don't see any color, just people'; that although the ugly face of discrimination is still with us, it is no longer the central factor determining minorities' life chances . . ." (p. 1).

9. P. L. Reichel, "Southern Slave Patrols as a Transitional Police Type," *American Journal of Police* 7 (1988): 51.

10. Ibid.

11. Sally Hadden, *Slave Patrols* (Cambridge, MA: Harvard University Press, 2001), 60.

12. Carol Archbold, *Policing: A Text/Reader* (Thousand Oaks, CA: Sage Publications, 2013), 5.

13. Ibid., 4.

14. R. R. Banks, J. L. Eberhardt, and Lee Ross, "Discrimination and Implicit Bias in a Racially Unequal Society," *California Law Review* 94 (2006): 1169.

15. E. Frenkel-Brunswik, "Intolerance of Ambiguities as an Emotional and Perceptual Personality Variable," *Journal of Personality* 18 (1949): 108–43.

16. P. Devine, "Stereotypes and Prejudice: Their Automatic and Controlled Components," *Journal of Personality and Social Psychology* 56 (1989): 5.

17. See, e.g., Kirwan Institute for the Study of Race and Ethnicity, "State of the Science: Implicit Bias Review 2014," http://kirwaninstitute.osu.edu/wp-content/uploads/2014/03/2014-implicit-bias.pdf (last accessed Nov. 1, 2015); Kenneth Lawson, "Police Shootings of Black Men and Implicit Racial Bias: Can't We All Just Get Along," *University of Hawai'i Law Review* 37 (2015): 339; J. T. Clemons, "Blind Injustice: The Supreme Court, Implicit Racial Bias and the Racial Disparity in the Criminal Justice System," *American Criminal Law Review* 51 (2014): 689.

18. *Saturday Night Live* transcript, season 1, episode 7, http://snltranscripts.jt.org/75/75ginterview.phtml, aired on Dec. 13, 1975 (last accessed October 31, 2015).

19. J. Eberhardt, A. Goff, V. Purdie, and P. Davies, "Seeing Black: Race, Crime and Visual Processing," *Journal of Personality and Social Psychology* 87 (2004): 876, 886 (see 885–88 for more details of this study).

20. Ibid., 888.

21. Ibid., 889.

22. Ibid., 876.

23. E. A. Plant and B. M. Peruche, "The Consequences of Race for Police Officers' Responses to Criminal Suspects," *Psychological Science* 16, no. 3 (2005).

24. B. M. Peruche and E. A. Plant, "The Correlates of Law Enforcement Officers' Automatic and Controlled Race-Based Responses to Criminal Suspects," *Basic and Applied Social Psychology* 28, no. 2 (2006): 193–99.

25. J. Correll et al., "Across the Thin Blue Line: Police Officers and Racial Bias in the Decision to Shoot," *Journal of Personality and Social Psychology* 92 (2007): 1006.

26. M. Sadler et al., "The World Is Not Black and White: Racial Bias in the Decision to Shoot in a Multiethnic Context," *Journal of Social Issues* 68 (2012): 286. This discussion only includes findings from research on police officers.

27. Ibid.

28. In 2016, the Office of Management and Budget submitted a proposal to add a U.S. Census category for "Middle Eastern and North African." Gregory Korte, "White House Wants to Add New Racial Category for Middle Eastern People," *USA Today*, Oct. 2, 2016, http://www.usatoday.com/story/news/politics/2016/09/30/white-house-wants-add-new-racial-category-middle-eastern-people/91322064/.

29. K. Spencer, A. Charbonneau, and J. Glaser, "Implicit Bias and Policing," *Social and Personality Psychology Compass* 10, no. 1 (2016): 50–63.

30. http://www.fairimpartialpolicing.com/.

31. L. Wallace, "DOJ Division of Law Enforcement 90-Day Review," 2015, 2, https://cbsla.files.wordpress.com/2015/04/90-day-review-doc_final.pdf (last accessed Nov. 13, 2015); "Principled Policing: Procedural Justice and Implicit Bias Training," https://oag.ca.gov/sites/all/files/agweb/pdfs/law_enforcement/principled-policing -white-paper.pdf.

32. J. Sim, J. Correll, and M. Sadler, "Understanding Police and Expert Perfor-mance: When Training Attenuates (vs. Exacerbates) Stereotypic Bias in the Decision to Shoot," *Journal of Personality and Social Psychology* 39 (2012): 291.

33. R. Smith, "Reducing Racially Disparate Policing Outcomes: Is Implicit Bias Training the Answer?" *University of Hawai'i Law Review* 37 (2015): 295, 306.

34. M. Bennett, "Unraveling the Gordian Knot of Implicit Bias in Jury Selection: The Problems of Judge-Dominated Voir Dire, the Failed Promise of *Batson* and Pro-posed Solutions," *Harvard Law and Policy Review* 4 (2010): 149.

35. Ibid., 169.

36. For research on the impact of implicit bias on judicial decision-making, see J. Rachlinski, S. Johnson, A. J. Wistrich, and C. Guthrie, "Does Unconscious Racial Bias Affect Trial Judges?" *Notre Dame Law Review* 84 (2009): 1195. See also National Center for State Courts, "Helping Courts Address Implicit Bias: Addressing Implicit Bias in the Courts," 2012 report on strategies judges can use to reduce influence of implicit bias, http://www.ncsc.org/~/media/Files/PDF/Topics/Gender%20and%20 Racial%20Fairness/IB_Summary_033012.ashx.

37. A number of studies have examined the impact of skin color on political, socio-economic, education, and family status. See, e.g., Jennifer Hochschild, "The Skin Color Paradox and the American Racial Order," *Social Forces* 86, no. 2 (2007): 643.

38. Findings by Eberhardt et al. ("Seeing Black," 886, 888) demonstrate that stereotypes of blackness and criminality are tied to several physical features, includ-ing a person's lips, nose, hair texture, and skin tone.

39. J. D. Levinson and D. Young, "Different Shades of Bias: Skin Tone, Implicit Bias, and Judgments of Ambiguous Evidence," *West Virginia Law Review* 112 (2010): 308.

40. Ibid., 309.

41. Ibid., 331–34.

42. K. Barsamian Kahn and P. Davies, "Differentially Dangerous? Phenotypic Racial Stereotypicality Increases Implicit Bias Among Ingroup and Outgroup Mem-bers," *Group Processes & Intergroup Relations* 14 (2010): 1–12.

43. Ibid.

44. K. Gyimah-Brempong and G. Price, "Crime and Punishment: And Skin Hue Too?" *American Economic Review* 96 (2006): 246. The researchers also examine the impact of dark skin on criminal offending. They find that when compared with lighter-skinned blacks, dark-skinned blacks face disadvantages that make it more likely they will choose to engage in crime.

45. T. Burch, "Skin Color and the Criminal Justice System: Beyond Black-White Disparities in Sentencing," *Journal of Empirical Legal Studies* 12, no. 3 (2015): 395–420.

46. In an unexpected finding, Burch notes that when compared with whites,

lighter-skinned blacks received sentences that were twenty days *shorter* than those assigned to whites. See ibid., 408.

47. For a thoughtful and provocative consideration of the costs and benefits of skin color, see Jennifer Hochschild, "The Skin Color Paradox and the American Racial Order," *Social Forces* 86, no. 2 (2007): 643.

48. R. J. Smith, J. D. Levinson, and Z. Robinson, "Implicit White Favoritism in the Criminal Justice System," *Alabama Law Review* 66 (2015): 871. For an additional discussion of implicit white favoritism, see L. S. Richardson, "Police Racial Violence: Lessons from Social Psychology," *Fordham Law Review* 83 (2015): 2961, 2962–66.

49. Smith, Levinson, and Robinson, "Implicit White Favoritism," 874.

50. For a recent instance, see the story involving a McGraw-Hill geography textbook. The text referred to slaves as "workers." See, e.g., Manny Fernandez and Christine Hauser, "Texas Mother Teaches Textbook Company a Lesson on Accuracy," *New York Times*, Oct. 5, 2015. See also K. Russell-Brown, "To Combat Racism in Law Enforcement, Start Young," *New York Times*, Sept. 1, 2014, http://www.nytimes.com/roomfordebate/2014/09/01/black-and-white-and-blue/to-combat-racism-in-law-enforcement-start-young. Some state codes require the inclusion of Latino history (California, Colorado, Connecticut, Nebraska, Ohio, Oklahoma, and Oregon) or Asian American history (California, Nebraska, and Oregon).

51. Florida Education Code (2015), Sect. 1005.42 (2)(h).

52. Ibid., Sect. 1003.42(2)(g).

53. Montana, for example has a constitutional amendment that requires teachers to integrate information on Native American culture and history across the curriculum, for all students (not just Native Americans). MCA 20-1-501 (2015).

Policing: A Model for
the Twenty-first Century

TRACY MEARES AND TOM TYLER

THE MOMENT IS ripe for a reconsideration of policing in America. What have been the successes and failures of policing over the last several decades? What works and what does not work in policing today? And, perhaps most importantly, what should policing be about in the twenty-first century? While there are disagreements about all of these issues, there is widespread agreement that reexamination of American policing is as pivotal today as it was in 1968, when the Kerner Commission issued an influential report following a period of urban unrest throughout American cities. As was true then, many long-held assumptions about the purposes and methods of policing are being questioned.

It is fair to say that in every era the criminal justice system, and policing in particular, faces distinct issues that need to be addressed. The key law enforcement concern of the last era was control of violent crime. We are now emerging from that period. The concern over violent crime control is an important framing because the roots of current policing models lie in the high levels of crime over three decades starting in the 1960s and the feelings of disorder and fear that these high crime levels created in many American communities.[1] For many in policing circles, the idea that police could and therefore should do something about such crime was the primary or even the sole criterion for innovation in the field. Thus, crime reduction became a goal against which policies and practices have been evaluated in recent years.

For more than two decades, the level of violent crime has steadily declined,[2] due in part to efforts by the police. At the same time, the police have generally become more professional and effective, as documented in the National Academy of Sciences report "Fairness and Effectiveness in Policing: The Evidence."[3] There is a great deal to be proud of in American policing and in the role the police played in meeting the challenges of this earlier era.

But while it is clear that police have played some role in the recent dramatic reduction in crime across the United States, there has been almost no change in the level of public trust in the police. For the last few decades, as crime has fallen precipitously, about 50–60 percent of adult Americans express trust and confidence in the police. Further, there has been a large and persistent racial gap in trust, with African Americans 20–30 percent less likely to express trust in the police than are whites. There are many things to note about this gap, but probably the most notable aspect of it is the fact that though African Americans as a group benefit more than other groups as violent crime rates fall because African Americans disproportionately are victims of violent crime, this gap has not disappeared or even diminished in any significant way as the crime rate has fallen.[4] These data strongly suggest that police effectiveness at reducing crime is not strongly related to public trust and confidence in the police. Given the emphasis and focus in the industry on police performance in crime reduction—especially as it benefits the public— this is unexpected.

One might ask then, if police effectiveness does not drive public trust, what does? One answer might be police lawfulness. In light of the repeated incidents of quite shocking police brutality—consider here the tragic death in North Charleston,

South Carolina, of Walter Scott, who was shot in the back by a white police officer as he fled—we might think that commitment to the rule of law and especially constitutional constraints that shape engagements between the public and the police would support public trust.

There are at least two problems with a potential relationship between levels of public trust and police commitment to lawfulness. The first is an objective measure of the extent to which police obey relevant law over time. While apparently unlawful incidents shown repeatedly across social media understandably cause people to question the extent to which police obey the law with respect to their use of deadly force, there is some evidence that over time—in the last forty years or so—changes in police policy have led to fewer civilians being killed by police officers.[5]

The second problem is the public's perception of the extent to which police actually obey the law. Research suggests that the public is not, unsurprisingly, very good at making these assessments. Our research with Jacob Gardener demonstrates that public judgments of police legitimacy leading to public trust and confidence are not very sensitive to whether police behavior is consistent with constitutional law. The public does not define lawfulness or make decisions regarding punishment of police behavior they deem wrongful through the same lens of legality that police and other legal authorities use.[6]

So what does form the basis of public trust in policing? Fortunately, we know a lot about how to strengthen trust in the police. Research has made it very clear that the public's evaluations focus on whether they feel that the police—either police departments or individual police officers—are exercising their authority fairly.[7] Decades of research show that people care both about whether the police make decisions fairly and about whether they treat members of the public respectfully. This body of evidence, called the social psychology of "procedural justice," has been widely replicated in many contexts.[8]

In terms of fair decision-making, the public wants to be listened to when policies are being created, as well as to have an opportunity to state their case when dealing with individual police officers. They also want explanations for police actions that allow them to determine that the police are acting in unbiased ways and in accordance with policies that connect to understandable and shared objectives. They need to have information that will allow them to make an assessment about whether they feel that the law is applied consistently and appropriately across people and situations.

In the case of quality of treatment, people look for an acknowledgment of their needs and concerns, as well as for evidence of an officer's or agency's sincere efforts to act on behalf of the community. The issue of respect has been particularly important to recent public controversies involving the police, where people believe that the police treat members of the public, especially those belonging to minority groups, in demeaning, discourteous, illegal, and otherwise disrespectful ways.

If people believe that the police are fair, they will trust them and defer to their authority.[9] They will also cooperate by reporting crimes and criminals, providing testimony, and otherwise helping to hold offenders accountable. Given these benefits, it is reasonable to expect that violent confrontations with the police similar to those experienced in the aftermath of the police killings in Ferguson and on Staten Island are less likely to occur. And when there is less likelihood of these kinds of confrontations, it is reasonable to assume that it is less likely that the public will react to those incidents with immediate anger.[10] If the police are trusted, then people are more likely to give them the benefit of the doubt, allowing them time to investigate and respond to contentious law enforcement actions. Overall, the public is willing to give trusted police officers greater discretion in their efforts to enforce the law.

Importantly, this argument does not presume or assume that

public disagreement with policy or government leaders or even protest is a negative or undesirable outcome. Indeed, creation of opportunities for public dialogue about important policy is a signal to the public that a legal authority is committed to the tenets of procedural justice, voice, and transparent process in particular. When legal authorities welcome opportunities for dialogue, that behavior is a signal to the public that the authority is behaving fairly.

The bottom line is this: members of the public want to believe that the authority they are dealing with—let's say a police officer—believes that they matter. And the public makes this assessment by evaluating how the police officer treats them. The nature and quality of this treatment conveys the officer's view of their social standing and status. A person in good standing within the community should receive respectful and fair treatment. This includes respect for their rights, respect for them as a person, and acknowledgment of their right to come before legal authorities and have their needs and concerns taken seriously.

This dynamic is inherently relational, not instrumental. If the dynamic were primarily instrumental then the actors would care most about outcomes and individual maximization of utility, but the research is clear that most people don't think about fairness in these terms. We see from the research that legitimacy-based compliance centers on how people view themselves instead of on eventual outcomes that will benefit them. That is, people's perceptions of the fairness of legal authorities are tied up with how they manage their identities. People tend to seek a favorable social identity within the groups to which they belong, whether that group is a workplace group (law professors), a racial group (African Americans), or a gender group (women). People want to be thought of highly within any group they belong to. They also want the groups to which they belong to have a favorable social status vis-à-vis other groups. Our deep interest in social identity undergirds the reasons why people so deeply care about procedural justice. Psychologists Allan Lind and Tom Tyler explain that procedural justice is important to people because it provides important informational signals that they view as relevant to their identities. For example, if a police officer treats a person rudely during an encounter, that person will process that treatment as information relevant to how legal authorities tend to view both her as an individual and the group to which she belongs. The conclusion will be a negative one.

According to this view, pride and respect are much more important motivators of behavior than formal punishment, for loss of status can occur without punishment. On the other hand, status enhancement can occur even in the face of punishment. Tyler and Fagan demonstrate that the police can enhance police legitimacy while giving a person a ticket or even arresting him or her if they are respectful and fair to the person they are dealing with.[11] By affirming and enhancing a person's status within society, the police give that person something valuable—a positive sense of self and identity—that is more important to them than whether the outcome of the interaction is personally beneficial, such as whether or not the person receives a ticket.

These findings have clear policy implications. They suggest that policing is more effective when every implemented policy and practice is evaluated not only in terms of its crime-control utility, but also in terms of its perceived fairness. Procedural justice theory teaches us that every encounter with the public is a teachable moment, and police departments and officers should ask what they are teaching the public about the police in each interaction. In other words, legitimacy is something that is earned, much like any form of capital is accrued, and the consent of the governed is earned through experiences with the police that are imbued with dignity, respect, and fairness. When police generate good feelings in their everyday contacts, people are motivated to help them fight crime.[12] A focus on the public and public concerns has advantages for the police because it leads to a more cooperative relationship between the police and the community, something envisioned in early discussions of community policing but often lacking in police-citizen relationships today.

Clearly, focusing on public trust and confidence in the context of policing is not inconsistent with a police agency's commitments to other goals, including crime reduction. Indeed, building police legitimacy can be a different and, studies suggest, equally or even more effective way to manage crime. Recent research reviews make clear both that aggressive, force-based policing is at best minimally useful as a crime management strategy[13] and that such an approach does not build trust and confidence in the police. Studies similarly suggest that building trust in the police, the courts, and the law is as effective or even more effective as a long-term crime-control approach.[14] When people have greater trust in the police, they are more likely both to obey the law and to cooperate with the police and engage with them.[15] Legitimacy facilitates crime control both directly, because it lowers people's likelihood of committing crimes, and indirectly, because it increases public cooperation, which allows the police to solve more crimes.

We think this approach provides a new perspective on issues that have created ongoing controversy between citizens and police, including racial profiling, broken-windows policing, aggressive street stops, and police use of force.[16] In each case, the public perception of—and reaction to—what the police are doing, apart from the impact on crime statistics of the police actions themselves, is central to the conversation we are not currently having about the role of police in society. In today's media climate and in a world in which seemingly every encounter with the police is recorded by someone, it is inevitable that public perceptions become increasingly important. This reality makes essential the requirement that police reflect in advance upon how their actions are likely to be viewed by the public, including both those likely to have contact with officers and those in the community at large. The results of this reflection should shape both what the police do and, perhaps more important, how they do it. In particular, when the police have reasons for taking action that will impact peoples' lives, they should do so in ways that the public will experience as fair.

Legitimacy-based policing is also valuable because it facilitates the achievement of a broader set of community goals. One is to provide a framework for reshaping police forces to help address the challenges currently facing American cities. Those challenges involve addressing issues of economic development and include high-quality education, adequate municipal services, and support for new and small businesses. As crime has ebbed, the need for a large and insular police force has declined, providing an opportunity to rethink the structure of police forces. Promoting legitimacy is first a path to building the type of cooperation with the public that allows for the co-policing of communities to maintain social order. Working closely with the community will allow police officers to more efficiently maintain the gains in crime control that have already been achieved, freeing up scarce public resources to meet other challenges. For example, resources that are currently being used to support the police can be used to support economic development in the community. This is another way of thinking about good policing.

Good policing, rightful policing, is not the only important result of law enforcement authorities and other representatives of government treating people with dignity and fairness, although that goal certainly is a worthy one. Another result is healthy and democratic communities.[17] Amy Gutmann, president of the University of Pennsylvania, trenchantly observes, "We earn each other's respect as citizens in some very basic ways. We show ourselves capable of abiding by the results of fair procedures, honoring the rights of others, and supporting the passage of laws and public policies that we can justify to one another."[18]

Policing in ways that the public recognizes as legitimate is one of the many ways that legal authorities build and replicate strong government.

Gutmann's observation is critical, because it makes clear that public safety is not the sole goal of policing. One of us had the honor of serving on President Obama's Task Force on 21st Century Policing. The recommendations in the task force's report were informed by some of the ideas expressed in this chapter; indeed, the report's key pillar is the building of public trust and legitimacy by policing. In the section devoted to community policing, the report notes that "public safety is not self-justifying." Focusing upon that idea, we argue here that legitimate policing must devote attention not only to public safety but also to *public security*.[19] While police professionals typically emphasize public safety primarily in terms of limiting the amount of crime citizens experience, too often these professionals glide over the fact that the public also desires security from government repression and violence. Public security and public safety, achieved through state-sanctioned lawful police behavior, are interdependent; each can enhance the other when policing is done the right way consistent with procedural justice. The path to public security emphasizes the centrality of law to the police officer's task. The police officer must not only carry out his or her duties lawfully but also understand that he or she is a legal authority who conveys critical information to members of the public about their role and status as citizens.

Thus, in terms of the police role in helping people to understand their own identities within the groups they belong to and the status of their groups vis-à-vis other groups, Bradford, Murphy, and Jackson offer a compelling metaphor: police officers as "mirrors." Their argument is quite straightforward. Fair treatment by the police increases a person's identification with national identity, while poor treatment undermines it.[20] Legitimate policing makes people safer and more secure and confirms their citizenship in their communities. While we may have framed the issue somewhat differently here than it has been framed in the past, the idea is that legitimacy must be central to the self-conception of police. During his early efforts to organize the police in London, Robert Peel famously talked about "policing by consent" and argued for the virtues of public support for police activities.[21] This theme has been a part of policing ever since. It was particularly prominent in America during the twentieth century, when community policing policies were developed.[22]

We hope we have made clear that models of policing for the twenty-first century should be based upon the recognition that "you cannot arrest your way out of crime."[23] Crime control is dependent upon economic and social development. And a trusted police force is central to providing the background of reassurance that encourages people to join together to revitalize their communities socially and economically by motivating people to work in them, shop in them, go out for entertainment in them, and otherwise actively participate in community life.[24] Fear of crime undermined communities in an earlier era, but today the police can help build communities by projecting safety and reassurance. And as key figures in government, police help people to understand their role as citizens in a healthy democracy.

To achieve these gains police officers need to be trained to recognize the importance of fair treatment; they must be taught skills and tactics to achieve the goal of strengthening public trust. Police training can enable commanders to identify policies that build trust and help officers on the street know how to conduct themselves in ways that achieve the same goal. This training benefits officers as well as the public. Better-trained officers steeped in tactics for de-escalating conflict and building trust are less likely to encounter resistance and hostility on the street, less likely to need to resort to the use of force, and therefore more likely to be safe.

When we adopt policies consistent with the theories we have

laid out here, it is critical to understand that our mechanisms for evaluation must include how the public experiences these policies in addition to their impact on crime. For example, being repeatedly stopped by the police on the street or in a car leads people to question law enforcement policies regardless of how fairly the police officers involved are acting.[25] Again, the point is that when policies and practices are being evaluated, the evaluation should include not only a consideration of the immediate impact of a policy on crime, but also an analysis of the impact of that same policy on trust in the police with its long-term impact on crime and the community as a whole.

Understanding the impact of law enforcement policies has become a critical issue in recent years because the police have increasingly sought to prevent crime through proactive policing. Proactive policing involves efforts to deal with future crime by searching for guns and drugs with community participation, as well as communicating the risks involved in criminal activity, with a view toward lowering the rate of subsequent misconduct.

This approach necessarily brings the police into more frequent contact with the public, either through broken-windows approaches that focus on arrests for minor crimes or broad stop-and-search practices aimed at illegal drugs and guns. Research findings suggest that a long-term consequence of these broader proactive police practices has been to undermine trust and build hostility toward the police.[26] This is especially true when the police engage in widespread stops of innocent people. Additionally, arrest for minor crimes brings more people into contact with the criminal justice system, especially those who are young, which has the effect of undermining police legitimacy.[27] It can cause psychological harm and inflict indignity upon suspects who are treated in a humiliating or demeaning way.[28]

The nature of police contact with young people is particularly important because young people are more likely than other groups to be involved in offending behavior and in groups.[29]

Research on adolescent development shows that young people lack the cognitive and emotion-management skills needed to make good judgments about rule-breaking.[30] When young people have contact with criminal justice authorities, such as the police, the courts, and the prison system, the likelihood of positive development among the young goes down, and the probability of future criminal conduct goes up.[31] But that negative impact is greatly diminished when police are sensitive to the fairness of their decision-making and the quality of their interpersonal treatment.

Beyond juveniles, there are several other groups about which the police should be especially mindful. One is the general population of high-crime neighborhoods. A key finding of recent research on crime is that even in high-crime areas most violent crime is the work of only a small proportion of the people, who are identifiable through techniques such as network analysis.[32] This means that in any area there is a large group of residents whose cooperation can be engaged through trust-building strategies, while a small group of violent offenders is managed through surveillance and sanctioning. In such situations, targeted strategies against violence are the most productive. Police activity can lower the rate of particular crimes in targeted neighborhoods in the short term.[33]

The other smaller group of concern is that of persistent violent offenders. If the police have the trust of most of the people in the community, they can concentrate their resources to respond to the behavior of those who are multiple offenders of violent crime. However, it should not be assumed that only the threat or the use of force matters. Recent studies by Tracey Meares, Andrew Papachristos, and Jeffrey Fagan show that even those with a history of violence respond favorably to trust-building strategies based on respectful treatment.[34]

Finally efforts to change the culture of policing need to focus on addressing police officers' job-related concerns.[35] Two such concerns are safety and health. Policing can be, of course, a dangerous, life-threatening job and not only on the street. The stress of policing leads to high levels of suicide, alcoholism, divorce, and physical and mental health maladies.[36] The risk of being shot may be low, but, unfortunately, it is not the only danger that policing poses even though it may be the most visible and salient. The daily task of policing under sometimes hostile conditions promotes stress, which has broad negative consequences for the lives of officers and their loved ones.[37]

Interviews with police officers suggest that police officers want from their commanders the same sort of fairness that the public wants from them.[38] And, like members of the public, officers often feel that they do not receive their due even in their own station houses. Hence, it is also important to rethink the organization of police forces to give field officers more opportunities to express their views, better explanations of the goals of department policies, more transparent procedures for discipline and promotion, and, in general, more respectful treatment.[39] Procedural justice is beneficial at three levels: within the organization, where it promotes better on-the-job performance; in the life of the officer, who is safer and healthier; and in the community, where a style of policing that is more cooperative is less likely to create anger and lead to conflict.

All the same, public policy should be evidence-informed, especially regarding policing. Evidence-informed criminology provides a research platform for evaluating policies and practices related to crime and to policing. Policing should be informed by empirical studies that tell us what can work. Such studies should have a broader focus than just the crime rate. We also have to study what shapes legitimacy. Community trust and confidence metrics also need to be collected on a systematic basis. If this were commonly done, it would be possible to benchmark police performance against public views and not just in terms of crime rate statistics.

We have offered a few examples of specific approaches agencies can take in service of the vision we offer here, but we want to be clear: we are not suggesting that agencies simply adopt a set of new strategies. Instead, agencies must commit to a new mission statement—one that makes all citizens feel counted as members of the polity. While many changes that follow from what we suggest here are not especially expensive to adopt, that doesn't mean that it will be easy for agencies to make them. Decades of choices that reinforce differences in treatment between groups are difficult to undo. Old practices and attitudes will not disappear overnight because people often are committed to doing the same things that they have always done. But the path is clear if steep, and the cost of not taking the right step forward is just too high to countenance.

NOTES

1. David H. Bayley and Christine Nixon, "The Changing Environment for Policing, 1985–2008," in *New Perspectives in Policing: Papers from the Harvard Kennedy School Executive Session on Policing and Public Safety* (2010), available at https://www.ncjrs.gov/pdffiles1/nij/ncj230576.pdf.

2. "Sourcebook of Criminal Justice Statistics Online," table 3.106.2012, available at http://www.albany.edu/sourcebook/pdf/t31062012.pdf.

3. National Research Council, *Fairness and Effectiveness in Policing: The Evidence*, eds. Wesley Skogan and Kathleen Frydl (Washington, DC: National Academies Press, 2004), 309.

4. Public views about the police have been surveyed by a variety of groups, including the Gallup Poll and the Pew Research Center. Results are available from those groups directly or through the "Sourcebook of Criminal Justice Statistics Online," table 2.12.2011, available at http://www.albany.edu/sourcebook/pdf/t2122011.pdf.

5. It is extremely difficult to ascertain a good national measure of police killings of civilians, whether lawful or unlawful, but consider one area of police use of force that has been well litigated over the years: police car chases. New policies to restrict police from engaging in high-speed car chases have resulted in many lives saved. See National Institute of Justice, "Restrictive Policies for High-Speed Police Pursuits," at https://www.ncjrs.gov/pdffiles1/Digitization/122025NCJRS.pdf.

6. See Tracey L. Meares, Tom R. Tyler, and Jacob Gardener, "Lawful or Fair? How Cops and Laypeople Perceive Good Policing," *Journal of Criminal Law and Criminology* 105 (2016): 297, 300.

7. R. K. Brunson and J. M. Gau, "Race, Place, and Policing the Inner-City," in *The Oxford Handbook of Police and Policing*, eds. M. Reisig and R. J. Kane (New York: Oxford University Press, 2014), 362–82; M. Dai, J. Frank, and I. Sun, "Procedural Justice During Police-Citizen Encounters: The Effects of Process-Based Policing on Citizen Compliance and Demeanor," *Journal of Criminal Justice* 39 (2011): 159–68; J. M. Gau and R. K. Brunson, "Procedural Justice and Order Maintenance Policing," *Justice Quarterly* 27 (2010): 255–79; L. Hinds, "Youth, Police Legitimacy and Informal Contact," *Journal of Police and Criminal Psychology* 24 (2009): 10–21; J. Jackson, B. Bradford, B. Stanko, and K. Hold, *Just Authority? Trust in the Police in England and Wales* (New York: Routledge, 2013); L. Mazerolle, S. Bennett, J. Davis, E. Sargeant, and M. Manning, "Procedural Justice and Police Legitimacy: A Systematic Review of the Research Evidence," *Journal of Experimental Criminology* 9 (2013): 245–74; M. D. Reisig and C. Lloyd, "Procedural Justice, Police Legitimacy, and Helping the Police Fight Crime," *Police Quarterly* 12, no. 1 (2009): 42–62; M. D. Reisig, J. Tankebe, and G. Mesko, "Compliance with the Law in Slovenia: The Role of Procedural Justice and Police Legitimacy," *European Journal of Criminal Policy Research* 20 (2013): 259–76; T. R. Tyler, *Why People Obey the Law* (Princeton, NJ: Princeton University Press, 2006); T. R. Tyler and J. Fagan, "Why Do People Cooperate with the Police?," *Ohio State Journal of Criminal Law* 6 (2008): 231–75; T. R. Tyler and Y. J. Huo, *Trust in the Law* (New York: Russell Sage, 2002).

8. J. Sunshine and T. R. Tyler, "The Role of Procedural Justice and Legitimacy in Shaping Public Support for Policing," *Law and Society Review* 37 (2003): 513–48; T. R. Tyler and J. Fagan, "Why Do People Cooperate," 231–75; T. R. Tyler and J. Jackson, "Popular Legitimacy and the Exercise of Legal Authority: Motivating Compliance, Cooperation and Engagement," *Psychology, Public Policy and Law* 20 (2014): 78–95.

9. Tyler and Huo, *Trust in the Law*.

10. Katrin Hohl, Betsy Stanko, and Tim Newburn, "The Effect of the 2011 London Disorder on Public Opinion of the Police and Attitudes Towards Crime, Disorder, and Sentencing," *Policing: A Journal of Policy and Practice* 7 (2013): 12; Jonathan Jackson, Aziz Z. Huq, Ben Bradford, and Tom R. Tyler, "Monopolizing Force? Police Legitimacy and Public Attitudes toward the Acceptability of Violence," *Psychology, Public Policy, and Law* 19 (2013): 479.

11. See Tom R. Tyler and Jeffrey Fagan, "Legitimacy and Cooperation: Why Do People Help the Police Fight Crime in Their Communities?," *Ohio State Journal of Criminal Law* 6 (2008): 231, 275.

12. Ibid., 231.

13. R. Paternoster, "How Much Do We Really Know About Criminal Deterrence?," *Journal of Criminal Law and Criminology* 100 (2006): 765–824; Travis C. Pratt, Francis T. Cullen, Kristie R. Blevens, Leah E. Daigle, and Tamara D. Madensen, "The Empirical Status of Deterrence Theory: A Meta-Analysis," in *Taking Stock: The Status of Criminological Theory*, eds. Francis T. Cullen, John Paul Wright, and Kristie R. Blevins, 367–96 (New Brunswick, NJ: Transaction Publishers, 2008), 383; J. D. McCluskey, *Police Requests for Compliance: Coercive and Procedurally Just Tactics* (New York: LFB Scholarly Publishing, 2003).

14. T. R. Tyler, "Legitimacy and Criminal Justice: The Benefits of Self-

Regulation," *Ohio State Journal of Criminal Law* 7 (2009): 307–59; T. R. Tyler and J. Jackson, "Popular Legitimacy and the Exercise of Legal Authority: Motivating Compliance, Cooperation and Engagement," *Psychology, Public Policy, and Law* 20 (2014): 78–95.

15. J. Fagan and A. R. Piquero, "Rational Choice and Developmental Influences on Recidivism Among Adolescent Felony Offenders," *Journal of Empirical Legal Studies* 4, no. 4 (2007): 715–48; J. Jackson, B. Bradford, M. Hough, A. Myhill, P. Quinton, and T. R. Tyler, "Why Do People Comply with the Law? Legitimacy and the Influence of Legal Institutions," *British Journal of Criminology* 52 (2012): 1051–71; Jackson et al., *Just Authority?*; J. Sunshine and T. R. Tyler, "The Role of Procedural Justice and Legitimacy in Shaping Public Support for Policing," *Law and Society Review* 37 (2003): 513–48; Tyler and Fagan, "Why Do People Cooperate"; T. R. Tyler, J. Fagan, and A. Geller, "Street Stops and Police Legitimacy," *Journal of Empirical Legal Studies* 11, no. 4 (2014): 751–85.

16. T. R. Tyler and C. Wakslak, "Profiling and the Legitimacy of the Police: Procedural Justice, Attributions of Motive, and the Acceptance of Social Authority," *Criminology* 42 (2004): 13–42; Tracey L. Meares, "The Law and Social Science of Stop and Frisk," *Annual Review of Law and Social Science* 10 (November 2014): 335–52.

17. See Amy Gutmann, "Why Should Schools Care About Civic Education," in *Rediscovering the Democratic Purposes of Education*, eds. L. McDonnell, P. Timpane, and R. Benjamin (Lawrence: University Press of Kansas, 2000), 74 (stating, "Fair procedures are essential to a healthy democracy").

18. Ibid., 79.

19. T. L. Meares, "Policing in the Twenty-first Century: The Importance of Public Security," keynote address, *University of Chicago Legal Forum*, vol. 2016: 1–13.

20. Ben Bradford, Kristina Murphy, and Jonathan Jackson, "Officers as Mirrors: Policing, Procedural Justice and the (Re)Production of Social Identity," *British Journal of Criminology* 54, no. 4 (2014): 527–50.

21. S. A. Lentz and R. H. Chaires, "The Invention of Peel's Principles: A Study of Policing 'Textbook' History," *Journal of Criminal Justice* 35 (2007): 69–79.

22. C. Fischer, *Leadership and Procedural Justice: A New Element in Police Leadership*. A report by the Police Executive Research Forum, 2014.

23. Bill Geller and Lisa Belsky, *Building Our Way Out of Crime: The Transformative Power of Police-Community Developer Partnerships* (Washington, DC: COPS, 2011).

24. T. R. Kochel, "Can Police Legitimacy Promote Collective Efficacy?," *Justice Quarterly* 29, no. 3 (2012): 384–419; T. R. Tyler and J. Jackson, "Popular Legitimacy and the Exercise of Legal Authority: Motivating Compliance, Cooperation and Engagement," *Psychology, Public Policy, and Law* 20 (2014): 78–95.

25. C. R. Epp, S. Maynard-Moody, and D. Haider-Markel, *Pulled Over: How Police Stops Define Race and Citizenship* (Chicago: University of Chicago Press, 2014); J. Glaser, *Suspect Race: Causes and Consequences of Racial Profiling* (New York: Oxford University Press, 2014); T. R. Tyler et al., "Street Stops and Police Legitimacy."

26. Tyler and Fagan, "Why Do People Cooperate"; Tyler et al., "Street Stops and Police Legitimacy."

27. Issa Kohler-Hausmann, "Misdemeanor Justice: Control Without Convic-

tion," *American Journal of Sociology* 119 (2013): 351, available at http://www.jstor.org/stable/pdfplus/10.1086/674743.pdf?acceptTC=true&jpdConfirm=true; and http://users.soc.umn.edu/~uggen/Kohler_Hausmann_.pdf.

28. A. Geller, J. Fagan, T. R. Tyler, and B. G. Link, "Aggressive Policing and the Mental Health of Young Urban Men," *American Journal of Public Health* 104, no. 12 (2014): 2321–27. Also see William J. Stuntz, "Terry and Substantive Law," *St. John's Law Review* 72 (2012): 1362.

29. Robert Brame, Michael G. Turner, Raymond Paternoster, and Shawn D. Bushway, "Cumulative Prevalence of Arrest from Ages 8 to 23 in a National Sample," *Pediatrics* 129, no. 1 (2012): 21, available at http://pediatrics.aappublications.org/content/129/1/21.full.pdf.

30. L. Steinberg, *Age of Opportunity: Lessons from the New Science of Adolescence* (Boston: Houghton Mifflin Harcourt, 2014).

31. A. Petrosino, S. Guckenburg, and C. Turpin-Petrosino, "Formal System Processing of Juveniles: Effects on Delinquency," *Campbell Collaborative Review*, 2010.

32. Papachristos, Braga, and Hureau, "Social Networks and the Risk of Gunshot Injury," *Journal of Urban Health* 89, no. 6 (2012): 992–1003.

33. A. Braga and D. L. Weisburd, *Policing Problem Places: Crime Hot Spots and Effective Prevention* (New York: Oxford University Press, 2010).

34. See T. L. Meares, A. Papachristos, and J. Fagan, "Attention Felons," *Journal of Empirical Legal Studies* 4, no. 2 (2007): 223–72; A. V. Papachristos, T. L. Meares, and J. Fagan, "Why Do Criminals Obey the Law?," *Journal of Criminal Law and Criminology* 102 (2012): 397–440.

35. One concern the police have that is easy to address is that it costs little to nothing to give greater public recognition to their successes in doing a difficult and often thankless job.

36. Police officers, for example, are more likely to die through suicide than in the line of duty.

37. I. Komarovskaya, S. Maguen, S. E. McCaslin, T. J. Metzler, A. Madan, A. D. Brown, I. R. Galatzer-Levy, C. Henn-Haase, and C. R. Marmar, "The Impact of Killing and Injuring Others on Mental Health Symptoms Among Police Officers," *Journal of Psychiatric Research* 45 (2011): 1332–36; R. M. MacNair, "Perpetration-Induced Traumatic Stress in Combat Veterans," *Peace and Conflict: Journal of Peace Psychology* 8 (2002): 63–71; H. M. Robinson, M. R. Sigman, and J. P. Wilson, "Duty Related Stressors and PTSD Symptoms in Suburban Police Officers," *Psychological Reports* 81 (1997): 831–45.

38. T. R. Tyler, P. Callahan, and J. Frost, "Armed, and Dangerous(?): Can Self-Regulatory Approaches Shape Rule Adherence Among Agents of Social Control," *Law and Society Review* 41, no. 2 (2007): 457–92; Akiva Liberman, Suzanne Best, Thomas Metzler, Jeffrey Fagan, Daniel Weiss, and Charles Marmar, "Routine Occupational Stress and Psychological Distress in Police," *Policing* 25, no. 2 (2002): 421–41.

39. Trinkner, Tyler, and Goff. "Justice from Within: The Relations Between a Procedurally Just Organizational Climate and Police Organizational Efficiency, Endorsement of Democratic Policing, and Officer Well-Being," *Psychology, Public Policy, and Law* 22 (2) (2016): 158–72.

The Prosecution of Black Men

ANGELA J. DAVIS

THE CRIMINAL JUSTICE SYSTEM polices black men at every step of the process. Police officers stop, question, search, and arrest black men. Prosecutors bring charges. Judges decide whether they will be held in jail or serve a prison sentence. Many other officials (probation and parole officers, prison officials, and legislators) make decisions that impact the lives of black men in fundamental and often devastating ways. Although all of these officials play a significant role in the process, prosecutors are the most powerful, and their decisions have the greatest and most lasting impact.

Most people understandably see police officers as the most powerful officials in the system. Cops appear to be omnipresent and omnipotent. They seem to be everywhere, and they appear to have the power to do whatever they want—especially in black neighborhoods. Police officers have almost limitless discretion, and they use it frequently and in ways that disproportionately affect black men. The power to stop, search, and even arrest is totally discretionary and the evidence of police officers using that power disproportionately against black men is overwhelming.[1]

However, the reality is that prosecutors are the most powerful officials in the criminal justice system, bar none. Police officers have the power to arrest and bring individuals to the courthouse door. But prosecutors decide whether they enter the door and what happens to them if and when they do. Through their charging and plea bargaining powers, prosecutors control the criminal justice system and frequently predetermine the outcome of criminal cases. Police power receives more attention than prosecutorial power because police officers are in the public eye and much of what they do is in public space. Prosecutors, on the other hand, make the most important decisions in the criminal process—whether to charge and offer a plea bargain and what the charge and plea offer should be. They make these decisions behind closed doors and are not required to justify or explain their choices to anyone. The consequences can be life-changing for everyone involved—criminal defendants, crime victims, and the families of both.

The Charging and Plea Bargaining Powers

The decision to charge a person is totally discretionary and is made solely by the prosecutor. Police officers have the discretion to arrest a person if they have probable cause to believe that person has committed a crime. They may then make a recommendation to the prosecutor about what the charge or charges should be, but the prosecutor makes the ultimate decision. The prosecutor may decide to charge the person with the crime recommended by the police officer or with a more or less serious crime. Or the prosecutor may decline prosecution altogether. This decision is made behind closed doors and the prosecutor is not required to explain or justify his or her decision.

There are certainly legitimate reasons for a prosecutor to decline to prosecute a case. The American Bar Association has established "standards for the prosecution function" which serve as guidelines for prosecutors as they perform their various functions.[2] The standards list a number of factors that prosecutors should consider as they are deciding whether to charge an individual with a crime. These factors include the seriousness of the offense, the interest of the victim in prosecution, and the likelihood of conviction.³ However, because the prosecutor is not required to consider these factors or provide a reason for declining to prosecute, the potential for abuse is great.

There also may be sound reasons for a prosecutor to charge an individual with a different or more or less serious offense than the one recommended. Police officers usually are not trained lawyers with comprehensive knowledge of the criminal laws, so they make mistakes. Or it may be that the prosecutor decides to charge a person with a less serious offense than recommended because that person is a first offender, or with a more serious offense because the individual is a repeat offender or because the prosecutor is aware of evidence of additional or more serious crimes.

For example, if a police officer arrests a person for possession of a large quantity of cocaine, the prosecutor has many choices. She might decline prosecution altogether. If she decides to bring charges, she might charge the defendant with possession with intent to distribute—a serious felony offense with a harsh penalty and a mandatory minimum sentence. However, she also has the option of charging the defendant with simple possession of cocaine—a misdemeanor with no mandatory sentence. These options have dramatically different consequences for the defendant. The difference between a misdemeanor and a felony could be the difference between freedom and imprisonment, a job and unemployment, housing and homelessness, the ability to vote and disenfranchisement. There may be appropriate reasons for making one choice over the other—a first offender gets a break while a repeat offender does not, for example. But because prosecutors are not required to justify their decisions, they often make these decisions arbitrarily or for the wrong reasons. And sometimes these choices produce unwarranted disparities—differences in treatment that often appear to be based on class or race.

Prosecutors also control the plea bargaining process. Plea

bargaining involves prosecutors making deals with defendants, permitting them to plead guilty to a less serious charge. The defendant may be charged with several offenses. If the defendant pleads guilty to one (or more) of the charges, the prosecutor agrees to dismiss the remaining charges. In theory, plea bargains offer benefits to both sides. The prosecutor gets a guaranteed conviction without the risk of a jury finding the defendant not guilty and saves her the time and resources that would otherwise be devoted to a trial. Trials sometimes last days or even weeks. Guilty plea hearings are usually over in a matter of minutes. Guilty pleas also offer benefits to the defendant. If the defendant is charged with numerous offenses and is convicted of all charges after a trial, the judge has the option of sentencing him to time in prison for all of the charges. But if the defendant pleads guilty to one offense and the rest of the charges are dismissed, he only faces time on that one charge. The prosecutor gets fewer convictions but avoids the possibility of losing altogether. The defendant gives up the right to a trial and the possibility that he will be found not guilty of everything, but he also avoids the possibility of being convicted of everything.

In theory, plea bargaining sounds like a fair practice that benefits all involved. In practice, it is frequently an unfair and one-sided process. Like the charging decision, the decision to offer a plea bargain is controlled entirely by the prosecutor. A prosecutor is not required to offer a plea bargain to a defendant, nor is he required to justify his decision. The defense attorney may of course ask for a plea bargain and even suggest the terms, but the final decision rests with the prosecutor. Judges may not order the prosecutor to offer a deal and are usually not involved with the bargaining process at all.

Defendants frequently feel pressured to plead guilty when facing an overwhelming number of charges, each of which may carry a long prison term and/or a mandatory minimum sentence. Going to trial is risky business because no one ever knows what a judge or jury may decide, regardless of the strength or weakness of the evidence. So a defendant facing a possible life sentence might plead guilty to a charge that carries a maximum of fifteen years—even if he is not guilty.[4]

Prosecutors need only meet the low standard of probable cause (more likely than not) to bring charges against the defendant. This standard is much lower and much easier to meet than the proof beyond a reasonable doubt that the prosecutor must establish to get a conviction at a trial. So frequently prosecutors will bring charges that they know they cannot prove beyond a reasonable doubt, just to give themselves leverage in the plea bargaining process. Frightened by a long list of serious charges, defendants represented by overworked court-appointed attorneys with few or no resources to investigate cases may plead guilty in cases where they may very well have prevailed at trial, simply because their lawyers do not have the time or resources to mount either an investigation that might reveal the weaknesses in the government's case and/or a viable defense. And prosecutors often increase the pressure by putting deadlines on plea bargains, requiring the defendant to accept or reject the plea by a certain time or the offer "expires." This puts defense attorneys in the untenable (and unethical) position of advising their clients about whether to accept an offer before they have had the opportunity to investigate the case and establish whether there is a viable defense.

The plea bargaining process is neither balanced nor fair, but it goes on in courtrooms across the country every day. Judges, prosecutors, and defense attorneys with overwhelming caseloads facilitate a system that masquerades as justice. And guilty pleas are very much the norm. Very few individuals exercise their constitutional right to a jury trial. In fact, 95 percent of all criminal cases are resolved with a guilty plea.[5]

So the prosecutor's total control over the charging and plea bargaining stages of the process gives her more control over the criminal justice system than any other official. When one considers the fact that 95 percent of all criminal cases result in a guilty plea, it is not a stretch to say that prosecutors not only control the process but come close to predetermining the outcome of most criminal cases. This is especially true with offenses that carry mandatory minimum sentences requiring the judge to impose a certain number of years, regardless of the circumstances of the case or the defendant's criminal history.

The Impact of Prosecutorial Decisions on Black Men

There are tremendous racial disparities in the criminal justice system at every step of the process, from arrest to sentencing and beyond. Over 60 percent of people in prison are people of color, and on any given day one in ten black men in their thirties are in prison or jail in the United States.[6] Police officers engage in racial profiling, and black men are the overwhelming majority of their targets.[7] Cops stop and search black men at higher rates than their similarly situated white counterparts, and unfortunately the law permits them to engage in this insidious behavior.

Cops are permitted to forcibly stop an individual if they have what's called "reasonable suspicion" to believe that the person is engaged in or about to engage in criminal behavior.[8] The "reasonable suspicion" standard is very easy to meet. For example, if a black man is running in a so-called "high-crime" area, that otherwise innocent behavior may be sufficient to permit a police officer to stop and question him or maybe even frisk him for weapons.[9] If a black man is driving his car and changes lanes without signaling, a police officer has the legal right to stop him. Once stopped, the officer can peer into the car, ask for consent to search, and engage in all kinds of behaviors that can lead to conflict and, as recent events have shown, even death. When cops engage in this type of racial profiling—stopping and searching black men at much higher rates than whites—unwarranted racial disparities throughout the process are the inevitable result. If they are only stopping black men—or stopping them at much higher rates—they will inevitably arrest them at higher rates, even if whites are engaging in the very same behaviors.

Prosecutors also engage in behaviors that contribute to and exacerbate the unwarranted racial disparities in the criminal justice system. And because the prosecutorial decisions drive the entire system, the impact on black men can be particularly severe. From charging and plea bargaining to recommending sentences, prosecutors make decisions that result in black men being treated worse than their similarly situated white counterparts—both as criminal defendants and as victims of crime.

As Criminal Defendants

Like police officers, prosecutors exercise discretion in ways that produce unwarranted and unjustifiable racial disparities, especially when making charging and plea bargaining decisions. If a prosecutor charges a black man more harshly than a white man who is alleged to have committed the same offense and is similarly situated in every other way (same criminal record, etc.), then the prosecutor is creating an indefensible racial disparity. Unfortunately the law provides no meaningful remedy for victims of this kind of racial discrimination.

In 1992, an African American man named Christopher Armstrong was charged in federal court in Los Angeles with distribution of crack cocaine, several firearms offenses, and other felonies. Armstrong's lawyer was an attorney in a public defender office that had been keeping track of the number of African Americans who had been charged with these types of offenses in federal court. They noticed that it appeared that all African Americans charged with these offenses were charged in federal court while white defendants charged with the same offenses were charged in state court. The significance of this difference cannot be overstated. Federal crack charges carried much higher sentences than similar charges in state court. In addition, the federal cases were subjected to the harsh federal sentencing guidelines and mandatory minimum prison terms that required judges to mete out extremely harsh and lengthy sentences. In contrast, the sentences in state court were not as harsh and judges had at least some discretion and the power to be more lenient in appropriate cases.

Based on their anecdotal evidence, Armstrong's lawyers believed that the prosecutors were engaging in selective prosecution—pursuing harsher charges against African Americans based solely on their race. The Supreme Court had ruled that this practice violated the Constitution but only if the prosecutors intentionally or purposefully discriminated against a defendant because of his race.[10] The public defenders knew that they would need strong evidence to prove their suspicions. So they filed a motion requesting that the prosecutors provide their criteria for deciding whether to bring charges in federal court and the number and racial identity of all defendants charged with crack offenses in both federal court and state court. The prosecutors opposed the motion without giving a reason why they did not want to provide the information. The case made its way to the United States Supreme Court, and the highest court in the land sided with the prosecutors, ruling that in order to get this information, the defendant had to prove that similarly situated white defendants could have been charged, but were not[11]—a virtually impossible task. In fact, if a defendant had such information, he most likely would be able to prove that the prosecutors had engaged in unconstitutional selective prosecution. In other words, the Court appeared to be requiring the defendant to produce the very evidence that he was asking the prosecutor to turn over.

Mr. Armstrong's case was not the first in which the Supreme Court considered the racial impact of prosecutorial decisions. Warren McCleskey, an African American man, was convicted of the murder of a police officer in Georgia in 1978 and was sentenced to death. In his appeal to the United States Supreme Court, he argued that the Georgia prosecutor discriminated against him based on his race. Specifically, he argued that the prosecutor sought the death penalty in his case because he was a black man charged with the murder of a white man. In support of his argument in the lower court, he presented a sophisticated statistical study conducted by a law professor named David Baldus. The "Baldus Study" examined over two thousand murder cases in the state of Georgia during the 1970s. One of its major findings was that defendants charged with murdering white victims were 4.3 times more likely to receive the death penalty than those charged with murdering black victims. Mr. McCleskey argued that the prosecutor discriminated against him in violation of the Equal Protection Clause of the Fourteenth Amendment of the Constitution.[12]

The Court rejected Mr. McCleskey's argument. In a 5–4 decision, the Court held that Mr. McCleskey had to prove that the prosecutor intentionally discriminated against him because of his race and that the Baldus study only demonstrated the racial impact of the prosecutor's decision.[13] This holding was consistent with the Court's previous rulings that individuals claiming racial discrimination had to prove discriminatory intent rather than simply proving that a particular practice had a discriminatory impact. Of course Mr. McCleskey most likely would never be able to prove that the prosecutor sought the death penalty in his case because he was black. Prosecutors are not required to state their reasons for seeking the death penalty or even for bringing charges. And even if there were such a requirement, it is doubtful that any prosecutor would admit such motives.

In fact, it is likely that many prosecutors who make these decisions do so because of unconscious racism. Professor Charles Lawrence defines unconscious racism as the ideas, attitudes, and beliefs developed in American historical and cultural heritage that cause Americans unconsciously to attach significance to an individual's race and which induce negative feelings and opinions about nonwhites.[14] Unconscious racism is a type of implicit bias—the more general term used to describe the unconscious biases of people of all races which cause us to harbor certain views about others based on all kinds of characteristics, including race, ethnicity, gender, and physical appearance. These subconscious views are developed over a lifetime as a result of exposure to stereotypes in the media, our environment, and life experiences.[15] No one is immune from implicit bias or unconscious racism, and these subconscious views may cause individuals to act in ways that result in great harm to others. This is especially true for criminal justice officials—judges, defense attorneys, parole and probation officers, and prosecutors—whose decisions can have a life-changing impact on the lives of others.

A prosecutor's unconscious racial biases may affect her charging and plea bargaining decisions in ways that may produce unwarranted and unjustifiable racial disparities and unfair treatment of black men—both as defendants and victims of crime. For example, suppose a prosecutor is considering the prosecution of two similar cases. One involves an eighteen-year-old white college student named Todd arrested for selling small amounts of cocaine in his college dorm. The other is Jamal, an eighteen-year-old African American high school dropout, arrested for selling small amounts of cocaine on the streets of his neighborhood. Neither Todd nor Jamal has any prior criminal convictions, but Jamal has been arrested numerous times for minor offenses, all of which were dismissed. The prosecutor has numerous options. She might charge either or both with possession of cocaine—a misdemeanor with a maximum one-year sentence. She might also charge either or both with either possession with intent to distribute cocaine or distribution of cocaine—both felonies that carry mandatory minimum sentences and many years in prison. The prosecutor also has the option of dismissing either or both cases.

A white prosecutor may very well empathize with Todd the

college student—perhaps seeing himself and remembering his own "youthful indiscretions." Understanding the consequences of a felony conviction for someone with a promising future, the prosecutor might be more inclined to be lenient with Todd than with Jamal, whose prospects as a high school dropout are already bleak. Perhaps the prosecutor will justify harsher treatment of Jamal because of his arrest record, although the chances that Jamal was a victim of unlawful racial profiling are high, especially since he was not charged with a crime after any of his prior arrests. Other factors might come into play as well. Suppose both young men were also addicted to cocaine and were selling to support their drug habits. It is more likely that Todd will be able to afford a drug treatment program and have an attorney who will advocate on his behalf for an alternative to incarceration, while Jamal would most likely be represented by an overworked public defender and have no resources to pursue an alternative result. A prosecutor might very well agree to dismiss Todd's case upon the successful completion of a drug program while going forward with Jamal's case—even though Todd committed the same crime. Thus, implicit bias as well as race-neutral factors with unintended racial consequences may all play a role in the prosecutor's decision to prosecute Jamal more harshly than Todd. The result is a difference in treatment with the black man being treated worse for no justifiable reason.

Despite the disparity in treatment, Jamal has no legal remedy. After the Supreme Court decisions in *Armstrong, McCleskey*, and other cases that addressed selective prosecution, Jamal would have to prove that the prosecutor intended to prosecute him because he is black—an impossible task and perhaps not even true. Nonetheless, implicit bias may have played a role and the resulting inequity is unfair.

The hypothetical example of Todd and Jamal illustrates a phenomenon that occurs in prosecutor offices and courthouses across the country every day. One high-profile example of race-based selective prosecution was the prosecution of the so-called "Jena Six" in Jena, Louisiana, in 2006. The incident that ultimately led to the prosecution of six African American students in Jena happened on September 1, 2006, at Jena High School. Although black and white students attended Jena High School (the school was about 85 percent white and 15 percent black at that time), they did not usually interact with each other socially. In fact, many of the white students had a practice of gathering under a very large tree on the school grounds, and the black students gathered in a different area near the auditorium. On August 31, one of the black students asked the principal if he was allowed to sit under the tree where the white students gathered, and the principal assured him that he could. Some of the white students got wind of the request and decided to send a different message. The following day, some of the white students hung nooses from the tree, sending a very clear and threatening message to the black students. The principal recommended expulsion for the white students who had committed the racist act, but his decision was overturned by the Board of Education and the school superintendent, who called the act "an adolescent prank."[16] The principal then imposed in-school detention for the white students, but the black students and their parents considered this punishment inadequate. The black students organized a peaceful protest that involved gathering and standing silently under the tree.

The principal of the school called a school assembly and for some reason invited the local prosecutor, Reed Walters, to speak at the assembly. Walters delivered a threatening and frightening message to the students, and the black students believed that he was speaking to them. Walters said, "I can be your friend or your worst enemy." And while holding a pen in the air, he added, "I can make your lives disappear with the stroke of a pen." Walters ultimately tried to make good on that threat.

In the ensuing weeks, there was a series of confrontations and fights between black and white students, and there were stark differences in how the prosecutor handled these cases. The black students were consistently treated more harshly than white students who were alleged to have committed similar and sometimes much more serious offenses. On one occasion, when a black student named Robert Bailey (who would eventually become one of the Jena Six) attempted to attend a party, he was allegedly attacked by a white student. The white student was charged with misdemeanor simple assault and received probation instead of jail time. One of the most shocking of Walters's prosecutorial decisions was his response to an incident that occurred the very next day. On that day, Bailey and some of his friends entered a grocery store and were approached by a white man carrying a sawed-off shotgun. Bailey and his friends disarmed the man in self-defense. Walters actually charged Bailey and his friends with robbery and theft for taking the gun; the white man who brandished the shotgun was not charged with anything.

The incident that led to the prosecution of the Jena Six was a fight at the school involving a number of students. A white student named Justin Barker was attacked and knocked unconscious. He was taken to the emergency room, treated for a concussion, cuts, and bruises, and released the same day. Later that night, he attended a school function.

Despite the fact that Barker was immediately released from the hospital, Walters charged six black students with extremely serious felonies, including conspiracy to commit second-degree murder, attempted second-degree murder, and assault with a dangerous weapon. They were not carrying or using weapons during the fight, but Walters later argued to the jury that Mychal Bell kicked Barker and that the tennis shoes he was wearing were weapons! In addition, Walters chose to charge five of the students as adults—a discretionary decision that meant they would end up in an adult prison for many years if convicted.

Mychal Bell (who was charged as an adult) went to trial

first and was convicted. An all-white jury found him guilty of aggravated second-degree battery and conspiracy to commit aggravated second-degree battery. The trial judge vacated the conspiracy conviction on the ground that Bell should have been tried as a juvenile. The battery conviction was overturned on appeal on the same ground and the case was sent to juvenile court for retrial. At this point Bell had been in jail for ten months on a $90,000 bond. The judge reduced the bond to $45,000 and he was released pending trial. Bell ultimately pled guilty to battery and was committed to a juvenile facility for eighteen months. The remaining five defendants ultimately pled "no contest" to the reduced charge of simple battery (a misdemeanor) and were sentenced to a $50 fine and seven days of unsupervised probation.

The incidents at Jena High School and the subsequent racially discriminatory treatment of the Jena Six inspired nationwide protests. On September 20, 2007, close to twenty thousand people from around the nation came to Jena to participate in one of the largest civil rights marches in history. Civil rights leaders Al Sharpton and Jesse Jackson attended, as did artists and civic leaders from all over the country. The NAACP, the Southern Poverty Law Center, and other organizations lent their support to the Jena Six. There were calls for a federal investigation and numerous online petitions calling for various actions against Reed Walters. Congressman John Conyers even held a congressional hearing with the goal of pressuring the Justice Department to take some kind of action. Other members of the Congressional Black Caucus asked the governor of Louisiana to pardon the Jena Six.

Despite the clear evidence that Reed Walters singled out black students for much harsher treatment than whites (even though both white and black students were involved in fights and other criminal behavior), there was no claim of race-based selective prosecution. Even if the lawyers for the Jena Six had brought such a claim, it likely would have failed because of the prevailing case law. Walters's decisions were unfair and racially discriminatory, but not illegal. Despite a national march with twenty thousand people, numerous petitions, and a congressional hearing, there was no justice for the Jena Six. Just as significantly, the prosecutor suffered no consequences. He was reelected, winning a fourth term after running unopposed.

As Victims of Crime

The dominant narrative of young black men in the criminal justice system portrays them as criminal defendants—perpetrators of crime who are disproportionately represented at every stage of the criminal process. But very little attention is paid to the fact that black men are also disproportionately victims of crime. The Centers for Disease Control and Prevention reports that homicide is the leading cause of death for young black males ages fifteen to thirty-four.[17] Statistics collected by the Justice Department between 1996 and 2007 showed that young black men were the most likely of any demographic to be robbed every year and the most likely to be victimized by violence overall in six of the eleven years.[18] Unfortunately, black men are treated no better as victims than they are as defendants.

Prosecutors do not serve as lawyers for victims of crime. They represent the state, which includes crime victims, criminal defendants, and all members of the community. Although everyone has an interest in enforcing the criminal laws, victims of crime who have suffered personal harm are naturally more invested in the conviction and punishment of the person or persons who harmed them. Prosecutors meet and interview victims and prepare them for testimony before the grand jury and at trial, so they often develop relationships of trust with victims and their families.

However, class, race, and implicit bias may influence the relationship between prosecutors and victims of crime as well as the decisions prosecutors make at the charging, plea bargaining, and other crucial stages of the process. The Baldus Study from the *McCleskey* case discussed earlier was as much about discrimination against black victims as black defendants. The study concluded that the one factor that was the greatest influence on whether prosecutors sought the death penalty was the race of the victim. Regardless of the race of the defendant, if the victim was white, the prosecutor was more likely to seek the death penalty.[19] There have been a number of similar studies conducted since the Baldus study and all have reached the same result: prosecutors are more likely to seek the death penalty in cases involving white victims.[20] Studies of other categories of crime have reached the same result: cases involving black victims are not prosecuted as zealously and the perpetrators of crimes with black victims are not punished as harshly as those in cases involving white victims.[21]

Like criminal defendants, victims of crime have very few legal options when challenging prosecutorial decisions that produce racial disparities. The same case law that permits these decisions that have a negative impact on criminal defendants applies to victims. In addition, victims of crime don't have the legal right to sue or take other legal action against prosecutors who make decisions that discriminate against a victim based on his race.[22] Although most states have laws that protect victims' rights in criminal courts, these laws give victims procedural rights such as the right to be informed of the proceeding, to consult with the prosecutor, and to speak at sentencing hearings. None address the issue of racial disparities.[23]

Consider the hypothetical case of a prosecutor considering how to resolve an armed robbery case. The robbery victim, Sean Jones, is walking home from the store when someone comes up to him, points a gun at his head, and demands that he hand over his leather jacket. Sean complies and the robber runs off. Sean immediately calls the police and identifies the suspect as someone he knows from the neighborhood. The suspect is caught, arrested, and charged with one count of armed robbery. The prosecutor sends a letter to Sean's apartment asking him to come to the prosecutor's office for a witness conference and to testify before the grand jury. After interviewing him, the prosecutor decides that Sean won't be a persuasive or credible witness because he uses a lot of slang, is not very articulate, and has a criminal record that will be disclosed to the jury when he testifies. In addition, Sean tells the prosecutor that he doesn't really want to testify in court. The prosecutor decides that she doesn't want to try the case. It would take too much time to work with Sean and prepare him to be a good witness, and he might not show up on the trial date. Also, she knows that most of the people who report for jury duty are middle-aged or older white people who she believes would have a negative reaction to Sean. The prosecutor offers a very favorable plea to the defendant which will result in very little prison time.

Suppose the victim of the armed robbery had been a white lawyer, Bob Smith, who was robbed of his briefcase and wallet while walking to his car after work. Bob shows up for the witness conference wearing a suit and tie. He is educated and articulate, and the prosecutor believes that he will do well on the witness stand. In addition, Bob is adamant that the prosecutor take the case to trial rather than offering the defendant a deal. Of course, the prosecutor doesn't have to follow the wishes of the victim, but she may certainly take them into account. In a case with an interested victim who will be a persuasive witness and who will not require much preparation, most prosecutors would likely take the case to trial and seek convictions on all of the charges.

Implicit bias and unconscious racism may have played a role in the outcome of these two hypothetical cases. The prosecutor felt more comfortable with the white lawyer and decided that the young black man would not make a good witness. This may have been a reflection of her own unconscious bias or a practical decision based on her belief that the jury would most likely include people with their own biases, or both.

Perhaps unconscious racism did not come into play. The American Bar Association Standards for the Prosecution Function suggest that prosecutors should take a number of factors into account in making charging and plea bargaining decisions. Those factors include the likelihood of conviction and the interest of the victim in prosecution. If the prosecutor concludes that she is more likely to get a conviction with an articulate, appealing witness who is motivated and highly interested in cooperating, then one might conclude that her decision was an appropriate one, uninfluenced by class or race.

Regardless of the reasons for the decision, the result is the same—the harm to the black victim who appears to have been undervalued as compared to his similarly situated white counterpart. Even if race did not play a role in the prosecutor's decision-making process, there is still a racial impact. Race-neutral decisions can produce racially disparate results.

These hypothetical examples accurately portray how many prosecutors make these decisions, but there are plenty of well-known examples of the undervaluing of the lives of black men who are victims of crime. There have been numerous killings of unarmed black men by white police officers, and in recent years these killings have provoked outrage, nationwide protests, and an ongoing movement called Black Lives Matter. Michael Brown, an unarmed eighteen-year-old black man, was killed by a white police officer in Ferguson, Missouri, on August 9, 2014. Police officers left his body lying in the street for four hours. Darren Wilson, the white police officer who killed him, was never charged with a crime. Eric Garner, a forty-three-year-old unarmed black man, was choked to death on Staten Island on July 17, 2014, by a white police officer named Daniel Pantaleo as other officers surrounded him. Pantaleo was never charged with a crime. Tamir Rice, a twelve-year-old black boy, was playing alone with a toy gun in Cleveland, Ohio, on November 22, 2014, when he was shot in the chest and killed by a white police officer. The killing was captured on videotape. The officer was not charged with a crime. These are just a few examples of the many cases in which police officers have killed unarmed black men with impunity.

In other cases involving police officers killing unarmed black men, charges have been brought, but the officers rarely have been convicted.[24] The officers charged with the April 19, 2015, death of Freddie Gray in Baltimore, Maryland, either were acquitted or had their cases dismissed. Michael Slager was charged with murder for shooting unarmed Walter Scott in the back in North Charleston on April 4, 2015. His trial ended in a mistrial on December 5, 2016, because the jury was unable to reach a unanimous decision. Slager's retrial is scheduled for August 28, 2017. Other cases are still pending. University of Cincinnati officer Ray Tensing was charged with murder and manslaughter in the shooting death of Sam DuBose on July 19, 2015. He stood trial but the jury could not agree on a verdict and the judge declared a mistrial on November 12, 2016. The retrial is scheduled to start on May 25, 2017. Alton Sterling was killed by police officers in Baton Rouge, Louisiana, on July 5, 2016. The Justice Department opened an investigation, which remains pending. Officer Jeronimo Yanez killed Philando Castile in St. Paul, Minnesota, on July 6, 2016, and was charged with second-degree manslaughter. Videotaped footage shows Terence Crutcher with his hands in the air when Officer Betty Shelby shot and killed him in the middle of a road in Tulsa, Oklahoma, on September 16, 2016. Shelby was charged with first-degree manslaughter. The cases against Yanez and Shelby are pending.

A Shortage of Black Prosecutors

The Women Donors Network released a study on July 7, 2015, that revealed a startling lack of diversity among elected prosecutors nationwide. According to the study, of 2,437 elected prosecutors, 95 percent are white and 79 percent are white men.[25]

Only 4 percent of all elected prosecutors are men of color. With the exception of Virginia and Mississippi, which have the highest concentration of black prosecutors, only 1 percent of all elected prosecutors are African American.[26]

In a press release announcing the study, the organization suggests that if there were more prosecutors of color, there would be more racial justice in the criminal justice system: "In the context of such skewed numbers, when a white male prosecutor fails to secure an indictment in Ferguson and another sends a woman of color in Indiana to prison for 20 years for feticide, we have to ask serious questions about systemic bias."[27] The prosecutors who failed to secure indictments against the police officers who killed Michael Brown, Eric Garner, and Tamir Rice are all white men.

Would black men be treated more fairly at the prosecution stage of the criminal process—as defendants and victims of crime—if there were more black prosecutors? There have been no studies to demonstrate whether there are more or fewer racial disparities as a result of the decision-making in the offices of the few black elected prosecutors so there is no statistical evidence one way or the other. The anecdotal evidence is mixed.

Former attorney general Eric Holder—the first African American attorney general of the United States—was a very vocal advocate for reducing racial disparities in the criminal justice system. From the time he became attorney general in 2009 until he left office in 2015, Holder repeatedly spoke out against unwarranted racial disparities and implemented policies that he believed would address the problem. In 2013, in a speech at the American Bar Association's annual meeting, Holder said, "[P]eople of color often face harsher punishments than their peers . . . Black male offenders have received sentences nearly twenty percent longer than those imposed on white males convicted of similar crimes. This isn't just unacceptable—it is shameful."[28] He went on to note that he planned to implement a number of reforms, including ordering federal prosecutors to refrain from charging low-level drug offenders with offenses that carry long, mandatory prison terms. By 2014, the number of federal prosecutions in these cases was slightly lower, and federal prosecutors sought mandatory minimum sentences in about half of drug-trafficking cases, down from two-thirds the previous year.[29] Attorney General Loretta Lynch—the first African American woman to serve as attorney general of the United States—continued Holder's criminal justice reform agenda.[30]

Attorney General Holder initiated an investigation of the killing of Michael Brown to determine whether federal charges should be brought against Officer Darren Wilson. The Justice Department ultimately concluded that there was not sufficient evidence to bring charges under the relevant federal statute.[31] However, Holder also initiated an investigation of the Ferguson Police Department and determined that it engaged in a pattern and practice of violating the First, Fourth, and Fourteenth amendments to the Constitution.[32] After the killing of Freddie Gray, Attorney General Lynch ordered an investigation of the Baltimore Police Department that resulted in similar findings.[33] The Justice Department secured consent decrees with each city that establish plans for overhauling both police departments.

Some point to Marilyn Mosby, the African American state's attorney of Baltimore, as evidence that black prosecutors are more likely to achieve racial justice in criminal cases. When Freddie Gray died at the hands of Baltimore police officers in April 2015, the streets of Baltimore erupted with protests and rioting. Numerous individuals were arrested, and the mayor imposed a curfew. On May 1, just twelve days after Freddie Gray's death, Mosby held a press conference in which she presented the results of her investigation and her intention to charge six police officers with various forms of homicide, including second-degree unintentional murder. Her swift action sharply contrasted with that of the prosecutors in Ferguson, Staten

Island, and Cleveland—none of whom brought charges in cases that were arguably clearer cases of homicide. Although none of the officers were convicted, many praised Mosby for bringing charges against them.

But should Mosby's response to the killing of Freddie Gray be the true measure of her commitment to racial justice in the prosecution of criminal cases in Baltimore? Baltimore's incarceration rate is three times that of the state of Maryland and the national average.[34] African Americans are over 5.6 times more likely to be arrested for marijuana possession than whites, even though marijuana use among the races is similar.[35] African Americans make up 92 percent of all marijuana possession arrests in Baltimore—one of the highest racial disparities in the country.[36]

Mosby has not taken steps to reduce the racial disparities in Baltimore's criminal justice system, nor has she announced any plans to do so. She has implemented a pilot diversion program—Aim to B'More—for first-time nonviolent felony drug offenders. The program offers participants a chance to get a job and expungement of their criminal record if they successfully complete the program.[37] This program could potentially reduce the number of people going to prison, but that number is a drop in the bucket since the program only includes first-time nonviolent drug offenders. The program does nothing to directly address the stark racial disparities at every step of the criminal process.

A number of well-known black prosecutors have implemented similar diversion programs. Prince George's County, Maryland, state's attorney Angela Alsobrooks; former Brooklyn, New York, district attorney Kenneth Thompson; and former California attorney general Kamala Harris all have promoted and implemented various types of diversion programs with the goal of providing alternatives to incarceration and a criminal conviction for some offenders. However, these programs are all very limited in scope, and none directly address the racial disparity issue. These programs and other initiatives that these and other prosecutors are starting to implement are definitely positive steps in the right direction that will have at least a marginal effect on reducing racial disparities because they result in fewer African Americans going to prison, even though that number is a small fraction of the number of incarcerated African Americans. Attorney General Holder's actions resulted in a slight improvement in federal cases, but 90 percent of all criminal cases are processed in state courts, not on the federal level.[38] Without more direct and aggressive measures and fundamental changes in charging policies on the state level, the impact of these efforts will be minimal.

Of the few elected black prosecutors, not all are working to reduce racial disparities or the incarceration rate. Paul Howard, the African American district attorney for Fulton County in the Atlanta Judicial District of Georgia since 1997, is well known for his punitive charging policies. Howard prosecuted thirty-five African American educators (a superintendent, teachers, and other staff) in connection with a cheating scandal in the Atlanta public school system in 2013.[39] He was criticized for what some believed to be overcharging when he brought RICO (the Racketeer Influenced and Corrupt Organizations Act) charges against the educators in a sixty-five-count indictment. RICO charges are traditionally brought against members of organized crime enterprises and drug dealers. These educators had no criminal record and most had served in the school system for years; the superintendent had been named National Superintendent of the Year in 2009.[40]

One judge expressed frustration with Howard's harsh charging policies in a case in which he charged a man with armed robbery for using an air gun during a robbery. Because the man had three prior felony convictions, under Georgia law the judge would have been required to sentence him to life in prison without the possibility of parole if he had been convicted. During the trial, the judge urged the prosecutor from Howard's office to work out a plea deal that would not require her to impose the harsh sentence. When no deal was reached, the judge took the unusual step of telling the jury that if they convicted the man of armed robbery, she would have no choice but to sentence him to life without parole. The prosecutor objected and even filed an emergency appeal with the Georgia Court of Appeals asking it to halt the jury's deliberations. The appellate court denied the prosecutor's request and the jury returned a verdict of guilty on the lesser offense of robbery. The judge sentenced the defendant to ten years in prison.

A number of black prosecutors were elected in November 2016 and some ran on themes of racial justice. Kim Foxx unseated Anita Alvarez to become Cook County's first black woman state's attorney. During her campaign, she criticized Alvarez for failing to indict the police officer accused of the shooting death of Laquan McDonald until a judge ordered the release of the videotape of the shooting.[41] Foxx also pledged to institute reforms to address the racial disparities in Cook County's criminal justice system. Aramis Ayala defeated incumbent Jeff Ashton of Florida's Ninth Judicial Circuit on November 8, 2016, to become Florida's first black elected state's attorney. Like Foxx, Ayala pledged to address racial disparities.[42] Kimberly Gardner, who became St. Louis's first black circuit attorney, ran on a similar theme.[43] Time will tell whether these black prosecutors make good on their promises.

Paul Howard is just one example that demonstrates why electing more black prosecutors will not necessarily result in a more just criminal justice system with fewer racial disparities. Of course, unwarranted racial disparities cannot be eliminated or even reduced by a single official in the criminal process. The most effective strategy would be a concerted effort by legislators, police officers, prosecutors, judges, and correctional officials. But the problem cannot be solved without the active participation of prosecutors who are willing to make significant changes in their charging policies, regardless of their race. In fact, the prosecutor who arguably has shown the most leadership in directly addressing unwarranted racial disparities is a white man, Milwaukee County district attorney John Chisholm.

African Americans make up only 6 percent of the population in Wisconsin but are 37 percent of the state's prison population.[44] Over half of the African American men in Milwaukee County have served time in state prison.[45] John Chisholm was disturbed by these statistics and wanted to do what he could to address the problem. The Prosecution and Racial Justice Program provided him with some help.

The Prosecution and Racial Justice Program

The Prosecution and Racial Justice Program (PRJ) was a pilot program conceptualized and implemented by the Vera Institute of Justice, a New York–based nonprofit organization that works to improve justice systems. PRJ was an innovative program that involved statisticians collecting and analyzing data in prosecution offices to determine the impact of discretionary decisions. According to the program's website:

> Vera's Prosecution and Racial Justice Program (PRJ) enhances prosecutorial accountability and performance through partnerships with prosecutors' offices nationwide. PRJ works collaboratively with its partners to analyze data about the exercise and impacts of prosecutorial discretion; assists in developing routine policies and practices that promote fairness, efficiency and professionalism in prosecution; and provides technical assistance to help prosecutors implement those measures. By collaborating with prosecutors, analyzing data, and devising solutions, PRJ works alongside prosecutors to improve their performance and related criminal justice outcomes.[46]

The PRJ staff developed a series of performance indicators that focused on four significant points in the prosecutorial process that involve the exercise of discretion: initial case screening, charging, plea offers, and final disposition. The program's methodology revealed whether similarly situated defendants were being treated differently based on race at each of these steps. The goal was to help prosecutors exercise discretion in a way that reduced the risk of racial disparity in the decision-making process.

The program started in 2005 and continued for ten years. During that ten-year period, PRJ formed partnerships with chief prosecutors in three jurisdictions: Mecklenburg County, North Carolina; Milwaukee County, Wisconsin; and New York County, New York. The statistical studies revealed racial disparities at various points in the process in all three offices. By all accounts, John Chisholm, the Milwaukee County prosecutor, invested the most time, energy, and resources in the program and implemented the most significant changes in his office to address the problem. The Vera Institute ended the Prosecution and Racial Justice Program in 2015, but published a guide for prosecutors interested in implementing the program.

The partnership with Milwaukee County began with Chisholm's predecessor, Michael McCann. McCann resigned shortly after the work began. When Chisholm was elected in 2007, he was eager to continue working with PRJ, and gave the PRJ staff full access to the data necessary to conduct the study. The results were eye-opening. The study revealed the starkest racial disparities in the prosecution of four offenses: possession of drug paraphernalia, prostitution, resisting or obstructing an officer, and domestic violence.[47]

Chisholm immediately took action, implementing a number of changes and programs. One of the most significant is an early intervention program that results in either dismissal or reduction of charges. The biggest difference between Chisholm's diversion program and those implemented by most other prosecutors is that he does not limit it to low-level drug offenders. Individuals charged with very serious violent offenses are not eligible for the program, but according to Chisholm, these individuals only constitute 10 to 15 percent of offenders in Milwaukee County.[48] However, individuals charged with a wide range of offenses, including felonies, may be considered for the program. Eligibility is determined by a detailed assessment of each defendant involving the completion of one or more questionnaires that explore the individual's background, habits, lifestyle, and other relevant factors. Instead of focusing on the charge recommended by the arresting police officer, Chisholm's model focuses on the individual. The diversion program involves close supervision and participation in some kind of program that seeks to address the participant's needs, such as drug treatment or education programs.

As a result of Chisholm's efforts, there has been significant progress. He prosecutes many fewer low-level drug offenses and stopped prosecuting possession of drug paraphernalia altogether. Chisholm drastically reduced the number of misdemeanor prosecutions—from nine thousand to fifty-two hundred. [49] And the number of African Americans sent to prison for drug offenses has been cut in half since 2006.[50]

Conclusion

Prosecutors make decisions that can have a grave, life-changing impact on the lives of black men—whether they are victims of crime or charged with a crime. These decisions are often made in ways which produce unwarranted racial disparities between African American and white victims and defendants. Sometimes implicit racial bias plays a role, but sometimes race-neutral decision-making produces these disparities. Eliminating them is a difficult and complex task, but it will not happen without the acknowledgment that they exist and the will to implement significant changes in prosecutorial practices.

There are very few African Americans or other people of color serving as chief prosecutors. This disgraceful lack of diversity should be remedied, and the increase in the number of African American chief prosecutors in the 2016 election demonstrates progress toward that goal. But more diversity will not automatically result in fairer treatment of black men in the criminal justice system. The solution lies in the election of prosecutors who care about racial fairness and who are committed to making it a priority, regardless of their race or ethnicity. Racial justice cannot be achieved without prosecutors who are willing to significantly change their charging policies and implement programs to reduce the number of black men in the criminal justice system.

NOTES

1. John T. Clemons, "Blind Injustice: The Supreme Court, Implicit Racial Bias, and the Racial Disparity in the Criminal Justice System," *American Criminal Law Review* 51 (Summer 2014): 694–95; Geoffrey P. Alpert, John M. MacDonald, and Roger Dunham, "Police Suspicion and Discretionary Decision Making During Citizen Stops," *Criminology* 43 (2005): 408–409.

2. American Bar Association Criminal Justice Standards Committee, *ABA Standards for Criminal Justice Prosecution Function and Defense Function* (Washington, DC: American Bar Association, 1993), 4.

3. Ibid., 70.

4. Campbell Robertson, "Deal Frees 'West Memphis Three' in Arkansas," *New York Times*, Aug. 19, 2011, http://www.nytimes.com/2011/08/20/us/20arkansas.html; Keith Morrison, "A 20-Year Quest for Freedom," *NBC News*, June 11, 2007, http://www.nbcnews.com/id/19161103/ns/dateline_nbc-crime_reports/t/-year-quest-freedom/#.VfSxOVNViko; "When the Innocent Plead Guilty," Innocence Project, http://www.innocenceproject.org/news-events-exonerations/when-the-innocent-plead-guilty; John H. Blume and Rebecca K. Helm, "The Unexonerated: Factually Innocent Defendants Who Plead Guilty," *Cornell Law Review* 100 (2014): 158–62.

5. "Plea and Charge Bargaining," Bureau of Justice Assistance, U.S. Department of Justice, last modified Jan. 24, 2011, https://www.bja.gov/Publications/PleaBargainingResearchSummary.pdf.

6. "Racial Disparity," Sentencing Project, accessed Sept. 12, 2015, http://www.sentencingproject.org/publications/trends-in-u-s-corrections/.

7. "The Reality of Racial Profiling," Leadership Conference on Civil Rights, accessed Sept. 14, 2015, http://www.civilrights.org/publications/reports/racial -profiling2011/the-reality-of-racial.html; "Justice on Trial: Racial Disparities in the American Criminal Justice System," Leadership Conference on Civil Rights, accessed Sept. 14, 2015, http://www.civilrights.org/publications/justice-on-trial/race.html.

8. *Terry v. Ohio*, 392 U.S. 1, 27 (1968).

9. *Illinois v. Wardlow*, 528 U.S. 119, 121–24 (2000).

10. *Oyler v. Boles*, 368 U.S. 448, 456 (1962).

11. *United States v. Armstrong*, 517 U.S. 456, 465 (1960).

12. *McCleskey v. Kemp*, 481 U.S. 279, 292 (1987).

13. *McCleskey v. Kemp*, 481 U.S. 279, 291–99 (1987).

14. Charles R. Lawrence III, "The Id, the Ego, and Equal Protection: Reckoning with Unconscious Racism," *Stanford Law Review* 39 (1987): 322.

15. "Understanding Implicit Bias," Kirwan Institute for the Study of Race and Ethnicity, accessed Sept. 13, 2015, http://kirwaninstitute.osu.edu/research/ understanding-implicit-bias.

16. Howard Witt, "Racial Demons Rear Heads," *Chicago Tribune*, May 20, 2007, http://articles.chicagotribune.com/2007-05-20/news/0705190058_1_white -students-black-students-nooses.

17. "Leading Causes of Death by Age Group, Black Males—United States, 2010," Centers for Disease Control and Prevention, accessed Sept. 13, 2015, http://www .cdc.gov/men/lcod/2010/LCODBlackmales2010.pdf.

18. "Criminalization in the United States—Statistical Tables, Table 10: Number of Victimizations and Victimization Rates for Persons Age 12 and Over, by Race, Gender, and Age of Victims and Type of Crime, 1996–2007," Bureau of Justice Statistics, last modified Sept. 13, 2015, http://www.bjs.gov/content/pub/sheets/cvsprshts .cfm.

19. David C. Baldus, Charles Pulaski, and George Woodworth, "Comparative Review of Death Sentences: An Empirical Study of the Georgia Experience," *Journal of Criminal Law and Criminology* 54 (1983): 661.

20. Stephen B. Bright, "The Failure to Achieve Fairness: Race and Poverty Continue to Influence Who Dies," *University of Pennsylvania Journal of Constitutional Law* 11 (2008–2009): 23; Raymond Paternoster, "Race of Victim and Location of Crime: The Decision to Seek the Death Penalty in South Carolina," *Journal of Criminal Law & Criminology* 74 (1983): 754; "Evaluating Fairness and Accuracy in State Death Penalty Systems: The Pennsylvania Death Penalty Assessment Report," American Bar Association, accessed Sept. 13, 2015, http://www.americanbar.org/content/dam/aba/ migrated/moratorium/assessmentproject/pennsylvania/finalreport.authcheckdam .pdf.

21. Randall Kennedy, *Race, Crime, and the Law* (New York: Vintage Books, 1997), 73–75.

22. Andrew Karmen, *Crime Victims: An Introduction to Victimology*, 9th ed. (Boston: Cengage Learning, 2015), 241–44.

23. "Fundamentals of Victims' Rights: A Summary of 12 Common Victims' Rights," *National Crime Victim Law Institute*, last modified November 2011, https:// law.lclark.edu/live/files/11823-fundamentals-of-victims-rights-a-summary-of-12.

24. Celisa Calacal, "This Is How Many People Police Have Killed So Far in 2016," July 6, 2016, https://thinkprogress.org/this-is-how-many-people-police -have-killed-so-far-in-2016-7f1aec6b7098#.ibr1l1esz.

25. Jenifer Fernandez Ancona, "New WDN Study Documents the Paucity of Black Elected Prosecutors," *WDN*, last modified July 7, 2015, http://www.women donors.org/new-wdn-study-documents-the-paucity-of-black-elected-prosecutors/.

26. "White Men Dominate Elected Prosecutor Seats Nationwide; 60% of States Have No Elected Black Prosecutors," *WDN*, July 7, 2015, http://www.jetmag.com/ wp-content/uploads/2015/07/Justice-For-All-7.7.15-Report.pdf.

27. Ibid.

28. "Attorney General Eric Holder Delivers Remarks at the Annual Meeting of the American Bar Association's House of Delegates," U.S. Department of Justice, Aug. 12, 2013, http://www.justice.gov/opa/speech/attorney-general-eric-holder-delivers -remarks-annual-meeting-american-bar-associations.

29. "In Milestone for Sentencing Reform, Attorney General Holder Announces Record Reduction in Mandatory Minimums Against Nonviolent Drug Offend- ers," U.S. Department of Justice, Feb. 17, 2015, http://www.justice.gov/opa/pr/ milestone-sentencing-reform-attorney-general-holder-announces-record-reduction -mandatory.

30. "Attorney General Loretta Lynch Delivers Remarks at the National Asso- ciation of Attorneys General Annual Winter Conference, *U.S. Department of Justice*, Feb. 23, 2016, https://www.justice.gov/opa/speech/attorney-general-loretta-e-lynch -delivers-remarks-national-association-attorneys-general.

31. "Justice Department Announces Findings of Two Civil Rights Investiga- tions in Ferguson, Missouri," U.S. Department of Justice, March 4, 2015, https:// www.justice.gov/opa/pr/justice-department-announces-findings-two-civil-rights -investigations-ferguson-missouri.

32. Ibid.

33. "Justice Department Announces Findings of Investigation Into Baltimore Police Department," U.S. Department of Justice, Aug. 10, 2016, https://www.justice .gov/opa/pr/justice-department-announces-findings-investigation-baltimore-police -department.

34. "The Right Investment?: Corrections Spending in Baltimore City," *Prison Policy Initiative*, last modified Feb. 2015, http://www.prisonpolicy.org/origin/md/ report.html.

35. Bill Quigley, "The 'Shocking' Statistics of Racial Disparity in Baltimore," *Common Dreams*, April 28, 2015, http://www.commondreams.org/views/2015/04/28/ shocking-statistics-racial-disparity-baltimore.

36. Ibid.

37. Saliqa Khan, "Marilyn Mosby Announces Aim to B'More Program," *Justice Center*, May 14, 2015, http://www.wbaltv.com/article/marilyn-mosby-announces -aim-to-b-more-program/7093587.

38. George Cole, Christopher Smith, and Christina Jong, *The American System of Criminal Justice*, 13th ed. (Boston: Cengage Learning, 2015), 364.

39. Valerie Strauss, "List of Charges Against 35 in Atlanta Test Cheating Indict- ment," *Washington Post*, March 3, 2013, https://www.washingtonpost.com/blogs/

answer-sheet/wp/2013/03/30/list-of-charges-against-35-in-atlanta-test-cheating
-indictment/.

40. "Atlanta School Leader Beverly Hall Named 2009 National Superintendent
of the Year," *AASA*, Feb. 20, 2009, http://www.aasa.org/content.aspx?id=1592.

41. Micah Uetricht, "The Criminal-Justice Crusade of Kim Foxx," *Chicago Reader*,
March 9, 2016, http://www.chicagoreader.com/chicago/kim-foxx-bid-unseat-anita
-alvarez-cook-county/Content?oid=21359641.

42. Renata Sago, "In the Black Lives Matter Era, an Effort to Elect More Diverse
Prosecutors," *NPR*, Nov. 6, 2016, http://www.npr.org/2016/11/05/500714709/
in-the-black-lives-matter-era-an-effort-to-elect-more-diverse-prosecutors.

43. Yamiche Alcindor, "After High-Profile Shootings, Blacks Seek Prosecutor Seats," *New York Times*, Nov. 5, 2016, http://www.nytimes.com/2016/11/06/us/
politics/black-prosecutors.html.

44. Jeffrey Toobin, "The Milwaukee Experiment: What Can One Prosecutor Do
About the Mass Incarceration of African-Americans?," *New Yorker*, May 11, 2015,
http://www.newyorker.com/magazine/2015/05/11/the-milwaukee-experiment.

45. Ibid.

46. "A Prosecutor's Guide for Advancing Racial Equity," Vera Institute of Justice, last modified November 2014, http://www.vera.org/sites/default/files/resources/
downloads/prosecutors-advancing-racial-equity.pdf.

47. Ibid.

48. Toobin, "Milwaukee Experiment."

49. Ibid.

50. Ibid.

The Grand Jury and Police Violence Against Black Men

ROGER A. FAIRFAX, JR.

THE GRAND JURY is an enigmatic yet prominent feature of the administration of criminal justice. This citizen body, with a heritage stretching back to the twelfth century, historically has played the role of injecting popular representation into the criminal justice system.[1] The grand jury traditionally has possessed robust investigative powers and can obtain and review a wide range of evidence in a case. However, the grand jury was designed primarily as a shield between the power of the government and the individual. In those jurisdictions requiring grand jury indictment, the prosecutor may not pursue charges against the accused unless the lay members of the grand jury find probable cause and consent to the prosecution. This protection was meant to prevent the government from forcing an individual to defend against meritless or baseless allegations.

Despite its theoretical power, however, the grand jury does not often enjoy a reputation for resisting prosecutions. In fact, statistics consistently show that grand juries very rarely turn back a prosecutor's request to bring a case to trial.[2] Because of this, the grand jury has often been described as serving as a "rubber stamp" for the prosecutor and, as the cliché goes, seems willing to "indict a ham sandwich."[3] Although there are legitimate disagreements about whether these characterizations of the grand jury are deserved, it is beyond dispute that the grand jury indicts in nearly all cases in which it is asked to do so.[4]

Against this backdrop, there have been recent high-profile examples of grand juries declining to indict police officers accused of unjustified violence against African American men.[5] The cases in Ferguson, Missouri, and on Staten Island, New York, gripped the nation and left many to ponder why the grand juries in those cases failed to indict officers who had taken the lives of Michael Brown and Eric Garner, both unarmed black men. These incidents led to a flurry of criticism of the grand jury as an institution and raised the questions of whether grand juries are equipped for cases involving police violence against African American men, and what obstacles work to frustrate efforts to obtain indictments against law enforcement officers in this context.[6] Among these are the close working relationship between prosecutors and law enforcement, and the high respect we have for police officers, who President Obama rightly described as "the heroic backbone of our communities."[7] This chapter explores these questions, taking into account the role and function of the grand jury, and the issues and realities associated with the prosecution of police violence, particularly when the victim is an African American male.

The chapter begins with a discussion of the grand jury's historical role in state violence against racial minorities in this country. This history is crucial to an understanding of the role the grand jury plays in these contemporary cases of police violence against African American men. The chapter then examines the challenges facing attempts to obtain grand jury indictments in cases involving police violence against African American men. Using selected contemporary cases as models, the chapter will identify common themes and certain obstacles to grand jury indictment in these cases—in particular, certain structural features of the grand jury and, most importantly, the role of the prosecutor.

The Historical Role of the Grand Jury in the Prosecution
of Violence Against African Americans

The grand jury consists of lay jurors convened by the court, in secret, to determine whether there is probable cause supporting the prosecutor's allegations against the defendant. The prosecutor utilizes the grand jury's subpoena power to compel witness testimony and tangible and documentary evidence. The prosecutor also largely controls the pace and manner of presentation of evidence to the grand jury. The grand jurors then vote on whether probable cause exists and whether an indictment will be returned against the defendant. In the federal system and roughly half of the states, a grand jury indictment is required before a defendant can be forced to stand trial on felony criminal charges.

The American grand jury has a proud history, tracing back to the colonial grand juries that rejected Crown prosecution of American colonists accused of violating unfair British laws. The grand jury had a prominent role in the political development of the nation, interjecting itself in political controversies and sometimes rejecting prosecutions under controversial laws such as the Alien and Sedition Acts.[8] The grand jury was present in cases giving shape to the regulation of industry and the rise of organized labor during and after the Industrial Revolution, the battles over Communism and its perceived influence in the post–World War II era, and the fight against public corruption in the big-city political machines of the early twentieth century and during the Watergate era.

However, perhaps a less obvious role played by the grand jury in American history involves the protection of the rights of African Americans. Federal grand juries in the North sometimes resisted prosecutions of those being prosecuted for not complying with the Fugitive Slave Act. During Reconstruction, grand juries indicted southern state and local officials who participated in violence against African Americans and the deprivation of civil rights guaranteed under the Thirteenth, Fourteenth, and Fifteenth amendments. Even when public officials and private individuals responsible for the lynching of African Americans during the Jim Crow era were acquitted of murder by sympathetic petit juries, it should be remembered that, in many cases, they first had been indicted by grand juries. Additionally, when the civil rights advances of the 1960s were being frustrated by racial violence and jury nullification in southern states, the U.S. Department of Justice brought federal civil rights criminal cases against defendants who first had to be indicted by grand juries drawn from those same communities that were unable to obtain convictions in the state cases.[9]

Are There Obstacles to Grand Jury Indictments in Cases of Police Violence Against Black Men?

Even assuming this anecdotal evidence supports the notion that the grand jury historically has not necessarily been an impediment to protecting African Americans from official violence, could there be cause for concern that, in more recent times, the grand jury has frustrated efforts to hold law enforcement officers accountable for the unjustified killings of African American males? Although the secrecy of the grand jury makes it somewhat difficult to know whether grand juries in these cases decline prosecution at a rate much higher than they do for criminal cases in general, we do know that African American males are much more likely (seven times more likely, according to some estimates) to be the victims of police violence than are whites in the United States.[10] Recent egregious examples of police violence against African American males have brought the issue to the forefront of the American consciousness.

The heightened attention paid to these cases has prompted scrutiny of how the justice system performs when law enforcement officers are accused of unjustified killings of African American males. In particular, high-profile cases in Ferguson,

Missouri, and on Staten Island, New York, in which grand juries declined to indict the police officers accused of killing African American men, have brought the grand jury front and center. What follows are brief descriptions of six recent cases that present a variety of issues relevant to the question of whether the grand jury is equipped for such cases and what obstacles might exist in this context.

FREDDIE GRAY

On the morning of April 12, 2015, Freddie Gray, a young African American man, was approached by four police officers on bicycles in Baltimore, Maryland. Gray initially fled, but when officers gave chase, he voluntarily stopped, was arrested "without force or incident," and was loaded into the back of a police transport van.[11] Minutes later, the van made a stop and Gray's legs were placed in irons. According to prosecutors, Gray allegedly was taken on a "rough ride," the alleged traditional method for meting out unofficial punishment to uncooperative suspects. This is done by placing suspects in the back of the transport van (which has a Spartan interior with hard metal surfaces) and taking them on a "bumpy" ride which, particularly for those not restrained by seat belts, can cause the individual to suffer anything from bruises and abrasions to broken bones and more serious injuries.

By the time the van arrived at the police station, Gray was unconscious and an ambulance was dispatched to transport him to the hospital. Gray would undergo spinal surgery and would remain in a coma until his death one week later. Autopsy reports determined that Gray suffered a nearly severed spine and fractured vertebrae. The community and national responses were immediate and intense. Protests and civil unrest gripped Baltimore, and only days later did calm return to the streets. Perceived gaffes and missteps in the aftermath of the incident and unrest would cost the Baltimore police commissioner, Anthony

Batts, his job, and prompt the promising young mayor of Baltimore, Stephanie Rawlings-Blake, to announce that she would not run for re-election.[12]

Meanwhile, Marilyn Mosby, the young, recently elected Baltimore City prosecutor, moved swiftly to investigate Gray's death. Within three weeks of the incident, Mosby announced that she had concluded that there was probable cause to charge six police officers with criminal homicide and other offenses.[13] The quick and forceful announcement was embraced by the many who felt that justice had been delayed or denied in too many other cases involving deaths of black men at the hands of police officers.[14] However, others—particularly those in law enforcement circles—condemned the decision as political pandering and lacking in evidentiary support. Some even called for Mosby, who is married to the city councilman who represented the district in which the arrest occurred, to recuse herself and appoint an independent prosecutor.[15] Just three weeks following Mosby's announcement, the grand jury returned indictments against all six of the officers, with substantially the same charges originally advanced by Mosby.[16] Ultimately, none of the six officers was convicted of the charges; after a hung jury in the trial of the first officer, three officers were acquitted in bench trials, and the charges against the remaining two officers and the first officer to stand trial were dropped.[17]

MICHAEL BROWN

On August 9, 2014, Officer Darren Wilson, a member of the police force of Ferguson, Missouri, a town outside St. Louis, shot and killed Michael Brown, an eighteen-year-old unarmed African American man. There are conflicting accounts regarding the moments leading up to the shooting, including whether there had been a struggle between Brown and Wilson for the officer's weapon, and whether Brown was in a posture of retreat with his hands up at the time of the fatal shooting. However, it is undisputed that Brown was unarmed and a distance away from Wilson when he was fatally shot with at least six rounds. The killing of Michael Brown prompted protests fueled, in part, by the horrific image of Brown's body being left in the middle of the street for hours on a hot August afternoon.

Despite the fact that, in Missouri, the prosecutor is able to bring murder charges without the intervention of the grand jury, St. Louis County chief prosecutor Robert McCulloch chose to present the charges to a grand jury, entrusting the presentation to two deputies. As the grand jury investigation got under way, McCulloch was the target of calls for his recusal on the grounds that he was biased in favor of law enforcement (his late father was a police officer who had been killed in the line of duty) and, therefore, could not be impartial.[18] McCulloch resisted these calls, asserting that he could weigh the evidence fairly.[19]

Because McCulloch took the virtually unprecedented step of releasing the grand jury transcripts, we have a rare inside view of the grand jury process, which was atypical from the very beginning.[20] First, the prosecution called pro-prosecution witnesses to testify before the grand jury and attempted to discredit them, using statements attributed to them in the media to impeach them. In addition, the government seemed to make little or no use of forensic evidence or chain-of-custody irregularities, the probing of which might have been helpful to the government's case against Wilson. Third, and most glaringly, the target of the grand jury investigation, Darren Wilson, testified under oath, and the prosecutors declined to cross-examine him. Finally, the prosecutors' legal instructions to the grand jury were both pro-defendant and arguably erroneous.[21] In the end, the grand jury declined to indict Darren Wilson for the killing of Michael Brown.[22]

ERIC GARNER

On July 17, 2014, a forty-three-year-old unarmed African American man named Eric Garner was approached by plainclothes New York Police Department (NYPD) officers Justin Damico and Daniel Pantaleo for allegedly selling loose, untaxed cigarettes outside a store on Staten Island, New York. Following a brief verbal exchange, the officer attempted to take down the much larger Garner, with Officer Pantaleo placing him in a choke hold, a maneuver prohibited under NYPD policy. After Garner was brought to the pavement, Officer Pantaleo still applied pressure to Garner's head and neck area as Garner gasped that he could not breathe. During the course of the interaction, Garner said "I can't breathe" repeatedly before being rendered unconscious and going into cardiac arrest. All of these events were captured on video. The emergency medical care rendered by the ambulance personnel was unsuccessful and Garner was pronounced dead shortly thereafter.[23]

Richmond County (Staten Island) district attorney Daniel M. Donovan Jr. brought before the grand jury manslaughter and criminally negligent homicide charges against Officer Daniel Pantaleo. According to reports of witnesses before the grand jury, prosecutors seemed to challenge witness accounts that concluded that Pantaleo had applied a choke hold, and focused attention on Garner's prior health ailments.[24] Officer Pantaleo testified before the grand jury and, according to reports from his attorney, characterized his physical encounter as a wrestling takedown move and emphasized that he did not intend to harm Garner. Pantaleo admitted he heard Garner's declarations that he could not breathe but insisted that he released Garner as soon as possible.[25] On December 3, 2014, it was announced that the grand jury had declined to indict.[26]

WALTER SCOTT

On April 4, 2015, in North Charleston, South Carolina, a fifty-year-old unarmed African American man named Walter Scott was shot and killed by Officer Michael Slager. As captured on the dashboard video camera of a police cruiser, Scott fled on foot from a traffic stop for a broken taillight and Slager gave chase, also on foot. After a brief and close encounter, Slager fatally shot Scott. Although Slager reportedly initially told fellow officers that Scott had taken his Taser prior to the shooting and that he shot him in self-defense, a passerby with a camera phone captured on video what actually happened. The video recording of the incident shows clearly that Slager shot Scott in the back as he fled.[27] Scott died at the scene. Slager was indicted by a South Carolina grand jury for murder on June 8, 2015.[28] A federal grand jury later indicted Slager for federal civil rights criminal offenses.[29] The trial judge in the state case declared a mistrial when the jury could not reach a unanimous verdict.[30] At the time of this writing, the state was planning to retry Slager for murder.[31]

TAMIR RICE

On November 22, 2014, a twelve-year-old African American boy named Tamir Rice was playing with a toy gun in a park in Cleveland, Ohio. An eyewitness called 911 and told the dispatcher that there was someone in the park waving a gun, describing the person as "probably a juvenile" and the gun as "probably fake."[32] One of the responding officers, Tim Loehmann, exited the cruiser just feet away from Tamir and fired two rounds, one of which struck and killed him.[33] Pursuant to a petition filed under an Ohio state procedure, a county judge reviewed the evidence in the case and concluded that there was probable cause to believe that Officer Loehmann committed criminal homicide.[34]

It is believed that Cuyahoga County prosecutor Tim McGinty began grand jury proceedings in the fall of 2015. In an atypical maneuver, McGinty commissioned four separate expert reports on the question of whether the shooting was justified. Each of the reports was made by individuals perceived as "pro-police" based on their prior experience and expert testimony in other cases. In addition, the expert reports, all of which concluded that the shooting of Tamir Rice was justified, were released to the public, as was an analysis of still photos taken from a surveillance video of the deadly encounter.[35] The attorney for the family of Tamir Rice subsequently released contrary expert reports that the family had commissioned,[36] and repeatedly called for an independent prosecutor in the case.[37]

The grand jury ultimately followed McGinty's recommendation against charging Loehmann and did not return an indictment.[38] It was later revealed that the grand jurors concluded that the shooting was justified and therefore did not vote on the individual criminal charges presented to them.[39]

LAQUAN MCDONALD

On October 20, 2014, a seventeen-year-old African American boy named Laquan McDonald was reported to have been breaking into cars and in possession of a knife in Chicago, Illinois. As police dashcam video shows, the teen was walking down the middle of a wide street with an object in his right hand. Two officers emerged from a patrol car stopped several feet away from, and perpendicular to, the teen's walking path. Seconds after exiting the passenger side of the police vehicle, Officer Jason Van Dyke opened fire on McDonald, as the teenager walked on a line away from the officers. The first volley of shots spun McDonald around and knocked him to the ground. Over the next few seconds, Van Dyke emptied the remaining ammunition in his sixteen-round weapon into the fallen body of the teenager.[40]

In the wake of the shooting, Officer Van Dyke was placed on paid administrative duty, but was not charged in the shooting. While Cook County state's attorney Anita Alvarez conducted an investigation, the city of Chicago settled a lawsuit with the family of Laquan McDonald for $5 million.[41] Amid concerns that Officer Van Dyke's actions constituted excessive force and the criminal deprivation of McDonald's civil rights, the federal authorities became involved in the case, and the Federal Bureau of Investigation began investigating the incident.[42]

While all of this transpired, very few individuals had been given access to the footage from the dashcam during the night of McDonald's killing. The family, investigators, and some public officials had viewed it, but it had not been made available to the general public, despite a clamor for it. However, a journalist's Freedom of Information Act request compelled the release of the dashcam video pursuant to a judge's order. The video was released to the public two days before the judge's deadline, but one day after State's Attorney Alvarez suddenly charged Van Dyke with first-degree murder in the shooting of Laquan McDonald.[43] Van Dyke was indicted by a grand jury for first-degree murder on December 16, 2015.[44] The following year, a special prosecutor sought a grand jury investigation of an alleged cover-up of the incident within the Chicago Police Department.[45]

Lessons to Be Learned

What binds all of these cases together, obviously, is the tragic loss of life, in circumstances in which the killing was either unnecessary or unjustified. In all of these cases, the victim was an African American male. Each of these incidents was marked by intense media scrutiny brought about, in part, by outcry in the African American community and beyond, demanding justice in these cases. New approaches toward activism, represented in social media campaigns and groups like Black Lives Matter, helped to maintain attention on these cases that in the not-too-distant past would have quickly faded from the headlines.

The similarities seem to stop there, however. In three of the cases, the grand jury declined to indict the officer primarily responsible for the killing. In the three others, a grand jury indictment was obtained and, in two of those cases, that indictment came relatively swiftly on the heels of the killing and the initial investigation. There are many factors involved in the disparate outcomes in the grand jury, to be sure. Identifying these factors will be instructive for determining what might contribute to the challenges in obtaining grand jury indictments in cases involving police violence against African American men.

Structural and Functional Issues Related to the Grand Jury

Are there structural issues that may make it more difficult to obtain grand jury indictments in cases involving police violence against African American men? Interestingly, most of the criticism of the grand jury revolves around the fact that it tends to indict far too *often*. The lack of judicial oversight of the prosecutor's conduct, the absence of defense counsel participation, the lack of transparency, and grand jurors' lack of empowerment are all cited as reasons why grand juries will "indict a ham sandwich" if prosecutors ask them to. As the argument goes, these structural features of the grand jury lead to more indictments, not fewer. However, in cases involving police violence against African American men, some of these structural features of the grand jury may work in the other direction, frustrating efforts to obtain indictments. These obstacles can be grouped into two categories: problems posed by the structure and function of the grand jury, and issues related to the role of the prosecutor in the grand jury process.

Demographic Makeup of the Grand Jury

The demographic makeup of the grand jury could contribute to its reluctance to indict in a given case. The grand jury is designed to serve as the "voice of the community."[46] Usually larger than the petit jury and sitting for a longer time across many different cases, the grand jury is meant to infuse the criminal justice system with popular perspective. However, although grand jurors today typically are selected by lot and summoned for service in the same way as petit jurors, there is no voir dire process for shaping the actual group of grand jurors who will serve.

The less diverse the community that the grand jury represents, the greater the chance that the grand jurors will reflect a particular viewpoint—and if that viewpoint is pro–law enforcement, indictments against police officers may be more difficult to obtain. For example, in the Eric Garner case, the grand jury was drawn from the Staten Island community, which is home to a relatively substantial population of New York Police Department officers. Although we cannot be sure, it would not be surprising if a significant number of grand jurors were related to or were social companions of police officers. Whether or not these relationships necessarily would bias the grand jurors in favor of police officer defendants, an affinity with the law enforcement community certainly could impact grand jury decision-making in these cases.

Secrecy of the Grand Jury

Given the secrecy of the grand jury process, we usually know very little, if anything, about the reasons for the failure of any given grand jury to return an indictment. Unlike in the petit jury context, where we can sometimes guess (or at least form sound opinions about) what the salient issues were, the grand jury is truly a black box. While there can be any number of reasons that indictments are more difficult to come by in these cases, the secrecy of the grand jury process may play a significant role in cases involving police violence against African Americans.

For instance, to the extent that there is a pro-law-enforcement bias among the grand jurors in a given case, the secrecy of the proceedings gives the grand jury greater opportunity to resist charges against law enforcement. To be sure, the grand jury's secrecy is designed to protect grand jurors from external pressure. In fact, the grand jury earned its early reputation as a protection for defendants when the London grand jury famously rejected charges sought by the Crown against the Earl of Shaftesbury, a religious rival of the king. Given the tremendous pressure placed upon the English grand jurors, the fact that they were permitted to deliberate in secret was a key factor in their ability to resist the wishes of the Crown.[47]

As demonstrated by the seventeenth-century English case, this rationale for secrecy is a legitimate one, and it protects grand jurors in the exercise of their duties, permitting them to consider the evidence and the law without undue outside influence. Thus, the grand jury's function is enhanced by both the secrecy of deliberations and the fact that grand jurors' identities are generally not disclosed. However, if a grand jury were predisposed not to approve charges against law enforcement despite the evidence in the case, the cover of secrecy and anonymity certainly would also facilitate their nullification. In other words, the lack of transparency leads to a lack of accountability on the part of the grand jurors for their decision.

Legal Instructions to the Grand Jury

Another aspect of secrecy that could work to frustrate indictments in these cases is the lack of transparency around the instructions that prosecutors give to the grand jury. As discussed below, the prosecutor has a dual role before the grand jury, serving as both an advocate of the government's position on the criminal charges and the legal advisor to the grand jury. The legal advisor role includes instructing the grand jurors on the law they must apply to the evidence presented to them. If the prosecutor's explanations of the law are either unclear or inaccurate, the grand jurors may be misled.

Particularly in cases involving law enforcement's justification defenses to homicide charges, the grand jurors need to be clear on the governing legal standards controlling their assessment of the evidence. However, because those instructions are generally secret and cannot be disclosed without a judicial order, it is difficult to ascertain whether the grand jury is correctly instructed. For example, in the Ferguson case, which provided a rare window into the usually secret instructions, we saw a jumbled and arguably incorrect articulation of the law of when deadly force is justified. The grand jurors in that case very easily could have been confused as they applied the law to the evidence. If secret legal instructions are inaccurate, they could work to frustrate the grand juries' return of indictments.

The Primacy of the Prosecutor in the Grand Jury Process

Although there are structural elements of the grand jury that might contribute to the failure of some grand juries to indict in cases involving police violence against African American males, the single most important factor is the prosecutor. Not only does the prosecutor have plenary discretion to pursue charges in these cases, he or she also has complete control over the grand jury process itself. The grand jury sees no evidence or hears from no witness unless the prosecutor wants it to do so. This tremendous power over the conduct—and outcome—of grand jury proceedings makes the prosecutor the primary determinant of whether an indictment will be returned.

Prosecutorial Motivations

Most prosecutors in the United States are elected.[48] This might make prosecutors especially sensitive to pressure from the public or the media in high-profile cases. Given the level of media attention paid to the cases involving police killings of African American men, it would not be surprising if decisions to prosecute in these cases are sometimes colored, in part, by assessments of public reaction and the anticipation of backlash. Such considerations, however, could have a distorting effect on prosecutorial discretion in relation to the grand jury. On the one hand, public pressure could cause a prosecutor to charge in a case where it is not warranted, or to overcharge and risk losing credibility before the grand jury. The other reaction might be a reluctance to charge an officer even where it is warranted, given the public's general support for law enforcement. Such reluctance might lead to the prosecutor's offering a watered-down effort in persuading the grand jury to endorse the potential charges.

From the grand jury transcripts released in the Ferguson case and from what can be gleaned about the Staten Island case, the prosecutors there were neutral at best in their presentation to the grand jury; in other words, they did not seem to be advocating that the grand jury return an indictment.[49] The Ferguson prosecutors did not seem to challenge the officer's version of events when he testified before the grand jury, despite the obvious incentive to do so in a case involving an asserted defense of justifiable homicide. Reports from some with knowledge of the Staten Island grand jury in the Eric Garner case also describe a less than aggressive attempt to challenge the officer's narrative.

It is a fair matter for debate whether the neutral approach seemingly taken by prosecutors in these cases is superior to that taken in cases involving civilians accused of criminal conduct. Indeed, some have argued that the treatment that Officer Darren Wilson received before the grand jury should be extended to all criminal defendants.[50] Nevertheless, it is clear that the "kid gloves" approach toward criminal defendants in the grand jury room seems to be reserved exclusively for these types of cases.

Transparency

Because the grand jury process is secret, it is usually very difficult, if not impossible, to determine whether a prosecutor has made an aggressive presentation of evidence to the grand jury in an effort to obtain an indictment. However, the secrecy of proceedings prevents outside observers from judging whether the grand jury's decision is appropriate under the circumstances. Indeed, a prosecutor could easily use the lack of transparency in the grand jury process to dispose of a case she did not want to bring in the first place.

Another phenomenon, seen in more than one of the aforementioned cases, has involved the prosecutor sharing more than is typical in grand jury investigations. For example, in the Ferguson case, the prosecutor released information regarding witness statements throughout the grand jury investigation and ultimately released the grand jury transcripts. In the Tamir Rice case, the prosecutor released expert reports his office commissioned on the question of the reasonableness of the officer's conduct.

In light of the premium on secrecy in grand jury proceedings, why would prosecutors disclose such matters? While there could be less than admirable motives for sharing too much information, it could simply be a matter of trust—or lack thereof. Given the history of the handling of cases involving official force against black men, well-intentioned prosecutors might feel compelled to be more transparent than is necessary—or appropriate—in such cases. In addition, these actions may be prompted by the intense media scrutiny these cases sometimes receive. This added external pressure is likely even greater in the age of social media, with activists and casual observers alike able to follow every development in the case without depending on the mainstream media.

Length of Investigations

Prosecutors understandably prefer to carefully evaluate the evidence and deliberate before making the decision to charge a police officer with a serious offense. However, a number of these cases involve videotaped evidence of the encounter between the police officer and the individual. Indeed, often these cases are under serious consideration only because video footage is available. In cases in which there is objective evidence of what took place, the public can become frustrated with prosecutorial delay in bringing charges to the grand jury and obtaining an indictment. For example, in the case involving the killing of Laquan McDonald, prosecutors waited more than a year before announcing charges against the officer and seeking a grand jury indictment, despite the existence of a videotape of the encounter. In the case involving the killing of Tamir Rice, which also had videotape evidence, the prosecutor reportedly waited a substantial amount of time before conducting grand jury proceedings. Prosecutors in both of these cases have been the subject of criticism for these delays.

On the other hand, the swift and certain approach to indicting police officers in such cases may not be a foolproof strategy. For example, the prosecutor in the Freddie Gray case bucked convention and, not long after the incident, boldly announced charges against the officers involved in the events leading to Gray's death. Her announcement was followed by a swift grand jury indictment. Although this aggressive approach was applauded in many circles, particularly after other high-profile cases involving police killings of African American men seemed to drag along, the decision to indict in these cases was not subsequently affirmed by guilty pleas or guilty verdicts. Of course, it is not necessarily the case that the failure to obtain a conviction means that the grand jury's decision to indict was unsound; other factors that develop after the grand jury process can work to derail a conviction. However, acquittals at three officers' trials and dismissals of charges against other officers have led some to call into question whether the initial decision to charge and indict was arrived at too hastily, without sufficient deliberation, or as a result of external pressure and not for reasons grounded in evidence.[51]

The Lack of Independence of the Prosecutor

Prosecutors work hand in hand with police officers in their shared mission of law enforcement. Police officers investigate prosecutors' cases, interview their witnesses, gather their evidence, conduct their search warrants, and testify at their trials. With prosecutors and law enforcement being so closely aligned in the common goal of fighting crime, there are serious concerns about the ability of prosecutors to fairly and impartially bring criminal cases against police officers when they are accused of criminal conduct. This is particularly so when the prosecutors and police officers work together in the same jurisdiction.

Therefore, it is of utmost importance to ensure the independence of those prosecutors called upon to investigate and prosecute wrongdoing by police officers. There are a number of ways this independence can be furthered. For example, a jurisdiction facing the need to prosecute one of its own law enforcement officers could bring in a prosecutor from a neighboring jurisdiction. Although all prosecutors likely have a healthy respect for, and affinity with, law enforcement, utlizing a nonlocal prosecutor diminishes the chance that a personal or working relationship could serve as a barrier to an impartial prosecution.

Another way to enhance independence in cases against police officers is to employ a private lawyer who could be designated as a special prosecutor in these types of cases. This private attorney could be granted investigative resources and be authorized to conduct grand jury proceedings in order to gather evidence. However, there are significant concerns associated with vesting private actors with the tremendous resources of the government and the ability to exercise prosecutorial discretion.[52]

Yet another approach to ensuring the independence of prosecutors in these cases is to establish a permanent independent prosecutor dedicated solely to the investigation and prosecution of police officers accused of unjustified violence. This independent prosecutor would be in a position not only to handle these cases without the concern about conflict of interest, but he or she would have the opportunity to gain particular expertise in these types of prosecutions.[53]

Regardless of which approach is pursued to ensure greater independence of the prosecutor, some argue that, unlike local elected prosecutors, independent prosecutors lack accountability to the community. Indeed, Baltimore City state's attorney Marilyn Mosby consistently rejected calls for an independent prosecutor in the case against the officer involved in the death of Freddie Gray, arguing that a special prosecutor would not have the same accountability to the local community that she has as an elected official. Prosecutors in other cases, such as those related to the killings of Tamir Rice and Laquan McDonald, also resisted calls for the appointment of an independent prosecutor.[54] Whatever the concerns about accountability, however, the potential conflicts of interest inherent in prosecutions of law enforcement officers and the near crisis in public confidence dictate that ensuring the independence of prosecutors in these cases becomes a top priority.

Conclusion

A common reaction to the frustration and puzzlement over recent grand jury decisions not to indict has been to call for the overhaul or abolition of the grand jury itself. One proposal, advanced by New York State's top judge, would involve the installation of a judge in the grand jury to oversee the process and monitor prosecutorial conduct. California passed a law prohibiting use of the grand jury in most cases involving police violence against civilians. Both of these approaches are well-meaning but flawed. The New York proposal inches toward transforming the grand jury into a trial-like venue, which undermines the purpose of the grand jury. The California law simply removes the popular participation from the process and puts the decision to prosecute solely in the hands of the prosecutor. This further underscores the importance of prudence in considering the appointment of independent prosecutors wherever there is any concern that a conflict of interest could be an issue.

As a possible alternative, one might consider looking to a long-standing but often dormant power of the grand jury to investigate matters of public concern. In some of these cases, a federal civil rights investigation has followed. It is becoming commonplace now for these investigations to conclude that, even if there is not sufficient evidence to meet the extraordinarily high threshold for a federal civil rights prosecution, there are serious problems in the police departments in question.[55] This would be an appropriate subject for investigation by grand juries, which could use their investigative authority to probe matters of concern and issue reports that could prompt accountability among law enforcement and prosecutors alike.

In the end, however, it will take much more than grand jury reform to address the scourge of unjustified police violence against African American men. The grand jury is but a preliminary step in the formal judicial process. We need to focus a great deal of attention on how to transform the institutional norms that permit a small handful of rogue actors to tarnish the badges of the vast majority of heroic law enforcement officers who discharge their duties with honor and bravery. Indeed, perhaps nothing short of *cultural* reform may help avoid the types of tragedies that seem to capture our attention with depressing and ever-increasing frequency.[56]

NOTES

1. See Roger A. Fairfax Jr., "The Jurisdictional Heritage of the Grand Jury," *Minnesota Law Review* 91 (2006): 398, 408–11. This chapter is based upon research also used in my article "The Grand Jury's Historical Role in the Prosecution of Unjustified Police Killings—Challenges and Solutions," which will appear in volume 52

of the *Harvard Civil Rights-Civil Liberties Law Review*. Portions appear here with permission.

2. See Roger A. Fairfax Jr., "Grand Jury Innovation: Toward a Functional Makeover of the Ancient Bulwark of Liberty," *William & Mary Bill of Rights Journal* 19 (2010): 339, 342–44.

3. See *U.S. v. Navarro-Vargas*, 408 F.3d 1184, 1195 (9th Cir. 2005).

4. See Bureau of Justice Statistics, Federal Justice Statistics 2010—Statistical Tables (December 2013), 12; Ben Casselman, "It's Incredibly Rare for a Grand Jury to Do What Ferguson's Just Did," *Five Thirty Eight* (Nov. 24, 2014).

5. As the book for which this chapter was prepared is focused on the issue of policing African American males, the inquiry here is more narrow. However, recent stories have emphasized the growing incidence of African American women as victims of police violence. See Jesse J. Holland, "Police Brutality Against Black Women Comes into National Spotlight," Associated Press, Oct. 31, 2015; and Kirsten West Savali, "Black Women Are Killed by Police Too," *Salon*, Aug. 23, 2014.

6. See, e.g., letter from Sherrilyn Ifill, director-counsel, NAACP Legal Defense and Educational Fund, to Judge Maura McShane, 21st Judicial Circuit, Clayton, Missouri (Jan. 5, 2015), available at www.naacpldf.org/document/ldf-open-letter-judge-maura-mcshane.

7. See Barack Obama, "The President's Role in Advancing Criminal Justice Reform," *Harvard Law Review* 130 (2017): 840.

8. See Roger A. Fairfax Jr., "Grand Jury Discretion and Constitutional Design," *Cornell Law Review* 93 (2008): 722.

9. Ibid., 715 n. 49, 722.

10. See "Black and Unarmed," *Washington Post*, Aug. 8, 2015; Kimberly Kindy, "Fatal Police Shootings in 2015 Approaching 400 Nationwide," *Washington Post*, May 30, 2015; "Thousands Dead, Few Prosecuted," *Washington Post*, April 11, 2015; see also Devon W. Carbado and Patrick F. Rock, "What Exposes African Americans to Police Violence?," *Harvard Civil Rights-Civil Liberties Law Review* 51 (2016): 159.

11. Baltimore Police Department Incident Report, Freddie Gray case (April 12, 2015).

12. See Sheryl Gay Stolberg, "Baltimore's Mayor, Stephanie Rawlings-Blake, Won't Seek Re-election," *New York Times*, Sept. 11, 2015; Scott Calvert, "Baltimore Mayor Fires Police Commissioner Anthony Batts," *Wall Street Journal*, July 8, 2015.

13. See Jean Marbella, "Six Baltimore Police Officers Charged in Freddie Gray's Death," *Baltimore Sun*, May 2, 2015; "National and Local Reaction to Charges in Freddie Gray Case," *Baltimore Sun*, May 2, 2015.

14. "National and Local Reaction to Charges in Freddie Gray Case," *Baltimore Sun*, May 2, 2015.

15. Ibid.; Doug Donovan, "FOP Calls on Prosecutor to Recuse Herself, Defends Officers," *Baltimore Sun*, May 1, 2015.

16. See Justin Fenton, "Six Baltimore Police Officers Indicted in Death of Freddie Gray," *Baltimore Sun*, May 21, 2015.

17. See Kevin Rector, "Charges Dropped, Freddie Gray Case Concludes with Zero Convictions Against Officers," *Baltimore Sun*, July 27, 2016; Sheryl Gay Stol-

berg and Jess Bidgwood, "All Charges Dropped Against Baltimore Officers in Freddie Gray Case," *New York Times*, July 27, 2016; Wil S. Hylton, "Baltimore vs. Marilyn Mosby," *New York Times Magazine*, Sept. 28, 2016.

18. See Jamelle Bouie, "Protesting the Prosecution," *Slate*, Aug. 21, 2014; Ed Silverstein, "Attorneys, Law Professors Weigh In on Whether McCulloch Should Step Aside in Fatal Shooting Case," *Inside Counsel*, Aug. 21, 2014.

19. See Frances Robles, "St. Louis County Prosecutor Defends Objectivity," *New York Times*, Aug. 20, 2014.

20. See, e.g., Kate Levine, "How We Prosecute the Police," *Georgetown Law Journal* 104 (2016): 760–62.

21. See Ruth Steinhardt, "Missouri Grand Jury Declines to Indict Police Officer in Fatal Shooting," *GW Today*, Nov. 26, 2014.

22. "Ferguson Police Officer Won't Be Charged in Fatal Shooting," *Washington Post*, Nov. 25, 2014.

23. "Beyond the Chokehold: The Path to Eric Garner's Death," *New York Times*, June 13, 2015.

24. Ibid.

25. J. David Goodman and Michael Wilson, "Officer Daniel Pantaleo Told Grand Jury He Meant No Harm to Eric Garner," *New York Times*, Dec. 3, 2014.

26. J. David Goodman and Al Baker, "Wave of Protests After Grand Jury Doesn't Indict Officer in Eric Garner Chokehold Case," *New York Times*, Dec. 3, 2014.

27. "Video Shows Fatal Police Shooting," *New York Times*, April 7, 2015.

28. See Bruce Smith, "Ex-SC Officer Indicted for Murder in Shooting of Walter Scott," *The State* (Columbia, SC), June 8, 2015.

29. See Chris Dixon and Tamar Lewin, "South Carolina Officer Faces Federal Charges in Federal Shooting," *New York Times*, May 11, 2016.

30. See Alan Blinder, "Mistrial for South Carolina Officer Who Shot Walter Scott," *New York Times*, Dec. 5, 2016.

31. See Andrew Knapp, "State Retrial of Michael Slager Set for March 1, 2017, Ahead of Federal Proceeding," *The Post and Courier*, Dec. 29, 2016.

32. See Mitch Smith, "Lawyers for Tamir Rice's Family Release Outside Reports Criticizing Shooting," *New York Times*, Nov. 29, 2015.

33. See Emma G. Fitzsimmons, "12-Year-Old Boy Dies After Police in Cleveland Shoot Him," *New York Times*, Nov. 23, 2014.

34. See Mark Berman and Wesley Lowery, "Cleveland Judge Finds Probable Cause of Murder Charge in Tamir Rice Shooting," *New York Times*, June 11, 2015.

35. Mark Gillispie, "Images, Analysis Released of Cleveland Officer Shooting Boy," *Washington Post*, Nov. 29, 2015.

36. See Mitch Smith, "Lawyers for Tamir Rice's Family Release Outside Reports Criticizing Shooting," *New York Times*, Nov. 29, 2015.

37. See Jaeah Lee, "Outrage Is Growing Over the Tamir Rice Investigation," *Mother Jones*, Oct. 28, 2015.

38. See Timothy Williams and Mitch Smith, "Cleveland Officer Will Not Face Charges in Tamir Rice Shooting Death," *New York Times*, Dec. 28, 2015.

39. See Mark Berman, "Grand Jurors in the Tamir Rice Case Voted That the

Shooting Was Justified, Did Not Vote on Specific Criminal Charges," *Washington Post*, Jan. 20, 2016.

40. See Annie Sweeney and Jason Meisner, "A Moment-by-Moment Account of What the Laquan McDonald Video Shows," *Chicago Tribune*, Nov. 25, 2015.

41. See Fran Spielman, "City Council Approves $5 Million Settlement Stemming from Fatal Police Shooting," *Chicago Sun-Times*, April 15, 2015.

42. See Dan Hinkel and Matthew Walberg, "Long Inquiry Before Charges in Laquan McDonald Shooting Prompts Scrutiny," *Chicago Tribune*, Nov. 25, 2015.

43. "Chicago Releases Dash-Cam Video of Fatal Shooting After Cop Charged with Murder," *Chicago Tribune*, Nov. 24, 2015.

44. See Steve Schmadeke, "Chicago Cop Indicted on 6 Murder Counts in Laquan McDonald Slaying," *Chicago Tribune*, Dec. 16, 2015.

45. See Steve Schmadeke, "Grand Jury to Look into Possible Cover-up by Chicago Police in Laquan McDonald Shooting," *Chicago Tribune*, Sept. 12, 2016.

46. See Susan W. Brenner, "The Voice of the Community: A Case for Grand Jury Independence," *Virginia Journal of Social Policy & the Law* 3 (1995): 67.

47. See George J. Edwards, *The Grand Jury: An Essay* (Philadelphia: George T. Bisel Company, 1906), 28–30; Fairfax, "Grand Jury Discretion," 721–22.

48. See Angela J. Davis, *Arbitrary Justice: The Power of the American Prosecutor* (New York: Oxford University Press, 2007).

49. See Jeffrey Toobin, "How Not to Use a Grand Jury," *The New Yorker*, Nov. 25, 2014.

50. See Kristin Henning, "Race and the Rule of Law in the Grand Jury Process," *Howard Law Journal* 58 (2015).

51. See, e.g., Ericka Blount Danois, "The Vilification of Marilyn Mosby," *The Root*, Oct. 6, 2016; Yvonne Wenger and Justin Fenton, "Rawlings-Blake Accuses Mosby of Bowing to Political Pressure, Charging Baltimore Officers Too Soon," *Baltimore Sun*, Sept. 28, 2016; Luke Broadwater, "As Acquittals Add Up, Freddie Gray Prosecutor Feels the Heat," *Los Angeles Times*, July 10, 2016.

52. See Roger A. Fairfax Jr., "Outsourcing Criminal Prosecution? The Limits of Criminal Justice Privatization," *University of Chicago Law Forum* (2010): 265.

53. See Erica Orden, "Lead Prosecutor Named for N.Y. Police Deadly-Force Cases," *Wall Street Journal*, July 9, 2015.

54. The original prosecutor in the Laquan McDonald case eventually capitulated to pressure to transfer the matter to a special prosecutor. See Steve Schmadeke, "Alvarez Requests Special Prosecutor in Laquan McDonald Shooting by Police," *Chicago Tribune*, May 5, 2016.

55. See, e.g., Jason Meisner, Annie Sweeney, Dan Henkel, and Jeremy Gorner, "Justice Report Rips Chicago Police for Excessive Force, Lax Discipline, Bad Training," *Chicago Tribune*, Jan. 13, 2017; Investigation of the Chicago Police Department, United States Department of Justice, Civil Rights Division and United States Attorney's Office, Northern District of Illinois, January 13, 2017; Investigation of the Ferguson Police Department, United States Department of Justice, Civil Rights Division, March 4, 2015; Investigation of the Baltimore City Police Department, United States Department of Justice, Civil Rights Division, August 10, 2016.

56. Although grand jury reforms are not among the reform measures mentioned by President Obama in his recent article summarizing his criminal justice legacy, he did acknowledge that the Task Force on 21st Century Policing was launched "in the wake of events in Ferguson, Cleveland, and New York City." Barack Obama, "The President's Role in Advancing Criminal Justice Reform," *Harvard Law Review* 130 (2017): 840. See also President's Task Force on 21st Century Policing, *Final Report of the President's Task Force on 21st Century Policing* (2015).

Elected Prosecutors and Police Accountability

RONALD F. WRIGHT

PROSECUTORS DON'T EXACTLY supervise the police—at least not in the sense that bosses supervise employees—but prosecutors do advise and train law enforcement officers. They decide whether to file criminal charges after the police arrest a suspect. Prosecutors also develop opinions about the reliability of different officers, and decide when to trust their work and to call them as witnesses at trial.

And then there are the difficult moments in the relationship. Prosecutors review the facts when somebody accuses an officer of misconduct, such as excessive use of force. Some police misconduct amounts to a crime; in those cases, prosecutors can file criminal charges against individual police officers.

Criminal prosecutors, therefore, can hold the police accountable to the public. But who watches the watchers? How do we make sure that prosecutors evaluate the work of police officers in ways that truly enforce the criminal law while responding to the values and priorities of the public?

In the state courts of the United States, unlike the court systems almost everywhere else in the world, the chief prosecutors are elected. Most are elected at the local level. They do not answer to an attorney general or to some other state official; chief prosecutors are accountable only to the local voters for their choices about how to enforce (or not to enforce) the criminal laws.

Sad to say, this accountability system for prosecutors does not work especially well. Elections do not, in most places in the United States, convince prosecutors to strengthen their oversight of local law enforcement. Elections have little impact because incumbents who decide to run for re-election almost always win. In fact, they usually run unopposed. As a result, incumbent prosecutors typically do not have to explain to the voters their relationship with local law enforcement agencies. In most cities and counties in the United States, nobody asks an elected prosecutor to defend his or her record on police accountability.

One result of this sputtering election system is a racial divide between prosecutors and voters. While African American voters have achieved some success in electing sympathetic candidates as mayors and city council members to implement their priorities in local government, the same is not true of local prosecutors. There are surprisingly few African American chief prosecutors in the United States, fewer than 5 percent of those who hold the office. And few prosecutors of any race build the sort of relationships with law enforcement that minority communities would like to see. Unresponsive prosecutors do not see the damaged and distrustful relationships between communities and their law enforcement officials, and they cannot cure what they cannot see.

Election law changes might improve the connection between prosecutors and voters. In particular, states might revise their election laws to create smaller prosecutorial districts and to align the prosecutor election cycle with the presidential election cycle. These and other structural changes could make prosecutors responsive to the entire community, including the portion of the community with the most direct stake in criminal law enforcement. A prosecutor who hears and responds to minority communities could push the police toward better partnerships with those communities.

The Elected Prosecutor's Place in Police Accountability

Police officers work in bureaucracies and answer to their superiors within the department. The head of the department, in turn, answers to the public in one way or another. Sheriffs, the chief law enforcement officials at the county level, are normally elected, while police chiefs are normally appointed by local elected officials, such as mayors or city councils. The result is an extremely fragmented organizational picture, with over seventeen thousand separate law enforcement agencies in the United States.[1]

Prosecutors in the United States do not sit at the top of any police hierarchy and therefore do not directly supervise police work.[2] Instead, a prosecutor receives a file (the end product of a police investigation) and decides whether to start a criminal case based on the facts that the police uncovered. If the police develop criminal cases in ways that reflect racial bias—for instance, by stopping black motorists and asking for consent to search their cars more often than they do other motorists—the prosecutor can push back.[3] A prosecutor might dismiss cases more often if they derive from questionable police practices; prosecutors could also reduce their sentencing recommendations to address concerns about the racial effects of mass incarceration.[4] Or they can prioritize some crimes over others to reflect the current worries and safety priorities of the local community. The criminal prosecutor, better than any other single official in criminal justice, can shift the racial impact of criminal enforcement.

Because prosecutors hold the final decision over whether to use police work-product in criminal cases, as a practical matter they train and advise law enforcement agencies in their local areas. If a new court case or some other legal development calls for a change in police techniques, the local prosecutor is likely to educate the officers about the new law. Prosecutors also stay in contact with police officers during their most complex and extended investigations, advising them how to stay clear of legal troubles. Individual prosecutors for some types of cases (particularly homicides, serious sexual assaults, and drug-trafficking matters) talk by phone routinely with the officers who investigate those cases, and sometimes go to the scene of the crime themselves to offer advice. Prosecutors also exert influence after the investigation ends. If some police officers ignore the prosecutor's training and do unreliable work, the prosecutor might discount cases from those officers or refuse to call them as witnesses at trial.

When it comes to the excessive use of force by police officers, local prosecutors once again have only indirect control. The police department itself trains officers in the use of force, or arranges for its officers to get training and certification from regional or statewide groups. The police department also declares and enforces its own policies on the use of force.

If an officer uses too much force during an arrest or some other encounter, the police department collects the relevant facts. The leadership in the department then decides how to respond internally to a misbehaving officer, considering the full range of bureaucratic tools, including demotion, further training, reassignment, or doing nothing.

The local prosecutor supplements this internal review by police supervisors in a potential case of excessive police force. In extreme cases, a prosecutor might file charges against the officer for a crime such as assault or a civil rights violation. In most states, the prosecutor can file charges directly without getting permission from anybody else. In other jurisdictions, the prosecutor might present the evidence to a grand jury and ask those citizens to decide whether to endorse criminal charges.[5] In various ways, therefore, prosecutors can shape the work of police departments and individual officers as they police black men.

While all prosecutors share in this work to some degree, most of the responsibility goes to prosecutors who work in state courts. The greatest share of criminal cases in the United States pass through the state courts rather than federal courts: more than 90 percent of all felony convictions and virtually all misdemeanor convictions happen in state courts. Not surprisingly, the states employ far more prosecutors than the federal government does—about five times more.[6] The state courts also take the lead in cases with special meaning for police work: police misconduct cases generally land in state court based on criminal charges such as assault or extortion.

To be sure, federal prosecutors do have the legal authority to file criminal charges in federal court against state or local police officers who violate the federal civil rights of the public. Those federal cases, however, are rare.[7] There simply are not enough federal prosecutors assigned to police misconduct complaints to process all the potential cases. The proof of intent required under the federal civil rights law is also extremely difficult to find. By default, prosecutors working in the state courts have the best resources and the most ready legal tools to respond when extreme police misconduct violates the criminal law.

Holding State Prosecutors Accountable Through Elections

If state prosecutors occupy such an important place in shaping police conduct, how do we make sure that prosecutors do the job well? Surprisingly, the answer does not come from the criminal law itself. The criminal codes in the United States are both too broad and too deep to control the work of prosecutors very closely. The criminal codes in each state are broad, in the sense that statutes use ambiguous terms that could possibly cover a great deal of conduct. The codes are also deep, because they pile up so many charging options for prosecutors to consider in a given factual situation; in effect, prosecutors can choose among several different punishment levels for a single criminal incident.[8] In this world of broad and deep criminal codes, we necessarily depend on prosecutors to use their discretion and to apply the criminal law in some cases, but not in every case that the language might conceivably reach. They must use their broad powers with wisdom and restraint.

Because the language in the criminal code does not set up serious guideposts for prosecutors, other methods are necessary to make sure that prosecutors enforce the criminal law in a way that the community accepts. In the United States, we accomplish this through local election of state court prosecutors. In forty-five of the fifty states, the chief prosecutors are elected at the local level. Their titles vary—district attorney, state's attorney, county attorney, or commonwealth attorney—and their offices vary enormously in size, from fewer than a half-dozen assistant prosecutors to more than eight hundred prosecuting attorneys in a single office. But in each case, the chief prosecutor in the local office sets the charging priorities and the litigation policies for all prosecutions of state crimes that happen within that local district. The district boundaries might reach only a single county, or they might encompass a few less-populated counties.

Local prosecutor elections create a radically decentralized criminal justice system. While the budgets for state prosecutors' offices depend largely on state funds in most states, or a blend of state and local tax dollars for other offices, the ultimate political responsibility for spending that budget rests with the chief prosecutor in the local district. Once elected to a term of office, the chief prosecutor has no boss other than the local voters. The district office is not part of a single hierarchy that answers to the state attorney general or to the governor of the state. Instead, the local office of the prosecutor applies the state criminal code by filing charges in state court, trying to prove the case to the judges and juries.

The attorney general in some states has the authority to

prosecute certain specialized cases (for instance, environmental crimes or public corruption cases), and the chief prosecutors in local offices can invite the attorney general's office to help with cases involving conflicts of interest.[9] Such "referrals" probably offer the best method of prosecuting police misconduct cases. The local prosecutor needs to maintain smooth working relationships with police departments in the district, and the filing of criminal charges against an officer could sour those relationships. The state attorney general can evaluate a possible case against a local police officer without such a conflict of interest.[10] This solution to the conflict-of-interest problem, however, remains the exception rather than the rule. Most local prosecutors keep for themselves the decision about whether to file charges when a police officer allegedly violates the criminal law. They point out that criminal cases based on alleged police misconduct are the ultimate test of prosecutor independence and offer a real chance to earn the community's trust.

In the five states that do not elect prosecutors at the local level, the chief prosecutor who runs the local office is one or two steps removed from the voters. In Alaska, Delaware, and Rhode Island, the elected state attorney general appoints the supervising prosecutor, who sets office policies and priorities for each local district. In New Jersey, the governor appoints the county attorneys, who run their local offices. And in Connecticut, the Criminal Justice Commission, which is composed of several gubernatorial nominees, appoints all of the state's attorneys.[11]

The federal courts represent an exception to the rule for American prosecutors. The prosecutors who enforce the federal criminal laws by filing charges in federal court—known as United States Attorneys—are appointed rather than elected. The president appoints the United States Attorneys who supervise each of the ninety-three district offices around the country. Those U.S. Attorneys, unlike the chief state prosecutors, all work within a single bureaucracy—the U.S. Department of Justice—and answer to the U.S. attorney general.

This system of a single bureaucracy for prosecutors is familiar in other parts of the world, where new prosecutors join a national bureaucracy when they enter the profession and spend their entire careers as prosecutors. Their careers as civil servants depend on following the priorities and policies of the Ministry of Justice. Thus, most countries promote responsible prosecution through bureaucratic oversight rather than prosecutor elections.[12]

Do Elections Work?

When viewed from afar, through the telescopic lens of political theory, the election of prosecutors looks promising. Prosecutors deal with a limited range of public policy questions that are important to the voters, those affecting their physical safety. Prosecutors also answer to small, localized constituencies. This combination of conditions—issues with salience to voters, happening at the local level—should in theory force prosecutors to listen to and carry out the voters' wishes. If the election system could work as designed, prosecutors would respond vigorously to police misconduct.

Unfortunately, prosecutor elections do not operate according to the political theory textbook. In the United States, local elections do not tell voters very much about the basic policy priorities and enforcement strategies in the prosecutor's office. Chief prosecutors do not hear any mandate from local voters to monitor police officers more closely. These elections fail because they produce low turnover and few challenges.

Nationwide surveys of chief prosecutors tell us in general terms that turnover in office happens slowly. According to the most recent national census of state prosecutors, the average chief prosecutor is in office for nine and a half years, a number that has slowly increased over the years.[13] The typical prosecutor's office is run by a veteran, not by a person recently put into office by the voters: only about one-third of prosecutor's offices have leaders who have been in office for less than five years.

Chief prosecutors stay in office for a long time because the voters keep them there. On the basis of election outcome data I have collected from sixteen states, it appears that incumbent prosecutors win re-election at an extremely high rate.[14] Incumbents win 94 percent of the races they enter and 69 percent of the races they run against challengers, even higher than the incumbency success rates for state legislators.

It is not just that incumbents win their races so often: incumbent prosecutors rarely face challengers at all. As table 1 indicates, 80 percent of prosecutor incumbents run unopposed in general elections and 82 percent in primaries. State legislative incumbents, by comparison, run unopposed in only 35 percent of their elections.[15] When challengers fail to appear on the scene, the incumbents never have to discuss or justify their office procedures or priorities to the public, and they receive no voter feedback in response. Thus, an elected prosecutor who does a poor job of holding law enforcement accountable probably does not become a larger target for the next campaign season. Even when the prosecutor's relationship to law enforcement agencies fails to match the public's expectations, the voters don't notice and don't switch their votes to a campaign challenger.

Are these results typical for all categories of prosecutors? Many chief prosecutors lead offices that employ few attorneys, in districts with relatively low populations. Table 2 sets those smaller offices aside and describes the election outcomes in the largest urban jurisdictions where the prosecutors' decisions most often affect black residents. Incumbent prosecutors in high-population districts ran for re-election at about the same rate as the incumbents from smaller districts (just over 70 percent of the time). A difference appears, however, in the number of

Table 1: Opposition to Incumbents in Prosecutor Elections

	GENERAL ELECTIONS	PRIMARY ELECTIONS
All Races	2653	2138
Incumbent Runs	2014	1522
	(76% of all races)	(71% of all races)
Incumbent Unopposed	1612	1253
	(80% of incumbent races)	(82% of incumbent races)
Incumbent Wins	1891	1429
	(94% of incumbent races)	(94% of incumbent races)
Incumbent Wins when opposed	279	176
	(69% of opposed incumbent races)	(65% of opposed incumbent races)

challenges that the incumbents faced in larger jurisdictions. The percentage of unopposed incumbents went down from 80 percent for all races to 55 percent for races in the larger districts. On the other hand, incumbent prosecutors won a higher percentage of contested elections in the urban districts (78 percent of them, compared to 66 percent in the smaller districts). Apparently, larger districts attract weaker challengers.

Table 2: Outcomes in Prosecutor Elections, Districts with Over 100K Votes Cast

All Races	263
Incumbent Runs	193
	(73% of all races)
Incumbent Unopposed	106
	(55% of all incumbent races)
Incumbent Wins	174
	(90% of all incumbent races)
Incumbent Wins When Opposed	68
	(78% of all opposed incumbent races)

One reason for the high rate of unopposed incumbents in prosecutor elections generally may be the difficulty of recruiting challengers. The pool of interested candidates might remain small because challengers have a great deal to lose from an unsuccessful electoral bid.[16] Based on a study of fifty-four contested general elections, more than half of the challengers had prosecutorial experience, and about 20 percent of them worked in the incumbent's office at the time of the election. Most of the other challengers worked as criminal defense attorneys.

In this setting, a challenger who runs against the incumbent and loses will pay a price after election day. The assistant prosecutor who unsuccessfully tries to unseat the boss will likely have to leave the office and find new employment. Those few challengers who remain in the office are not likely to get further promotions or plum assignments. Given these costs, it is a wonder that incumbents face challengers in almost 20 percent of the elections after they decide to run.

Even in the small number of campaigns that produce challengers to the incumbents, campaign rhetoric during the election cycle does not create real prosecutor accountability either. Candidates tend to focus on their individual qualifications rather than the performance of the entire office. For instance, candidates talk about their number of years in practice, with particular emphasis on the number of years spent in prosecution.

When the campaign rhetoric does turn to office performance, the candidates usually discuss a handful of recent prominent criminal trials, such as a newsworthy murder trial or public corruption charges against a local mayor or other government official. The candidates rarely discuss any topics related to office management, such as the backlog of cases awaiting disposition in court or the practices of the office related to plea bargaining or screening of cases that the local police recommend for prosecution. Campaign speeches and debates generally remain silent about the prosecutor's relationship to the local police department. The forest is lost for the trees.[17]

In sum, the chief prosecutor in most cities or counties can expect to keep the job for many years and to run unopposed most of the time. Over 90 percent of the incumbents who want to return to prosecutorial office are re-elected, even in the largest and most competitive jurisdictions. The typical incumbent prosecutor will cruise to re-election and will not have to explain her performance to voters in a competitive atmosphere. Thus, the relationship between the prosecutor and local law enforcement agencies does not attract voter attention in most election campaigns. A prosecutor who is too protective of the police or indifferent to their abusive investigations or improper uses of force does not, in most places, have to explain those choices to the voters.

Granted, elections might affect prosecutors despite the overwhelming advantages that incumbents hold. District attorneys might look over their shoulders and perform their duties *as if* a challenger could appear in the next election cycle. The potential for a voter revolt might keep the prosecutor focused on local views. Studies do show some election-season effects: prosecutors' offices produce slightly more trials and convictions, and slightly fewer dismissals, during the year before an election.[18] Those effects, however, appear to be small. With success rates over 90 percent for incumbents, one must wonder how much a possible loss on a future election day could truly matter to chief prosecutors as they set office priorities and their relationships with local law enforcement agencies.

The Racial Divide Between Communities and Their Prosecutors

As we have seen, there is a potential gap between prosecutor office policies and the views of the local voters. Elections do not force prosecutors to explain their policies to the voters very often, and the voters do not often reject incumbents. At the same time, chief prosecutors talk and act as if majority community views matter. So the bottom line for police accountability is equivocal: public views about the proper relationship between the prosecutor and the police might matter, or they might not.

The impact of elections is even more complex when we consider the different ways that prosecutors might interact with voters from minority communities. Elections place different pressures on prosecutors, depending on whether black voters amount to a majority of voters in the district or make up only a small portion of the voters in the larger community. Let us consider each of these scenarios.

First, state election law sometimes draws the boundaries of the prosecutorial district to place black voters into a small voting bloc. In that situation, the views of black voters about the best way to run the local prosecutor's office tend to get outvoted. For those districts, prosecutor elections likely make no difference for the black community, even in those rare times when elections operate as well as they should.

Minority voters in St. Louis County recently found themselves in this quandary. The jurisdiction received intense national media coverage after the death of a young black man, Michael Brown, during an altercation with a police officer in the suburb of Ferguson in August 2014. The elected prosecutor for the county, Robert McCulloch, asked a grand jury to decide whether to charge the officer with homicide or some other crime. In the view of some observers (myself included), McCulloch manipulated the grand jury into refusing to indict the officer. Whether or not that is a fair assessment, it is certainly true that minority voters in Ferguson and elsewhere in St. Louis County were unhappy with McCulloch's response to police misconduct, both in this case and in other similar cases over the years.

Despite this voter unhappiness, McCulloch had been reelected every four years since the early 1990s. Indeed, he cleared a nominal challenge in the Democratic primary election earlier in 2014, and ran unopposed in the 2014 general election. Given that African American residents (living mostly on the north side of the county) make up about a quarter of the county's population and typically account for only 15 percent of the vote, McCulloch had little reason to respond to their views.[19] The views of black voters about the relationship between McCulloch and the local police presented no threat. The incumbent prosecutor was safe so long as the majority of voters from the south side of the county approved of his dealings with the police—or so long as they remained ignorant or indifferent, as voters often do.

There is, however, a second scenario. In some prosecutorial districts, African American residents amount to a majority of the voters in the district. Even where they do not account for the majority of registered voters, they might combine with a coalition of other voters who have similar preferences for police oversight and criminal law enforcement. In districts such as these, a tighter connection between the voters and the performance of the prosecutor might produce better results for the African American community. Better prosecutor elections could mean better criminal justice priorities and better prosecutor supervision of the local police.

One example comes from the city of St. Louis, where city residents (including a stronger minority voter presence than in McCulloch's suburban district) in 2016 elected a new prosecutor. Kimberly Gardner campaigned on a promise to "restore trust in the criminal justice system" after the events surrounding Michael Brown's shooting. Although her opponent had more prosecutorial experience and received an endorsement from the St. Louis Police Officers' Association and the city's principal newspaper, Gardner handily won in the primary and faced no opposition in the general election. She described her election as a chance to "heal" the relationships between the community and its police and prosecutors.[20]

Other examples suggest how minority voters might demand more from their prosecutors, insisting on a different sort of relationship with the police. In the 2016 electoral cycle, a few challengers in major cities defeated incumbent prosecutors, based in part on campaigns calling for more serious oversight of police. For instance, challenger Kim Foxx won a primary election in Chicago after she criticized the incumbent, Anita Alvarez, for a slow and non-transparent response to the police shooting of an unarmed teenager, Laquan McDonald. Alvarez had charged an officer, but only after an investigation lasting over a year; she filed the charges only hours before the court-ordered release of a graphic video recording of the shooting. Foxx declared her intentions to hold more bad cops "accountable for their actions" and lamented that "trust in our criminal justice system has been broken." The *Chicago Tribune* treated Foxx's easy primary victory as "a referendum on [Alvarez's] handling of high-profile prosecutions, particularly when police misconduct is alleged."[21]

The same could be said for the 2016 election loss of incumbent Cleveland prosecutor Tim McGinty, who did not charge a police officer who shot and killed Tamir Rice, a twelve-year-old African American child who was playing with a toy gun outside a city recreation area. While challenger Michael O'Malley did not claim that he would have decided differently in the Rice case, he did criticize McGinty's poor relationships with the community and the police. O'Malley promised that he would "build bridges in communities." He also declared that he would lobby for a statewide law to require the state attorney general to handle all investigations and prosecutions of officer-involved cases of deadly force.[22]

Election outcomes in a few cities do not amount to a sustainable national trend in prosecutor elections. At this point, the stories remain more anecdote than data. How many districts include a large bloc of minority voters who might begin to take prosecutor elections more seriously? There is no national database that reveals how many prosecutorial districts include enough black voters to translate their political power into the election of chief prosecutors with compatible views. One database, assembled in 2015 by the Women Donors Network, reports the name, gender, and race of the elected prosecutors in over 2,400 districts. Their analysis indicates that over 95 percent of the elected prosecutors are white.[23]

In some districts, it seems, prosecutor elections could draw more attention and energy among minority voters, making them more like elections for other citywide or countywide offices. Given the success of African American voters in electing mayors and city council members, there are probably districts where the voting power of the black community has not yet reached the prosecutor elections. In those places, replacing an incumbent with a challenger who better reflects the views of black voters could make a difference for police accountability.

Election Law and Locally Responsive Prosecutors

The current system of prosecutor elections does not reliably create prosecutors who know and respond to the views of the entire community. Instead, incumbent prosecutors can stay in office even when they listen to some voters in the district but not to others.

A few changes to election law could make a difference. With a better set of rules, election campaigns for prosecutors might become more competitive. They could give prosecutors more reason to listen broadly to the voters in their district, because even small blocs of voters might be necessary for victory when the elections tend to be closer. Given the right voting rules, minority voters could truly become part of the "public" that gives marching orders to the prosecutor.

A first step would address the laws that disenfranchise people who are convicted of a felony, even after they complete their sentence and return to society. These felon disenfranchisement laws have a disproportionate impact on African American men.

Changes to these laws that restore voting rights to felons on a routine basis at the successful conclusion of their criminal sentence would profoundly change the racial profile of the electorate in some states.[24] Prosecutors who answer to this expanded group of voters might hear a different set of priorities about how to monitor the police.

Another change to election laws might be to schedule more prosecutor elections in high-turnout presidential election years. Again, this structural change would broaden the base of citizens who raise their voices to set the enforcement priorities of a local prosecutor. The timing would have a stronger impact in minority communities, where the difference in voting turnout between presidential elections and off-year elections is more pronounced.

Perhaps the most important change to consider would be to create new boundaries for prosecutorial districts. A great deal of thought and litigation goes into the drawing of district lines for state and local legislative bodies. Both federal and state law encourage boundaries that do not dilute the political power of minority voters in city councils, county commissions, and state legislatures. The same level of care should go into the drawing of prosecutorial districts.

New boundaries of voting districts could offer better protection to impoverished neighborhoods by making the minority of voters from a larger district into the majority of voters in a smaller district. Each of the prosecutors in the new smaller districts would deliver a different blend of enforcement priorities, intrusions, expenditures, and public safety, customized to the preferences of their own communities.

Alternatively, a state might achieve the same objective of a locally responsive prosecutor through a single statewide election for the state's chief prosecutor, who then appoints the chief of each local district office for the prosecutorial service. This approach characterizes the prosecutorial services in Alaska, Connecticut, Delaware, and New Jersey. In each of these states, the voters choose a single chief prosecutor for the state (either the attorney general or the chief state's attorney). This elected official provides the necessary popular control, assuring the voters that prosecutors throughout the state will carry out the public's highest priorities for public safety. At the same time, the elected statewide prosecutor appoints (or, in Connecticut, heads a commission that appoints) the chief prosecutor for each of the local district offices around the state.

The realities of geographic dispersion of local offices and a busy agenda for the attorney general mean that the local offices necessarily have some autonomy. They are free to develop their own cultures and local community ties. Under the right circumstances, this hybrid system of elections and appointments can produce prosecutors who are responsive both to the needs of their local communities and to the input from local courtroom actors. Prosecutors who answer to smaller communities are more likely to respond to the concerns and hopes of minority voters—at least if those smaller communities are defined with a sensitivity to the distinctive wishes of the African American community.

Whether a state adopts smaller electoral districts for local prosecutors or instead asks local appointees to run regional offices of a single statewide prosecutorial service, the larger strategy is a prosecutor who responds to local concerns. Those local priorities for criminal enforcement may differ across regions and communities in the state, because the urban-rural divide reflects a serious distance in terms of values. Burglaries might be the highest concern for residents of some areas, while residents in other parts of the same state might put more weight on assault cases. Police use of force or aggressive stop-and-frisk techniques might attract more community concern in some parts of the state than in others.

In short, the same criminal code in a state might look quite different in everyday practice, depending on the choices of the local prosecutor to allocate resources. The coexistence of different "criminal procedures" in a single state is not lawless or troubling. It is the essence of prosecutorial discretion in the United States.

Conclusion

A slender thread runs from the black community, through the local prosecutor's office, to the local police. Too often, this cord breaks and policing is untethered from community views. The ties between communities and their prosecutors do matter, however, and there are unexplored methods for strengthening those ties. Part of the answer lies in voter education and mobilization. African American communities need to recognize that the local prosecutor occupies one of the most important lines on the election ballot.

More vigorous control over prosecutors by an alert and determined set of voters may, under the right conditions, give those voters the sort of police accountability that they want. The conditions for success are not always present. In the suburbs of St. Louis County, African American voters will probably not be able to elect a prosecutor who supervises the local police in the way that they prefer. They will simply be outvoted.

On the other hand, the criminal justice system in the United States is remarkably fragmented. There are over 2,400 prosecutor offices and more than 17,000 law enforcement agencies in this country, each of them answerable to local voters. Somewhere within that intricate and chaotic collection of organizations, there are spaces for African Americans to use their votes and to obtain the blend of police accountability and crime control that suits them best.

RESOURCES

Asp, Peter. "The Prosecutor in Swedish Law." *Crime and Justice* 41 (2012): 141–66.
Bandyopadhyay, Siddhartha, and Bryan McCannon. "The Effect of the Election of Prosecutors on Criminal Trials." *Public Choice* 161 (2014): 141–56.
Barkow, Rachel E. "Federalism and Criminal Law: What the Feds Can Learn from the States." *Michigan Law Review* 109 (2011): 519–80.

Byrne, John, and Hal Dardick. "Foxx: Cook County State's Attorney Win About 'Turning the Page.'" *Chicago Tribune*, March 16, 2016.

Currier, Joel. "Former Prosecutor Turned State Rep Takes St. Louis Circuit Attorney Primary." *St. Louis Post-Dispatch*, Aug. 3, 2016.

Dyke, Andrew. "Electoral Cycles in the Administration of Criminal Justice." *Public Choice* 133 (2007): 417–37.

Ellis, Michael J. "The Origins of the Elected Prosecutor." *Yale Law Journal* 121 (2012): 1528–69.

Harmon, Rachel. "Limited Leverage: Federal Remedies and Policing Reform." *St. Louis University Public Law Review* 32 (2012): 33–56.

Levine, Kate. "Who Shouldn't Prosecute the Police." *Iowa Law Review* 101 (2016): 1447–96.

Manza, Jeff, and Christopher Uggen. *Locked Out: Felon Disenfranchisement and American Democracy*. New York: Oxford University Press, 2006.

Miller, Marc L., and Ronald F. Wright. "The Black Box." *Iowa Law Review* 94 (2008): 125–96.

Perry, Steven W., and Duren Banks. *Prosecutors in State Courts, 2007—Statistical Tables*. Washington DC: Office of Justice Programs, Bureau of Justice Statistics, 2011.

Reaves, Brian A. *Census of State and Local Law Enforcement Agencies, 2008*. Washington, DC: Office of Justice Programs, Bureau of Justice Statistics, 2011.

Shaffer, Cory. "Tamir Rice Looms over Debate for Cuyahoga County Prosecutor." *Cleveland Plain Dealer*, Feb. 23, 2016.

Somashekhar, Sandhya. "Black Voters in St. Louis County Direct Their Anger at the Democratic Party." *Washington Post*, Oct. 14, 2014. Available at https://www.washingtonpost.com/politics/black-voters-in-st-louis-county-direct-their-anger-at-the-democratic-party/2014/10/14/e6957b8a-4f02-11e4-aa5e-7153e466a02d_story.html.

Squire, Peverill. "Uncontested Seats in State Legislative Elections." *Legislative Studies Quarterly* 25 (2000): 131.

Stuntz, William J. "The Pathological Politics of Criminal Law." *Michigan Law Review* 100 (2001): 505–600.

Tonry, Michael. "Prosecutors and Politics in Comparative Perspective." *Crime and Justice* 41 (2012): 5–23.

Wright, Ronald F. "Beyond Prosecutor Elections." *SMU Law Review* 67 (2014): 593–615.

———. "Public Defender Elections and Public Control of Criminal Justice." *Missouri Law Review* 75 (2010): 803–29.

———. "How Prosecutor Elections Fail Us." *Ohio State Journal of Criminal Law* 6 (2009): 581–610.

NOTES

1. Reaves, *Census*, 2.

2. In most parts of the world, prosecutors have formal authority to supervise the

work of the police. As the case file develops, the prosecutor can order the police to develop some leads and to ignore others. If the police elsewhere in the world do their jobs badly, prosecutors can discipline them. Asp, "Prosecutor in Swedish Law," 147.

3. Sharon LaFraniere and Andrew W. Lehren, "The Disproportionate Risks of Driving While Black," *New York Times*, Oct. 24, 2015.

4. Miller and Wright, "Black Box," 161–66.

5. See Roger A. Fairfax Jr., "The Grand Jury and Police Violence Against Black Men," in this volume.

6. State prosecutor offices employ over 27,000 full-time attorneys; U.S. attorneys employ about 6,000 attorneys, both civil and criminal. Perry and Banks, *Prosecutors*, 2; Executive Office for United States Attorneys, "United States Attorneys' Annual Statistical Report, Fiscal Year 2010," 2.

7. Harmon, "Leverage," 33.

8. Stuntz, "Pathological," 512.

9. Barkow, "Federalism," 545.

10. Levine, "Prosecute," 18.

11. Wright, "Beyond Prosecutor Elections." For a history of the use of elections for state prosecutors in the United States, see Ellis, "Origins," 1528.

12. Tonry, "Comparative," 5.

13. Perry and Banks, *State Prosecutors*, table 5.

14. The data are drawn from elections held between 1998 and 2015 in the following states: California, Colorado, Florida, Georgia, Hawaii, Idaho, Indiana, Maine, Massachusetts, Minnesota, New Mexico, New York, North Carolina, Oregon, Texas, and Wisconsin.

15. Squire, "State Legislative Elections," 132–33.

16. Wright, "Public Defender Elections."

17. Wright, "How Prosecutor Elections Fail."

18. Dyke, "Electoral Cycles"; Bandyopadhyay and McCannon, "Effect of Election."

19. Somashekhar, "Black Voters in St. Louis."

20. Currier, "Former Prosecutor."

21. Byrne and Dardick, "Foxx."

22. Shaffer, "Rice Looms over Debate."

23. The data appear at http://wholeads.us/justice/.

24. Manza and Uggen, *Locked Out*.

Do Black Lives Matter to the Courts?

JIN HEE LEE AND SHERRILYN A. IFILL

Hands Up, Don't Shoot[1] . . . Again and Again

On September 15, Johnny Robinson, a sixteen-year-old black teenager, was among hundreds—if not thousands—of protesters demanding justice for the African American community in Birmingham, Alabama.[2] As protests broke out in the city, the governor ordered five hundred members of the National Guard and three hundred state troopers to support city police and sheriff's deputies at the request of local authorities.[3] Police arrested nineteen black men and women for charges that included "refusing to obey the command of an officer" and "disorderly conduct."[4] Young Johnny Robinson purportedly had been throwing stones at a car when he fled from police down an alley.[5] As he was running, Officer Jack Parker shot him in the back and killed him.[6] A grand jury was convened, but it declined to indict Officer Parker.[7]

The year was 1963, and the protests were in response to the horrific and infamous bombing of the 16th Street Baptist Church in Birmingham, which killed four young black girls. That was more than fifty years ago, but the shooting death of Johnny Robinson—and the failure to indict Officer Parker—could have been taken from today's headlines. The undeniable truth is that black men, women, and children have long been the victims of state violence. Government-sanctioned slavery, which took the lives of millions of Africans forced into servitude, gave way to a government-sanctioned convict leasing system[8] and lynchings[9] during the Jim Crow era. The pervasiveness of lynchings across the Deep South led the NAACP to unfurl that now famous flag outside its New York City office, declaring "A Man Was Lynched Yesterday."[10]

The NAACP Legal Defense and Educational Fund* has been at the heart of the struggle against state-sanctioned violence against black men, women, and children from the early days of its founding by Thurgood Marshall, who would later become the first African American appointed to the United States Supreme Court. Gilbert King's Pulitzer Prize–winning book, *Devil in the Grove: Thurgood Marshall, the Groveland Boys, and the Dawn of a New America*,[11] masterfully retells Justice Marshall's death penalty representation of Walter Irvin, one of four young black men who were falsely accused of raping a white woman in Lake County, Florida. In 1951, Mr. Irvin and a co-defendant, Samuel Shepherd, were shot and left for dead by the county sheriff, Willis McCall, while they were in his custody.[12] Mr. Shepherd died from the shooting, but Mr. Irvin survived by pretending to be dead.[13] Like so many law enforcement officers who have used excessive force on black bodies, Sherriff McCall was never held accountable for his crime and went on to serve another twenty years.[14]

The number of black individuals brutalized or killed at the hands of law enforcement is too numerous to recount fully, in large measure because there is no mandatory reporting requirement or database that provides reliable information on police-involved killings. The 1991 videotaped beating of Rodney King by Los Angeles Police Department officers unleashed a brewing outrage among communities of color across the country that had suffered from police abuse, culminating in the 1992 civil unrest,

---

* The NAACP Legal Defense Fund is an entirely separate organization from the NAACP and has been since 1975.

often referred to as the "LA Riots," which ensued after the officers involved in the King beating were acquitted of all criminal
charges.[15] Mass protests also erupted after the brutal assault of
Abner Louima, who had been forcibly sodomized with a broom
handle by New York City Police Department (NYPD) officers
in 1997.[16] Two years later, in 1999, plainclothes NYPD officers
shot Amadou Diallo forty-one times as he was taking his wallet out of his jacket.[17] In 2006, Sean Bell was shot and killed by
NYPD officers the night before his wedding.[18] On New Year's
Day in 2009, Oscar Grant was shot in the back by a Bay Area
Rapid Transit (BART) police officer in Oakland, California,
while being restrained on a subway platform.[19]

On July 17, 2014, Eric Garner died on Staten Island, New
York, after stating repeatedly "I can't breathe" as Officer Daniel
Pantaleo placed him in a choke hold while trying to arrest him
for selling loose cigarettes.[20] Less than a month later, eighteen-
year-old Michael Brown was shot and killed by Officer Darren
Wilson on August 8, 2014, in Ferguson, Missouri—his body left
on the street for four hours—sparking widespread protests.[21]
On April 4, 2015, in North Charleston, South Carolina, Officer
Michael Slager fatally shot Walter Scott in the back as he was
running away.[22] Freddie Gray died from a spinal cord injury on
April 12, 2015, while in custody in a police van in Baltimore,
Maryland,[23] which unleashed days of civil unrest.[24] And in two
consecutive days of tragedy—July 5 and July 6, 2016—Alton
Sterling was killed from close-range gunshots in the back while
restrained on the ground by two officers in Baton Rouge, Louisiana,[25] and Philando Castile was driving in a suburb of St. Paul,
Minnesota, when he was shot and killed by an officer during a
traffic stop in front of his girlfriend and four-year-old daughter.[26] These are merely a few of the incidents that have captured
media attention in the past few years, but it is unclear how many
more police-involved deaths and beatings of black individuals
have occurred without widespread public notice.[27]

Throughout history, the police-involved killings of black

individuals have been intimately connected to the racially discriminatory policing that has plagued communities of color for generations. The National Advisory Commission on Civil Disorders (known as the "Kerner Commission" after the commission's chair, Illinois governor Otto Kerner Jr.) was established by President Lyndon Johnson on July 28, 1967, in response to the widespread civil unrest in black communities all across the United States in the summer of 1967.[28] After an exhaustive study, the Kerner Commission concluded that "[o]ur nation is moving towards two societies, one black, one white—separate and unequal."[29]

As part of its findings, the commission noted:

> The police are not merely a "spark" factor. To some Negroes police have come to symbolize white power, white racism and white repression. And the fact is that many police do reflect and express these white attitudes. The atmosphere of hostility and cynicism is reinforced by a widespread belief among Negroes in the existence of police brutality and in a "double standard" of justice and protection—one for Negroes and one for whites.[30]

The Kerner Commission further opined that the police had become "a symbol not only of law, but of the entire system of law enforcement and criminal justice," such as the "assembly-line justice in teeming lower courts"; "widespread disparities in sentences"; "antiquated correctional facilities"; and "the basic inequities imposed by the system on the poor."[31] At the core of the commission's recommendations was the need for a national agenda to address and remedy the entrenched racial inequality in employment, education, the welfare system, and housing.[32]

Almost fifty years later, the United States Department of Justice's (DOJ) investigations of the Ferguson Police Department and the Baltimore Police Department detailed similar systemic racial discrimination that reflects the "'double standard' of justice" identified by the Kerner Commission. On March 4, 2015, the DOJ's Civil Rights Division issued an exhaustive report of its investigation of the Ferguson Police Department in the aftermath of Michael Brown's shooting death, concluding

> Ferguson's approach to law enforcement both reflects and reinforces racial bias, including stereotyping. The harms of Ferguson's police and court practices are borne disproportionately by African Americans, and there is evidence that this is due in part to intentional discrimination on the basis of race. Ferguson's law enforcement practices overwhelmingly impact African Americans.[33]

The following year, the Civil Rights Division issued another report, detailing the results of its comprehensive investigation of the Baltimore Police Department after Freddie Gray's death.[34] The report found that officers had "engage[d] in a pattern or practice of . . . (1) making unconstitutional stops, searches, and arrests; (2) using enforcement strategies that produce severe and unjustified disparities in the rates of stops, searches, and arrests of African Americans; (3) using excessive force; and (4) retaliating against people in constitutionally-protected expression."[35]

Similar to the findings of the Kerner Commission, the racial injustices of Ferguson's criminal justice system did not rest solely with the police department, but also implicated city officials and municipal courts in their focus on generating revenues from municipal fines and fees.[36] Thus, "[o]ver time, Ferguson's police and municipal court practices have sown deep mistrust between parts of the community and the police department, undermining law enforcement legitimacy among African Americans in particular."[37] And echoing the Kerner Commission's "two societies," the Baltimore Report noted "a long history of social and economic challenges that impact much of [Baltimore], including the perception that there are 'two Baltimores:' one wealthy and largely white, the second impoverished and predominately black."[38]

The police-involved killings of black individuals are merely the tip of the iceberg in terms of the systemic racial discrimination in law enforcement agencies across the country. At the heart of this discrimination is the automatic association between "blackness" and criminality that is the product of the long-standing dehumanization of black people throughout American history.[39] Burgeoning scientific studies on "implicit bias" have proven this to be the case: people unconsciously connect black people with dangerous weapons, animals, and aggressive behavior.[40] The activist cry that "Black Lives Matter,"[41] therefore, urges a fundamental reconfiguring of the societal hardwiring that presumes the dangerousness and criminality of black people by virtue of their race.[42]

Yet, despite the need for court intervention to remedy the entrenched racial discrimination within the criminal justice sphere, the American judicial system has done a poor job of protecting and vindicating the rights of people of color victimized by police. Through a series of regressive judicial opinions, the United States Supreme Court has embraced a color-blind vision of American society that is patently at odds with the lived experiences of people of color, especially in the context of our criminal justice system. As a result, the courts function in a distorted reality that only recognizes racial discrimination in a specific and distinct form: overt racial animus by a specific actor. This completely ignores the systemic racism that has endured throughout our nation's history.

Race matters. It matters in our daily lives, and it matters in our social institutions. And it certainly matters in people's interactions with the police. Yet, despite the common knowledge that the black community has a specific history with racism in law enforcement—a history that informs current police-community relations—the courts' resistance to meaningfully redress systemic racial discrimination has created a disconnect between law and reality. Amid the current crisis with "policing the black man,"[43] this disconnect compels us to question whether the courts can be a driving force in the adjudication of justice for black people who have suffered at the hands of law enforcement. In other words, do Black Lives Matter to the courts?

Equal Protection's Unfulfilled Promise

For most of its history, the United States Supreme Court has had a sordid history of dealing with race in this country. In the infamous 1857 case of *Dred Scott v. Sanford*, the Supreme Court did not recognize black people—whether free or slave—as American citizens with rights under the United States Constitution.[44] Dred Scott was a black slave who was taken by his owner from Missouri, a slave state, to Illinois, where slavery was illegal under the Missouri Compromise. After returning to Missouri, Mr. Scott and his wife, Harriet, attempted to sue for their freedom in federal court; however, the lower court ruled that, as a slave, Mr. Scott was not a citizen and was not entitled to seek redress of any kind in the court system. The Scotts appealed, but the lower court was affirmed by the Supreme Court in a 7–2 decision, declaring that black people "are not included, and were not intended to be included, under the word 'citizens' in the Constitution, and can therefore claim none of the rights and privileges which the instrument provides for and secures to citizens of the United States."[45]

The Supreme Court went on to state that black individuals "had for more than a century before" the adoption of the United States Constitution "been regarded as beings of an inferior order, and altogether unfit to associate with the white race, either in social or political relations; and so far inferior, that they had no rights which the white man was bound to respect."[46] Thus, a state "may give the right to free [N]egroes and mulattoes, but that does not make them citizens of the States, and still less of the United States. And the provision in the Constitution giving privileges and immunities in other states, does not apply to them."[47] In other words, it made no difference whether a free state prohibited slavery within its borders: even free African Americans were not "citizens"—and, thus, had no rights—under the Constitution.

It took the Civil War and ratified amendments to the United States Constitution before the equal rights of black people were secured. The ratification of the Thirteenth Amendment (prohibiting slavery and involuntary servitude),[48] the Fourteenth Amendment (recognizing birthright citizenship and the "due process" and "equal protection" rights of all persons),[49] and the Fifteenth Amendment (guaranteeing the right to vote regardless of race, color, or prior servitude)[50] following the end of the Civil War heralded a radical reordering of power in our country and ensured the full citizenship of former slaves and other African Americans. The language of these "Reconstruction Amendments" established a new limitation on state power. In particular, the words "no state shall" in the Fourteenth Amendment recognized that the states constituted a powerful threat to black citizenship, thus requiring the "equal protection of the laws" to establish the equality of all persons regardless of race.

Ratification of the Reconstruction Amendments—combined with the provisions of the Civil Rights Act of 1866,[51] which enumerated an array of rights that the Reconstruction Congress associated with the exercise of citizenship, and the Freedmen's Bureau Act,[52] which established a government agency to assist former slaves in their transition from enslavement to freedom—produced a legal framework that would protect the physical safety, voting rights, and economic rights of African Americans. The result was the most profound and sweeping change in the American electorate as millions of new citizens were added to this country after the 1868 ratification of the Fourteenth Amendment, which guaranteed the citizenship of "*[a]ll* persons born or naturalized in the United States.[53] The rights to vote, serve on juries, testify in court, enter into contracts, and own property were some of the key guarantees of that citizenship.

But, in short order, this period of an expansive imagining of black citizenship gave way to retrenchment and ultimately reversal. Reconstruction—and the project of black citizenship—ended with the removal of federal troops from key southern states as part of the Compromise of 1877[54] and a series of Supreme Court decisions that gutted the equal protection provisions of the Fourteenth Amendment.[55] It would take decades of painstaking litigation and the civil rights movement to return to the promise of the Reconstruction Amendments. But even with the passage of expansive new legislation protecting employment[56] and voting[57] rights and outlawing segregated public accommodations[58] and housing,[59] key elements of the backlash against Reconstruction proved to be stubbornly resilient due to three powerful and consistent interpretive impediments that have hindered the development and application of robust civil rights legal protections: racial exhaustion, the intent standard, and the narrative of reverse discrimination. These interpretive elements, which have their roots in the Supreme Court's early post-Reconstruction jurisprudence, reemerged in the years after the retirement of Chief Justice Earl Warren in 1969[60] to narrow and constrict the potential and reach of legal protections of civil rights.

Racial Exhaustion

A creeping sense of what the scholar Darren Hutchinson calls "racial exhaustion"[61] was in full effect by 1883 when the Supreme Court decided the *Civil Rights Cases*, a consolidation of five cases challenging the refusal of private business owners to serve African Americans at a public lodging, theater, and railroad car.[62] These discriminatory acts were in direct violation of the Civil Rights Act of 1875,[63] which were intended to protect the rights

of newly freed slaves. In its interpretation of this critical legislation, the Supreme Court took an unnecessarily narrow view of
the Thirteenth and Fourteenth amendments, finding that they
did not authorize Congress to enact legislation that prohibited
discriminatory acts by private individuals, as opposed to governmental actors. Thus, the Supreme Court struck down the Civil
Rights Act of 1875 and paved the way for the Jim Crow laws
throughout the Deep South.

Shockingly, less than twenty years after Emancipation, the
Supreme Court's decision in the *Civil Rights Cases* began criticizing the "special protections" sought by African Americans after
generations of dehumanization and forced servitude:

> When a man has emerged from slavery, and by the aid of
> beneficent legislation has shaken off the inseparable con-
> comitants of that state, there must be some stage in the
> progress of his elevation when he takes the rank of a mere
> citizen, and ceases to be the special favorite of the laws, and
> when his rights as a citizen, or a man, are to be protected
> in the ordinary modes by which other men's rights are
> protected. There were thousands of free colored people
> in this country before the abolition of slavery, enjoying all
> the essential rights of life, liberty, and property the same as
> white citizens; yet no one, at that time, thought that it was
> any invasion of their personal *status* as freemen because they
> were not admitted to all the privileges enjoyed by white
> citizens, or because they were subjected to discriminations
> in the enjoyment of accommodations in inns, public con-
> veyances, and places of amusement. Mere discriminations
> on account of race or color were not regarded as badges of
> slavery.[64]

By the time the Supreme Court decided *Plessy v. Ferguson* in
1896, upholding the "separate but equal" justification for state-

sanctioned racial segregation,[65] it had fully abdicated any significant role in ensuring equality for black people. In this case, Mr. Plessy, the person challenging the *de jure* segregation, was seven-eighths white and one-eighth black.[66] Even though "the mixture of colored blood was not discernible in him," Mr. Plessy was still "forcibly ejected" and "imprisoned" for refusing to leave the coach of a passenger train reserved for white passengers.[67] In upholding this separation of races, the Supreme Court in *Plessy*, like in the *Civil Rights Cases*, continued its retreat from the robust vision of equality contemplated by the Reconstruction Congress. Indeed, the Supreme Court in *Plessy* commented that any "assumption that the enforced separation of the two races stamps the colored race with a badge of inferiority" is "solely because the colored race chooses to put that construction on it."[68] By delineating a false distinction between political equality and social equality, the Court surrendered its responsibility to ensure the full measure of equal citizenship: "If the civil and political rights of both races be equal, one cannot be inferior to the other civilly or politically. If one race be inferior to the other socially, the constitution of the United States cannot put them upon the same plane."[69]

Thus, what we now see as successful twentieth-century civil rights litigation—with *Brown v. Board of Education*[70] at its center—was largely a project focused on compelling the federal courts to accept its proper role to ensure that the promise of the Reconstruction Amendments would not be subverted and derailed by the states. It was only after nearly a hundred years and a decades-long strategic battle by civil rights lawyers that the Supreme Court returned the federal courts to the proper role of protecting the rights guaranteed by the Reconstruction Amendments.

Meanwhile, outside the courtroom, grassroots activists were waging a similar battle in Congress. Beginning with the Civil Rights Act of 1957,[71] which created the DOJ's Civil Rights Division, a series of hard-fought and stunning legislative victories—the Civil Rights Act of 1964,[72] the Voting Rights Act of 1965,[73] and the Fair Housing Act of 1968[74]—created an infrastructure of civil rights protections. The Supreme Court, led by Chief Justice Earl Warren, played a powerful role in the constitutional affirmation of the civil rights movement by upholding both the Voting Rights Act of 1965 and the Civil Rights Act of 1964 after they were subjected to immediate and sustained legal challenges.[75]

But in the years following Chief Justice Warren's tenure, the Supreme Court once again evinced its impatience with the effort to achieve the promises of equality. For example, in cases challenging affirmative action, questions about "how long" ameliorative efforts would need to be made to combat and prevent racial discrimination began to appear with frequency and force in the Supreme Court's decisions.[76] This obsession with identifying an expiration date for the legal mechanism enforcing racial equality was most expressly stated by Justice Sandra Day O'Connor in her 2003 majority opinion in *Grutter v. Bollinger*, which upheld race-conscious admissions at the University of Michigan Law School, but predicted "that 25 years from now, the use of racial preferences will no longer be necessary to further the interest" of student diversity.[77] Amid the current crises of heightened educational[78] and residential[79] segregation, income and job inequality,[80] and mass incarceration,[81] that prediction seems hardly within reach.

Discriminatory Intent

The centerpiece of the Supreme Court's approach to antidiscrimination protections has been to confine the definition of illegal discrimination to those acts that are motivated by intentional racial animus. The "intent" requirement—or the conscious desire to discriminate—has led the Supreme Court to burden civil rights plaintiffs with the obligation to prove the unspoken motivation of a defendant supervisor, school board, election registrar, or law enforcement officer. The primacy of "discriminatory intent," as necessary to prove racial discrimination, was established by the Supreme Court in *Washington v. Davis*,[82] a constitutional challenge to a personnel test used to hire and promote police officers in Washington, D.C., based on the facts that black test takers were four times as likely to fail as their white counterparts and that the test was not proven to be an adequate measure of job performance.

The Supreme Court rejected the idea that the discriminatory impact of the test was sufficient to establish a constitutional violation.[83] Writing for the majority in *Washington v. Davis*, Justice Byron White declared that "we have not held that a law, neutral on its face and serving ends otherwise within the power of government to pursue, is invalid under the Equal Protection Clause simply because it may affect a greater proportion of one race than of another."[84] Proof of discriminatory intent, the Supreme Court held, was the key to invalidating a statute or practice that negatively affected racial minorities.

In a concurring opinion, Justice John Paul Stevens agreed with the disposition of the case but expressed skepticism about the discriminatory purpose requirement, suggesting that courts should instead adopt a flexible approach that is adaptive to the circumstances of the case. He cautioned:

> [I]t is unrealistic, on the one hand, to require the victim of alleged discrimination to uncover the actual subjective intent of the decisionmaker or, conversely, to invalidate otherwise legitimate action simply because an improper motive affected the deliberation of a participant in the decisional process. . . . [T]he line between discriminatory purpose and discriminatory impact is not nearly as bright, and perhaps not quite as critical, as the reader of the Court's opinion might assume.[85]

He went on to say that this is true "when the disproportion" is so "dramatic" that "it really does not matter whether the standard is phrased in terms of purpose or effect."[86]

Justice Stevens's skepticism has been echoed by critics of the "discriminatory intent" framework, which fails to acknowledge how racial discrimination actually exists within American society and the nature of its harm to people of color.[87] As Professor Charles Lawrence aptly noted, "By insisting that a blameworthy perpetrator be found before the existence of racial discrimination can be acknowledged, the Court creates an imaginary world where discrimination does not exist unless it was consciously intended."[88] The discriminatory intent doctrine impedes enforcement of constitutional protections against racial discrimination by imposing an almost impossible burden given that discriminatory motives are easily hidden and multiple decision-makers are often involved.[89] Moreover, focusing on discriminatory intent ignores the fact that victims of racial discrimination suffer from very real injuries regardless of whether those injuries were intentionally inflicted: "Does the black child in a segregated school experience less stigma and humiliation because the local school board did not consciously set out to harm her? Are blacks less prisoners of the ghetto because the decision that excludes them from an all-white neighborhood was made with property values and not race in mind?"[90]

Color Blindness and Reverse Discrimination

Justice John Marshall Harlan famously dissented from *Plessy v. Ferguson*, declaring that "our Constitution is color-blind."[91] However, in the 1970s and 1980s, that declaration was turned on its head in the name of "protecting" white students, contractors, and employees.[92] The narrative and manufactured reality of a "reverse discrimination" entitled to legal protection was a skillful manipulation of antidiscrimination principles. The concept of "reverse discrimination" not only used the Fourteenth

Amendment to deny opportunity and legal protection to African Americans in direct contravention of the Reconstruction Amendments' purpose, it was also put on the same doctrinal footing as the use of race to promote opportunity and equality for African Americans. Notwithstanding the radically divergent histories of discrimination experienced by black and white individuals in the United States, both were viewed as "suspect" and received the Supreme Court's "strict scrutiny," meaning that consideration of either race is constitutionally invalid under the Constitution unless narrowly tailored to meet a compelling state interest—a standard that is very difficult to meet.[93]

The historical inconsistency of this logic was eloquently explained by Justice Thurgood Marshall: "The Congress that passed the Fourteenth Amendment is the same Congress that passed the 1866 Freedmen's Bureau Act, an Act that provided many of its benefits only to Negroes. . . . Indeed, the bill was bitterly opposed" by many congressmen "on the ground that it 'undertakes to make the negro in some respects . . . superior . . . and gives them favors that the poor white boy in the North cannot get.'"[94] Thus, opponents of affirmative race conscious legislation were claiming "reverse discrimination" shortly after the Civil War, but the same Congress that passed the Fourteenth Amendment soundly defeated those claims.

Although equating actions designed to fulfill the intent of the Equal Protection Clause of the Fourteenth Amendment (that is, actions designed to remediate the impact of slavery and ensure that black individuals have full and fair access to the rights of citizenship) with actions designed to subordinate black people and deny their full citizenship might seem to be a doctrinal absurdity, the ahistorical principle that *any* consideration of race should be treated equally has become the guiding standard set by the Supreme Court. This adherence to the notion of color-blindness ensures that any actions taken by government actors to correct the imbalances created by white supremacy and complex policies of racial subordination are treated as harshly as the most diabolical efforts to subvert African American advancement.

The nadir of the Supreme Court's application of this doctrine came in its 2006 decision, *Parents Involved v. Seattle School District No. 1*,[95] which struck down even the modest, voluntary efforts of school districts in Seattle and Kentucky to promote integrated schools. A majority of the Supreme Court equated the school districts' laudable integration efforts with pernicious racial discrimination simply because the school districts considered the race of students in some aspects of their school-assignment plans in order to promote racial balance. The current chief justice, John Roberts, dismissed nearly 150 years of antidiscrimination efforts with a stunningly simplistic tautology, declaring that "the way to stop discrimination on the basis of race is to stop discriminating on the basis of race."[96] However, as Justice Sonia Sotomayor noted in her dissenting opinion in a separate case, "The way to stop discrimination on the basis of race is to speak openly and candidly on the subject of race, and to apply the Constitution with eyes open to the unfortunate effects of centuries of racial discrimination. As members of the judiciary tasked with intervening to carry out the guarantee of equal protection, we ought not sit back and wish away, rather than confront, the racial inequality that exists in our society."[97]

Criminal Injustice in Color-Blind Courts

Taken together, racial exhaustion, the search for intentional racism, and the narrative of reverse racism have strangled an expansive and flexible use of civil rights laws to protect people of color. Those obstacles prevent people of color, and black people in particular, from addressing racial inequalities within the criminal justice system. A contemporary example of how racial exhaustion and reverse discrimination remain obstacles to the achievement of racial justice and civil rights is the proclamation "All Lives Matter" in response to the Black Lives Matter movement. Rather than acknowledging the distinct, historical dehumanization of black people, which has been characterized by their treatment by law enforcement, the focus on "all lives" diminishes the specific injustices faced by "black lives."[98]

The Movement for Black Lives and similar movements, as well as the recent public focus on police-involved killings of black individuals, lay bare the racial discrimination that is inherent in police violence against black people. However, the Supreme Court's interpretation of "equal protection" under the Fourteenth Amendment imposes significant barriers to bringing claims of racially discriminatory policing in court. The requirement that victims of police abuse demonstrate the discriminatory intent of specific law enforcement actors thwarts the ability of courts to adjudicate and remedy the systemic discriminatory forces that are often endemic to police practices. Thus, racism—the elephant in the room—too often remains a silent courtroom witness even though it is at the forefront of public discourse and attention in the burgeoning movement for racial fairness in the criminal justice system.

The Search for Discriminatory Intent

In order to successfully prove race discrimination under the Fourteenth Amendment of the United States Constitution, a black victim of police violence must prove discriminatory intent. This means that statistics demonstrating even stark racial disparities are not, in and of themselves, sufficient evidence to prove discrimination. For example, in a 1987 Supreme Court case, *McCleskey v. Kemp*, the NAACP Legal Defense and Educational Fund presented extensive statistical evidence of racial disparities in Georgia's death penalty system: "prosecutors sought the death penalty in 70% of the cases involving black defendants and white victims; 32% of the cases involving white defendants and white victims; 15% of the cases involving black defendants and black victims; and 19% of the cases involving white defendants and black victims."[99] The Supreme Court specifically acknowledged that there was "a discrepancy that appears to correlate with race."[100] Nevertheless, in a 5–4 decision, the Supreme Court concluded that these compelling statistics alone were not sufficient to prove a "discriminatory purpose,"[101] and characterized the racial disparities as "an inevitable part of our criminal justice system."[102]

The Supreme Court also expressed concern that if it "accepted [the] claim that racial bias has impermissibly tainted the capital sentencing decision, we could soon be faced with similar claims as to other types of penalty," which "throws into serious question the principles that underlie our entire criminal justice system."[103] In other words, the more racial disparities existed throughout the criminal justice system, the less open the Supreme Court was to considering racial disparities as evidence of discrimination: otherwise, the entire criminal justice system would be in jeopardy. Justice William Brennan, in his dissenting opinion, called this line of thinking "a fear of too much justice."[104] And we now know—as we deal with the painful consequences of mass incarceration—that the Supreme Court's "fear of too much justice" has wreaked havoc in the black community. Indeed, Justice Lewis Powell—who authored the majority opinion and cast the deciding vote—famously conceded years later that *McCleskey* was the one case that he would have decided differently in his growing opposition to the death penalty during his retirement.[105]

Brown v. City of Oneonta is a racial profiling case decided in 2000 by a federal appeals court in New York that stands as another example of the obstacles imposed by the intent requirement.[106] The case arose in the small upstate New York town of Oneonta, which had a population of only 10,000 residents and 7,500 students in a local college, only about 2–3 percent of whom were black. On September 29, 1992, a seventy-seven-year-old woman was attacked by someone she described as a young black man with a cut on his hand from their struggle during the attack.[107] The victim admitted that she suspected that the assailant was young only because he walked quickly.[108] This vague description prompted the local police to stop and question every nonwhite person on the street and every black student at the local college.[109] The fact that this police action disproportionately affected the black residents and students of Oneonta was found to be insufficient to prove racial discrimination because the court found no evidence of discriminatory animus.[110] Even the fact that a black *woman* was stopped and questioned by police, which the appeals court conceded may have shown that the police "considered race more strongly than other parts of the victim's description," was not enough to establish racial discrimination under the Fourteenth Amendment.[111] There was little outcry when the Supreme Court refused to hear this case just a few weeks after the September 11 terrorist attacks in New York City and Washington, D.C.

Thus, the intent requirement has imposed substantial—and often insuperable—barriers for private citizens[112] seeking to attack structural discrimination in the criminal justice system, including claims of racial discrimination against police officers and police departments. Proof that discrimination is systemic and widespread necessarily relies on data of police activity, but court decisions like *McCleskey* and *Oneonta* require evidence of discriminatory intent or racial animus that is difficult to prove. While there have been successful race discrimination challenges to police practices—for example, the New York City "stop-and-frisk" case, *Floyd v. City of New York*, in which a district court concluded after a bench trial that "the NYPD has a policy of indirect racial profiling based on local criminal suspect data" and "that senior officials in the City and at the NYPD have been deliberately indifferent to the intentionally discriminatory application of stop and frisk at the managerial and officer levels"[113]— they are few and far between. The practical result has been closure of the courthouse doors to challenges to the kind of race discrimination that black people experience on a daily basis. As a result, there has been no meaningful opportunity to develop a body of law that substantively seeks to redress the injuries from that discrimination—all to the detriment of the many black people who have suffered at the hands of the police.

Criminal Prosecutions to Vindicate Rights

One of the most frequently articulated frustrations of the black community is the lack of accountability for police abuse, especially for the unjustified killings of black individuals. Despite the high burden of proof in criminal prosecutions—which requires proof "beyond a reasonable doubt"—the conviction of individual police officers would offer some vindication for the widespread misconduct faced by communities of color at the hands of police departments as a whole. Yet, because there is so little faith that local prosecutors—who routinely have close ties to local law enforcement—will fairly seek justice, questions persist about the existence of a double standard for law enforcement defendants. Examples of this include the local prosecutors' failure to indict Ferguson Officer Darren Wilson for the killing of Michael Brown and NYPD Officer Daniel Pantaleo for the murder of Eric Garner. Both decisions sparked widespread protests across the country.[114] Similarly, incumbent prosecutors in Chicago and Cleveland were voted out of office and replaced by lesser-known challengers, in large part due to criticisms of their handling of the prosecutions of police officers responsible for killing seventeen-year-old Laquan McDonald and twelve-year-old Tamir Rice.[115] Thus, as one scholar commented, "[a]s was true in the decade following the Civil War, the failure of states to police their police leaves to the federal government the task of pursuing prosecutions against those who abuse their official authority to brutalize civilians."[116]

The statute that authorizes federal prosecutions of police killings and other instances of excessive use of force by police is 18 U.S.C. § 242 ("Section 242"), which forbids "[w]hoever, under color of any law, statute, ordinance, regulation, or custom, [from] willfully subject[ing] any person in any State, Territory, Commonwealth, Possession, or District to the deprivation of any rights, privileges, or immunities secured or protected by the Constitution or laws of the United States."[117] As part of the Civil Rights Act of 1866,[118] Section 242 "increased the level of power and the presence that the federal government had over those states (and persons within those states) who were resistant to ensuring that the basic rights of African Americans were met."[119] In essence, "Section 242 is aimed at public officers who abuse the constitutional or statutory rights of others,"[120] especially emancipated slaves.

The seminal Supreme Court case explaining Section 242 is *Screws v. United States*,[121] which was decided over seventy years ago, in 1945. The majority opinion begins by stating that "[t]his case involves a shocking and revolting episode in law enforcement,"[122] and then describes the following facts:

Petitioner Screws was sheriff of Baker County, Georgia.[123] He enlisted the assistance of petitioner Jones, a policeman, and petitioner Kelley, a special deputy, in arresting Robert Hall, a citizen of the United States and of Georgia. The arrest was made late at night at Hall's home on a warrant charging Hall with theft of a tire. Hall, a young negro about thirty years of age, was handcuffed and taken by car to the court house. As Hall alighted from the car at the court house square, the three petitioners began beating him with their fists and with a solid-bar blackjack about eight inches long and weighing two pounds. They claimed Hall had reached for a gun and had used insulting language as he alighted from the car. But after Hall, still handcuffed, had been knocked to the ground they continued to beat him from fifteen to thirty minutes until he was unconscious.[124]

Robert Hall subsequently died from the injuries from this savage beating.[125]

In prosecuting Sheriff Screws and his accomplices, the federal government charged them with "'willfully' caus[ing] Hall to be deprived of 'rights, privileges, or immunities secured or protected' to him by the Fourteenth Amendment—the right not to be deprived of life without due process of law; the right to be tried, upon the charge in which he was arrested, by due process of law and if found guilty to be punished in accordance with the laws of Georgia."[126] In other words, federal prosecutors argued that the Constitution required law enforcement in Baker County to try and, if convicted, punish Mr. Hall through the court system rather than by beating him to death for the alleged offence of stealing a tire. Notably, willful deprivation of Mr. Hall's right to "equal protection under the laws," which prohibits discriminating against Mr. Hall under the Fourteenth Amendment, was not included in the charges—although the *Screws* Court noted in its recounting of Section 242's history that "[in origin it was an antidiscrimination measure . . . framed to protect negroes in their newly won rights."[127]

Sheriff Screws and his codefendants had been convicted by a jury, but the Supreme Court threw out the conviction and remanded the case for another trial because the jury did not have a proper understanding of the term "willfully." According to the Supreme Court in *Screws*, it was not sufficient that the defendants willfully killed Mr. Hall: the defendants must have also had the specific intent to willfully deprive him of a constitutional right, in this case "the right to be tried by a court rather than by ordeal."[128] Thus, in order to federally prosecute someone under Section 242, not only must "the suspect . . . have violated a person's rights," he or she must also have "intended to do so."[129]

The Supreme Court explicitly recognized that its interpretation of "willfully" made Section 242 "less severe."[130] In fact, the Supreme Court opined that "willfully" was added by Congress into the statute so that "its severity" would "be lessened by making it applicable only where the requisite bad purpose was present, thus requiring specific intent not only where discrimination is claimed but in other situations as well."[131] The Supreme Court recognized that there was a high bar to proving racial discrimination as a constitutional violation due to the intent requirement, and the *Screws* decision carried this high bar over to proving other forms of constitutional violations by also requiring proof of specific intent, thereby making it more difficult to federally prosecute someone for the deprivation of those constitutional violations.[132]

Forty years after the *Screws* decision, the Supreme Court began evaluating claims of excessive—and even deadly—force by police officers under the Fourth Amendment's prohibition against unreasonable search and seizure rather than other constitutional provisions.[133] As established by the Supreme Court, the "test of reasonableness under the Fourth Amendment . . . requires careful attention to the facts and circumstances of each particular case, including the severity of the crime at issue, whether the suspect poses an immediate threat to the safety of the officers or others, and whether he is actively resisting arrest or attempting to evade arrest by flight."[134] Moreover, when evaluating the reasonableness of an officer's actions, the Supreme Court cautioned "that police officers are often forced to make split-second judgments—in circumstances that are tense, uncertain, and rapidly evolving—about the amount of force that is necessary in a particular situation."[135]

Legal scholars have been critical of the Supreme Court's Fourth Amendment "reasonableness test" as it pertains to excessive force by police officers because, in practice, it provides insufficient guidance to lower courts handling these types of claims.[136] But what constitutes "reasonableness" should exact even more scrutiny in the context of police killings of black people, given the phenomenon of implicit bias.[137] Individuals such as police officers have a greater risk of interpreting ambiguous behavior of a black person as a threat, when compared to the behavior of a white person.[138] Indeed, a black person is more likely than a white person to be perceived to have a gun, as opposed to a tool,[139] and more likely to be shot when unarmed.[140] These automatic, yet baseless, associations between race and dangerousness—derived from generations of false and dehumanizing stereotypes of blackness—are even more likely to occur when making the type of "split-second judgments" that the Supreme Court acknowledged were common for police officers.[141]

History is replete with instances of police officers going unpunished for killing a black man. "[A]fter the conclusion of the *Screws* case, Claude Screws was elected to the Georgia State Senate."[142] Thus, justice was denied, as it had been in the killing of Johnny Robinson by Officer Jack Parker in Birmingham, Alabama, and the shooting of Walter Irvin by Sheriff Willis McCall in Lake County, Florida. More recently, the DOJ declined to prosecute Officer Darren Wilson under Section 242 for the killing of Michael Brown, concluding that Officer Wilson was justified in using lethal force because "it was not unreasonable for [him] to perceive that Brown posed a threat of serious physical harm, either to him or to others,"[143] and Officer Wilson did not act "willfully" or "for the specific purpose of violating the law"[144] because "his intent in shooting Brown was in response to a perceived deadly threat."[145] What exactly happened moments before Michael Brown's death has been disputed, as well as the purported threat that Officer Wilson claimed to have experienced. But missing from the analysis of Officer Wilson's culpability and the reasonableness of his actions is his employment and training in a police department with a now-documented history of persistent discrimination against the black residents of Ferguson,[146] as well as the role race may have played in Officer Wilson's perception of threat. Not surprisingly, race was not mentioned once in the DOJ's eighty-six-page report regarding the federal criminal investigation into the shooting death of Michael Brown.

Conclusion

Both the Fourteenth Amendment to the United States Constitution and Section 242 were enacted in the aftermath of the Civil War and the emancipation of millions of enslaved African Americans. Their express purpose was to ensure the equal rights of black people given a long-standing history of legally imposed and sanctioned racial inferiority and human degradation. Yet, despite the specific origins of these legal protections, the Supreme Court has, over the years, taken a restrictive and constrained view of the courts' ability and authority to address— and redress—the injuries emanating from twenty-first-century manifestations of racial discrimination. The Supreme Court's overly simplistic and formalistic understanding of racial discrimination has stunted the development of a more robust body of antidiscrimination law that would directly and substantively deal with the evolving nature of racism, especially as it pertains to the policing of black individuals.

As the courts become less available as a legal recourse for systemic racial discrimination in policing, communities have turned to prosecutions of individual officers as remedies for police abuse, especially police-involved killings of black people. Yet, these prosecutions have often been sources of great disappointment, whether from prosecutors' routine failure to seek or secure an indictment or from a judge or jury's decision not to convict. Criminal prosecutions are, of course, subject to the highest burden of proof in the judicial system (proof beyond a reasonable doubt), and criminal defendants (regardless of who they are) are entitled to a presumption of innocence. When it comes to prosecutions of police officers accused of killing black victims, however, there is a legitimate concern about the existence of a double standard with respect to how much evidence establishes a reasonable doubt and how much of a presumption of innocence officers receive, as compared to the black criminal defendants who come from the same communities as the black victims of police abuse.

For both civil actions challenging systemic racial discrimination in law enforcement agencies, as well as criminal prosecutions of individual police officers, courts—led by the Supreme Court—have made it difficult to litigate issues of race, especially the real-world forms of discrimination experienced by black individuals at the hands of law enforcement in the present day. The primacy of "discriminatory intent" as the only actionable form of racial discrimination under the Fourteenth Amendment's Equal Protection Clause presumes that discrimination exists only as deliberate and malicious acts by individuals, rather than embedded within the fabric of many of our social institutions, especially our law enforcement agencies with their long history of racial violence toward the black community. Additionally, criminal prosecutions for alleged acts of police abuse are often devoid of a race context that informs the reasonableness of an accused officer's perceptions of his or her own safety and the communities that are most heavily policed.

The challenge in the coming years for civil rights lawyers and activists alike is to advance a more effective body of equal protection and antidiscrimination law that directly tackles the messy, complicated, emotionally fraught, and eminently important problem of racial discrimination in our country. This is especially true in the context of our manifestly flawed and unfair criminal justice system, which for generations has magnified deep-seated racial stereotypes of black people as violent, dangerous, and criminal. It is, therefore, incumbent on all of us to continue the struggle that began with Emancipation and the passage of the Reconstruction Amendments to fully and substantively secure our nation's promise of equality for all. Through legal advocacy, we must not only protect the significant advances that have been made in battling race discrimination, but also push the courts to do more. Simultaneously, activists on the ground must document and demonstrate, in stark detail, the shortcomings of our legal system and demand real and meaningful progress for those who have suffered the most.

The road ahead will not be easy, especially given our increasingly conservative judiciary and the slowly evolving nature of constitutional jurisprudence. But there has recently been a glimmer of hope in a remarkable dissenting opinion, written in 2016 by Justice Sonia Sotomayor, the first Latina member of the Supreme Court. The case, *Utah v. Strieff*, concerned the admissibility of evidence seized during a search incident to an arrest for an outstanding warrant, where the initial investigatory stop was unquestionably illegal.[147] The majority of the Supreme Court held that such evidence was "admissible because the officer's discovery of the arrest warrant attenuated the connection between the unlawful stop and the evidence seized incident to arrest."[148] Justice Sotomayor's dissent begins by explaining how the majority ruling contradicted longstanding Supreme Court precedent "to exclude illegally obtained evidence" whenever " 'lawless police conduct' uncovers evidence of lawless civilian conduct" in order to "remove an incentive for officers to search us without proper justification."[149]

The extraordinary portion of Justice Sotomayor's dissent, however, was Part IV, which sadly no other Supreme Court Justice joined. She cataloged the many ways that condoning unlawful stops could lead to "treating members of our communities as second-class citizens": the degradation of being stopped for any pretextual justification that may include your ethnicity, residence, clothes, and behavior; possible searches of a bag or purse or frisks of your body in front of passersby; and all the indignities attendant to an arrest.[150] Most remarkably, Justice Sotomayor wrote directly about the racial implications of police malfeasance. Citing the work of Michelle Alexander, W.E.B. Du Bois, James Baldwin, and Ta-Nahesi Coates, Justice Sotomayor eloquently explained the particular harm of the Supreme Court's ruling on people of color:

> The white defendant in this case shows that anyone's dignity can be violated in this manner. . . . But it is no secret that people of color are disproportionate victims of this type of scrutiny. . . . For generations, black and brown parents have given their children "the talk"—instructing them never to run down the street; always keep your hands where they can be seen; do not even think of talking back to a stranger—all out of fear of how an officer with a gun will react to them. . . . We must not pretend that the countless people who are routinely targeted by police are "isolated." . . . Until their voices matter too, our justice system will continue to be anything but.[151]

We should not underestimate the power of a member of our highest court writing so specifically and pointedly about the Supreme Court's impact on those whom the Reconstruction Amendments were aimed to protect. Harkening back to the revelatory opinions of Justice Thurgood Marshall, Justice Sotomayor undoubtedly drew upon her experiences as both a litigator and a person of color in her effort to ground Supreme Court jurisprudence in the lived experiences of actual people. As Justice Sotomayor expressly recognized, Supreme Court decisions do not exist in a vacuum, but instead have real and significant consequences on people's daily lives. Those consequences are no less important for black individuals who fall victim to police abuse and who should be able to turn to the courts to protect and vindicate their rights as equal members of our society.

NOTES

1. "Hands up, don't shoot" has been a rallying cry for those protesting the shooting death of Michael Brown on August 8, 2014, as well as other unarmed black individu-

als, despite the controversy as to whether Michael Brown actually held his hands up when he was shot by Officer Darren Wilson. See Cheryl Corely, "Whether History or Hype, 'Hands Up, Don't Shoot' Endures," National Public Radio, August 8, 2015, http://www.npr.org/2015/08/08/430411141/whether-history-or-hype-hands-up -dont-shoot-endures.

2. Claude Sitton, "Birmingham Bomb Kills 4 Negro Girls in Church; Riots Flare; 2 Boys Slain," *New York Times*, September 16, 1963, http://www.nytimes.com/learning/ general/onthisday/big/0915.html#article; UPI, "Six Dead After Church Bombing," *Washington Post*, September 16, 1963, http://www.washingtonpost.com/wp-srv/ national/longterm/churches/archives1.htm.

3. Sitton, "Birmingham Bomb Kills."

4. "23 Negroes Arrested," *Birmingham Post-Herald*, September 16, 1963, http:// bplonline.cdmhost.com/u?/p4017coll2,537.

5. UPI, "Six Dead After Church Bombing."

6. Sitton, "Birmingham Bomb Kills"; Carrie Johnson, "Johnny's Death: The Untold Tragedy in Birmingham," National Public Radio, September 15, 2010, http://www.npr.org/templates/story/story.php?storyId=129856740.

7. Johnson, "Johnny's Death."

8. See generally David M. Oshinsky, *"Worse Than Slavery": Parchman Farm and the Ordeal of Jim Crow Justice* (New York: Simon & Schuster, 1997); Douglas A. Black- mon, *Slavery by Another Name: The Re-Enslavement of Black Americans from the Civil War to World War II* (New York: Doubleday, 2008).

9. See generally Equal Justice Initiative, *Lynching in America: Confronting the Leg- acy of Racial Terror* (2d ed. 2015).

10. The artist Dread Scott explicitly made the link between this famous flag and the recent crisis of police-involved shootings of black men and women. See Corinne Segal, "This Flag Once Protested Lynching. Now It's an Artist's Response to Police Violence," *PBS NewsHour*, July 10, 2016, http://www.pbs.org/news hour/art/this-flag-once-protested-lynching-now-its-an-artists-response-to-police -violence/.

11. Gilbert King, *Devil in the Grove: Thurgood Marshall, the Groveland Boys, and the Dawn of a New America* (New York: HarperCollins, 2012).

12. Ibid., 232–33, 242–43.

13. Ibid.

14. Ibid., 357.

15. "The L.A. Riots: 24 Years Later," *Los Angeles Times*, April 28, 2016, at http:// timelines.latimes.com/los-angeles-riots/.

16. Vinette K. Pryce, "A Week of Outrage, Pain and Celebration: Thousands March Across B'klyn Bridge in Search of Justice," *Amsterdam News*, September 10, 1997, 1.

17. Michael Cooper, "Officers in Bronx Fire 41 Shots, and an Unarmed Man Is Killed," *New York Times*, February 5, 1999, http://www.nytimes.com/1999/02/05/ nyregion/officers-in-bronx-fire-41-shots-and-an-unarmed-man-is-killed.html.

18. Robert D. McFadden, "Police Kill Man After a Queens Bachelor Party," *New York Times*, November 26, 2006, http://nyti.ms/2a7YLgb.

19. Jill Tucker, Kelly Zito, and Heather Knight, "Deadly BART Brawl—Officer

Shoots Rider, 22," *San Francisco Chronicle*, January 2, 2009, http://www.sfchronicle
.com/bayarea/article/Deadly-BART-brawl-officer-shoots-rider-22-3178373.php.

20. Al Baker, J. David Goodman, and Benjamin Mueller, "Beyond the Choke-hold: The Path to Eric Garner's Death," *New York Times*, June 13, 2015, https://www
.nytimes.com/2015/06/14/nyregion/eric-garner-police-chokehold-staten-island
.html.

21. "Tracking the Events in the Wake of Michael Brown's Shooting," *New York Times*, November 24, 2014, http://www.nytimes.com/interactive/2014/11/09/us/10
ferguson-michael-brown-shooting-grand-jury-darren-wilson.html.

22. Michael S. Schmidt and Matt Apuzzo, "South Carolina Officer Is Charged with Murder of Walter Scott," *New York Times*, April 7, 2015, http://www
.nytimes.com/2015/04/08/us/south-carolina-officer-is-charged-with-murder-in
-black-mans-death.html.

23. Kevin Rector, "The 45-Minute Mystery of Freddie Gray's Death," *Baltimore Sun*, April 25, 2015, at http://www.baltimoresun.com/news/maryland/freddie-gray/
bs-md-gray-ticker-20150425-story.html.

24. Jon Swaine, "Baltimore Freddie Gray Protests Turn Violent as Police and Crowds Clash," *The Guardian*, April 26, 2015, https://www.theguardian.com/us-news/
2015/apr/25/baltimore-freddie-gray-protests-violence-police-camden-yards.

25. Richard Fausset, Richard Pérez-Peña, and Campbell Robertson, "Alton Ster-ling Shooting in Baton Rouge Prompts Justice Dept. Investigation," *New York Times*, July 6, 2016, http://www.nytimes.com/2016/07/06/us/alton-sterling-baton-rouge
-shooting.html.

26. Kyle Potter, "AP News Guide: Details about the Philando Castile Shoot-ing," *Minneapolis Star Tribune*, July 8, 2016, http://bigstory.ap.org/article/e0ba0539c
b924e0ca3709ca96849f679/ap-news-guide-details-about-philando-castile-shooting.

27. According to *The Guardian*'s "The Counted," an online resource of people killed by police in the United States, 266 black individuals were killed in 2016, con-stituting 6.66 per million black persons killed, as compared to 2.9 per million white individuals killed by police. "The Counted," *The Guardian*, https://www.theguardian
.com/us-news/ng-interactive/2015/jun/01/the-counted-police-killings-us-database.

28. National Advisory Commission on Civil Disorders, *Report of the National Advisory Commission on Civil Disorders* (Washington, DC: U.S. Government Printing Office, 1968), 1.

29. Ibid.

30. Ibid., 5.

31. Ibid., 157.

32. Ibid., 229–63.

33. U.S. Department of Justice, Civil Rights Division, "Investigation of the Fer-guson Police Department" (Washington, DC: 2015), 4, https://www.justice.gov/sites/
default/files/opa/press-releases/attachments/2015/03/04/ferguson_police_depart
ment_report.pdf. The report details shocking racial disparities in the Ferguson Police Department's law enforcement activities: (1) "African Americans account for 85% of vehicle stops, 90% of citations, and 93% of arrests made by FPD officers, despite comprising only 67% of Ferguson's population"; (2) "African Americans are more

than twice as likely as white drivers to be searched during vehicle stops . . . , but are found in possession of contraband 26% less often than white drivers"; (3) "African Americans are more likely to be cited and arrested following a stop regardless of why the stop was initiated and more likely to receive multiple citations during a single incident"; and (4) "[n]early 90% of documented force used by FPD officers was used against African Americans." Ibid., 4–5. These disparate results do not reflect "any difference in the rate at which people of different races violate the law," but rather "occur, at least in part, because of unlawful bias against and stereotypes about African Americans" (5).

34. U.S. Department of Justice, Civil Rights Division, "Investigation of the Baltimore City Police Department" (Washington, DC, 2016), https://www.justice.gov/opa/file/883366/download; see also Del Quentin Wilber and Kevin Rector, "Justice Department Report: Baltimore Police Routinely Violated Civil Rights," *Baltimore Sun*, August 9, 2016, http://www.baltimoresun.com/news/maryland/baltimore-city/bs-md-ci-doj-report-20160809-story.html.

35. Baltimore Investigation, 3. As part of its findings, the report noted that police "stops are concentrated in predominately African-American neighborhoods and often lack reasonable suspicion," "officers frequently pat-down or frisk individuals as a matter of course, without identifying necessary grounds to believe that the person is armed and dangerous," "officers make warrantless arrests without probable cause . . . [or] make arrests for misdemeanor offenses . . . without providing the constitutionally required notice," "[r]acially disparate impact is present at every stage of BPD's [Baltimore Police Department's] enforcement actions, from the initial decision to stop individuals on Baltimore streets to searches, arrests, and uses of force," BPD uses excessive or unreasonable force against "individuals with mental health disabilities or in crisis," "juveniles," and "people who present little or no threat to officers or others," and BPD "violates the First Amendment by retaliating against individuals engaged in constitutionally protected activities," such as exercises of free speech. Ibid., 5–9.

36. Ferguson Investigation, 2–4. The report identified striking racial disparities in municipal court practices: (1) "African Americans are 68% less likely than others to have their cases dismissed by the court"; (2) "African Americans are at least 50% more likely to have their cases lead to an arrest warrant, and accounted for 92% of cases in which an arrest warrant was issued by the Ferguson Municipal Court"; and (3) "of those actually arrested by FPD [Ferguson Police Department] only because of an outstanding municipal warrant, 96% are African American." Ibid., 5.

37. Ibid., 2.

38. Baltimore Investigation, 4–5.

39. See, e.g., Jennifer L. Eberhardt, et al., "Seeing Black: Race, Crime, and Visual Processing," *Journal of Personality and Social Psychology* 87, no. 6 (2004): 876.

40. See, e.g., Jennifer L. Eberhardt, et al., "Looking Deathworthy: Perceived Stereotypicality of Black Defendants Predicts Capital-Sentencing Outcomes," *Psychological Science* 17, no. 5 (2006); R. Richard Banks, et al., "Discrimination and Implicit Bias in a Racially Unequal Society," *California Law Review* 94, no. 4 (2006): 1169 (2006); Philip Atiba Goff, et al., "Not Yet Human: Implicit Knowledge, Historical

Dehumanization, and Contemporary Consequences," *Journal of Personality and Social Psychology* 94, no. 2 (2008): 292–306.

41. Black Lives Matter is a movement founded by Patrisse Cullors, Opal Tometi, and Alicia Garza in response to the shooting death of seventeen-year-old Trayvon Martin in 2012. It has grown into a chapter-based national organization that seeks black liberation from racial discrimination and oppression. For more information, go to the Black Lives Matter website at http://blacklivesmatter.com/. See also Jelani Cobb, "The Matter of Black Lives," *The New Yorker*, March 14, 2016, http://www .newyorker.com/magazine/2016/03/14/where-is-black-lives-matter-headed.

42. In October 2016, the NAACP Legal Defense and Educational Fund argued before the Supreme Court on behalf of our client, Duane Buck, who was sentenced to death based, in part, on testimony from the defense expert that he was more likely to be a future danger because he is black. See generally "Duane Buck: Sentenced to Death Because He Is Black," http://www.naacpldf.org/case -issue/duane-buck-sentenced-death-because-he-black. On February 22, 2017, the Supreme Court ruled in Mr. Buck's favor, finding that such testimony "appealed to a powerful racial stereotype—that of black men as 'violence prone.'" *Buck v. Davis*, no. 15-8049, 2017 WL 685534 (Feb. 22, 2017).

43. While this book is titled *Policing the Black Man*, the racial discrimination suffered by black women and girls at the hands of law enforcement is no less severe or troubling, and is the subject of the #SayHerName movement. More information is available on the African American Policy Forum website at http://www.aapf.org/sayhernamereport/.

44. *Scott v. Sanford*, 60 U.S. 393 (1857).

45. Ibid., 404.

46. Ibid., 407.

47. Ibid., 422.

48. Section 1 of the Thirteenth Amendment provides: "Neither slavery nor involuntary servitude, except as a punishment for crime whereof the party shall have been duly convicted, shall exist within the United States, or any place subject to their jurisdiction." U.S. Const., amend. XIII, sec. 1.

49. Section 1 of the Fourteenth Amendment provides: "All persons born or naturalized in the United States, and subject to the jurisdiction thereof, are citizens of the United States and of the state wherein they reside. No state shall make or enforce any law which shall abridge the privileges or immunities of citizens of the United States; nor shall any state deprive any person of life, liberty, or property, without due process of law; nor deny to any person within its jurisdiction the equal protection of the laws." U.S. Const., amend. XIV, sec. 1.

50. Section 1 of the Fifteenth Amendment provides: "The right of citizens of the United States to vote shall not be denied or abridged by the United States or by any state on account of race, color, or previous condition of servitude." U.S. Const., amend. XV, sec. 1.

51. April 9, 1866, ch. 31, 14 Stat. 27, currently codified at 42 U.S.C. §§ 1982, 1987, 1988, 1991, and 1992, with subsequent amendments. The full text of the original legislation can be found at http://www.pbs.org/wgbh/amex/reconstruction/activism/ps_1866.html.

52. March 3, 1865, ch. 90, 13 Stat. 507. The full text of the legislation can be found at http://www.freedmen.umd.edu/fbact.htm.

53. U.S. Const., amend. XIV, sec. 1.

54. The Compromise of 1877 resolved the close presidential race between Samuel Tilden and Rutherford B. Hayes, in which southern states voted in favor of Hayes through a national commission in return for Hayes's promise to remove federal troops from the South. See Jack Greenberg, "A Crusader in the Court: Comments on the Civil Rights Movement," *UMKC L.* Rev. 63 (1994): 207, 211–12.

55. See *Civil Rights Cases*, 109 U.S. 3 (1883).

56. See Title VII of the Civil Rights Act of 1964, 42 U.S.C. § 2000e *et seq.*

57. See Voting Rights Act of 1965, 52 U.S.C. § 10301 et seq.

58. See Title II of the Civil Rights Act of 1964, 42 U.S.C. § 2000a *et seq.*

59. See Fair Housing Act of 1968, 42 U.S.C. § 3601 *et seq.*

60. Chief Justice Earl Warren presided over the United States Supreme Court from 1953 to 1969, during which time it made significant advances in civil rights protections, including the landmark decision *Brown v. Board of Education*, 347 U.S. 483 (1954). See Morton J. Horwitz, "The Warren Court and the Pursuit of Justice," *Washington and Lee Law Review* 50 (1993): 5.

61. Darren Lenard Hutchinson, "Racial Exhaustion," *Wash. U. L. Rev.* 86 (2009): 917.

62. *Civil Rights Cases*, 109 U.S. 3 (1883).

63. March 1, 1875, ch. 114, §§ 3-5, 18 Stat. 336, 337. The full text of the legislation can be found at http://www.pbs.org/wgbh/amex/reconstruction/activism/ps_1875 .html.

64. 109 U.S. at 25.

65. *Plessy v. Ferguson*, 163 U.S. 537 (1896), overruled by *Brown v. Board of Education*, 347 U.S. 483 (1954).

66. Ibid., 541.

67. Ibid., 541–42.

68. Ibid., 551.

69. Ibid., 551–52.

70. *Brown v. Board of Education*, 347 U.S. 483 (1954) (striking down racial segregation of public schools as unconstitutional).

71. Civil Rights Act of 1964, Pub. L. 85-315, September 9, 1957, 71 Stat. 634. The full text of the legislation can be found at https://www.law.umaryland.edu/marshall/usccr/documents/civriac.pdf.

72. Civil Rights Act of 1964, Pub. L. 88-352, July 2, 1964, 78 Stat. 241, 42 U.S.C. §§ 2000a-2000h-6.

73. Civil Rights Act of 1965, Pub. L. 89-110, August 6, 1965, 79 Stat. 437, 52 U.S.C. § 10301 *et seq.*

74. Civil Rights Act of 1968, Pub. L. 90-284, Title VIII, April 11, 1968, 82 Stat. 81, 42 U.S.C. § 3601 *et seq.*

75. See *South Carolina v. Katzenbach*, 383 U.S. 301 (1966) (upholding the constitutionality of the Voting Rights Act of 1965 under the Fifteenth Amendment), abrogated by *Shelby County, Alabama v. Holder*, 133 S. Ct. 2612 (2013); *Heart of Atlanta Motel Inc., v. United States*, 379 U.S. 241 (1964) (declaring the Civil Rights Act of

1964's prohibition against discrimination in public accommodations to be valid under the Commerce Clause). For almost fifty years since the passage of the Voting Rights Act of 1965, certain states that had literacy tests and low voter registration or turnout were required to obtain approval from the United States Department of Justice or a federal court in Washington, D.C. (called "preclearance") before enacting any new voting laws or procedures, to ensure that those laws or procedures were not racially discriminatory. Shockingly, the Supreme Court recently gutted this crucial, prophylactic voting rights protection in its 2013 decision, *Shelby County, Alabama v. Holder*, by invalidating the formula that determined which states were subject to preclearance. The NAACP Legal Defense and Education Fund represented black residents of Shelby County in this case, and is now actively engaged in remedying this tremendous setback in securing the right to vote.

76. See, e.g., *Regents of the University of California v. Bakke*, 438 U.S. 265 (1978) (invalidating medical school's admission program reserving certain number of positions to disadvantaged applicants of color, but recognizing race can be one of multiple factors to consider under certain circumstances); *Wygant v. Jackson Board of Education*, 476 U.S. 267 (1986) (striking down provision of collective bargaining agreement that, in some circumstances, protected employees of color from layoffs despite lesser seniority); *City of Richmond v. J. A. Croson Co.*, 488 U.S. 469 (1989) (finding requirement to award certain percentage of contracts to minority businesses to be unconstitutional); *Parents Involved in Community Schools v. Seattle School District No. 1*, 551 U.S. 701 (2007) (holding that school districts improperly considered race in student assignments). However, the Supreme Court recently upheld the consideration of race, among multiple factors, in the University of Texas's undergraduate admissions policy to further the compelling interest of student diversity. See *Fisher v. University of Texas at Austin*, 136 S. Ct. 2198 (2016).

77. *Grutter v. Bollinger*, 539 U.S. 306, 343 (2003).

78. The educational segregation of present-day black students is comparable to their segregation in the late 1960s. Reed Jordan, "America's Public Schools Remain Highly Segregated," Urban Institute, *Urban Wire: Children*, August 27, 2014, http://www.urban.org/urban-wire/americas-public-schools-remain-highly-segregated. According to the Urban Institute, "public schools are highly segregated by race and income, with the declining share of white students typically concentrated in schools with other white students and the growing share of Latino students concentrated into low-income public schools with other students of color." Ibid. Likewise, a recent study by the Government Accountability Office found that, "[f]rom schools years 2000–01 to 2013–14 . . , both the percentage of K–12 public schools that were high-poverty and comprised of mostly Black or Hispanic students . . . and the students attending these schools grew significantly." Government Accountability Office, "K–12 Education: Better Use of Information Could Help Agencies Identify Disparities and Address Racial Discrimination," GAO-16-345 (Washington, DC: 2016), 10. The percentage of schools with mostly black or Hispanic students "increased steadily from 9 percent in 2000–01 (7,009 schools) to 16 percent in 2013–14 (15,089 schools)." Ibid. (footnote omitted). Moreover, the number of students attending schools with mostly black or Hispanic students "more than doubled, increasing by about 4.3 million students,

from about 4.1 million to 8.4 million students," and "the number of schools where 90 to 100 percent of the students were eligible for free or reduced-price lunch and 90 to 100 percent of the students were black or Hispanic grew by 143 percent." Ibid., 12.

79. For example, one study has found that "[d]eclining segregation at the neighborhood level may be offset by growing segregation between places or other levels of geography, such as the exurban fringe or small towns, which are typically excluded from metro-centric segregation studies." Daniel T. Lichter, et al., "Toward a New Macro-Segregation? Decomposing Segregation within and between Metropolitan Cities and Suburbs," *American Sociological Review* Vol. 80(4), 2015, at 845; see also ibid., 855–57. The fact that "recent segregation declines were located primarily . . . from neighborhood to neighborhood . . . seem[s] to reflect continuing patterns of white depopulation from many large cities, growing place-to-place economic differentiation, and the emergence of a new 'political economy of place' that emphasizes cities and communities rather than neighborhoods as political actors that exclude undesirable populations, including historically disadvantaged minorities." Ibid., 868. Moreover, there are notable exceptions to declining segregation within metropolitan areas: "Some metropolitan areas—like Chicago, Detroit, and Milwaukee—continued to have exceptionally high levels of black-white segregation." Ibid., 868. See also John R. Logan, "Separate and Unequal: The Neighborhood Gap for Blacks, Hispanics and Asians in Metropolitan America," *US2010 Project*, July 2011 (1) ("As black-white segregation has slowly declined since 1990, blacks have become less isolated from Hispanics and Asians, but their exposure to whites has hardly changed. . . . [And] [a]ffluent blacks and Hispanics live in poorer neighborhoods than whites with working class incomes").

80. According to the Pew Research Center, "Black and Hispanic men . . . have made no progress in narrowing the wage gap with white men since 1980. . . . [B]lack men earned the same 73% share of white men's hourly earnings in 1980 as they did in 2015, and Hispanic men earned 69% of white men's earnings in 2015 compared with 71% in 1980." Eileen Patten, "Racial, Gender Wage Gaps Persist in U.S. Despite Some Progress," Pew Research Center, *FacTank: News in the Numbers*, July 1, 2016, http://www.pewresearch.org/fact-tank/2016/07/01/racial-gender-wage-gaps-persist -in-u-s-despite-some-progress/. These disparities persist among college graduates: "College-educated black and Hispanic men earn roughly 80% of the hourly wages of white college educated men ($25 and $26 vs. $32, respectively)," and "black and Hispanic women with a college degree earn only about 70% of the hourly wages of similarly educated white men ($25 and $22, respectively)." Ibid. With respect to wealth disparities, "white families on average had seven times the wealth of African American families and six times the wealth of Hispanic families in 2013." Urban Institute, "Nine Charts About Wealth Inequality in America," February 2015, http://apps.urban.org/ features/wealth-inequality-charts/. Additionally, "[i]n 1963, the average wealth of white families was $117,000 higher than the average wealth of nonwhite families. By 2013, the average wealth of white families was over $500,000 higher than the average wealth of African American families . . . and of Hispanic families." Ibid. And the unemployment rate for African Americans has consistently been double the rate for whites from 1954 (when the Bureau of Labor Statistics began reliably documen-

ing unemployment by race) until the present. Drew Desilver, "Black Unemployment Rate Is Consistently Twice That of Whites," Pew Research Center, *FacTank: News in the Numbers*, August 21, 2013, http://www.pewresearch.org/fact-tank/2013/08/21/through-good-times-and-bad-black-unemployment-is-consistently-double-that-of -whites/.

81. See generally Michelle Alexander, *The New Jim Crow: Mass Incarceration in the Age of Colorblindness* (New York: The New Press, 2010).

82. *Washington v. Davis*, 426 U.S. 229 (1976).

83. This case concerned *constitutional* rights, as opposed to *statutory* rights under Title VII of the Civil Rights Act of 1964, which prohibits employment policies and practices that have a discriminatory impact without an adequate business justification. Ibid., 235.

84. 426 U.S. at 242.

85. Ibid., 253–54.

86. Ibid., 254.

87. See, e.g., Alan David Freeman, "Legitimizing Racial Discrimination Through Antidiscrimination Law: A Critical Review of Supreme Court Doctrine," *Minnesota Law Review* 62 (1978): 1049; Neil Gotanda, "A Critique of 'Our Constitution Is Color-Blind,'" *Stanford Law Review* 44 (1991): 1; Kenneth L. Karst, "Foreword: Equal Citizenship Under the Fourteenth Amendment," *Harvard Law Review* 91 (1977): 1; Robert G. Schwemm, "From *Washington* to *Arlington Heights* and Beyond: Discriminatory Purpose in Equal Protection Litigation," *University of Illinois Law Forum* (1977): 961.

88. Charles R. Lawrence III, "The Id, the Ego, and Equal Protection: Reckoning with Unconscious Racism," *Stanford Law Review* 39 (1987): 317, 324–25.

89. Ibid., 320.

90. Ibid., 319.

91. *Plessy*, 163 U.S. at 559. Justice Harlan was prescient in his prediction that the *Plessy* decision would "in time, prove to be quite as pernicious as the decision made by this tribunal in the Dred Scott Case." However, his otherwise laudable dissent has been marred by his explicitly racist observations of Chinese immigrants: "There is a race so different from our own that we do not permit those belonging to it to become citizens of the United States. Persons belonging to it are, with few exceptions, absolutely excluded from our country. I allude to the Chinese race." Ibid., 561. See also Gabriel J. Chin, "The Plessy Myth: Justice Harlan and the Chinese Cases," *Iowa Law Review* 82 (1996): 151.

92. Philip L. Fetzer, " 'Reverse Discrimination:' The Political Use of Language," *National Black Law Journal* 12 (1990): 212, 215.

93. Professor Gerald Gunther coined the phrase that "strict scrutiny" was " 'strict' in theory and fatal in fact." Gerald Gunther, "Forword: In Search of Evolving Doctrine on a Changing Court: A Model for a Newer Equal Protection," *Harvard Law Review* 86 (1972): 1, 8. See also Adam Winkler, "Fatal in Theory and Strict in Fact: An Empirical Analysis of Strict Scrutiny in the Federal Courts," *Vanderbilt Law Review* 59 (2006): 793.

94. *Regents of the University of California v. Bakke*, 438 U.S. 265, 397 (1978) (Marshall, J., concurring in part and dissenting in part).

95. *Parents Involved in Community Schools v. Seattle School District No. 1*, 551 U.S. 701 (2007).

96. Ibid., 748.

97. *Schuette v. Coalition to Defend Affirmative Action, Integration and Immigrant Rights and Fight for Equality by Any Means Necessary (BAMN)*, 134 S.Ct. 1623, 1676 (2014) (Sotomayor, S., dissenting).

98. See, e.g., Daniel Victor, "Why 'All Lives Matter' Is Such a Perilous Phrase," *New York Times*, July 15, 2016, http://www.nytimes.com/2016/07/16/us/all-lives -matter-black-lives-matter.html.

99. *McCleskey v. Kemp*, 481 U.S. 279, 287 (1987).

100. Ibid., 312.

101. Ibid., 295–99.

102. Ibid., 312.

103. Ibid., 314–15.

104. Ibid., 339.

105. Opinion, "Justice Powell's New Wisdom," *New York Times*, June 11, 1994.

106. *Brown v. City of Oneonta*, 221 F.3d 329 (2000). The NAACP Legal Defense and Educational Fund filed an amicus brief in this case in support of the plaintiffs.

107. Ibid., 334.

108. Ibid.

109. Ibid.

110. Ibid., 338.

111. Ibid., 338–39.

112. Although private individuals are required to prove discriminatory intent in claims of racial discrimination against the police, state and federal governments may not. Regulations promulgated under Title VI of the Civil Rights Act of 1964 permit governmental entities—but not private individuals—to bring claims of racial discrimination against recipients of federal funding based on statistical evidence that a protected group, such as people of a certain race, is disproportionately harmed by a particular action, regardless of intent. See *Alexander v. Sandoval*, 532 U.S. 275 (2001).

113. *Floyd v. City of New York*, 959 F. Supp. 2d 540, 660 (2013). The NAACP Legal Defense and Education Fund is counsel in *Davis v. City of New York*, No. 10 Civ. 0699 (S.D.N.Y.), which is a federal class-action lawsuit that is related to the *Floyd* case and is now part of the court monitoring of the NYPD that was ordered in *Floyd*.

114. Monica Davey and Julie Bosman, "Protests Flare After Ferguson Police Officer Is Not Indicted," *New York Times*, November 24, 2014, http://www.nytimes .com/2014/11/25/us/ferguson-darren-wilson-shooting-michael-brown-grand-jury .html; J. David Goodman and Al Baker, "Wave of Protests After Grand Jury Doesn't Indict Officer in Eric Garner Chokehold Case," *New York Times*, December 3, 2014, http://www.nytimes.com/2014/12/04/nyregion/grand-jury-said-to-bring-no -charges-in-staten-island-chokehold-death-of-eric-garner.html.

115. Richard Pérez-Peña, "Angered by Cities' Handling of Police Shootings, Voters Oust Two Prosecutors," *New York Times*, March 16, 2016, https://www.nytimes .com/2016/03/17/us/angered-by-cities-handling-of-police-shootings-voters-oust -two-prosecutors.html.

116. John V. Jacobi, "Prosecuting Police Misconduct," *Wisconsin Law Review* (2000): 789, 806.

117. 18 U.S.C. § 242.

118. 18 U.S.C. § 242; see also note 51.

119. Brian R. Johnson and Phillip B. Bridgmon, "Depriving Civil Rights: An Exploration of 18 U.S.C. 242 Criminal Prosecutions, 2001–2006," *Criminal Justice Review* 34, no. 2 (June 2009): 197; see also Jacobi, "Prosecuting Police Misconduct," 806.

120. Johnson and Bridgmon, "Exploration," 198.

121. *Screws v. United States* 325 U.S. 91 (1945).

122. Ibid., 92.

123. It is notable that this case originated in Baker County, Georgia, which later became a center of civil rights activism, culminating in what has been called the "Baker County Movement," which was born in the summer of 1965. See Shirley Sherrod, *The Courage to Hope: How I Stood Up to the Politics of Fear* (New York: Atria Books, 2012), 89.

124. 325 U.S. at 92–93.

125. Ibid., 93–94.

126. Ibid.

127. Ibid., 98.

128. Ibid., 107.

129. Johnson and Bridgmon, "Exploration," 199.

130. 325 U.S. at 103.

131. Ibid.

132. Marshall Miller, "Police Brutality," *Yale Law and Policy Review* 17 (1998): 149, 153 (noting that the specific intent requirement presents "a significant obstacle" to federal criminal civil rights prosecutions); Jacobi, "Prosecuting Police Misconduct," 806 (suggesting that, due to specific intent requirement, Section 242 "is a tool that is rarely used in the fight against police misconduct").

133. *See Tennessee v. Garner,* 471 U.S. 1 (1985); *Graham v. Connor,* 490 U.S. 386 (1989); *Scott v. Harris,* 550 U.S. 372 (2007).

134. *Graham,* 490 U.S. at 396.

135. Ibid., 396–97.

136. See, e.g., Rachel A. Harmon, "When Is Police Violence Justified," *Northwestern University Law Review* 102 (2008): 1119; Brandon Garrett and Seth Stoughton, "A Tactical Fourth Amendment," *Virginia Law Review* 102 (2017) (forthcoming).

137. The NAACP Legal Defense and Educational Fund presented an *amicus curiae* brief to the Supreme Court on this issue in the case *Tolan v. Cotton,* No. 13-1551, which involved the police shooting of former Washington Nationals baseball player, Robbie Tolan, in the driveway of his parents' home after being mistakenly suspected of driving a stolen car. See generally http://www.naacpldf.org/case-issue/tolan-v-cotton. The Supreme Court ultimately ruled in favor of Mr. Tolan, finding his case to have been improperly dismissed. *Tolan v. Cotton,* 134 S. Ct. 1861 (2014); see also notes 39–40.

138. See Patricia G. Divine, "Stereotypes and Prejudice: Their Automatic and

Controlled Components," *Journal of Personality and Social Psychology* 56, no. 1 (1989): 5; *Kurt Hugenberg & Galen v. Bodenhausen*, "Facing Prejudice: Implicit Prejudice and the Perception of Facial Threat," *Psychological Science* 14, no. 6 (2003): 640, 643.

139. B. Keith Payne, "Prejudice and Perception: The Role of Automatic and Controlled Processes in Misperceiving a Weapon," *Journal of Personality and Social Psychology* 81, no. 2 (2001): 181, 183-86; Eberhardt, et al., "Seeing Black," 889-90.

140. See Anthony G. Greenwald, et al., "Targets of Discrimination: Effects of Race on Responses to Weapon Holders," *Journal of Personality and Social Psychology* 39 (2003): 399, 403; Joshua Correll, et al., "The Police Officer's Dilemma: Using Ethnicity to Disambiguate Potentially Threatening Individuals," *Journal of Personality and Social Psychology* 83. no. 6 (2002): 1314, 1319.

141. See L. Song Richardson and Phillip Atiba Goff, "Self-Defense and the Suspicion Heuristic," *Iowa Law Review* 98 (2012): 293, 301.

142. Frederick M. Lawrence, "Civil Rights and Criminal Wrongs: The Mens Rea of Federal Civil Rights Crimes," *Tulane Law Review* 67 (1993): 2113, 2174.

143. U.S. Department of Justice, "Department of Justice Report Regarding the Criminal Investigation into the Shooting Death of Michael Brown by Ferguson, Missouri, Police Officer Darren Wilson" (Washington, DC: 2015), 10–11, https://www.justice.gov/sites/default/files/opa/press-releases/attachments/2015/03/04/doj_report_on_shooting_of_michael_brown_1.pdf.

144. Ibid., 11 (quoting *Screws*, 325 U.S. at 101–107).

145. Ibid., 12.

146. Ferguson Investigation.

147. *Utah v. Strieff*, 136 S. Ct. 2056 (2016).

148. Ibid., 2059.

149. Ibid., 2065.

150. Ibid., 2069–70.

151. Ibid., 2070–71.

Poverty, Violence, and Black Incarceration

JEREMY TRAVIS AND BRUCE WESTERN

IN THE HUNDRED and fifty years since Emancipation, the two great markers of racial injustice have been violence and poverty. Violence encompasses the community violence of street crime in African American neighborhoods richly documented since W.E.B. DuBois's (1899) analysis of the social problems of Philadelphia's ninth ward, the political violence of the Klan, and other domestic terrorism that wreaked havoc through the first half of the twentieth century, and the state violence of law enforcement and imprisonment.[1] Just as the physical security of African Americans has always been tenuous, material well-being has also been elusive. Statistics on black employment and poverty reflect a stubborn disadvantage that withstood great twentieth-century efforts at social improvement through the New Deal and the Great Society.

Mass incarceration occupies a special place in the long historical contest over African American citizenship. Blacks have always been imprisoned at much higher rates than whites, at least since Reconstruction.[2] In 1900, the imprisonment rate was three times higher for blacks than whites, and the racial disparity in incarceration climbed steadily throughout much of the twentieth century.[3] But the penal system has acquired a historically new significance over the last two decades. Racial inequality in incarceration peaked in the 1990s as African Americans had become about seven times more likely to be imprisoned than whites.[4] And in the current era of mass incarceration, imprisonment is not just unequally distributed between blacks and whites; incarceration is pervasive in poor communities of color. For recent birth cohorts, born since the late 1970s, about a fifth of all black men have served time in prison. Among high school dropouts, lifetime chances of imprisonment are even higher, approaching 70 percent.[5]

Mass incarceration now lies at the intersection of violence and poverty in contemporary African American life. The historic expansion of state violence with rising prison and jail populations was concentrated almost entirely among the economically disadvantaged.[6] In American cities, very high rates of incarceration came to characterize very poor, mostly African American neighborhoods that were also struggling with high rates of crime, profound joblessness, family instability, poor schools, and inadequate health care.[7,8]

We argue that mass incarceration grew out of social conditions of poverty and violence, and has created a novel kind of social inequality in which full participation in American life has been foreclosed in poor black communities. Like earlier chapters in African American history—slavery, Jim Crow, and the emergence of the northern ghetto—the racial inequality produced by mass incarceration has been perpetuated by the levers of law and political control. Reversing mass incarceration, too, will require significant political will. Our analysis suggests that such a political project must confront the central importance of violence and poverty to American race relations. A project for racial justice must simultaneously provide for the physical safety of African American children and adults, and improve the level of material well-being in black communities. The excessive use of prison as a response to the problem of violence and other crime has done little to advance the safety of those communities and now looms large as a barrier to any hopes for economic, political, and social advancement of Americans of African descent.

The Social, Political, and Legal Origins of the Prison Boom

Mass incarceration is often traced to a combination of three conditions: rapid social and economic change in American cities, a conservative backlash to civil rights politics of the 1960s, and since the 1970s a transformation of criminal justice policy that intensified the prosecution and punishment of drug offenses, required prison time for minor offenses, and implemented very long sentences, particularly for violence.

The African American community, and black men in particular, were central to each of these developments. High rates of violent crime emerged in minority neighborhoods of concentrated disadvantage. The collapse of urban manufacturing industries propelled high rates of unemployment for black men with low levels of schooling. In the wake of social protest and the passage of the Civil Rights Acts, conservative politicians curried favor with white voters by touting an often racialized politics of law and order. Finally, the war on drugs and tough-on-crime sentencing policy were intended to address the problem of inner-city crime and had disastrous effects on the incarceration of black men.

American urban life was roiled in the 1960s and 1970s by a sustained rise in crime, episodes of severe civil disorder, and the collapse of urban labor markets for unskilled workers in inner cities. Crime rates had always been higher in urban areas than in the suburbs and rural America, but the early 1960s ushered in an increase in crime that was to last over two decades. The national homicide rate more than doubled from 4.5 (per 100,000) in the early 1960s to its peak year of 10.2 in 1980. The increase was even larger in cities, rising in Chicago, for example, from 10.3 in 1960 to 25.0 in 1975.[9] The murder rate for African Americans was 6 to 10 times higher than for whites, and Gurr found the increase in violence in the 1960s and 1970s to be associated with a disproportionate rise in black murder rates.[10] Murder rates for young black men in particular reached extremely high levels— around 150 per 100,000 in 1980—making homicide the leading cause of death among blacks aged 15 to 34 by the early 1990s.[11]

Urban life in the 1960s also became more volatile in other ways. The sixties were marked by acute episodes of urban disorder. Riotous summertime unrest in U.S. cities culminated in the Kerner Commission report on civil disorders, which surveyed dozens of incidents of disorder in twenty-three cities. Concluding famously that the nation was moving to "two societies, one black, one white—separate and unequal," the report warned that racial polarization threatened the destruction of basic democratic values.

The civil disorder of the sixties foreshadowed a long economic malaise in American cities, particularly in poor communities of color. American cities passed through a long eclipse in the 1970s and 1980s. The out-migration of working-class and middle-class families for the suburbs and shrinking employment in urban manufacturing left pockets of severe and spatially concentrated poverty.[12,13] Joblessness, nonmarital birth rates, and rates of violent crime all increased in poor inner-city neighborhoods. It was in these poor communities that incarceration rates climbed highest, yielding extraordinary rates of involvement in the criminal justice system, particularly among young minority men with very little schooling.

Rising incarceration rates are closely linked to the burgeoning employment problems of young, low-skilled men. Persistent employment problems began to emerge through the 1970s, concentrated among workers with just a high school education or less. In part this could be seen in the growing race gap in unemployment between black and white workers. But more fundamental changes were also unfolding in urban labor markets as labor force participation declined among young, less-educated black men.[14,15,16] In a careful review of labor market data from the 1970s and 1980s, Richard Freeman and John Bound found growing racial gaps in earnings and employment that extended from the mid-1970s to the end of the 1980s. Anticipating the close interconnection between economic opportunity and incarceration that was to flourish over the following decade, Freeman and Bound also observed how the prevalence of criminal records among young black men with little schooling was itself becoming a major cause of reduced employment.

How did the employment problems of inner-city youth contribute to the growth in incarceration rates? Researchers focused on two main channels. First, in a context depleted of legitimate economic opportunities, young inner-city residents increasingly turned to drug dealing and other crime as a source of income. Thus econometric studies interpret high rates of arrest and incarceration as indicating high levels of criminal involvement among disadvantaged youth.[17,18] Consistent with the quantitative research, ethnographers vividly described the proliferation of drug dealing and violence in the high-unemployment ghettoes of the 1980s and 1990s.[19,20,21]

Second, the shifting conditions of urban life—the emergence of mass unemployment among young men in poor urban neighborhoods, and a flourishing street trade in drugs, combined with a real increase in violent crime—produced a punitive response from criminal justice authorities. How did this happen in practice? Researchers have long observed intensive police scrutiny of poor neighborhoods.[22,23] Under conditions of mass unemployment, more of daily life, and illegal activity, transpires in public space. Ethnographers suggest that the purchase and consumption of drugs, drunkenness, and domestic disturbances are more likely to take place in public in urban areas, but in private homes in the suburbs. Consequently, poor urban residents are more exposed to police attention and risk arrest more than their suburban counterparts.[24,25] The great social distance between the police and poor urban minorities also contributes to distrust on both sides. Police tend to view disadvantaged blacks and Hispanics and the communities in which they live as unsafe.[26,27] The poor are treated with more suspicion as a result. A parallel set of findings indicates judges treat poor defendants more harshly in the courts. Poor defendants have been found to be viewed as more culpable and having fewer prospects for rehabilitation.[28,29,30,31] As a consequence, the incarceration rates of young black men were found to rise with their unemployment rates, and incarceration rates increased most in states where black unemployment problems were most severe.[32]

These social and economic trends accompanied a change in the politics of crime. The cultural trope of black criminality had deep historical roots that were nourished not just by popular stereotypes but also by academic criminology and official statistics on crime that had been recording arrests separately for blacks and whites since the early twentieth century.[33] Ideas about the criminal predisposition of African Americans gained a special political significance in reaction to the rapid social and political change of the sixties. Conservative politicians drew a close connection between social protest, civil disorder, and crime and argued for a get-tough approach.[34,35,36] In presidential politics, Barry Goldwater in the 1964 election warned of "the growing menace in our country . . . to personal safety, to life, to limb, and property." Goldwater vowed that "liberty lacking order will not become the license of the mob and of the jungle."[37,38,39] In his third-party campaign George Wallace used similar imagery to paint civil rights activists as the enablers of criminals: "[We] find the nation's capital becomes a jungle where citizens fear to walk the streets at night," resulting in "the astounding spectacle of . . . high officials calling for the passage of the so-called civil rights bill for fear of mob violence."[40] Speaking to trends in crime, Richard Nixon in 1968 also conjured up images of wild savages in which "the city jungle will cease to be a metaphor; it will become a barbaric reality."[41]

Racially charged political talk about crime demanded a punitive response. Three policy changes, originating in the 1970s and continuing through the 1990s, drove the increase in incarceration: the intensified enforcement and punishment of drug crimes, the widespread adoption of mandatory prison time for less serious offenses, and the adoption of very long sentences, especially for serious violence.[42] President Nixon declared a "war on drugs" in 1971, expanding the size and capacity of federal drug control agencies. Drug arrest rates escalated sharply through the 1980s and remained at a high level through the 1990s. During this period, drug arrest rates for blacks were more than twice as high as for whites. States widely adopted prison sentences for drug offenses, and mandatory minimum prison sentences for drug crimes were established in the federal system. The war on drugs came to have large racially disparate effects on incarceration. Just as mandatory minimum sentences were legislated for drug crimes, mandatory prison sentences were also passed for a large number of non-serious crimes. The main effect of the widespread adoption of mandatory minimum sentences was to make incarceration the presumptive punishment for a felony offense. Finally, very long sentences were passed through the 1990s. In part, this involved increasing sentences for violent crimes and restricting eligibility for parole release. In part, it involved the adoption of very long sentence enhancements, especially for defendants with prior felony records. California's three-strikes enhancement, in which third-time felony defendants could be given life sentences, was widely emulated around the country. The net result was that individuals already sentenced to prison terms were kept in prison longer.

The social and economic deterioration of American cities, the emergence of racialized tough-on-crime politics, and the adoption of more punitive sentencing policies all set the stage for the emergence of very high rates of incarceration. The social landscape (dotted with poor, high-crime, African American neighborhoods), the politics (raising the specter of black criminality), and policy (focused on the street trade in drugs and violence) made the pervasive incarceration of poorly educated black men overwhelmingly likely.

Race and the Growth of Incarceration

Prison incarceration is the deep end of the criminal justice system. Prisons are state or federal facilities holding people convicted of felony offenses, typically for a minimum of twelve months, twenty-nine months on average, with about 10 percent serving life sentences.[43,44] Prisons account for about two-thirds of all U.S. incarceration, with the remaining penal population held in local jails either serving short sentences or awaiting trial.

Two main facts stand out in research on the social contours of imprisonment. First, the U.S. incarceration rate today is unparalleled by comparative and historical standards. The scale of a penal system is typically measured by an incarceration rate that records the number of people who are locked up on a given day as a fraction of the total population. In 2012, the U.S. prison and jail incarceration rate was the highest in the world at 707 per 100,000, significantly exceeding incarceration rates in Western Europe. From Germany (77 per 100,000) to the United Kingdom (148 per 100,000), incarceration rates were nearly an order of magnitude lower than in the United States.

Historically, data on the state and federal imprisonment rate go back to the 1920s. In 1925, the U.S. imprisonment rate was close to today's Western European average, around 100 per 100,000. Imprisonment rates remained stable until the early 1970s. In the period from 1972 to 2012 the imprisonment rate increased fivefold, from 93 to 471 per 100,000. In absolute numbers there were 1.5 million people in U.S. prisons in 2012 and another 700,000 in local jails. Thus, the total penal population in the United States stands at 2.2 million. Although the United States accounts for just 5 percent of the world's population, U.S.

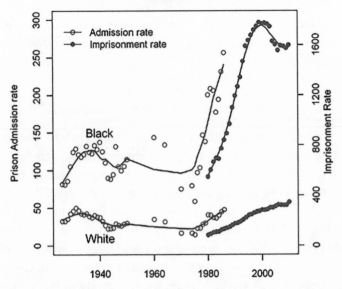

Figure 1. State and federal prison admission rates, 1926 to 1986, and state and federal imprisonment rates, 1980 to 2010, for blacks and whites. Source: Admissions rates are from Langan (1991). Black and white imprisonment rates are from Blumstein and Beck (2012). This figure is reproduced from Travis, Western, and Redburn (2014, p. 57).

prisons and jails account for 23 percent of the incarcerated population worldwide.

In addition to a historically and comparatively unprecedented rate of incarceration, the penal population is marked by large racial and other disparities. As a result, the effects of incarceration are concentrated in a disproportionately poor and minority segment of the population. Combining historical data on race and prison admissions with contemporary data on imprisonment rates, figure 1 provides a long historical time series on incarceration for blacks and whites. Over much of the twentieth century, blacks have been two to three times more likely to be incarcerated than whites. The racial disparity in incarceration grew substantially from the 1970s, peaking in the late 1990s. Throughout the 1990s, African Americans were about seven times more likely to be incarcerated than whites. In the 2000s, racial disparity declined, but black arrest rates have declined more than among whites, indicating that the relatively punitive treatment of black arrestees has increased in the recent period.[45]

To account for racial disparity in incarceration rates, researchers have studied the patterns of arrests, charging, convictions, sentencing, and imprisonment. Research on sentencing has mostly focused on the racial differences in receiving a custodial sentence for black and white defendants, controlling for legally relevant factors. Although blacks are more likely to receive prison sentences than whites, much of the racial disparity is explained by differences in the severity of offenses and criminal history.[46,47]

Sentencing research provides only a partial explanation of racial disparities in incarceration because the analysis begins relatively late in the processing of a criminal case. Other studies of racial differences in imprisonment begin with patterns of arrest, upstream from the criminal trial. Research comparing racial disparities in arrest and incarceration began with a seminal paper by Blumstein, who studied state imprisonment across a range of offenses. Where the distribution of imprisonment is proportionate to the distribution of arrests, we can conclude that the level of African American incarceration reflects the level of arrests. Using this method, Blumstein concluded that 80 percent of the disparity in state imprisonment is attributable to racial differences in arrests. Langan replicated this analysis, using victimization data to answer criticism that disparities in arrest may result from police discrimination rather than racial differences in offending. Langan concluded that the high rate of African American incarceration was not reducible to discriminatory patterns of arrest and instead reflected the relatively high rate of crime among African Americans. Recent data from the 1990s and 2000s, however, suggest that the racial disparity attributable to offending has declined significantly. Tonry and Melewski find that the unexplained component of incarceration disparity has increased and only 60 percent of the recent disparity in imprisonment is attributable to the racial differences in arrest.

While these analyses are helpful for linking incarceration to arrests, they fail to encompass the effects of sentencing policy on exacerbating the racial disparities in incarceration rates. In the first instance, the policy decisions taken over the past four decades, particularly in the 1990s, to increase sentence length for those convicted of violent crimes have resulted in more African Americans, mostly men, spending more of their lives in prison for crimes that in earlier years would have been punished less severely. Thus, through the 1990s and early 2000s, African Americans accounted for half or more of all state prisoners who were convicted of murder, robbery, or aggravated assault.[48] From the 1980s to the 2000s, the proportion of prisoners serving at least ten years for each of these violent offenses increased by 57, 236, and 90 percent.[49] Thus, time served in prison increased disproportionately for African Americans.

Drug policy also played a large role in the prison build-up. Over the same period that overall incarceration rates were increasing fivefold, the rate of incarceration for drug offenses increased tenfold.[50] The ballooning of the population in prison for drug offenses exacerbated racial disparities. At the beginning of the prison build-up, African Americans were arrested for drug crimes at a rate about double that of whites. By 1989, the African American arrest rate for drug crimes had surged to 1,460 per 100,000, nearly four times the rate for whites, which was 365 per 100,000.

As policymakers reacted to the introduction of crack cocaine into urban communities with harsher enforcement and stiffer sentences, racial disparities became even more pronounced. The spike in arrest rates of African Americans was visible at the front door of America's prisons. In 1987, nearly equal numbers of whites and African Americans were admitted to state prisons for drug crimes, about 20,000. By 1990, the admissions of African

Americans had quadrupled to nearly 80,000 per year; for whites, the increase was to about 30,000 a year.[51] These stark racial disparities in arrest and incarceration rates for drug offenses do not mirror observable racial differences in drug use or drug sales. On the contrary, national surveys report stable levels of drug use with little or no racial differences. Although the measures of drug-selling activity are highly inadequate, longitudinal surveys of youth show that white youth actually report slightly higher levels of drug sales than their African American counterparts.[52,53]

Crack cocaine was also the target of harsh sentencing policy. In 1986, the federal Anti-Drug Abuse Act mandated a five-year prison sentence for five grams of crack, while imposing the same sentence for five hundred grams of cocaine. The 100 to 1 disparity fell heavily on black defendants. In 1993, for example, blacks made up 88.3 percent of federal convictions for crack distribution, compared to 4.1 percent for whites.[54] Only in 2010 was the extreme sentencing disparity moderated when the crack-to-powder ratio was reduced from 100 to 1 to 18 to 1, and the federal five-year mandatory minimum sentence for crack possession was eliminated.

Beyond the racial divide, incarceration is also distributed unequally within the African American community. About 93 percent of prison and jail inmates are men, over half are in their twenties and thirties, and most have less than a high school education. Disparities of age, race, and education have created extraordinarily high rates of imprisonment among young African American men who have dropped out of high school. Figure 2 shows the probability of imprisonment by age thirty-five for two cohorts of men, one born in the late 1940s, growing up before the prison boom, and the other born in the late 1970s, growing up through the prison boom. These cumulative risks of imprisonment are reported for three levels of education: at least some college (C), completed high school (HS), or less than high school (DO). The figure shows that for African American men

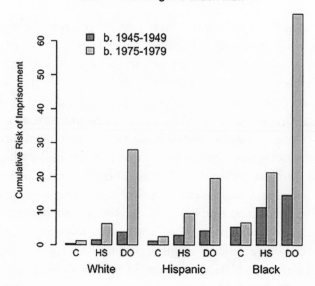

Figure 2. Cumulative risks of imprisonment by 1979 for men born in 1945–1949 and by 2009 for men born in 1975–1979, by race and education.

Note: C = at least some college; HS = completed high school or general equivalency diploma (GED); DO = no high school diploma or GED. Source: Western and Wildeman, 2009. This figure is reproduced from Travis, Western, and Redburn (2014, p. 67).

born in the late 1970s who failed to complete high school, about two-thirds had prison records by age thirty-five. In short, mass incarceration has involved the pervasive institutionalization of young men of color with very little schooling.

As the incarceration rate increased, conditions of penal confinement deteriorated in important respects. Prisons became safer as the number of deaths in custody declined, but prisons also became more overcrowded. Overcrowding reflects the stark reality that America did not build enough prisons to accommodate the expanding prison and jail populations mandated by a newly punitive sentencing regime. As the prison population increased beyond the design capacity of correctional facilities, prison administrators, with approval from the federal courts, increased the use of double and triple cells (meaning two or three individuals lived in a cell built for one), commandeered cafeterias and gymnasiums as dormitories, and added bunk beds to minimum-security housing.

Beyond the statistics of overcrowding, the quality of prison life has also changed significantly. The portion of the prison population suffering from mental illness has increased, and some prison systems have experienced the growth of gangs defined by race and ethnicity. Under these conditions, correctional administrators cut services, and the rehabilitative ideal—central to correctional philosophy in an earlier era—lost its persuasive power.[55] Perhaps most telling was the rise of a correctional philosophy called the "penal harm" movement, which viewed the time in prison as a time for more punishment.[56,57] The tough-on-crime rhetoric that defined the new American punitiveness penetrated the walls of correctional practice as some prisons removed air conditioners, abolished furloughs, banned televisions, abandoned conjugal visits, eliminated work-release programs, and generally made life inside prisons harsher than before.

Although the mortality rate inside prisons declined, most other indicators of prison life painted a picture of longer sentences, less contact with the outside world, and fewer program opportunities. In this environment, African American prisoners encountered another system of justice, not unlike that on the outside. They have been more likely to be disciplined for infractions, rules violations, and reports of misconduct, which in turn has led to more punishment within the prison. The ultimate expression of the penal harm movement has been the growth of solitary confinement, also known as administrative segregation. This deprivation of liberty—confinement to a small cell, twenty-three hours a day, with no human contact, sometimes for years—represents the deep end of the deep end. Although data are scarce, there is also evidence of racial disparities in this form of punishment too. In New York State, for example, African

American prisoners make up 49 percent of the prison population but constitute 59 percent of those in solitary confinement.[58] A survey of eighteen jurisdictions reveals similar patterns: African American prisoners represented 39 percent of the prison population, but 47 percent of those in administrative segregation units.[59] Recent figures from the Bureau of Justice Statistics indicate that, compared to whites, African American prisoners are 25 percent more likely to have spent time in segregation in the last twelve months. Not just a more punitive type of confinement, long periods of segregation are associated with elevated levels of anxiety, mood disorder, and serious psychological distress.[60] This prison-to-solitary pipeline, infused with racial disparity, defines the extreme instance of state violence short of capital punishment.

The Consequences of Incarceration
for Social and Political Life

The effects of incarceration extend well beyond the loss of liberty suffered during a period of confinement. Social researchers have studied the effects of incarceration on crime, on the well-being of individuals after incarceration, and on communities.

To estimate the effect of incarceration on crime, a large literature has studied deterrence and incapacitation—the two channels through which incarceration might reduce crime. For deterrence, would-be criminals are thought to weigh the benefits of crime against the costs of incarceration. Research finds, however, that those involved in crime respond more to the certainty and speed of punishment, rather than its severity.[61] For incapacitation, incarceration takes those off the street who might otherwise be involved in crime. This assumes that those incarcerated (street corner drug dealers, say) would not be replaced if locked up, and that people would continue to actively offend if not for their incarceration. In reality, street corners often repopulate with drug dealers after a street sweep, and offending declines with age so additional time on long sentences has little incapacitative effect. Against this background, most studies of the growth in incarceration find the crime reduction effect to be small.[62] Thus, estimates indicate that for the large crime decline of the 1990s—which contributed to the public safety of blacks and whites in similar proportion—between 70 and 90 percent was unrelated to the fivefold growth in incarceration rates.[63]

If we cannot be certain that mass incarceration appreciably improved public safety, what about its other social and economic consequences? Some studies have focused on incarcerated individuals, their families, or the communities from which they are drawn. Legal scholars have examined the so-called civil disabilities (loss of legal rights) associated with a prior criminal conviction. Still others have cast a wider net, looking at the impact of high rates of incarceration on the efficacy of democratic institutions and the larger social fabric.

This research encompasses related ideas about collateral consequences, invisible punishment, social stigma, or social exclusion. Given the massive expansion of imprisonment, the attendant reach of the criminal justice system into American society, and the extreme racial disparities in imprisonment and justice involvement, this research takes on elevated urgency.

At the core of this research stand discrete inquiries into topics such as the effects of incarceration on earnings, employment, physical health, mental health, housing, education, mortality, and child well-being.[64] Unfortunately, only a few studies have extrapolated the findings to consider the aggregate consequences of incarceration on racial inequality. Here, research has focused on labor markets, the children of incarcerated parents, and communities.

In the labor market, incarceration has often been found to be associated with diminished earnings and employment. Incarceration is thought to reduce economic opportunities by diminishing job skills, undermining physical and mental health, constricting social networks, eroding family support, and conferring stigma.[65] The most direct evidence on these causal pathways isolates the effects of the stigma of a criminal record. Audit studies, typically used to study race discrimination in employment or housing, estimate the effects of a criminal record on the hiring behavior of employers. Pager's audit studies in Milwaukee sent trained job applicants—randomly assigned to résumés, with and without evidence of a criminal record—to apply for entry-level jobs. Pager found that a white job applicant with a felony conviction was more likely to be called for an interview than an African American applicant with no criminal record. Moreover, the negative effects of a job seeker's criminal record were larger for blacks than whites.

Building on research on the negative employment effects of incarceration, Western studied the aggregate consequences of incarceration for racial inequality in the labor market. Analyzing survey data, he found that incarceration was associated with a 40 percent reduction in annual earnings after release from prison. Because incarceration is overwhelmingly concentrated among poor men with very little schooling, the aggregate effect of incarceration is not so much to exacerbate income inequality between blacks and whites, but to increase income inequality among black men between the college-educated middle class and those with little schooling.

Research on children provides stronger evidence of the effects of incarceration on racial inequality. In 2008, the Bureau of Justice Statistics reported that 3.6 percent of all minor children in America now have a parent in prison or jail, up from 0.8 percent in 1980. This increase has cut deeply into the population of African American children. In 1980, 2.7 percent of black children had a parent incarcerated. By 2008, parental incarceration had increased to a staggering 11.4 percent of all black children.[66] As striking as these figures are, they cannot capture the disruption experienced by these children as they adjust to the absence of a parent, are often placed in the care of grandparents or in foster care, and experience the stigma of explaining the absence of a parent.[67]

Wakefield and Wildeman estimated the effects of parental incarceration on children's behavior, homelessness, and infant mortality. The research on child well-being anticipates the inter-generational character of the inequalities of mass incarceration. Could high and racially disparate levels of incarceration contribute to racial inequality from one generation to the next? Their analysis of aggregate inequalities shows that incarceration is unlikely to contribute significantly to racial differences in behavioral problems in children, but may increase racial inequality in child homelessness by between 50 and 100 percent and increase racial inequality in infant mortality by about 50 percent.[68]

Other research points to the possibility of damage to the African American family across generational lines. Incarceration drains financial resources from a family that often loses the earnings of a breadwinner while simultaneously shouldering the costs of collect calls, travel to faraway prisons, and contributions to commissary. Donald Braman has argued that this financial burden has impeded the ability of the African American family to accumulate capital and transfer that to the next generation.

In addition to the financial burden on families, processes of family formation have also been distorted in African American communities experiencing high rates of incarceration. In Braman's (2002) study of neighborhoods in Washington, D.C., he found that in neighborhoods with high rates of incarceration, there were only 62 men for every 100 women, as opposed to a 94-to-100 ratio in low-incarceration neighborhoods. According to Braman, this gender imbalance has had damaging effects, "encouraging men to enter into relationships with multiple women, and encouraging women to enter into relationships with men who are already attached."[69] It will likely take another generation before researchers can fully assess the long-term consequences of these challenges to the self-concepts of young men and women, dating patterns, and family relationships.

The spatially concentrated effects of incarceration in poor black communities have also been shown by Robert Sampson. In a landmark analysis of Chicago-area neighborhoods, Sampson found that incarceration was overwhelmingly focused in areas that were very poor, had high rates of violent crime, and were highly racially segregated. These same poor, high-crime neighborhoods had been Chicago's most disadvantaged for generations. In the era of mass incarceration, the character of community life had changed such that enduring neighborhood poverty was not just associated with segregation, joblessness, and crime but with pervasive penal confinement as well. Todd Clear, studying spatially concentrated incarceration in Tallahassee, Florida, argues that the population turnover associated with incarceration not only adds to social and economic disadvantage; it also reduces public safety, contributing to a cycle of crime and punishment in very poor communities.

Taken together, the social research on the racially disparate effects of incarceration on economic well-being, on families, and on community life suggest that the nature of black urban poverty has been transformed by very high rates of incarceration. The prospects of upward mobility have been restricted for poor black workers. Poor black children face relatively higher risks of homelessness and mortality because of parental incarceration. In short, African American neighborhoods of concentrated poverty have become the focal point of the prison system. In profound ways, pervasive incarceration has transformed the relationship of poor African Americans to the state, cementing inequality over the life course, from one generation to the next, and in urban space.

Legal researchers observe a similar transformation of the political and civil rights of poor African American citizens. Research on civil and political rights initially focused on the voting bans for citizens with felony records. Interest in felon disenfranchisement peaked following the 2000 presidential election, in which at least 600,000 ex-felons in Florida, mostly African American, were legally barred from voting.[70] Following the 2000 elections, many states took steps to limit felon disenfranchisement and assist in the restoration of voting rights for those with criminal records. Still, ten states retain a permanent ban on voting rights, disenfranchising an estimated 2.6 million citizens with felony records.[71] The large racial disparity in incarceration is reflected in the racial disparity in disenfranchisement. Christopher Uggen and his colleagues estimated that by 2010, about 7.7 percent of all adult African Americans were disqualified from voting by felon disenfranchisement laws compared to 1.8 percent of the non–African American population.[72] In Florida, Kentucky, and Virginia, disenfranchisement of black voters exceeds 20 percent.

While felon disenfranchisement laws have deep historical roots in southern states aiming to limit voting rights of a newly freed black population, many restrictions on civil rights date from the period of mass incarceration itself. The 1994 crime bill, besides tying federal prison funding to enhanced sentences, also limited access to public housing and federal housing vouchers, educational benefits and grants, and welfare benefits for those with prior drug convictions.[73,74] The full extent of civil disabilities ranges from restricted access to the social safety net to limitations on occupational licenses.[75,76]

Conclusion

The causes, scope, and consequences of mass incarceration have contributed to a cycle of poverty and violence, producing a novel kind of embedded social inequality that prevents the full participation of blacks in American social and political life. Mass incarceration emerged in inner-city neighborhoods marked by segregation, crime, unemployment, and other social problems.

The new reality of pervasive incarceration can be traced to harsh sentencing policies which grew out of a racialized politics that often stoked deep-seated fears of white voters about black criminality. The problems of violence in poor African American communities are real and serious, exacting a massive toll on young black men in their late teens and early twenties. Yet research on crime trends show that the great increase in prison populations—which made incarceration a near certainty for black men who dropped out of high school—did not produce a significant increase in public safety. What's more, mass incarceration undermined economic opportunities, broke up families, and contributed to childhood disadvantage for boys and girls with incarcerated parents. In civic life, the stigma of a criminal record was formalized in law as voting and other rights were taken away, particularly in southern states where African American populations were largest and where incarceration rates were highest.

The close connection between poverty and an escalating problem of serious violence in poor African American communities in the 1960s and 1970s presented a deep public policy challenge. Certainly, some policymakers called for new commitments to improving employment opportunities and reducing poverty in response to the new kinds of racial inequality that were emerging in American cities. But these efforts were defeated by a harsh politics of social policy retrenchment and the turn to punitive criminal justice. In response to the problems of violence and poverty, mass incarceration—a massive and concentrated expansion of state violence—emerged to fill a social-policy vacuum.

This analysis of race and incarceration highlights the challenges faced by the current conversation about criminal justice reform. One approach to reform would simply try to reduce sentences to the 1970s level and scale back the level of incarceration to its historic average. Such an approach, however, would ignore history, and overlook the real problems of violence and poverty that propelled the emergence of mass incarceration in the first place.

The challenge, then, is one of social and political imagination—envisioning how justice institutions might help extinguish rather than fan the flames of poverty and violence in African American communities. Two goals are central to this challenge: reimagining justice and promoting peace. Justice demands basic fairness in social and economic life. Just communities ensure the wide distribution of social and economic opportunity and preserve full social membership for all, even for those who have been involved in crime. Crime is exclusionary for both victims and offenders, and indeed these are often revolving roles in poor communities, where social contexts can be ripe with the potential for chaos and physical harm. Justice in this context should seek the social reintegration of victims and offenders alike. Peace demands a cessation of violence, most likely not through the force of interdiction but, like any successful peace process, under conditions of trust and consultation. Peaceful communities allow the development of routines in everyday interaction, allowing citizens to plan for tomorrow, and imagine a future. Peace and justice may sound like lofty goals for a criminal justice system with backlogged courts and overcrowded prisons. But we see this as a compelling cause, responsive to the injury that mass incarceration has inflicted on the progress of African American citizenship. If mass incarceration has grown out of, and perpetuated, the poverty and violence that lie at the heart of American race relations, an effective criminal justice reform agenda must necessarily advance the twin goals of justice and peace.

REFERENCES

Albonetti, Celesta A. "An Integration of Theories to Explain Judicial Discretion." *Social Problems* 38, no. 2 (1991): 247–66.

Anderson, Elijah. 1990. *Streetwise: Race, Class, and Change in an Urban Community*. Chicago: University of Chicago Press.

Angeli, David H. 1996. "Second Look at Crack Cocaine Sentencing Policies: One More Try for Federal Equal Protection." *American Criminal Law Review* 34: 1211.

Baumgartel, Sarah, Corey Guilmette, Johanna Kalb, Diana Li, Josh Nuni, Devon Porter, and Judith Resnik. 2015. "Time-In-Cell: The ASCA-Liman 2014 National Survey of Administrative Segregation in Prison." West Haven, CT: The Liman Program, Yale Law School.

Beck, Allen J. 2015. "Use of Restrictive Housing in U.S. Prisons and Jails, 2011–12." Bureau of Justice Statistics Special Report. NCJ 249209.

Beck, A. J., and A. Blumstein. 2012. "Trends in Incarceration Rates: 1980–2010." Presentation to the National Research Council Committee on Causes and Consequences of High Rates of Incarceration. Washington, DC.

Beckett, Katherine. 1997. *Making Crime Pay: The Politics of Law and Order in the Contemporary United States*. New York: Oxford University Press.

Blumstein, Alfred. 1982. "On the Racial Disproportionality of United States' Prison Populations." *The Journal of Criminal Law & Criminology* 73, no. 3: 1259–81.

Bonczar, Thomas P. 2011. "National Corrections Reporting Program: Time Served in State Prison, by Offense, Release Type, Sex, and Race." Washington, DC: Bureau of Justice Statistics.

Bourgois, Philippe. 2003. *In Search of Respect: Selling Crack in El Barrio*. Cambridge: Cambridge University Press.

Braman, Donald. 2002. "Families and Incarceration." Ph.D. dissertation, Yale University. Available at https://www.ncjrs.gov/pdffiles1/nij/grants/202981.pdf.

Chambliss, William J. 2001. *Power, Conflict, and Crime*. Boulder, CO: Westview Press.

Clear, Todd. 2007. *Imprisoning Communities: How Mass Incarceration Makes Disadvantaged Neighborhoods Worse*. New York: Oxford University Press.

Cullen, Francis T. 1995. "Assessing the Penal Harm Movement." *Journal of Research in Crime and Delinquency* 32: 338–58.

Donohue, John J., III. 2009. "Assessing the Relative Benefits of Incarceration: Overall Changes and the Benefits on the Margin." In *Do Prisons Make Us Safer? The Benefits and Costs of the Prison Boom*, eds. Steven Raphael and Michael A. Stoll, 269–342. New York: Russell Sage Foundation.

DuBois, W. E. B. 1899. *The Philadelphia Negro*. New York: Lippincott.

Duneier, Mitchell, and Ovie Carter. 1999. *Sidewalk*. New York: Macmillan.

Edsall, Thomas Byrne, and Mary D. Edsall. 1992. *Chain Reaction: The Impact of Race, Rights, and Taxes on American Politics*. New York: W. W. Norton.

Fairlie, Robert W., and William A. Sundstrom. 1997. "The Racial Unemployment Gap in Long-Run Perspective." *American Economic Review* 87, no. 2: 306–10.

Flamm, Michael W. 2005. *Law and Order: Street Crime, Civil Unrest, and the Crisis of Liberalism in the 1960s*. New York: Columbia University Press.

Freeman, Richard. 1992. "Crime and the Employment of Disadvantaged Youth." National Bureau of Economic Research (NBER) Working Paper no. 3875.

General Accountability Office (GAO). 2005. *Drug Offenders: Various Factors May Limit the Impacts of Federal Laws That Provide for Denial of Selected Benefits*. Washington, DC: GAO (GAO-05-238).

Goldwater, Barry. 1964. "Speech Accepting the Republican Presidential Nomination." In *American Speeches: Political Oratory from Abraham Lincoln to Bill Clinton*, ed. Ted Widmer, 595–603. New York: Library of America. 2006.

Greenberg, David F. *Corrections and Punishment*. 1977. Beverly Hills, CA: Sage.

Griffith, Ezra E. H, and Carl C. Bell. 1989. "Recent Trends in Suicide and Homicide Among Blacks." *Journal of the American Medical Association* 262: 2265–69.

Gurr, Ted Robert. 1981. "Historical Trends in Violent Crime: A Critical Review of the Evidence." *Crime and Justice* (1981): 295–353.

Herbert, Steven Kelly. 1997. *Policing Space: Territoriality and the Los Angeles Police Department*. Minneapolis: University of Minnesota Press.

Jargowsky, Paul. 2005. "Stunning Progress, Hidden Problems: The Dramatic Decline of Concentrated Poverty in the 1990s." In *Redefining Urban and Suburban America: Evidence from Census 2000*, edited by Berube Alan, Bruce Katz, and Robert E. Lang, 137–72. Washington, DC: Brookings Institution Press.

Juhn, Chinhui. 1992. "Decline of Male Labor Market Participation: The Role of Declining Market Opportunities." *Quarterly Journal of Economics* 107, no. 1: 79–121.

Kluegel, James R. 1990. "Trends in Whites' Explanations of the Black-White Gap in Socioeconomic Status, 1977–1989." *American Sociological Review* 55, no. 4: 512–25.

Langan, Patrick. 1991. "Race of Prisoners Admitted to State and Federal Institutions, 1926-86." Bureau of Justice Statistics Special Report. NCJ 125618.

Levitt, Steven D., and Sudhir Alladi Venkatesh. 2000. "An Economic Analysis of a Drug-Selling Gang's Finances." *Quarterly Journal of Economics* 115, no. 3: 755–89.

Love, Margaret Colgate. 2006. *Relief from the Collateral Consequences of a Criminal Conviction: A State-by-State Resource Guide*. Getzville, NY: William S. Hein Publishing.

Love, Margaret C., Susan M. Kuzma, and Keith Waters. 1996. *Civil Disabilities of Convicted Felons: A State-by-State Survey*. Washington, DC: US Department of Justice, Office of the Pardon Attorney.

Manza, Jeff, and Christopher Uggen. 2006. *Locked Out: Felon Disenfranchisement and American Democracy*. New York: Oxford University Press.

Mauer, Marc. 1999. "The Crisis of the Young African American Male and the Criminal Justice System." Washington, DC: Prepared for U.S. Commission on Civil Rights.

Muhammad, Khalil Gibran. 2010. *The Condemnation of Blackness*. Cambridge, MA: Harvard University Press.

Muller, Christopher. 2012. "Northward Migration and the Rise of Racial Disparity in American Incarceration, 1880–1950." *American Journal of Sociology* 118, no. 2: 281–326.

Nagin, Daniel S. 2013. "Deterrence: A Review of the Evidence by a Criminologist for Economists." *Annual Review of Economics* 5, no. 1: 83–105.

Neal, Derek, and Amin Rick. 2013. "The Prison Boom and the Lack of Black Progress After Smith and Welch." Department of Economic Working Paper, University of Chicago. Chicago: University of Chicago Press.

Nellis, A. 2013. "Life Goes On: The Historic Rise in Life Sentences in America." Washington, DC: The Sentencing Project. Available at http://sentencingproject.org/wp-content/uploads/2015/12/Life-Goes-On.pdf.

Offner, Paul A., and Harry J. Holzer. 2002. "Left Behind in the Labor Market: Recent Employment Trends Among Young Black Men." The Brookings Institution, Center on Urban and Metropolitan Policy, Survey Series. April.

Pager, Devah. 2003. "The Mark of a Criminal Record." *American Journal of Sociology* 108, no. 2: 937–75.

Perlstein, Rick. 2010. *Nixonland: The Rise of a President and the Fracturing of America.* New York: Simon and Schuster.

Rohler, Lloyd Earl. 2004. *George Wallace: Conservative Populist.* Westport, CT: Praeger.

Sampson, Robert J. 2012. *Great American City: Chicago and the Enduring Neighborhood Effect.* Chicago: University of Chicago Press.

Sampson, Robert J., and Charles Loeffler. 2010. "Punishment's Place: The Local Concentration of Mass Incarceration." *Daedalus* 139, no. 3: 20–31.

Schlanger, Margo. "Prison Segregation: Symposium Introduction and Preliminary Data on Racial Disparities (June 28, 2013)." *Michigan Journal of Race & Law* 18: 241–50.

Schmitt, John and Kris Warner. 2010. "Ex-offenders and the Labor Market." Washington, DC: Center for Economic and Policy Research.

Smith, James P., and Finis R. Welch. 1989. "Black Economic Progress After Myrdal." *Journal of Economic Literature* 27, no. 2: 519–64.

Spohn, Cassia, and David Holleran. 2000. "The Imprisonment Penalty Paid by Young, Unemployed Black and Hispanic Male Offenders." *Criminology* 38, no. 1: 281–306.

Steffensmeier, Darrell, Jeffery Ulmer, and John Kramer. 1998. "Interaction of Race, Gender, and Age in Criminal Sentencing: The Punishment Cost of Being Young, Black, and Male." *Criminology* 36, no. 4: 763.

Tonry, Michael, and Matthew Melewski. 2008. "The Malign Effects of Drug and Crime Control Policies on Black Americans." *Crime and Justice* 37, no. 1: 1–44.

Travis, Jeremy. 2002. "Invisible Punishment: An Instrument of Social Exclusion." In *Invisible Punishment: The Collateral Consequences of Mass Imprisonment*, eds. Marc Mauer and Meda Chesney-Lind, 15–36. New York: The New Press.

———. 2005. *But They All Come Back: Facing the Challenges of Prisoner Reentry.* Washington, DC: Urban Insitute Press.

Travis, Jeremy, Bruce Western, and Steve Redburn, eds. 2014. *The Growth of Incarceration in the United States: Exploring Causes and Consequences.* Washington, DC: National Academies Press.

Uggen, Christopher, Sarah Shannon, and Jeff Manza. 2012. *State-Level Estimates of Felon Disenfranchisement in the United States, 2010.* Washington, DC: The Sentencing Project.

Wakefield, Sara, and Christopher Wildeman. 2013. *Children of the Prison Boom: Mass Incarceration and the Future of American Inequality.* New York: Oxford University Press.

Weaver, Vesla M. 2007. "Frontlash: Race and the Development of Punitive Crime Policy." *Studies in American Political Development* 21, no. 2: 230–65.

Weber, Max. 1946. "Politics as a Vocation." In *From Max Weber: Essays in Sociology*, eds. H. H. Gerth and C. Wright Mills, 77–128. New York: Oxford University Press. Originally published as "Politik als Beruf," 1921.

Western, Bruce. 2006. *Punishment and Inequality in America*. New York: Russell Sage Foundation.

Western, Bruce, and Becky Pettit. 2009. "Technical Report on Revised Population Estimates and NLSY79 Analysis Tables for the Pew Public Safety and Mobility Project." Unpublished manuscript. Harvard University, Department of Sociology, Cambridge, MA.

Western, Bruce, and Christopher Wildeman. 2009. "The Black Family and Mass Incarceration." *Annals of the American Academy of Political and Social Science* 621, no. 1 (2009): 221–42.

Wildeman, Christopher, and Sara Wakefield. 2014. "Long Arm of the Law: The Concentration of Incarceration in Families in the Era of Mass Incarceration." *Journal of Gender, Race & Justice* 17: 367.

Wilson, James Q. 1968. *Varieties of Police Behavior: The Management of Law and Order in Eight Communities*. Cambridge, MA: Harvard University Press.

Wilson, William Julius. 1987. *The Truly Disadvantaged: The Inner City, the Underclass, and Public Policy*. Chicago: University of Chicago Press.

NOTES

1. We use the term "state violence" to describe the criminal justice functions of policing and incarceration because they are obviously coercive, compelling citizens by force or the threat of force. As Weber (1946) observes, such coercion is regularly regarded by citizens as legitimate ("the state is considered the sole source of the 'right' to use violence"), but the term "state violence" also underlines that physical force is not somehow milder when it is deployed under public authority.

2. Muller, "Northward Migration," 286–87.

3. Ibid.

4. Travis, Western, and Redburn, *Growth of Incarceration*.

5. Western and Wildeman, "The Black Family and Mass Incarceration."

6. Western, *Punishment and Inequality in America*.

7. Sampson and Loeffler, "Punishment's Place."

8. Sampson, *Great American City*.

9. Gurr, "Historical Trends in Violent Crime," 323.

10. Ibid., 326.

11. Griffith and Bell, "Recent Trends in Suicide and Homicide Among Blacks."

12. Wilson, *The Truly Disadvantaged*.

13. Jargowsky, "Stunning Progress, Hidden Problems."

14. Smith and Welch, "Black Economic Progress After Myrdal."

15. Offner and Holzer, "Left Behind in the Labor Market."

16. Fairlie and Sundstrom, "The Racial Unemployment Gap."

17. Freeman, "Crime and the Employment of Disadvantaged Youth."

18. Juhn, "Decline of Male Labor Market Participation."

19. Bourgois, *In Search of Respect.*

20. Anderson, *Streetwise.*

21. Levitt and Venkatesh, "An Economic Analysis of a Drug-Selling Gang's Finances."

22. Wilson, *Varieties of Police Behavior: The Management of Law and Order in Eight Communities.*

23. Herbert, *Policing Space.*

24. Duneier, *Sidewalk*, 304–7.

25. Anderson, *Streetwise*, 193–98.

26. Wilson, *Varieties of Police Behavior*, ch. 2.

27. Chambliss, *Power, Conflict, and Crime*, ch. 3.

28. Kluegel, "Trends in Whites' Explanations."

29. Steffensmeier, Ulmer, and Kramer, "Interaction of Race, Gender, and Age," 770.

30. Greenberg, *Corrections and Punishment.*

31. Albonetti, "An Integration of Theories."

32. Western, *Punishment and Inequality.*

33. Muhammad, *The Condemnation of Blackness.*

34. Weaver, "Frontlash."

35. Flamm, *Law and Order.*

36. Mauer, "The Crisis of the Young African American Male," 50–54.

37. See Goldwater, "Speech Accepting the Republican Presidential Nomination."

38. See Beckett, *Making Crime Pay.*

39. See Edsall and Edsall, *Chain Reaction.*

40. Quoted in Rohler, *George Wallace*, 33.

41. Perlstein, *Nixonland*, 268.

42. Travis, Western, and Redburn, *Growth of Incarceration*, ch. 3.

43. Bonczar, "National Corrections Reporting Program."

44. Nellis, "Life Goes On."

45. Tonry and Melewski, "Malign Effects."

46. Spohn and Holleran, "Imprisonment Penalty."

47. Steffensmeier, Ulmer, and Kramer, "Interaction of Race, Gender, and Age."

48. Beck and Blumstein, "Trends in Incarceration Rates: 1980–2010," table 6.

49. Neal and Rick, "Prison Boom," table 7a.

50. Beck and Blumstein, "Trends in Incarceration Rates," table 6.

51. Travis, *But They All Come Back*, 28.

52. Travis, Western, and Redburn, *Growth of Incarceration*, 50.

53. Western, *Punishment and Inequality.*

54. Angeli, "Second Look at Crack Cocaine Sentencing Policies," 1213.

55. Travis, Western, and Redburn, *Growth of Incarceration*, 160–63.

56. Cullen, "Assessing the Penal Harm Movement."

57. Travis, Western, and Redburn, *Growth of Incarceration*, 163.

58. Schlanger, "Prison Segregation."

59. Baumgartel, et al. "Time-In-Cell."

60. Beck, "Use of Restrictive Housing."

61. Nagin, "Deterrence."

62. See, e.g., Donohue, "Assessing the Relative Benefits," 274–80.

63. Western, *Punishment and Inequality*.

64. See Travis, Western, and Redburn, *Growth of Incarceration*, chs. 6–9.

65. Schmitt and Warner, "Ex-Offenders."

66. Western and Pettit, "Technical Report on Revised Population Estimates."

67. Travis, *But They All Come Back*, 123–38.

68. Wildeman and Wakefield, "Long Arm of the Law," 138–39.

69. Braman, "Families and Incarceration," 123.

70. Manza and Uggen, *Locked Out*.

71. Uggen, Shannon, and Manza, *State-Level Estimates*.

72. Ibid., 1–2.

73. Travis, "Invisible Punishment."

74. General Accountability Office, *Drug Offenders*.

75. Love, Kuzma, and Waters, *Civil Disabilities of Convicted Felons*.

76. Love, *Relief from the Collateral Consequences*.

Contributor Acknowledgments

"The Prosecution of Black Men" by Angela J. Davis, copyright 2017 by Angela J. Davis. Used by permission of the author.

"The Grand Jury and Police Violence Against Black Men" by Roger A. Fairfax, Jr., copyright 2017 by Roger A. Fairfax Jr. Used by permission of the author.

"Boys to Men: The Role of Policing in the Socialization of Black Boys" by Kristin Henning, copyright 2017 by Kristin Henning. Used by permission of the author.

"Racial Profiling: The Law, the Policy, and the Practice" by Reneé McDonald Hutchins, copyright 2017 by Reneé McDonald Hutchins. Used by permission of the author.

"Do Black Lives Matter to the Courts?" by Sherrilyn A. Ifill and Jin Hee Lee, copyright 2017 by Sherrilyn A. Ifill and Jin Hee Lee. Used by permission of the authors.

"The Endurance of Racial Disparity in the Criminal Justice System" by Marc Mauer, copyright 2017 by Marc Mauer. Used by permission of the author.

"Policing: A Model for the Twenty-first Century" by Tracey Meares and Tom Tyler, copyright 2016 by Tracy Meares and Tom Tyler. Used by permission of the authors.

"Making Implicit Bias Explicit: Black Men and the Police" by Katheryn Russell-Brown, copyright 2017 by Katheryn Russell-Brown. Used by permission of the author.

"A Presumption of Guilt: The Legacy of America's History of Racial Injustice" by Bryan Stevenson, copyright 2017 by Bryan Stevenson. Used by permission of the author.

"Poverty, Violence, and Black Incarceration" by Jeremy Travis and Bruce Western, copyright 2017 by Jeremy Travis and Bruce Western. Used by permission of the authors.

"Elected Prosecutors and Police Accountability" by Ronald F. Wright, copyright 2017 by Ronald F. Wright. Used by permission of the author.

A Note About the Contributors

Angela J. Davis is a professor of law at American University and a former director of the D.C. Public Defender Service. She is the author of *Arbitrary Justice: The Power of the American Prosecutor*, the coauthor of several books on criminal law, and the author of numerous articles and book chapters on prosecutorial power and criminal justice.

Roger A. Fairfax, Jr., is senior associate dean for academic affairs and professor of law at George Washington University, where he teaches courses in criminal law, procedure, and policy. An elected member of the American Law Institute, his scholarship appears in leading journals and in his edited volume, *Grand Jury 2.0: Modern Perspectives on the Grand Jury*.

Kristin Henning is the Agnes N. Williams Research Professor of Law and director of the Juvenile Justice Clinic at Georgetown Law. Her scholarship has appeared in the *Cornell Law Review*, *California Law Review*, and *NYU Law Review* and in books such as *Punishment in Popular Culture*. She is currently writing a book on the criminalization of black adolescence.

Renée McDonald Hutchins is the codirector of the Clinical Law Program and the Jacob A. France Professor of Public Interest Law at the University of Maryland Carey School of Law. She is the author of several scholarly works, including two books, *Learning Criminal Procedure* and *Developing Professional Skills: Criminal Procedure*.

Sherrilyn Ifill is the president and director-counsel of the NAACP Legal Defense and Educational Fund, Inc. She was a professor of law at the University of Maryland and chair of the board of U.S. programs at the Open Society Institute. She is the author of *On the Courthouse Lawn: Confronting the Legacy of Lynching in the 21st Century*.

Jin Hee Lee is the deputy director of litigation at the NAACP Legal Defense and Educational Fund, Inc., where she supervises criminal justice and education matters. She also litigates death penalty, juvenile life without parole, and police reform cases, and speaks regularly on issues pertaining to the criminal justice system and racial justice.

Marc Mauer is the executive director of the Sentencing Project, a national nonprofit organization engaged in research and advocacy on criminal justice policy. He is the author of *Race to Incarcerate*, which was named a semifinalist for the

Robert F. Kennedy Book Award, and the coeditor of *Invisible Punishment: The Collateral Consequences of Mass Imprisonment*.

Tracey Meares is the Walton Hale Hamilton Professor of Law at Yale Law School. Together with Tom Tyler she directs the Justice Collaboratory at Yale Law School. In December 2015, President Obama appointed her to serve on his Task Force on 21st Century Policing.

Katheryn Russell-Brown is a professor of law and director of the Race Center at the University of Florida, Levin College of Law. She received a Soros Justice Advocacy Fellowship in 2009. Her books include *The Color of Crime*, *Protecting Our Own*, *Underground Codes*, and a children's book, *Little Melba and Her Big Trombone*.

Bryan Stevenson is the director of the Equal Justice Initiative. He has represented the poor and disadvantaged for over thirty years, winning several important criminal cases in the United States Supreme Court. He is the author of the number-one *New York Times* best seller *Just Mercy* and is leading a national project to address the history of racial injustice in America.

Jeremy Travis, president of John Jay College of Criminal Justice, has published widely on a variety of criminal justice topics. He coedited the landmark NRC report on U.S. incarceration rates. Travis served as director of the National Institute of Justice, general counsel of the NYPD, and senior fellow at the Urban Institute.

Tom Tyler is the Macklin Fleming Professor of Law and Professor of Psychology at Yale Law School. He is the author of several books, including *Why People Cooperate*, *Legitimacy and Criminal Justice*, *Why People Obey the Law*, *Trust in the Law*, and *Cooperation in Groups*.

Bruce Western is professor of sociology and the Daniel and Florence Guggenheim Professor of Criminal Justice Policy at Harvard University. He was the vice chair of the National Academy of Sciences consensus panel on the causes and consequences of high incarceration rates in the United States and is the author of *Punishment and Inequality in America*.

Ronald Wright is a professor of law at Wake Forest University. He is the coauthor of two casebooks in criminal procedure and sentencing. His empirical research concentrates on the offices of criminal prosecutors, along with the people, institutions, and habits that shape the work of prosecutors.